In Search of the Working Class

The Working Class in American History

Editorial Advisors
David Brody
Alice Kessler-Harris
David Montgomery
Sean Wilentz

*A list of books in the series appears
at the end of this book.*

IN SEARCH
OF THE
WORKING CLASS

*Essays in American Labor History
and Political Culture*

LEON FINK

UNIVERSITY OF ILLINOIS PRESS
Urbana and Chicago

Library of Congress Cataloging-in-Publication Data

Fink, Leon, 1948–
    In search of the working class / essays in American labor history
and political culture / Leon Fink.
        p.   cm.
    Includes index.
    ISBN 0-252-02077-4. — ISBN 0-252-06368-6 (paper)
    1. Labor—United States—History. 2. Labor movement—United
States—History. 3. Working class—United States—History.
4. Trade-unions—United States—Political activity—History.
5. Industrial relations—United States—History. I. Title.
HD8066.F544   1994
305.5'62'0973—dc20   93-29986
                                                          CIP

Contents

Introduction   vii

PART ONE

Point of Departure

1. John R. Commons, Herbert Gutman, and the
   Burden of Labor History   3

PART TWO

The Contest for Power

2. Class Conflict American-Style   15

3. Politics as Social History: A Case Study of Class
   Conflict and Political Development in
   Nineteenth-Century New England   33

4. A Labor Crusade behind the Magnolia Curtain:
   Hospital Workers and the Politics
   of Race and Class   51

PART THREE

Peculiarities of the Americans

5. The New Labor History and the Powers of Historical
   Pessimism: Consensus, Hegemony, and the
   Case of the Knights of Labor   89

6. Labor, Liberty, and the Law: Trade Unionism and
   the Problem of the American Constitutional Order   144

PART FOUR
*Strategic Reinventions of the
American Worker*

7. Looking Backward: Reflections on Workers' Culture
   and Certain Conceptual Dilemmas
   within Labor History   175

8. "Intellectuals" versus "Workers": Academic
   Requirements and the Creation of Labor History   201

9. Culture's Last Stand? Gender and the Search
   for Synthesis in American Labor History   236

Index   249

Introduction

When the director of the University of Illinois Press invited me, as one of the "second generation of New Labor historians," to assemble a collection of essays, I responded with mixed emotions. Amid pride I also felt a slight sense of dread. Much of my writing has been stimulated by scholarly or political debates tied to a particular time and place. As those moments of inspiration have faded, are their products still worthy of review? In considering materials for a collection, the closet I would be entering would be my own. How to arrange the costumes hanging there, created over the course of fifteen years?

This volume offers a tentative answer. Since the 1970s, historians of my generation have been regularly rediscovering the American working class. To be sure, what we found was not always what we were looking for, and what we were looking for often reflected as much about our own lives as it did the subjects under investigation. The very concept of the working class has enjoyed diverse and radically shifting meanings. The term has stood variously as a collective agent of social transformation, a socioeconomic categorization of occupations, a unified field of values or common culture, a set of segmented oppositions based on internal differences in power and status, an object of social policy and the law's discipline, and a historically conditioned creation of middle-class intellectuals. However instigated, each of these historical journeys, in my view, is worth undertaking so long as the vessel is seaworthy. The key criteria include purpose, argument, and evidence. A highly motivated enterprise, the labor history that attracts me at least is not likely to fall victim to the proverbial justification-gone-absurd (once actually encountered by journal editor Mark Perlman) that it "fills a much-needed gap in the literature."

In considering my own motivations for embarking on such work, a

shorthand set of associations substitutes for any better-considered auto-
biographical impulse. My first contact with the history of American
labor came through stories from my mother's parents, Russian-Jewish
immigrants who had passed through the peddler trade, garment shops,
and American Communist party in Toledo, Ohio. But for many years
that experience seemed altogether remote from my own. Growing up in
the Indianapolis suburbs of the 1950s, as the son of liberal parents (my
mother, a former newspaper reporter and Latin teacher; my father, a
lawyer), my first political activity came in organizing a pro-Stevenson
kickball team on the school playground. While "class" politics in high
school for the most part meant student council elections, I do remember
a couple moments of larger social discovery. Within a generally affluent
student body, there were a few "greasers" in my high school; during an
unofficial "Senior Slob Day," at which everyone tried to dress down to
the point of provoking the school monitors, one of these poor whites was
accidentally sent home for unself-consciously wearing his normal attire.
Then, a couple years later, while supervising the summer recreation
program at Max Bahr Park, I watched, contentedly, as a young black
high school basketball phenom named Steve Downing (assigned to the
same park as groundskeeper) successfully integrated what had been
strictly white, ethnic turf. In the same neighborhood the political yard
signs that summer of 1968 switched from Robert Kennedy to George
Wallace, and one of my favorites among the tougher, older kids was sent
off to Vietnam.

Like many of my generation, my first conscious consideration of
class-related issues and radical thought came in college. My college
experience at Harvard (1966–70) matched neither the warm sense of
belonging nostalgically trumpeted by alumni boosters nor the picture of
embittered alienation glimpsed in some of the sixties retrospective
narratives. As a British history major, I first encountered a diet of
Whiggish lectures delivered by elderly dons in a most entertaining way.
For a brief while, history served as a kind of anecdotal preserve, irrelevant but reassuring, from the gathering clouds of contemporary political
strife. It was in my sophomore year, while I was otherwise occupied with
antiwar meetings and the Eugene McCarthy campaign, that my history
tutor, Alice Mattice, assigned me E. P. Thompson's *The Making of the
English Working Class*. In important ways, the book broke down barriers
between different sections of my life, suggesting that academic work need
not be removed from political passions. I spent the following year at the
University of Warwick, enraptured by Thompson, his colleagues in
comparative labor history at the Centre for the Study of Social History,
and a motley crew of radical student activists. Ironically, it was the view

from abroad (and the influence of Visiting Professor David Montgomery) that first stimulated my interest in U.S. history. When I returned to Harvard for my senior year, my gaze was already fixed on a graduate career in American labor history. The Warwick experience facilitated my historical career in one other way: a draft-exempting injury to my trigger finger suffered while playing for the Warwick basketball team allowed me to proceed directly from college to graduate school at the University of Rochester.

When I began graduate work in 1970, the history department at Rochester was, indeed, a lively place. Although its three principal Americanists—Eugene Genovese, Christopher Lasch, and Herbert Gutman—proved temperamentally incompatible, their own conflicts (as well as superb historical talents) proved only further grist for the mill for a gaggle of students convinced that conflict, above all else, made the world go round. Although I taught for two semesters with Lasch and remained intrigued by his inquest into intellectual lives, Gutman's world of the American worker most fired my imagination. I followed Herb to City College in 1972, pursuing under his close direction both a dissertation on nineteenth-century labor politics and an oral history project documenting the lives of twentieth-century New York City immigrants and African-American southern migrants. A valiant if frustrated attempt to connect the new "history from the bottom up" to the needs of CCNY's new "open admissions" student body, the Working-Class Oral History Project became the seed for the later American Social History Project and the path-breaking *Who Built America?* texts.

It was through the oral history work that I first made contact with Moe Foner and New York City's Hospital Workers' Union, Local 1199. Soon fellow graduate student Brian Greenberg and I had embarked upon a full-scale study of an organization that seemed to bridge the militant idealism of earlier American labor history with the challenges of institution building among the "new working class." The connection of politics and scholarship in these years was regularly enlivened by the MARHO (Mid-Atlantic Radical Historians' Organization) network, including a monthly forum series and associated study groups. One other connection from the New York years deserves mention: Not long after I arrived at City College, I met a history graduate student who happened to be reading the *Journal of United Labor* at the time; within two years Susan Levine and I had married.

It was with a sense of nervous excitement that I accepted in 1977 the first labor history appointment ever offered at the University of North Carolina at Chapel Hill. While Chapel Hill was generally a very pleasant and liberal community, when it came to labor issues, Sue and I soon

asked ourselves if we were living in the past—or the future? Shortly after
we arrived, a labor studies program in the area for which Sue had been
hired was scuttled on account of business opposition; even more revealing
was the comment of the hapless college administrator who, while trying
to defend a program chartered in part to "serve the professional needs of
the labor movement," explained that "by labor movement we mean the
movement of labor from one place to another." In a state that regularly
vied for the designation of lowest-percentage-unionized-workforce in the
country, some people took me seriously when I suggested that it had
helped to be named "fink" in getting hired. (When the nearest labor
history colleague turned out to be Gary Fink at Georgia State, even I
began to wonder!) Regularly teaching an undergraduate course called
"The Worker and American Life," I initially saw it as my task to awaken
students to a social movement that carried little visible legacy in the
world they inhabited. Fortunately for me, there was no shortage of
interested graduate students, many of whom were attracted to the department through the Southern Oral History Project, whose magnificent
research culminated in *Like a Family: The Making of a Southern Cotton Mill
World.* My intellectual and political interests were also sustained by an
exceptionally able group of younger faculty, who supplemented individual friendship and encouragement with a shifting series of public forums
and discussion groups. When my tenure case aroused unanticipated
controversy and opposition in 1982–83, I was successfully defended by an
uncommon alliance of younger peers and, for want of a better term, older
southern gentlemen, as well as by many strong appeals from outside
scholars.

Even while pressing ahead with an agenda carved out in an earlier
time and place, both immediate surroundings and the changing national
political mood gradually weighed in with inevitable force. Just as I and
many other young faculty radicals had descended on the campuses, the
social and economic conservatism already at home in North Carolina
had come to dominate the nation. I became less the sure-footed crusader
and more the curious consumer of new influences: feminism, child care,
and the schools soon loomed as immediate political issues, while intellectually a renaissance of interdisciplinary social theory beckoned me beyond
the limits of my training in social history. A Fulbright year at the
American Studies Institute of the University of Munich in 1983–84
offered a further stimulus to see the world from new perspectives.

I was still writing the hospital workers' study when Herbert Gutman
died unexpectedly in 1985. While the earlier essays collected here openly
reflect and often borrow from his superior understanding of nineteenth-
century social and labor history, the latter ones also reflect something of

the discontinuity his death left within a field so stamped with his image. It seems appropriate, therefore, to begin this anthology with an affectionate tribute to the teacher and scholar who most inspired my efforts.

The essays in this collection were obviously not designed as a coherent whole, yet together I think they do more than merely coexist. I have organized the pieces along the lines of three themes that have dominated my professional-intellectual itinerary. The first I call the "Contest for Power"; the second, "The Peculiarities of the Americans"; and the last, "Strategic Reinventions of the American Worker."

I was first driven to examine the class divide within American society and to connect that divide to struggles for power, as evidenced at the workplace and in centers of government. My interest in this regard has focused on moments of working-class mobilization, when workplace-centered demands for recognition escalated into community-wide contests for authority and legitimation. While undertaking a doctoral study of a diverse set of communities engulfed in Gilded Age labor protest, I tried in the ensuing book—*Workingmen's Democracy: The Knights of Labor and American Politics* (1983)—to offer a refutation of classic American Exceptionalist denials of the centrality of class to the American political universe. By excerpting and reconcentrating several passages from the book, "Class Conflict American-Style" perhaps makes the most effective statement of the book's central argument.

In "Politics as Social History," written as an immediate afterthought to my dissertation, I sought to apply a neo-Marxist understanding of social conflict to American political history. The historical drama of the rise and fall of a workingmen's government in a Vermont marble town—composed against the contemporary backdrop of the hounding of the populist Dennis Kucinich in Cleveland and the memory of the extermination of Salvadore Allende in Chile—suggested a larger, and more permanent, dependency of political regime and political stability upon power relations in civil (i.e., class) society. It was with that concern in mind that I proposed an abbreviated typology of American urban political models according to their social-historical content.

In the hospital workers' project, Brian Greenberg and I, heretofore nineteenth-century historians, encountered the continuing resonance of class conflict in contemporary American society. The struggle for hospital unionization, however, also reflected a complexity of race politics, local political climate, institutional settings, and individual leadership. To make matters more complex, we discovered that the workplace and political strategies that worked for the union on its home turf of New York City frequently met a different reception in other locales. Nowhere was the struggle of union mobilization more intense nor the forms of resistance more sustained than in Charleston, South Carolina, in 1969. There, a "union-power, soul-power" strategy—the legacy of Local 1199's own long-time social activism—ran into the heart of southern conservative opposition to labor and civil rights agendas. In "A Labor Crusade behind the Magnolia Curtain," I include portions of a chapter I prepared for *Upheaval in the Quiet Zone: A History of Hospital Workers' Union, Local 1199.*

I have also been attracted to the distinctive aspects of American popular culture that have helped to define and limit our industrial and political history. Convinced by my early studies of the vitality of late nineteenth-century labor culture and political conflicts, I viewed with some distress the continuing ability of other historians to dismiss such evidence on the basis of the long-term "victory" of liberal individualism and capitalist hegemony. "The New Labor History and the Powers of Historical Pessimism" thus joins a debate extending well beyond the ranks of labor historians—as evident in the critical commentaries by T. J. Jackson Lears, John P. Diggins, George Lipsitz, and Mari Jo Buhle and Paul Buhle—over how to interpret dissenting voices within the larger political culture. As the exchange makes clear, the issue is not only how we interpret "republican" versus "liberal" messages within cultural texts but what integrity we attach to such texts in the first place.

If American workers from the Gilded Age factory to the post–World War II hospital did not fatally lack a common will or consciousness, they did face a peculiar, and often overwhelming, set of obstacles. One of the most continuingly debilitating of those obstacles was embedded in the doctrines of American law. "Labor, Liberty, and the Law" (a piece commissioned for the Constitutional bicentennial issue of the *Journal of American History*) suggests that legal culture and the courts have themselves helped to define—and scramble—U.S. labor strategy and action.

Finally, my work reflects a continuing interest in the very lenses we wear to study and write about labor history. Over the course of my meanderings, I have become ever more sensitive to the ways that the history of the working class is also a history of the intellectuals who have taken on that task. I have here included three attempts to take stock of major assumptions within the field. The first such effort, derived from readings completed in Germany, emphasizes a peculiar chronological divide I encountered in the literature. While documenting the integrity of a labor-republican consciousness stretching across nineteenth-century American labor protest—and indeed uniting U.S. workers' actions with those of their counterparts abroad—the new labor history appeared to stumble into something of a conceptual no-man's-land upon entering the twentieth century. The essay "Looking Backward" is, therefore, an attempt to synthesize a rich historiographical literature and to set some signposts for subsequent inquiry.

In following the historical fight to legitimate collective labor protest and sanction collective bargaining, I became fascinated with the extended cast of middle-class characters—lawyers, settlement workers, economists, etc.—who came to champion, and interpret, the workers' cause. First drawn, in fact, to consider the role of intellectuals and the labor question by a stimulating paper by George Fredrickson at the American Historical Association meetings in 1985, I have adopted a version of this theme in my ongoing work. " 'Intellectuals' versus 'Workers,' " a portrait of the early labor historians and their social context, represents the first installment of this project.

Since the mid-1980s, the sharpest intellectual challenge to the use of social class as a defining historical construct has derived from the ranks of women's history. Within the subfield of labor history, as well, a new revisionism raising the banner of gender is the occasion of a rich harvest of literature. Just how sharp is the challenge, and how possible is a reconciliation between class and gender as fields of understanding for workers' history and identity? This is the question I attempt to address in "Culture's Last Stand?" a paper delivered at the plenary session of the 1991 North American Labor History Conference at Wayne State University.

Except for minor editorial and cosmetic changes, I have kept to the original texts. Although hardly an unbiased commentator, I think the theses sustained here will bear further scrutiny, notwithstanding the obvious point that other scholars have subsequently extended and sometimes revised the thoughts expressed here. For those hypercritical readers anxiously looking to do battle, I have tried to provide some helpful fodder by updating references in the notes.

Beyond those specifically acknowledged for each entry, I am overwhelmed in considering the larger social debt that lies behind these pages. In rereading the essays, my thoughts drift back inexorably to the myriad friends, teachers, colleagues, and students who have sustained me. For their collaboration (both direct and indirect) during the years in Chapel Hill when these pieces were written, I should especially like to thank William Barney, James Barrett, Judith Bennett, Craig Calhoun, Charles Capper, Peter Coclanis, James Epstein, Judith Farquhar, Jacquelyn Hall, Cynthia Herrup, Gil Joseph, John Kasson, Robert Korstad, Paul Krause, Cliff Kuhn, James Leloudis, Steven Leonard, Michael Lienisch, Roger Lotchin, Donald Reid, Harry Watson; and for their special friendship, Mike and Melva Okun. Appreciation is extended, too, to Theresa L. Sears, managing editor at the University of Illinois Press for her exemplary preparation of the final manuscript. Finally, for collaboration verging on co-conspiracy, one person was always near. Susan Levine and I have passed from the Knights of Labor through the labor of nights—parenthood!—to the blizzard of a new world order without losing a common sense of humor. With respect and love, this book is dedicated to her.

PART ONE

Point of Departure

1

John R. Commons, Herbert Gutman, and the Burden of Labor History

Not being a brilliant and systematic lecturer, his success came from a more individual approach. Using his enthusiasm on individuals and small groups, he accomplished more than those who held large audiences spellbound. He did lecture and he often gave talks to large groups, but his success came from his marshalling of facts and from his enthusiasm for what he was advocating.

[Affectionately known by his first name], he was generous in his praise for conscientious effort and credited his students with ideas they got from him, or which he inspired. To many of us he was a second father, unselfishly interested in our welfare, in and out of the classroom. Nor did his interest cease when they left the university. He kept in touch with everything they were doing and gave them counsel and assistance whenever they sought his help, as they were constantly doing.[1]

How many books and articles in labor history in recent years introduced themselves with some reference to the contrast between John R. Commons and Herbert G. Gutman? The former was the representative of the "old," the latter the apostle of the "new." The former, product of a small-town Indiana and Presbyterian upbringing, from early on adopted Spencerian, evolutionist notions of social progress; the latter, a New York Jew and son of a Bolshevik partisan, re-emphasized the sources of inequality and class antagonism in American life. The former focused scholarly inquiry on the formal institutions of industrial relations, and, in doing so, on the skilled, "American," male workers who took part in them; the latter sought out the informal, community basis in a labor conflict and, in doing so, emphasized the pluralistic, immigrant-based cultures of the nation's wage-earning population. The former, a dedicated Progressive Era reformer, accepted the legitimacy of capitalist institutions in America; the latter, aligning himself with the wave of post-1960 insurgencies, questioned not only the immediate logic of capitalist structures but the degree of popular consent historically vested in them.

Yet, I think that the commonplace, almost instinctually summoned contrast between Commons and Gutman hides some similarities that are likely more than coincidental. One point they had in common, of course, was the University of Wisconsin, to which as a graduate student Gutman was attracted, in part, on account of the tradition of Commons and the "Wisconsin school" of labor history. Yet, while he apparently had some contact with Commons's protégé, Selig Perlman, and while he also shared with Commons an interest in the details of economic development, this influence appears more limited than one might have expected. I never heard Herb speak of Perlman, for example, and Gutman's seminars included precious little of the literature produced in the Commons mold.[2]

Rather, I suspect, if there was an underlying convergence in the careers of Commons and Gutman, it was "structurally determined," a product of both adversity and recognition encountered in the course of their extraordinary work. Despite the considerable differences of personal, social, and political contexts, in both cases young "radical" academics fought their way from the margins of their fields into positions of intellectual and professional respectability.[3] As intellectuals effectively asserting workers' claims on public policy (Commons) and historical consciousness (Gutman), moreover, they each implicitly accepted an added burden on their individual work. Their commitment to the advancement of a larger vision of human welfare in part accounts for the exceptional reputation each came to enjoy from those who knew them.

In Commons's case the path to academic security and acknowledged public stature came at the cost of both political and emotional turmoil. His first two appointments were cut short on account of his unacceptable political sympathies and economic theories.[4] Commons had willfully departed from the norms of neoclassical economics, following his mentor, Richard Ely, toward assimilation of German historicist influences as well as Henry Georgite economic doctrines, both of which contravened the supposedly immutable workings of iron economic laws. While never producing the sustained theoretical work he set as a goal, Commons contributed mightily to the practical reform of state welfare and industrial relations policy.[5]

Probably more than any other intellectual of his day, he contributed as well to the legitimacy of organized labor in the eyes of "polite society." Yet, despite his many accomplishments and acceptance within the public realm, Commons remained something of an enigmatic and marginal figure within his own discipline. In the course of his institutional economic studies in Madison, he found satisfaction less in his influence on other academic economists than in his own world of students where he was affectionately known as "John R."[6] And even as he threw himself energetically into numerous projects, Commons never entirely escaped a cloud of paralyzing depression, intermittently triggered since his college days from the pressure of work or other sources of intimate, private pain.[7]

Herbert Gutman, of course, traveled in very different circles from John R. Commons. He, too, however, was marked by an extended sojourn in the academic "wilderness." He watched for years as people with better degrees, better connections, more publications, more acceptable research interests, and much shallower minds gathered in the emoluments of the profession. Like a folksinger from the 1960s club scene, his reputation and cult-like student following began to emerge via the "underground" of state historical journals (as well as the circulation of unpublished manuscripts) through which he disseminated his early work. Shielded until mid-career from the attention of well-endowed senior scholars in American history, Gutman functioned as a feisty, even exuberant critic of mainstream work. Working indefatigably in his own laboratory, he regularly enthralled his students with the products of his research—narratives that not only had gone unnoticed but sharply challenged conventional wisdom about the structure, behavior, and beliefs of the American working class.

Even as John R. Commons regularly incorporated his students into his own projects (adding to their own sense of self-esteem), so did Gutman cultivate a pleasant feeling of conspiracy among his students and far-flung youthful admirers. In huddles at professional meetings, he regularly provided a wide-ranging and uncensored intelligence report on what was new or not so new on the historical hustings. His devastatingly humorous put-downs of academic shysters, pompous social scientists, and narrow-minded careerists (only slightly muted in face-to-face encounters with the same subjects) contrasted with his unstinting praise for budding young talents. For his friends' work he characteristically restricted himself to three reactions: "that's interesting" masked a range of responses from quizzical disbelief to outright scorn for the conclusion reached; "smart," widely proffered on creative research, offered a generous compliment to the author's originality but not necessarily final concurrence;

while "really smart" was tantamount to an initiation ceremony into a magic inner circle of serious talents.

As his student, I think his most powerful impact came during those evenings when I was invited to Herb and Judy Gutman's house for dinner. Sometime late in the evening, Herb would invariably excuse himself before his dinner guests, indicating he wanted to "show you something upstairs." There was always a sense of nervous excitement about those moments alone with Herb in his study. There, amid a mountain of books, notecards, and paper, lay a mystical world of buried treasure. Here was the quest that counted, where the unknown experience of the American people was being gathered, and unheard voices were waiting to cry out. Here was History-in-Creation.

Herb's method in his study normally began with a leading question— e.g., who were the prostitutes in Lynchburg?—to which he alone could provide an intelligent answer. Indeed, sometimes you gave him the most conventional response just because he would so enjoy its refutation. Herb would soon proceed into an extended and animated disquisition on his latest research topic. Then came the test of one's mettle as a Gutman student. Bedazzled by Herb's grasp and monopoly of information and swayed as well as by his determination and sureness in pursuit of his subject, could one nevertheless weigh in with a critical rejoinder or at least a probing question? Even a hesitating stutter on his part was signal enough that the thought had affected him, allowing the student to descend the stairs with dignity.

Intellectually, of course, Gutman was in rebellion against the confined respectability to which the Commons tradition had deposited the study of labor in the United States. With his primary graduate training in history rather than economics, Gutman from the beginning was more interested in "discovering" the world of American workers than in assimilating that world into a set of institutional matrices. Like Commons, however, Gutman also found inspiration for a new approach among foreigners, in particular, the Marxism of British scholars such as Christopher Hill, Eric Hobsbawm, Raymond Williams, and especially E. P. Thompson. While holding on to the basic categories of class analysis, Thompson's "New Left" perspective offered a window on the complex and shifting world of workers' lived experience and homegrown ideas and actions. Less systematic in his theoretical convictions, Gutman borrowed heavily from the British Marxists but also drew eclectically from emergent findings and theories of American social science, including modernization models, mobility studies, quantitative approaches to social structure, and ultimately cultural anthropology and kinship theory.

Gutman's research grasp was a thing of wonder. Spilling out over the conventional subcategories of specialization within U.S. history, his findings about nineteenth-century American life were richer and more complex than even his own ever-expanding analytic framework could contain. Indeed, in my view, he left unfinished (and unpublished) some of his best work because he could not fully come to grips with its implications. Let me illustrate my point with reference to one essay, completed during a most productive academic year (1966–67) while Gutman was in residence at Stanford's Center for Advanced Study in the Behavioral Sciences, now posthumously published through the diligent efforts of Ira Berlin.

In "Labor in the Land of Lincoln: Coal Miners on the Prairie," Gutman offers a fascinating *histoire totale* of the coal-mining community of Braidwood, Illinois. The themes of town building, immigration, class structure, social mobility, standards of living, women's place in community protests, racial divisions, and class and ethnic culture all receive extended treatment even as the author follows two Scottish-born miners, John James and Daniel McLaughlin, through a narrative focusing on labor conflict and political organization. Upon rereading this essay (a manuscript copy came into my possession years ago), I am struck simultaneously by Gutman's tenacity in the pursuit of evidence and by his apparent frustration in gaining satisfactory control or explanation of why things occurred in Braidwood as they did. On the first point, for example, Gutman scours the sources for an explanation of the town's history and workers' place in it, including their diet, dress, and degree of property ownership. He ingeniously uses a list of seventy-four miners killed in one set of pits during a severe flood in 1883 to test his hypothesis that the miners' world in Braidwood "tightened family ties but weakened ethnic distinctions." Lacking employment records, Gutman teases out of the disaster reports the fact that nearly a third of those killed were related to one another, but that otherwise hiring had been spread almost indiscriminately among white ethnic groups. Gutman's voracious appetite for historical truths of all kinds is likewise evident in footnotes that attest to the importance of free-roaming cows as "supplementary income for prairie workers" and that anecdotally identify the widowed washerwoman of Braidwood's John James as the stepmother of future United Mine Workers leader John Mitchell.[8]

I suspect, however, that Gutman was troubled by more than the run-on length of what he reported in "Labor in the Land of Lincoln." One of the mysteries that may have concerned him surrounds the figure of John James himself. On the one hand, James and McLaughlin, as Scottish working-class immigrants who take up leading positions in the Braidwood labor movement, pose a neat contrast (which Gutman exploits at both the beginning and the end of the essay) to the career of a third countryman, Allan Pinkerton (the former Chartist turned union-busting detective). Both James and McLaughlin contribute to the creation of Braidwood's "rude republic," a portrait of working-class culture as evocative as any study currently available.

Gutman neatly suggests the Braidwood miners' cycle from trade union experience in the Mother Country to immigrant faith in the American dream of individual mobility and material progress and finally to participation in a more critical community of interests among workers and other townspeople in the face of corporate power and wage cutting. James, in particular, a self-styled poet evicted from his company-owned house during the strike of 1868, emerges as an authentic voice of American worker disillusionment with the Age of Capital: "Let me tell the Chicago and Wilmington Coal Company [C&W] that they may drive me from their services—they no doubt can do without me and I without them—but whether I work for them or not, they can never control my opinions, nor stay my tongue, my brain, nor pen."[9] Unable to find work as a miner, James opened a general store and steamship agency but continued to play an important role in the workers' political community; in 1875 he even took an official position with the Miners' National Association.

And yet, over time, the apparently seamless web uniting the people of Braidwood against the coal company lost its most eloquent advocate. In the aftermath of a disastrous eight-month-long strike in 1877 (Gutman calls it the longest industrial dispute in the nation's history), suffering miners, led by Daniel McLaughlin, turned to Greenback-Labor politics and secret affiliation with the Knights of Labor. Braidwood and its county environs would, indeed, serve as a bastion of Greenback-Labor strength through the mid-eighties, and McLaughlin would ultimately take his place as a powerful labor lobbyist within the state legislature. But John James did not follow the trajectory of his politicized working-class neighbors. Apparently employed as a salesman for the coal companies by 1877, he attacked the strikers for listening to the "secret conclave" of the Knights of Labor and even supported a major-party fusion candidate against the Greenback-Labor slate. At odds with many of his old friends (although retaining the respect of Miners' National Association president John Siney), James left Braidwood in 1880 to take work as superintendent of an Ohio coal mine.[10]

Just what kind of society and what kind of culture produces, side by side, a Daniel McLaughlin and a John James? I suspect that Herbert Gutman had not yet satisfied himself with his answer when he lay "Labor in the Land of Lincoln" on his shelf in 1967. To be sure, there were other internal questions in the essay that he had also not yet resolved. Just how representative, and representative of what, was Braidwood? The struggles of the Braidwood miners across the 1870s, for example, were more than once weakened by the failure of nearby Streator, Illinois, miners to maintain a similar strike discipline. But other than the fact that Streator was a younger town apparently lacking in inspired leaders, it is not clear why Braidwood's rude republic had such restricted local boundaries.

While embedded in a rich and complicated narrative (reflecting Gutman's insistence on the ambiguities of history), the qualms listed above were not minor points but went to the heart of his project. How was the sympathetic historian to come to grips with the patterns as well as the variety of American working-class experience and with its defeats as well as triumphs? Although he never laid his answers to these questions out in a cut-and-dried way, I see Gutman's later work as an attempt to clarify some of the dilemmas he had exposed in earlier studies like the one on Braidwood.

The ethnic and racial conflict he encountered in the local studies (most apparent at Braidwood in the importation of black strikebreakers in 1877) received imaginative analytic treatment in his famous 1973 essay on the discontinuity of American working-class experience.[11] Afro-Americans, in particular, entered most of the early studies as peripheral characters, the agents of company manipulations in industrial warfare or victims caught in a crossfire of race and class anger.[12] Only by turning back in time toward slavery and the black family, it seems, could Gutman figure out how to clothe his black subjects with a full dignity as historical subjects, equipped with a parallel set of resources to those that he had already identified among the white working class. Similarly, his later quantitative excavations of class, immigrant, and occupational structure offered Gutman the chance to set his narrative view of the nineteenth century in a more systematic social context. Finally, even the problem of John James was one to which Gutman eventually returned. In his 1982 address to the Organization of American Historians, he identified a "central tension in all dependent groups over time" as that "between individualist (utilitarian) and collective (mutualist) ways of dealing with, and sometimes overcoming, dependence and inequality." Puzzling over the choices and costs of decisions faced by Nate Shaw, David Levinsky, and others struggling to "make it" in America, Gutman in the end boldly insisted that historians face the "tensions" embodied in the record of historical choices: "We are humanized by that encounter and so is American history."[13]

Like John R. Commons, Herbert Gutman assumed a considerable burden in undertaking to change the way historians, and eventually the larger public, understood American workers. Like Commons as well, Gutman was clearly nagged by certain ghosts in the course of his work, at times making it impossible for this normally joyful man to continue with his writing. Perhaps we as labor historians, caught up vicariously in the historical struggles of those removed from us in time and social space, tend to overlook, until too late, the inner turmoil besetting our own working lives. I am in no position to carry the comparison further except to note that our current burden is that much the lighter for the accomplishments of the likes of John R. Commons and Herbert Gutman.

NOTES

This essay originally appeared in *Labor History* 29 (Summer 1988): 313–22. Reprinted by permission.

1. Lafayette G. Harter, Jr., *John R. Commons: His Assault on Laissez-Faire* (Corvallis, Oreg., 1962), 77–78. The first quotation is Harter's own synthetic view; the second is drawn from Commons's famous student, Edwin W. Witte.

2. Herbert G. Gutman, *Power and Culture: Essays on the American Working Class,* ed. Ira Berlin (New York, 1987), 10. In Gutman's Rochester seminar, for example, one was more likely to read the economic histories of Caroline Ware, Richard Morris, Vera Shlakman, and Louis Hartz, or the social history of Oscar Handlin, than the early labor history of Richard Ely, Commons, and their students.

3. Lawrence J. Boyette, "The Roots of American Labor History: The Development of the Wisconsin School" (ms., University of Rochester, 1985), helped to alert me to the unappreciated side of the Ely-Commons tradition.

4. Harter, *Commons,* 20–21.

5. Beyond their empirical research, valuable for its collection of primary sources and its susceptibility to modern-day revisionism, Commons's writings have perhaps been too easily dismissed as conceptually outdated by labor historians. His emphasis, for example, on market expansionism (as opposed to the classic Marxist focus on changes in the mode of production) as the key to capitalist development receives unconscious reinforcement in the work of Paul Sweezy, Andre Gunder Frank, and Emmanuel Wallerstein, whom Robert Brenner critically labels "neo-Smithian Marxists" (Brenner, "The Origins of Capitalist Development: A Critique of Neo-Smithian Marxism," *New Left Review,* July–Aug. 1977, 25–93). Likewise, Commons's long-neglected economic works, *The Legal Foundations of Capitalism* (1924) and *Institutional Economics* (1934), which especially emphasize the larger sociological, legal, and administrative environment of economic growth, deserve another look from labor historians, themselves searching for a more systematic political-economic perspective on social conflict.

In retrospect, for I have not always held this view, I find myself at odds with the most serious recent dismissal of Commons's work. While Alan Dawley is no doubt correct in his revision of the Commons school research on the shoeworkers and Knights of St. Crispin, Dawley's view that Commons was "an efficiency expert in finessing class struggle" and that his "overriding objective was to achieve social harmony without disturbing basic property relations" is unfair to the specific political intervention that Commons was making in the affairs of his times. Commons and a few contemporaries were not revolutionaries, but, nevertheless, they offered a persuasive case, within the dominant idiom of the day, to vastly expand the role of organized labor within public life as well as to defend the legitimacy of the regulatory power of democratic government over the economy. See Dawley, *Classes and Community: The Industrial Revolution in Lynn* (Cambridge, Mass., 1976), 180–84.

6. Harter, *Commons*, 215, 209, 211, 77.

7. Ibid., 83, on Commons's "lifetime propensity to break down at intervals."

8. Gutman, *Power and Culture*, 134, 202, 196.

9. Ibid., 135, 141.

10. Ibid., 210–12, 194–96.

11. "Work, Culture, and Society in Industrializing America, 1815–1919," *American Historical Review* (June 1973), reprinted in Gutman, *Work, Culture, and Society in Industrializing America: Essays in American Working-Class and Social History* (New York, 1976), 3–78.

12. Gutman, *Power and Culture*, 175–84, 203–5. Gutman's fascination with race relations among industrial workers was first highlighted in his essay "The Negro and the United Mine Workers of America: The Career and Letters of Richard L. Davis and Something of Their Meaning, 1890–1900," in Julius Jacobson, ed. *The Negro and the American Labor Movement* (New York, 1968), reprinted in *Work, Culture, and Society*, 121–208.

13. Gutman, *Power and Culture*, 404, 408.

PART TWO

The Contest for Power

2

Class Conflict American-Style

Two well-traveled routes into the Gilded Age are likely to leave the present-day visitor with the same puzzled and unsatisfied feeling. One itinerary pursuing the political history of the era begins in 1876 with the official end of Reconstruction and winds through the election of William McKinley in 1896. The other route, this one taking a social prospectus, departs with the great railroad strikes of 1877 and picks its way through the drama and debris of an industrializing society. The problem is that the two paths never seem to meet. Compartmentalization of subject matter in most textbooks into "politics," "economic change," "social movements," and so on, only papers over the obvious unanswered question—what impact did an industrial revolution of unprecedented magnitude have on the world's most democratic nation?[1]

The question, of course, permits no simple answer. By most accounts the political era inaugurated in 1876 appears, except for the Populist outburst of the mid-1890s, as a conservative, comparatively uneventful time sandwiched between the end of Radical Reconstruction and the new complexities of the twentieth century. With the Civil War's financial and social settlement out of the way, a society desperately wanting to believe that it had removed its last barriers to social harmony by and large lapsed into a period of ideological torpor and narrow-minded partisanship. Political contests, while still the national pastime (national elections regularly drew 80 percent, state and local elections 60–80 percent of eligible voters, 1876–96), seem to have dwelt less on major social issues than on simple party fealty. Fierce rivalries engendered by the sectional, ethnocultural, and economic interest group divisions among the American people increasingly were presided over and manipulated by party professionals. To be sure, genuine policy differences—e.g., over how best to encourage both industry and trade, the degree of danger posed by the saloon, honesty in government—fueled a venomous political rhetoric. As echoed by both national parties from the late 1870s through the early 1890s, however, a complacent political consensus had emerged, stressing individual opportunity, rights in property, and economic freedom from constraints. The welfare of the American Dream, in the minds of both Democrats and Republicans, required no significant governmental tinkering or popular mobilization. Acknowledging the parties' avoidance of changing social and economic realities, a most compelling recent commentary on the late nineteenth-century polity suggests that the "distinct, social need" of the time was in part filled by heightened partisanship and the act of political participation itself.[2]

In contrast to the ritualistic quality of politics, the contemporary social world seems positively explosive. Consolidation of America's industrial revolution touched off an era of unexampled change and turmoil. As work shifted decisively away from agriculture between 1870 and 1890, the manufacturing sector, with a spectacular increase in the amount of capital invested, the monetary value of product, and the number employed, sparked a great economic leap forward. By 1880 Carroll D. Wright, U.S. commissioner of labor statistics, found that the application of steam and water power to production had so expanded that "at least four-fifths" of the "nearly 3 millions of people employed in the mechanical industries of this country" were working under the factory system. It was not just the places of production but the people working within them that represented a dramatic departure from preindustrial America. While only 13 percent of the total population was classified as foreign-born in 1880, 42 percent of those engaged in manufacturing and extractive industries were immigrants. If one adds to this figure workers of foreign parentage and of Afro-American descent, the resulting nonnative/nonwhite population clearly encompassed the great majority of America's industrial work force. Not only, therefore, had the industrial revolution turned a small minority in America's towns and cities into the direct employers of their fellow citizens, but the owners of industry also differed from their employees in national and cultural background. This sudden transformation of American communities, accompanied as it was by a period of intense price competition and unregulated swings in the business cycle, provided plentiful ingredients for social unrest, first manifest on a national scale in the railroad strike of 1877.[3]

The quintessential expression of the labor movement in the Gilded Age was the Noble and Holy Order of the Knights of Labor, the first mass organization of the North American working class. Launched as one of several secret societies among Philadelphia artisans in the late 1860s, the

Knights grew in spurts by the accretion of miners (1874–79) and skilled urban tradesmen (1879–85). While the movement formally concentrated on moral and political education, cooperative enterprise, and land settlement, members found it a convenient vehicle for trade union action, particularly in the auspicious economic climate following the depression of the 1870s. Beginning in 1883, local skirmishes escalated into highly publicized confrontations with the railroad financier Jay Gould, a national symbol of new corporate power. Strikes by Knights of Labor telegraphers and railroad shop craft workers touched off an unprecedented wave of strikes and boycotts that carried on into the renewed depression in 1884–85 and spread to thousands of previously unorganized semiskilled and unskilled laborers, both urban and rural. The Southwest Strike on Gould's Missouri and Texas-Pacific railroad lines, together with massive urban eight-hour campaigns in 1886, swelled a tide of unrest that has become known as the "Great Upheaval." The turbulence aided the efforts of organized labor, and the Knights exploded in size, reaching more than three-quarters of a million members. Although membership dropped off drastically in the late 1880s, the Knights remained a powerful force in many areas through the mid-1890s. Not until the Congress of Industrial Organizations' revival of the 1930s would the organized labor movement again lay claim to such influence within the working population.[4]

At its zenith the movement around the Knights helped to sustain a national debate over the social implications of industrial capitalism. Newspaper editors, lecturers, and clergymen everywhere addressed the Social Question. John Swinton, the leading labor journalist of the day, counted Karl Marx, Hawaii's king Kalakaua, and the Republican party's chief orator, Robert G. Ingersoll, among the enlightened commentators on the subject. Even the U.S. Senate in 1883 formally investigated "Relations between Labor and Capital." Nor was the debate conducted only from on high. In laboring communities across the nation the local press as well as private correspondence bore witness to no shortage of eloquence from the so-called inarticulate. One of the busiest terminals of communications was the Philadelphia office of Terence Vincent Powderly, general master workman of the Knights of Labor. Unsolicited personal letters expressing the private hopes and desperations of ordinary American citizens daily poured in upon the labor leader: an indigent southern mother prayed that her four young girls would grow up to find an honorable living; an unemployed New York cakemaker applied for a charter as an organizer; a Cheyenne chief sought protection for his people's land; an inventor offered to share a new idea for the cotton gin on condition that it be used cooperatively.[5]

Amid spreading agitation, massed strength, and growing public awareness, the labor issues ultimately took tangible political form. Wherever the Knights of Labor had organized by the mid-1880s, it seemed, contests over power and rights at the workplace evolved into a community-wide fissure over control of public policy as well. Indeed, in some 200 towns and cities from 1885 to 1888 the labor movement actively fielded its own political slates. Adopting "Workingmen's," "United Labor," "Union Labor," "People's party," and "Independent" labels for their tickets, or alternatively taking over one of the standing two-party organizations in town, those local political efforts revealed deep divisions within the contemporary political culture and evoked sharp reactions from traditional centers of power. Even as manufacturers' associations met labor's challenge at the industrial level, business response at the political level was felt in the dissolution of party structures, creation of antilabor citizens' coalitions, new restrictive legislation, and extralegal law and order leagues. In their ensemble, therefore, the political confrontations of the 1880s offer a most dramatic point of convergence between the world leading out of 1876 and that stretching from 1877. As a phenomenon simultaneously entwined in the political and industrial history of the Gilded Age, the subject offers an opportunity to redefine the main issues of the period.

The labor movement of the Gilded Age, not unlike its nineteenth-century British counterpart, spoke a "language of class" that was "as much political as economic." In important ways an eighteenth-century republican political inheritance still provided the basic vocabulary. The emphasis within the movement on equal rights, on the identity of work and self-worth, and on secure, family-centered households had informed American political radicalism for decades. A republican outlook lay at the heart of the protests of journeymen-mechanics and women millworkers during the Jacksonian period; it likewise inspired abolitionists and the woman suffrage and temperance movements and even contributed to the common-school crusade. Within the nineteenth-century political mainstream this tradition reached its height of influence in the free labor assault of the Radical Republicans against slavery. The fracture of the Radical Republican bloc, as David Montgomery has demonstrated, signaled a break in the tradition itself. The more conspicuous and politically dominant side of the schism reflected the growing ideological conservatism of America's industrialists and their steady merger into older socioeconomic elites. A less complacent message, however, also percolated through the age of Hayes, Harrison, and Hanna. Taking place largely outside the party system, this renewed radicalism found a home within an invigorated labor movement.[6]

Working-class radicalism in the Gilded Age derived its principles—as grouped around economic, national-political, and cultural themes—from the period of the early revolutionary-democratic bourgeoisie. Implicitly, labor radicals embraced a unifying conception of work and culture that Norman Birnbaum has labeled the *Homo faber* ideal: "an artisanal conception of activity, a visible, limited, and directed relationship to nature." The *Homo faber* ethic found its political embodiment in Enlightenment liberalism. "From that source," notes Trygve R. Tholfson in a commentary on mid-Victorian English labor radicalism, "came a trenchant rationalism, a vision of human emancipation, the expectation of progress based on reason, and an inclination to take the action necessary to bring society into conformity with rationally demonstrable principles." In the late nineteenth century, Enlightenment liberalism was harnessed to a historical understanding of American nationalism, confirmed by both the American Revolution and the Civil War. Together these political, economic, and moral conceptions coalesced around a twin commitment to the citizen-as-producer and the producer-as-citizen. For nearly a century Americans had been proud that their country, more than anywhere else in the world, made republican principles real. In this respect the bloody war over slavery served only to confirm the ultimate power of the ideal.[7]

Certain tendencies of the Gilded Age, however, heralded for some an alarming social regression. The permanency of wage labor, the physical and mental exhaustion inflicted by the factory system, and the arrogant exercise of power by the owners of capital threatened the rational and progressive march of history. "Republican institutions," the preamble to the constitution of the Knights of Labor declared simply, "are not safe under such conditions." "We have openly arrayed against us," a Chicago radical despaired in 1883, "the powers of the world, most of the intelligence, all the wealth, and even law itself." The lament of a Connecticut man that "factoryism, bankism, collegism, capitalism, insuranceism and the presence of such lump-headed malignants as Professor William Graham Sumner" were stultifying "the native genius of this state" framed the evil in more homespun terms. In 1883 the cigar-makers' leader Samuel Gompers, not yet accepting the inevitability of capitalist industry, bemoaned the passing of the day of "partners at the work bench" that had given way to "the tendency . . . which makes man, the worker, a part of the machine." The British-born journalist Richard J. Hinton, an old Chartist who had commanded black troops during the Civil War, also reflected on the sudden darkening of the social horizon. The "average, middle-class American," he complained, simply could not appreciate the contemporary position of American workers: "They all look back to the days when they were born in some little American village. . . . They have seen their time and opportunity of getting on in the world, and they think that is the condition of society today, when it is totally a different condition."[8]

In response the labor movement in the Gilded Age turned the plowshares of a consensual political past into a sword of class conflict. "We declare," went the Knights' manifesto, "an inevitable and irresistible conflict between the wage-system of labor and republican system of government." To some extent older demons seemed simply to have reappeared in new garb, and, as such, older struggles beckoned with renewed urgency. A Greenback editor in Rochester, New Hampshire, thus proclaimed that "patriots" who overturn the "lords of labor" would be remembered next to "the immortal heroes of the revolution and emancipation."[9]

To many outside observers in the 1880s, the American working class—in terms of organization, militancy, and collective self-consciousness—appeared more advanced than its European counterparts. A leader of the French Union des Chambres Syndicales Ouvrières compared the self-regarding, individualist instincts of the French workers to those of the Americans enrolled in the Knights of Labor (Ordre des Chevaliers du Travail):

> Unfortunately, the French worker, erratic as he is enthusiastic, of an almost discouraging indolence when it is a question of his own interests, does not much lend himself to organization into a great order like yours. He understands nevertheless their usefulness, even cites them as an example each time that he has the occasion to prove the possibility of the solidarity of workers; but when it comes to passing from the domain of theory to that of practice, he retreats or disappears. Thirsty for freedom he is always afraid of alienating any one party while contracting commitments toward a collectivity; mistrustful, he is afraid of affiliating with a group whose positions might not correspond exactly to those inscribed on his own flag; undisciplined, he conforms with difficulty to rules which he has given to himself. . . . He wants to play it safe and especially will not consent to any sacrifice without having first calculated the advantages it will bring to him.

Eleanor Marx and Edward Aveling returned from an 1886 American tour with a glowing assessment of the workers' mood. Friedrich Engels, too, in the aftermath of the eight-hour strikes and the Henry George campaign, attached a special preface to the 1887 American edition of *The Condition of the Working Class in England in 1844:*

In European countries, it took the working class years and years before they fully realized the fact that they formed a distinct and, under the existing social conditions, a permanent class of modern society; and it took years again until this class-consciousness led them to form themselves into a distinct political party, independent of, and opposed to, all the old political parties, formed by the various sections of the ruling classes. On the more favored soil of America, where no medieval ruins bar the way, where history begins with the elements of the modern bourgeois society as evolved in the seventeenth century, the working class passed through these two stages of its development within ten months.[10]

Nor was it only in the eyes of eager well-wishers that the developments of the 1880s seemed to take on a larger significance. Surveying the map of labor upheaval, the conservative Richmond *Whig* wrote in 1886 of "socialistic and agrarian elements" threatening "the genius of our free institutions." The Chicago *Times* went so far in its fear of impending revolution as to counsel the use of hand grenades against strikers.[11]

Revolutionary anticipations, pro or con, proved premature. That was true at least partly because both the movement's distant boosters as well as its domestic detractors sometimes misrepresented its intentions. Gilded Age labor radicals did not self-consciously place themselves in opposition to a prevailing economic system but displayed a sincere ideological ambivalence toward the capitalist marketplace. On the one hand, they frequently invoked a call for the "abolition of the wage system." On the other hand, like the classical economists, they sometimes spoke of the operation of "natural law" in the marketplace, acknowledged the need for a "fair return" on invested capital, and did not oppose profit per se. Employing a distinctly pre-Marxist economic critique that lacked a theory of capital accumulation or of surplus value, labor leaders from Ira Steward to Terence Powderly tried nevertheless to update and sharpen the force of received wisdom. The Knights thus modified an earlier radical interpretation of the labor-cost theory of value, wherein labor, being the source of all wealth, should individually be vested with the value of its product, and demanded for workers only an intentionally vague "proper share of the wealth they create." In so doing they were able to shift the weight of the analysis (not unlike Marx) to the general, collective plight of the laboring classes. In their eyes aggregation of capital together with cutthroat price competition had destroyed any semblance of marketplace balance between employer and employee. Under the prevailing economic calculus, labor had been demoted into just another factor of production whose remuneration was determined not by custom or human character but by market price. In such a situation they concluded, as Samuel Walker has noted, that "the contract was not and could not be entered into freely. . . . The process of wage determination was a moral affront because it degraded the personal dignity of the workingman." This subservient position to the iron law of the market constituted "wage slavery," and like other forms of involuntary servitude it had to be "abolished."[12]

Labor's emancipation did not, ipso facto, imply the overthrow of capitalism, a system of productive relations that the Knights in any case never defined. To escape wage slavery workers needed the strength to redefine the social balance of power with employers and their allies—and the will and intelligence to use that strength. One after another the Knights harnessed the various means at their disposal—education, organization, cooperation, economic sanction, and political influence—to this broad end: "To secure to the workers the full enjoyment [note, not the full return] of the wealth they create, sufficient leisure in which to develop their intellectual, moral and social faculties, all of the benefits of recreation, and pleasures of association; in a word to enable them to share in the gains and honors of advancing civilization."[13]

A wide range of strategic options was represented within the counsels of the labor movement. One tendency sought to check the rampant concentration of wealth and power with specific correctives on the operation of the free market. Radical Greenbackism (with roots in Kelloggism and related monetary theories), Henry George's single tax, and land nationalization, each of which commanded considerable influence among the Knights of Labor, fit this category. Another important tendency, cooperation, offered a more self-reliant strategy of alternative institution building, or, as one advocate put it, "the organization of production without the intervention of the capitalist." Socialism, generally understood at the time as a system of state as opposed to private ownership of production, offered a third alternative to wage slavery. Except for a few influential worker-intellectuals and strong pockets of support among German-Americans, however, socialism carried comparatively little influence in the 1880s. The argument of the veteran abolitionist and labor reformer Joseph Labadie—"To say that state socialism is the rival of co-operation is to say that Jesus Christ was opposed to Christianity"—met a generally skeptical reception. Particularly in the Far West, self-identified anarchists also agitated from within the ranks of the Order.[14]

If Gilded Age labor representatives tended to stop short of a frontal rejection of the political-economic order, there was nevertheless no mistaking their philosophic radicalism. Notwithstanding differences in emphasis, the labor movement's political sentiments encompassed both a sharp critique of social inequality and a broad-based prescription for a more humane future. Indeed, the labor representative who shrugged off larger philosophical and political commitments in favor of a narrow incrementalism was likely to meet with incredulity. One of the first, and most classic, enunciations of business unionism, for example, received just this response from the Senate Committee on Labor and Capital in 1883. After taking testimony from workers and labor reformers across the country for six months, the committee, chaired by New Hampshire senator Henry Blair, interviewed Adolph Strasser, president of the cigar-makers' union. Following a disquisition on the stimulating impact of shorter working hours on workers' consumption patterns, Strasser was asked if he did not contemplate a future beyond the contemporary exigencies of panic and overproduction, "some time [when] every man is to be an intelligent man and an enlightened man?" When Strasser did not reply, Senator Blair interceded to elaborate the question. Still Strasser rebuffed the queries: "Well, our organization does not consist of ideal-ists. . . . we do [not] control the production of the world. That is con-trolled by employers, and that is a matter for them." Senator Blair was taken aback.

> Blair. I was only asking you in regard to your ultimate ends.
> Witness. We have no ultimate ends. We are going on from day to day. We are fighting only for immediate objects—objects that can be realized in a few years. . . .
> Blair. I see that you are a little sensitive lest it should be thought that you are a mere theorizer. I do not look upon you in that light at all.
> Witness. Well, we say in our constitution that we are opposed to theorists, and I have to represent the organization here. We are all practical men.
> Blair. Have you not a theory upon which you have organized?
> Witness. Yes, sir: our theory is the experience of the past in the United States and in Great Britain. That is our theory, based upon actual facts. . . .
> Blair. In other words you have arrived at the theory which you are trying to apply?
> Witness. We have arrived at a practical result.
> Blair. But a practical result is the application of a theory is it not?[15]

On a cultural level, labor's critique of American society bore the same relation to Victorian respectability that its political radicalism bore to contemporary liberalism. In both cases the middle-class and working-class radical variants derived from a set of common assumptions but drew from them quite different, even opposing, implications. No contemporary, for example, took more seriously than the Knights of Labor the cultural imperatives toward productive work, civic responsibility, education, a wholesome family life, temperance, and self-improvement. The intellectual and moral development of the individual, they would have agreed with almost every early nineteenth-century lyceum lecturer, was a precondition for the advancement of democratic civilization. In the day of Benjamin Franklin such values may well have knit together master craftsmen, journeymen, and apprentices. In the age of the factory system, however, the gulf between employer and employee had so widened that the lived meanings of the words were no longer the same.

For the Knights the concept of the producing classes indicated an ultimate social division that they perceived in the world around them. Only those associated with idleness (bankers, speculators), corruption (lawyers, liquor dealers, gamblers), or social parasitism (all of the above) were categorically excluded from membership in the Order. Other social strata such as local merchants and manufacturers were judged by their individual acts, not by any inherent structural antagonism to the workers' movement. Those who showed respect for the dignity of labor (i.e., who sold union-made goods or employed union workers at union conditions) were welcomed into the Order. Those who denigrated the laborer or his product laid themselves open to the righteous wrath of the boycott or strike. Powderly characteristically chastised one ruthless West Virginia coal owner: "Don't die, even if you do smell bad. We'll need you in a few years as a sample to show how *mean* men used to be." This rather elastic notion of class boundaries on the part of the labor movement was reciprocated in the not inconsequential number of shopkeepers and small manuacturers who expressed sympathy and support for the labor movement.[16]

Idealization of hearth and home, a mainstay of familial sentimentality in the Gilded Age, also enjoyed special status within the labor movement. For here, as clearly as anywhere in the radicals' worldview, conventional assumptions had a critical, albeit ambivalent, edge in the context of changing social circumstances. Defense of an idealized family life as both moral and material mainstay of society served as one basis of criticism of capitalist industry. The machinist John Morrison argued before the Senate investigating committee that the insecurities of the unskilled labor market were so threatening family life as to make the house "more like a dull prison instead of a home." A self-educated Scottish-born leader of the type-founders, Edward King, associated trade union morality with the domestic "sentiments of sympathy and humanity" against the "business principles" of the age. Almost unanimously, the vision of the good life for labor radicals included the home.[17]

The importance of the domestic moral order to the late nineteenth-century radical vision also translated into an unparalleled opening of the labor movement to women. As Susan Levine has documented, the Knights of Labor beckoned to wage-earning women and workingmen's wives to join in construction of a "cooperative commonwealth," which, without disavowing the Victorian ideal of a separate female sphere of morality and domestic virtue, sought to make that sphere the center of an active community life.[18]

The Knights' self-improving and domestic commitments both converged in the working-class radicals' antipathy to excessive drinking. The oath of temperance, which became known as "the Powderly pledge," appealed in turn to intellectual development and protection of the family as well as to the collective interests of the labor movement. Like monopoly, the bottle lay waiting to fasten a new form of slavery upon the free worker. In another sense, as David Brundage has suggested, the growing capitalization of saloons together with expansion of saloon-linked variety theater directly threatened a family-based producers' community. While most radicals stopped short of prohibition, exhortations in behalf of temperance were commonplace. In part it was a matter of practical necessity. Tension between the mores of traditional plebeian culture and the need for self-discipline by a movement striving for organization and power were apparent in Thomas Barry's appeal to Saginaw Valley general strikers: "My advice has always been in favor of sobriety. . . . If a man wants a glass of beer he should take it, but it is this going to extremes that is dangerous. The danger that would threaten us on the [picnic] grounds would be the system of treating. . . . If you are invited often drink pop. When you don't want to drink pop drop your pipe and smoke a cigar for a change. . . . I expect you all to act as deputy marshalls."[19]

In general, then, the labor movement of the late nineteenth century provided a distinct arena of articulation and practice for values that crossed class lines. Two aspects of this use of inherited values for radical ends merit reemphasis. First, to the extent that labor radicalism shared in the nineteenth century's cult of individualism, it established a social and moral framework for individual achievement. The culture of the labor movement stressed the development of individual capacity but not competition with other individuals; while striving to elevate humanity, it ignored what S. G. Boritt has identified as the essence of the Lincoln-sanctified American Dream—the individual's "right to rise." The necessary reliance by the labor movement upon collective strength and community sanction militated against the possessive individualism that anchored the world of the workers' better-off neighbors. By its very nature, the labor movement set limits to the individual accumulation of wealth extracted from others' efforts and represented, in Edward King's words, "the graduated elimination of the personal selfishness of man."[20]

Second, in an age of evolutionary, sometimes even revolutionary, faith in progress and the future (a faith generally shared by labor radicals), the movement made striking use of the past. Without renouncing the potential of industrialism for both human liberty and material progress, radicals dipped selectively into a popular storehouse of memory and myth to capture alternative images of human possibility. The choice of the name "Knights of Labor" itself presented images of chivalry and nobility fighting the unfeeling capitalist marketplace. Appeals to the "nobility of toil" and to the worker's "independence" conjured up the proud village smithy—not the degradation of labor in the factory system. Finally, celebrations of historic moments of human liberation and political advancement challenged a political-economic orthodoxy beholden to notions of unchanging, universal laws of development. Indeed, so conspicuously sentimental were the celebrations of Independence Day and Memorial Day that Powderly had to defend the Order from taunts of "spread-eagleism" and "Yankee doodleism."[21]

This sketch of working-class radicalism in the Gilded Age raises one final question. Whose movement—and culture—was it? In a country as diverse as the United States, with a labor force and labor movement drawn from a heterogeneous mass of trades, races, and nationalities, any group portrait runs the risk of oversimplification. The articulate leadership of the Knights of Labor and the political movement that sprang from it included brainworkers (especially the editors of the labor press), skilled craft workers, and shopkeepers who looked to the labor movement as a source of order in a disorderly age. The self-conception of the radical labor leadership as a middle social stratum, balanced between the very rich and very poor, was evident in Powderly's 1885 characterization of his own ancestors—"they did not move in court circles; nor did they figure in police courts."[22]

This dominant stream within the labor movement included people who had enjoyed considerable control over their jobs, if not also economic autonomy, men who often retained claim to the tools as well as the knowledge of their trade. They had taken seriously the ideal of a republic of producers in which hard work would contribute not only to the individual's improved economic standing but also to the welfare of the community. So long as they could rely on their own strength as well as their neighbors' support, this skilled stratum organized in an array of craft unions showed economic and political resilience. But the spreading confrontations with national corporate power, beginning in the 1870s, indicated just how much erosion had occurred in the position of those who relied on custom, skill, and moral censure as ultimate weapons. Industrial dilution of craft skills and a direct economic and political attack on union practices provided decisive proof to these culturally conservative workingmen of both the illegitimacy and ruthlessness of the growing power of capital. It was they, according to every recent study of late nineteenth-century laboring communities, who formed the backbone of local labor movements. The Knights were, therefore, first of all a coalition of reactivating, or already organized, trade unions.[23]

For reasons of their own, masses of workers who had not lost full and equal citizenship—for they had never possessed it—joined the skilled workers within the Knights. Wherever the Order achieved political successes, it did so by linking semiskilled and unskilled industrial workers, including blacks and new immigrants, to its base of skilled workers and leaders. Although lacking the vote, the presence of women in the Order also undoubtedly strengthened its broader community orientation. The special strength of the Knights, noted the Boston *Labor Leader* astutely, lay "in the fact that the whole life of the community is drawn into it, that people of all kinds are together . . . , and that they all get directly the sense of each others' needs."[24]

Politically, the Knights of Labor envisioned a kind of producer democracy. The organized power of labor was capable of revitalizing democratic citizenship and safeguarding the public good within a regulated marketplace economy. Through vigilant shop committees and demands such as the eight-hour day, organized workers—both men and women—would ensure minimal standards of safety and health at the industrial workplace, even as they surrounded the dominant corporate organizational model of business with cooperative models of their own.[25] A pride in honest and useful work, rational education, and personal virtue would be nurtured through a rich associational life spread out from the workplace to meeting hall to the hearth and home. Finally, the integrity of public institutions would be vouchsafed by the workingmen in politics. Purifying government of party parasitism and corruption, cutting off the access to power that allowed antilabor employers to bring the state apparatus to their side in industrial disputes, improving and widening the scope of vital public services, and even contemplating the takeover of economic enterprises that had passed irreversibly into monopoly hands—by these means worker-citizens would lay active claim to a republican heritage.

The dream was not to be. At the workplace management seized the initiative toward the future design and control of work. A managerial revolution overcoming the tenacious defenses of the craft unions transferred autonomy over such matters as productivity and skill from custom and negotiation to the realm of corporate planning. Except for the garment trades and the mines, the national trade unions had generally retreated from the country's industrial heartland by 1920. In the local community as well, the differences, even antagonisms, among workers often stood out more than did the similarities. Segmentation of labor markets, urban ethnic and socioeconomic residential segregation, cultural as well as a protectionist economic disdain for the new immigrants, and the depoliticization of leisure time (i.e., the decline of associational life sponsored by labor organizations) all contributed toward a process of social fragmentation. In such circumstances working-class political cooperation proved impossible. The Socialist party and the Progressive slates could make little more than a dent in the hold of the two increasingly conservative national parties over the electorate. Only with the repolarization of political life beginning in 1928 and culminating in the New Deal was the relation of labor and the party system again transformed. By the late 1930s and 1940s a revived labor movement was beginning, with mixed success, to play the role of a leading interest group and reform conscience within the Democratic party.[26]

This impressionistic overview permits one further observation of a quite general nature. One of the favorite tasks of American historians has been to explain why the United States, alone among the nations of the Western world, passed through the industrial revolution without the establishment of a class consciousness and an independent working-class political movement. Cheap land, the cult of individualism, a heterogeneous labor force, social mobility, and the federal separation of powers comprise several of the numerous explanations that have been offered. While not directly denying the importance of any of the factors listed above, this study implicitly suggests a different approach to the problem of American exceptionalism.

The answer appears to lie less in a permanent structural determinism—whether the analytic brace be political, economic, or ideological—than in a dynamic and indeed somewhat fortuitous convergence of events. To understand the vicissitudes of urban politics, we have had to keep in mind the action on at least three levels: the level of working-class social organization (i.e., the nature and strength of the labor movement), the level of business response, and the level of governmental response. During the Gilded Age each of these areas took an incendiary turn, but only briefly and irregularly and most rarely at the same moment. The 1880s, as R. Laurence Moore has reiterated, were the international seed-time for the strong European working-class parties of the twentieth century. In America, too, the momentum in the 1880s was great. Indeed, examined at the levels of working-class organization and industrial militancy, a European visitor might understandably have expected the most to happen here first. At the political level, as well, American workers were in certain respects relatively advanced. In the 1870s and in the 1880s they established independently organized local labor regimes well before the famous French Roubaix or English West Ham labor-Socialist town councils of the 1890s. Then, a combination of forces in the United States shifted radically away from the possibilities outlined in the 1880s. The labor movement fragmented, business reorganized, and the political parties helped to pick up the pieces. The initiatives from without directed at the American working class from the mid-1890s through the mid-1920s—part repression, part reform, part assimilation, and part recruitment of a new labor force—at an internationally critical period in the gestation of working-class movements may mark the most telling exceptionalism about American developments.[27]

It would in any case be years before the necessary conditions again converged and labor rose from the discredited icons of pre-Depression America with a new and powerful political message. Workplace, community, and ballot box would all once again be harnessed to a great social movement. But no two actors are ever in quite the same space at the same time. The choices open to the CIO, it is fair to say, were undoubtedly influenced by both the achievement and failure of their counterparts a half-century earlier.

NOTES

This essay was excerpted from *Workingmen's Democracy* (Urbana: University of Illinois Press, 1983), pp. xi–xiv, 3–14, 228–30. For the creative thrust behind the cut-and-paste job required for this essay, I am indebted to Larry Madaras and James M. SoRelle, who offer a similar excerpt in their reader *Taking Sides: Clashing Views on Controversial Issues in American History,* vol. 2, (Guilford, Conn., 1989), 44–57.

1. For two other revisionist treatments of American class conflict, see Eric Foner, "Why Is There No Socialism in the United States?" *History Workshop* 17 (Spring 1984), 57–80; and Sean Wilentz, "Against Exceptionalism: Class Consciousness and the American Labor Movement, 1790–1920," with responses by Nick Salvatore and Michael Hanagan, in *International Labor and Working-Class History* 26 (Fall 1984), 1–36. For insightful comparative studies, see Ira Katznelson and Aristide Zolberg, *Working-Class Formation: Nineteenth-Century Patterns in Western Europe and the United States* (Princeton, N.J., 1986); and Gary Marks, *Unions in*

Politics: Britain, Germany, and the United States in the Nineteenth and Early Twentieth Centuries (Princeton, N.J., 1989).

2. Richard Hofstader, *The American Political Tradition and the Men Who Made It* (New York, 1948), 164–85; Morton Keller, *Affairs of State: Public Life in Late Nineteenth-Century America* (Cambridge, Mass., 1977), 532–33.

3. U.S. Tenth Census, 1880, *Report on Manufactures of the United States* (Washington, D.C., n.d.), 17, 36; U.S. Thirteenth Census, 1910, Pt. 4, *Population, Occupation Statistics* (Washington, D.C., 1914), 41; U.S. Eleventh Census, 1890, *Compendium of the Eleventh Census*, Pt. 3 (Washington, D.C., 1897), 68; Ira Berlin and Herbert G. Gutman, "The Structure of the American Urban Working Class in the Mid-Nineteenth Century: The South, the North" (paper presented at the annual meeting of the Organization of American Historians, Apr. 3, 1981, Detroit, Mich.); Philip S. Foner, *The Great Labor Uprising of 1877* (New York, 1977).

4. Jonathan Garlock, "A Structural Analysis of the Knights of Labor" (Ph.D. diss., University of Rochester, 1974), 194–210.

5. Mary J. Lockett to Powderly, Apr. 14, 1886; David Davidson to Powderly, Apr. 14, 1886; Powderly to D. W. Bushyhead, July 12, 1886; C. H. Merry to Powderly, Mar. 14, 1886, all in Terence V. Powderly Papers, Catholic University, Washington, D.C.

6. Iorwerth Prothero, *Artisans and Politics in Early Nineteenth-Century London: John Gast and His Times* (Baton Rouge, 1979), 4; James B. Gilbert, *Work without Salvation: America's Intellectuals and Industrial Alienation, 1880–1910* (Baltimore, 1977), viii–ix, 3–13; Daniel T. Rodgers, *The Work Ethic in Industrial America, 1850–1920* (Chicago, 1978). See, e.g., Thomas Dublin, *Women at Work: The Transformation of Work and Community in Lowell, Massachusetts, 1826–1860* (New York, 1979); Alan Dawley, *Class and Community: The Industrial Revolution in Lynn* (Cambridge, Mass., 1979); Robert Sean Wilentz, "Class Conflict and the Rights of Man: Artisans and the Rise of Labor Radicalism in New York City" (Ph.D. diss., Yale University, 1980); Eric Foner, *Free Soil, Free Labor, Free Men: The Ideology of the Republican Party before the Civil War* (New York, 1970); David Montgomery, *Beyond Equality: Labor and the Radical Republicans, 1862–1872* (New York, 1967); John N. Ingham, *The Iron Barons: A Social Analysis of an American Urban Elite, 1874–1965* (Westport, Conn., 1978); and Ellen Carol Dubois, *Feminism and Suffrage: The Emergence of an Independent Women's Movement in America, 1848–1869* (Ithaca, N.Y., 1978).

7. Norman Birnbaum, *The Crisis of Industrial Society* (London, 1969), 107–8; Trygve R. Tholfson, *Working-Class Radicalism in Mid-Victorian England* (New York, 1977), 25–28.

8. George McNeill, *The Labor Movement: The Problem of Today* (Boston, 1887), 491; John Swinton's Paper (hereafter JSP), Dec. 16, 1883, Nov. 15, 1885; *Report of the Committee of the Senate upon the Relations between Labor and Capital*, 3 vols. (Washington, D.C., 1885), I:290, II:438. Major recent monographs on the Knights of Labor include: Gregory S. Kealey and Bryan D. Palmer, *Dreaming of What Might Be: The Knights of labor in Ontario, 1880–1900* (New York, 1982); Richard Oestreicher, *Solidarity and Fragmentation: Working People and Class Consciousness in Detroit, 1875–1900* (Urbana, Ill., 1986); Shelton Stromquist, *A Generation of Boomers:*

The Pattern of Railroad Labor Conflict in Nineteenth-Century America (Urbana, Ill., 1987); Steven J. Ross, "The Politicization of the Working Class: Ideology, Culture, and Politics in Late Nineteenth-Century Cincinnati," *Social History* 11 (May 1986), 171–95. For a useful overview, see Bruce Laurie, "Rise and Fall of the Knights of Labor" in *Artisans into Workers: Labor in Nineteenth-Century America* (New York, 1989).

9. McNeill, *Labor Movement,* 459; Rochester (N.H.) *Anti-Monopolist,* Nov. 9, 1878.

10. *Journal of United Labor* (hereafter *JUL*), Aug. 9, 1988 (translation mine). Engels quoted in R. Laurence Moore, *European Socialists and the American Promised Land* (New York, 1970), 12–13.

11. Richmond *Whig,* Sept. 25, 1886; Chicago *Times* quote in Winfield (Kans.) *American Nonconformist,* Oct. 7, 1887.

12. Samuel Walker, " 'Abolish the Wage System': Terence V. Powderly and the Rhetoric of Labor Reform" (paper presented at the 1979 Knights of Labor Symposium, Newberry Library, Chicago), 8–10. For an older, eloquent, and still valuable assessment of these themes, see Chester McArthur Destler, *American Radicalism, 1865–1901* (Chicago, 1966), 1–31, esp. 25–27.

13. McNeill, *Labor Movement,* 486.

14. *JUL,* June 1882, Feb. 1884, Oct. 10, 1884; McNeill, *Labor Movement,* 485. For an upgrading of the role of the Socialists in the Knights of Labor, see Richard Oestreicher, "Socialism and the Knights of Labor in Detroit, 1877–1886," *Labor History* 22 (Winter 1981), 5–30; and Alan Dawley, "Anarchists, Knights of Labor, and Class Consciousness in the 1880s" (paper presented at the 1979 Knights of Labor Symposium, Newberry Library, Chicago).

15. *Report... Labor and Capital,* I:460.

16. "Some people think it unreasonable to exclude a lawyer from the Knights of Labor, because he is somewhat of a carpenter. He can file a bill, split a hair, chop logic, dovetail an argument, make an entry, get up a case, frame an indictment, empannel a jury, put them in a box, nail a witness, hammer a judge, bore a court, chisel a client, and when the job is finished he will demand the highest wages and take the property" (*JSP,* May 1, 1887; *JUL,* Mar. 1883).

17. *Report... Labor and Capital,* I:758–59, 688.

18. Susan Levine, *Labor's True Woman: Carpet Weavers, Industrialization, and Labor Reform in the Gilded Age* (Philadelphia, 1984).

19. Terence V. Powderly, *Thirty Years of Labor, 1859–1889* (1890; rpt., New York, 1967); David Brundage, "The Producing Classes and the Saloon: Denver in the 1880s," *Labor History* 26 (Winter 1985), 29–52; Saginaw *Courier,* July 19, 1885.

20. The notion of movement culture is borrowed from Lawrence Goodwyn, *Democratic Promise: The Populist Moment in America* (New York, 1976), 88; S. Gabor Boritt, *Lincoln and the Economics of the American Dream* (Memphis, 1978); Edward King, quoted in *Report... Labor and Capital,* II:888.

21. The Knights preferred to think of themselves as part of a Western tradition of innovators who included Galileo, Newton, Columbus, and Ben Franklin—"discontented" men who had made great contributions to "the progress of the world"

(*JUL,* Apr. 10, 1886). See also David Montgomery, "Labor and the Republic in Industrial America: 1860–1920," *Movement Social* 111 (Apr.–June 1980), 204; *JUL,* May 14, 1887.

22. Russell Hann, "Brainworkers and the Knights of Labor: E. E. Sheppard, Phillips Thompson, and the Toronto News, 1883–1887," in Gregory S. Kealey and Peter Warrian, eds., *Essays in Canadian Working-Class History* (Toronto, 1976), 35–57; *JUL,* Mar. 25, 1885.

23. See, e.g., Bryan D. Palmer, *A Culture in Conflict: Skilled Workers and Industrial Capitalism in Hamilton, Ontario, 1860–1915* (Montreal, 1979)

24. Boston *Labor Leader,* Feb. 5, 1887.

25. Paul Buhle, "The Knights of Labor in Rhode Island," *Radical History Review* 5 (Spring 1978), 39–73.

26. Richard Edwards, *Contested Terrain: The Transformation of the Workplace in the Twentieth Century* (New York, 1979), esp. 90–110, 163–83; David Montgomery, *Workers' Control in America* (New York, 1980), esp. 113–38; David Brody, *Workers in Industrial America: Essays on the Twentieth-Century Struggle* (New York, 1980), 3–81; John T. Cumbler, *Working-Class Community in Industrial America: Leisure and Struggle in Two Industrial Cities, 1880–1930* (Westport, Conn., 1979), esp. 41, 126, 161; Gareth Stedman Jones, "Working-Class Culture and Working-Class Politics in London, 1870–1900," *Journal of Social History* 7 (Summer 1974), 460–508; Samuel Lubell, *Future of American Politics* (New York, 1952). Roger W. Lotchin, "Power and Policy: American City Politics between the Two World Wars," in Scott Greer, ed., *Ethnics, Machines, and the Urban American Future* (Cambridge, Mass., 1981), notes that the rise of the new unions in the 1930s also sparked serious challenges to machine politics in Memphis, Jersey City, and Chicago.

27. R. Laurence Moore, *European Socialists and the American Promised Land* (New York, 1970), xv; Joan Wallach Scott, "Social History and the History of Socialism: French Socialist Municipalities in the 1890s," *Le Mouvement Social* 3 (1980), 145–55; Leon Fink, "The Forward March of Labour Started? Building a Politicized Class Culture in West Ham, 1898–1900," in Robert Malcolmson and John Rule, eds., *Protest and Survival* (London, 1994); James Holt, "Trade Unionism in the British and U.S. Steel Industries, 1888–1912: A Comparative Study," *Labor History* 18 (Winter 1977), 5–35.

3

Politics as Social History: A Case Study of Class Conflict and Political Development in Nineteenth-Century New England

The consolidation of the industrial revolution hit New England small-town society with particular force. An expanding national marketplace coupled with the intensification of agriculture doomed large areas of the countryside to a century of depopulation and demoralization while changes in manufacturing drastically altered the composition and character of the settlements that survived and prospered. In the second half of the nineteenth century a world once ordered by the personalism of book, bar, and magistrate disappeared forever as a society of independent householders gave way to a more complex set of economic dependencies. That the work force for the new mills, quarries, and workshops now derived less from Yankee farms than foreign soil added to the strangeness and abruptness of the arrival of a new age. Finally, the symbolic linchpin of the New England community, the town meeting, also fell by the wayside as more and more industrial towns incorporated and adopted the representative structures of urban government.

Contemporary observers as well as latter-day historians carefully noted the impact of economic "progress" on New England's distinct political and social heritage. Nostalgic late nineteenth-century commentators were apt to regard the urban-industrial transformation of small-town society as "a complete change in the character of the town . . . a change for the worse." In this view a small homogeneous community of freeholders gave way to a "heterogeneous mass of men" "with little knowledge of town traditions and less respect for them." Present-day scholars, of course, have offered a different, almost inverted assessment of New England institutional evolution. Colonial historians have made careful distinctions between village consensus and democratic decision making, noting the narrow access to power maintained by gentrylike county elites. Likewise, Stephan Thernstrom, among others, has emphasized the social hierarchy, religious closed-mindedness, and mercantile control exercised in the early nineteenth-century preindustrial town. Michael Frisch has argued that real "community"—implying areas of common public concern distinct from private interest—was experienced less in the good old days than in the very process of modernization or "town-building."[1]

Whether mourned as the dying ember of local democracy or hailed as its true beginning, the displacement of consensual town meeting politics by the more distant structures of representative government and competing professional political parties appears to latter-day observers as an inevitable corollary of modernization. In an inexorable continuum, so it seems, a kaleidoscope of interests replaced the traditional seats of authority; the resulting social dislocation, in turn, bred an anxious "search for order." Finally, stability was restored by a mixture of institutional and ideological adjustments to a more professional, urban, technocratic, and bureaucratic society.[2]

Whatever their unifying value, such assumptions also carry a severe risk of historicism. Process tends to overcome people, forces replace decisions, and conflicts among contemporaries are reduced to the tension of accommodating old ways to new circumstances. In the course of such a progressive *tableau vivant,* popular movements in particular play only the most minor role. Historical treatment of the Knights of Labor, whose dramatic rise and fall coincided with the crucial years of U.S. industrial consolidation, provides an instructive and immediately relevant example. Along the traditional-modern axis of the modernization yardstick, the Knights fit in either as a backward-looking remnant of the preindustrial order or, in Michael J. Cassity's modification, as a transitional expression caught somewhere in the middle. Either way, this leading working-class movement of the century figures less as historical subject than as captive to the assumedly larger social and political currents of the times.[3]

The political and institutional transformation of the town of Rutland, Vermont, however, offers a markedly different perspective on the dynamic of urban political development. Here, as throughout New England, the old consensual town meeting gave way to representative city government under the sway of a socially inclusive two-party competition. But the timing and significance of this transition derived neither from a general recognition that it was time for a change nor from any identifiable modernizing impulse. Rather, institutional change grew out of an intense contest shaking Rutland and much of the rest of the nation in the 1880s over the exercise of private power and public authority. The political and governmental reforms engendered by this period of conflict depended on who was able to reimpose order and what they had to overcome to do so. Throughout these events the presence of the Knights of Labor was of critical historical importance. Given the well-taken injunctions to reunite social with political history, it is hoped that the approach applied in this specific study may prove of more general application as well.[4]

By 1880 a combination of rail and rock had turned the small manufacturing town of Rutland into the state's largest metropolis (population 12,000) and political center of influence. In the railroad boom of the 1850s jealous rivals Troy and Albany built no fewer than six lines through Rutland seeking connections to the agriculture hinterland and a passage to Canada. (Even Jay Gould lived there for three years and accomplished enough to land his partner in a Vermont jail.) While crossing Rutland County land, the railroads opened the way to the full exploitation of mineral wealth buried beneath them. The largest marble company in the world began to take shape in the early 1870s when the lawyer and banker Redfield Proctor entered a fledgling quarrying and finishing industry based in the blue hills surrounding Rutland Village at West Rutland, Sutherland Falls, and Center Rutland (all four settlements lay within the borders of Rutland "town"). By 1880 Proctor's Vermont Marble Company controlled 55 percent of local production, rapidly expanding through technological innovation and vertical integration of marketing, and employed more than a thousand workers. In 1883 Proctor expanded horizontally as well, getting his rivals to join him temporarily in a marble producers' cartel. The influence of Rutland's leading marble manufacturer was also felt outside the business world. The town of Sutherland Falls was renamed Proctor in the early 1880s, during Redfield Proctor's tenure as governor of Vermont.[5]

In political affairs Rutland was dominated by a group of some thirty to fifty families who administered and adjudicated the public's business. United by deep native American roots (often including or at least claiming illustrious Revolutionary service), farming and/or merchant-banking backgrounds, membership in the less enthusiastic Protestant churches, fraternal connections with the Masons or the Elks Club, Civil War officership, a record of philanthropic contributions, and wives active in town benevolent societies and charitable affairs, the leading men of Rutland were nearly all Republican in the most Republican of U.S. states. A rare exception like Democratic attorney L. W. Redington might yet be accepted for being thoroughly "Republican" in his social life. Given the basic homogeneity of local representatives, town politics usually operated at the subparty level of factional rivalry or personal popularity. In 1884, for instance, an identical slate of officers was presented to and approved by both Republican and Democratic caucuses prior to the town meeting. The list, moreover, contained only a single change from the roster of incumbents. By occupational standing, only the top third of the social structure reaching down from capitalists and professionals through self-employed master craftsmen were actively involved in town government. Thus, despite substantial economic growth and development, Rutland town stewards continued to operate in the public realm as if nothing had changed. This political lag was highlighted by the fact that Rutland in the mid-1880s was the largest jurisdiction in the United States still operating under town government.[6]

In 1886, however, things did change dramatically. Beginning in January 1886, Rutland's skilled tradesmen and marble workers coalesced under the spreading national umbrella of the Knights of Labor. In and of itself this organizational achievement created the potential for a new political majority. When, in addition, widespread charges of waste and neglect beset the town's incumbent officers in February, the stage was set for a challenge to the lax and honorific tradition of conducting town business. "The time has come when we propose to have a share in the legislation by which we are governed," declared the quarryman and West Rutland master workman James Gillespie on August 26, 1886, at the town's first workingmen's convention. On September 7, the largest town meeting in Rutland's history elected a full slate of candidates from the United Labor ticket (taking its name from the Henry George movement in New York City), including a state assemblyman and fifteen justices of the peace. Fourteen of the justices identifiable by trade included four marble workers, three carpenters, two laborers, one shoemaker, one clerk, one meat market owner, one country store proprietor, and one small farmer—men who most likely would never have appeared on any other list of nominees for public office. Although their strength was clearly rooted in the 2,000-member local marble labor force, the Rutland Knights derived "from almost every department of work in town."[7]

The Knights saw United Labor government less as a radical transformation than a purification of the public trust. A republican heritage that linked the welfare of the nation to the economic and political independence of the citizenry was extended in the hands of the Gilded Age labor movement into a battle cry against industrial monopoly and governmental corruption. Rutland labor spokesmen compared their initiative to that of the "horny-handed sons of toil" who had once marched behind Andrew Jackson's assault on "ring rule." Their legislative program, in keeping with their self-image as respectable albeit unrecognized citizens, was in fact quite moderate. At the state level—a plane at which they could in any case expect little influence—they did propose various labor-related reforms, including an employers' liability act, weekly cash payments of wages, free evening schools, and a ten-hour law. Correspondingly, at the local level, they favored expanded appropriations and taxation for roads, schools, and a new town library. Wary of influence peddling and public debt, the workingmen in their platform simultaneously promised a balanced budget, equitable taxation, and "strict account of all public transactions . . . rendered so as to be perfectly understood." In a period characterized by unprecedented labor organization and economic downturn for the marble trade, the political arena, while not the point of departure for labor mobilization, must have beckoned to the Knights as a most inviting sphere of influence.[8]

Labor's self-delimited political intentions stood in striking contrast to the revulsion expressed toward the new government by the town's erstwhile political rulers—a feeling summed up in an oblique commentary by the local Republican daily on government by "the vomit of the saloons." The shift in the social locus of power entailed by the workingmen's movement did, in fact, make the 1886 events more than an ordinary succession of the "ins" by the "outs." Indeed, in this context proposals that might in themselves have been accepted as benign took on a more threatening cast. Given Rutland's past, the sudden assertion from below of the right to control public affairs represented a radical political departure.

Widening the chasm between the town's traditional governing elite and the new political forces was the fact that class differences in Rutland were reinforced by a sharp cultural divide. The ranks of capitalists, professionals, merchants, white-collar employees, and farmers occupied men 80 to 90 percent of whom were of native American background. But Yankee dominance of these upper strata masked the fact that by 1880 immigrants and their sons composed a majority of Rutland's adult male population, two-thirds of the town's wage earners, and a near monopoly of the lower rungs of manual labor. Most significant, nine out of ten marble workers were of foreign extraction. Six of ten were of Irish background; two of ten were French Canadians. The rest divided between English Canadians, Swedes, and native Americans. Among the latter, foremen and supervisors made up the single largest job categories.[9]

The Rutland Knights of Labor, not surprisingly, carried a strong ethnic, and especially Irish-American, character. Local sources estimated that "a majority" of the marble workers joined the Order in 1886, and two of four assemblies within Rutland town were based in the heavily Irish-Catholic marble-working community of West Rutland (there were two other assemblies based in other hamlets of the county). The Knights' political efforts signaled a kind of coming of age of the immigrant working-class community. Included on the labor ticket as a candidate for justice of the peace, for instance, was the only French-Canadian name on a list of local officeholders going back ten years. Even more representative of the social turnabout represented by the labor party was the unprecedented slating of the Irish-Catholic James F. Hogan, a clothing store owner and son of an Irish quarryman, for the state legislature. With utter condescension, Redfield Proctor saluted labor's nomination of "a colored man" for representative.[10]

Under these conditions the prospect of labor rule in Rutland summoned up less a loyal opposition than a counterrevolution. Within days of the town election, Redfield Proctor dusted off plans he had been nursing for some time to rid his business of potential legislative interference and unnecessary taxation by the central government in Rutland town. Through influential contacts at Montpelier, he began a vigorous lobbying effort to divide Proctor from Rutland's political jurisdiction, and he encouraged West Rutland to do likewise. As he put it in private correspondence, in a large town "interests are so mixed and varied that a large part of the voters have little interest in them and never understand them but are led by demagogues and go with the mob." Small-town citizens were less likely to make such mistakes because "the questions are brought right to their doors." In the one-industry village in which only thirty-five homes were independently owned, overwhelming endorsement of a prodivision petition circulated door to door by Redfield's son, Fletcher D. Proctor, tended to prove his point.[11]

The Proctor family picked the opportune moment to push their initiative. Business connections alone helped to corral other marble owners to their side. But Redfield Proctor also figured that labor's electoral success would soften natural commercial opposition in Rutland Village to a move (the division of both Proctor and West Rutland) that would deprive Rutland town of a third of its population and its largest revenue-producing properties. "Fear of foreign rule," Proctor advised his counsel, "had produced a wondrous change in public feeling." While a coalition of eminent elder citizens, independent businessmen, Democrats, and Knights of Labor did organize against the division plans, the *Rutland Herald,* scion of the town's (and much of the state's) older Republican elite, uttered not a word against the proposal. The disposition of the rural-dominated state legislature was apparently never in doubt. "From the fact that the laboring men elected a representative by such an overwhelming vote," reflected a disappointed antidivision spokesman, "they seemed to infer that we were in a state of anarchy down here." One legislator openly advised a group of antidivision Rutland businessmen:

"Division is your only salvation. You are in bad shape politically and something must be done for relief." In late November bills sailed smoothly through the legislature approving division for both Proctor and West Rutland.[12]

The basic decision probably surprised no one. But in the final hours of the closing legislative session, the lawmakers tacked on some unadvertised items affecting Rutland citizens. By an amendment to the original town charter, the state withdrew Rutland's right to elect a municipal judge, making it an appointed position. Another hurriedly enacted statute required local trustees to furnish bonds ranging from $1,000 to $5,000 before taking office. Finally, the tenure of the fifteen Rutland justices elected on the 1886 labor ticket was voided on grounds that they could not properly represent the newly created districts. The governor was authorized to appoint interim justices. While the division vote rested on a variety of motivation and justification, the object of the postdivision collateral actions was unmistakable. The presiding (Republican) municipal judge, Albert Landon, best expressed the combination of humiliation and indignation felt by many Rutland citizens: "The industrial classes have become sufficiently intelligent to undertake to right their wrongs at the ballot box. And this is a mad attempt to wrest that dreaded weapon from their grasp."[13] Forced to choose between political pacification and civic growth, the division forces betrayed fears that underlay the surface exuberance of the Age of Progress. The Rutland Knights of Labor, for their part, had been treated to an elementary lesson in the cost of inexperience among political professionals. It was as if they had sat down to dinner only to discover that the main course had just been removed. Political dismemberment, in itself, however, did not ensure the success of the stratagem. The degree of disruption in labor's political momentum would rest effectively on the specific social and political configurations to emerge in the new jurisdictions of Rutland, West Rutland, and Proctor.

As it happened, three distinct political climates and party alignments arose in the three new governmental units. Precisely because they grew out of the breakdown of an older order of social relationships, politics in the three towns may offer some general clues as to the social content of the political forms that emerged.

A magisterial rule—at once benevolent and arbitrary—quickly settled over the new town of Proctor. In the spring of 1887 the first local town meeting elected Redfield Proctor moderator and proceeded to endorse a company-backed slate by acclamation. For decades to come, the Proctor family, itself a bulwark of the state Republican party, would be able to count on solid, conservative Republican majorities in their town. An apparent absence of working-class organization and activity from 1887 seemed to signal the dispersal of what had always been a relatively weak Knights of Labor presence in Proctor's mills. Effective control of the town's social and political life henceforth emanated from a single center of power.[14]

Proctor family rule combined power with discretion. As early as 1886 the Vermont Marble Company chartered a company cooperative store and an employees' savings bank. While disclaiming direct liability for quarry accidents, it hired the country's first industrial nurse in 1895. Soon a fully equipped hospital was providing free medical care to all Proctor employees. The company also built and funded programs for the local YMCA. Redfield Proctor committed himself to his town and company and tried to ensure that the employees would do likewise. In December 1886, for example, "in these times of labor troubles," he bought back shares of stock from large shareholders to resell them at reduced rates to foremen and salesmen "to bind them all the more closely together." Proctor also worked hard, almost scientifically, at securing a docile labor force. He requested the Cunard Line in 1887 to send 200 to 300 Swedes to the quarrying center: "We want good rugged men and much prefer men from the country rather than such as go from the city." During the same period he took pains to recruit a particular Chicago building contractor known for employing "men who have not got the 8 hour craze and are not controlled by unions." Proctor pointedly did favors for the local clergy and as pointedly expected their loyalty in return. The ambivalent nature of acquiescence in the town of Proctor—rendered in part out of desperation and in part out of gratefulness—explains why the local marble workers paraded in welcome whenever the governor or his son entertained visiting dignitaries and why 3,000 people waited for hours through a severe March snowstorm in 1908 for the Marble King's casket to pass in final review.[15]

The political alignment in Proctor directly reflected its status as a company town. Community in such a town derived not from organic or voluntary ties but from mystique—the artificial attempt to recreate an older set of paternal-deferential social relationships in a new industrial environment. As such, the peculiar social solidarity exhibited there required the continuous and conspicuous exercise of an enlightened despotism. Politically, we might best describe the situation in Proctor as one of *paternalistic consensus,* a state of affairs where the lower classes participate but with little or no autonomy from the will of their employer(s).

Nearly twice the size of Proctor, with a well-organized working-class community owning their own homes and little plots of land, and lacking a single commanding center of political and economic authority, the new town of West Rutland possessed more of the substance and spirit of

democratic self-government. Indeed, evidence suggests that an over-⌐
whelming popular majority of West Rutlanders had favored town division.
While West Rutland merchants naturally wished specifically to regulate
the excursion trains that carried shoppers away to larger Rutland Village,
West Rutland workers shared in more general complaints of town inattention to roads, sidewalks, and other needs of their community. One other
factor also probably influenced prodivision sentiment in West Rutland.
An Irish political majority would almost certainly accompany political
separation of the community. An Irish-American marble worker who
had "always lived" in West Rutland had thus spoken approvingly before
a legislative committee of attaining "home rule," and two West Rutland
Knights of Labor leaders had joined the division forces. Apparently,
even disapproving Montpelier legislators fully expected that West Rutland
town government "would become more distinctly a working-men's experi-
ment than any other [town] in the state." And at the March 1, 1887,
inaugural town meeting, independent labor forces did sweep the field as
predicted. But then a new political pattern began to emerge in West
Rutland, one at once dominated by the unabashed assertiveness of its
Irish working-class constituency and by its limitations. In 1888 a Citizens
caucus acquired control of town government, while in national affairs the
town took on decidedly Democratic preferences; at least through the
mid-1890s, local affairs were untroubled by independent labor political
agitation.[16]

Several factors seem to have influenced the new town's unexpected
political quiescence. The need to establish fiscal solvency was perhaps
most important. Division left West Rutland with considerable debts
owed to the old town authority, and the new government had immediately issued bonds just to maintain local projects already under way. West
Rutland stood on an uncertain economic base in any case, as in Proctor
practically everyone depended on the health of the marble industry.
From the beginning of their tenure, therefore, West Rutland labor
selectmen cooperated with local businessmen and even deferred to the
advice of a marble company lawyer. One of their first acts budgeted
public funds for roads requested by local marble companies. M. W.
Cannon, a farmer (and former quarryman), Knights of Labor master
workman, and a leader of West Rutland labor political forces, boasted
that "there is no element of our population that will make greater efforts
for the maintenance of law and order, for the security of person and
property and for the economical administration of town affairs than the
workingmen. No action of the workingmen will ever mar the progress of
the new town."[17]

If labor's West Rutland representatives displayed a willingness to

work with other local interests, businessmen also accepted the necessity
for collaboration. Before the first West Rutland town meeting, several
Knights leaders were offered places on the businessmen's Citizens ticket.
When the Knights refused, other marble workers were nominated to take
their place. Indeed, the 1887 election amounted almost to a competition
in representation from below. In reaction to the Citizens call for a government of all the talents," the labor caucus pressed for election of "all
nationalities," adding two French Canadians (a carriage manufacturer
and a marble worker) to a ticket weighted with Irish marble workers.
Looking over the town's governors in 1887, a visitor noted that West
Rutland possessed "the most common representatives I have run across."
By the year's end, however, the workingmen's politicians appear to have
accepted the political hospitality of town elders. In 1890, for example,
Cannon was elected selectman alongside two other "non-partisan" candidates: one, a marble worker and former United Labor man; the other, a
superintendent of the Sheldon Marble Company. From the beginning
local Democratic politicians showed skill in accommodating to and making use of intraclass political formations in West Rutland. As early as
1886 Democratic businessmen like the cigar manufacturer A. H. Abraham
and the insurance executive W. L. Redington diplomatically contributed
gifts to a Knights of Labor raffle. That West Rutland was the only site in
the county to carry for Grover Cleveland in 1888 suggested the particular
turn that labor's political strength had taken there.[18]

West Rutland, in short, displayed political tendencies quite unlike
those of Proctor. A distinct working-class constituency, rooted in labor
and ethnic communal organization, created the basis for political pluralism.
But it was a most moderate pluralism. The conflict-ridden atmosphere of
1886 had given way to a climate of civic unity under adversity, in which
workers identified with the town's commercial welfare, while men of
commerce also accommodated to post-1886 political realities. In West
Rutland, as in other areas where urban immigrant demography clashed
with its surrounding native rural counterpart, the Democratic party
provided the warmest welcome for the ethnic working-class voter; still,
in local matters partisanship seemed scarcely to matter. West Rutland, by
all signs, had entered a period of *democratic consensus,* in which the lower
classes remained actively enfranchised on their own behalf (at least
relatively free from coercion from above) but nevertheless articulated no
independent class-oriented politics.

In taking stock of the relations between the labor movement and the
community power structure that gave rise to such a political juncture, it
is important to note that class conciliation in West Rutland took place not
in the flush of labor mobilization but during the ebb tide of organized

labor strength. As early as mid-1887 employer hostility and intransigence before labor wage demands were reportedly taking a heavy toll in
demoralization and loss of membership among area marble workers.
While four Knights assemblies, including two based in West Rutland,
survived until 1892, they did so with a much attenuated community
presence.[19] The collapse of labor leadership and mass discipline (following
the national fate of the Knights of Labor) left the movement without
confidence in its own future. In less polarized relation to local government,
the labor constituency henceforth served as a residual opposition, setting
limits rather than clear direction in the public sphere. From another
(and not contradictory) perspective we might want to emphasize the
conciliatory tendencies within the movement's (again, specifically the
Knights') ideology (though this is a subject that must be treated elsewhere).
A corollary to the last point would stress the effective blandishments that
ideologically amorphous American political parties continually have
held out to insurgents. And yet, perhaps more important than any of
these political deficiencies were the economic limits on labor political
autonomy in a small, one-industry town, even a class-conscious and
organized one. That such a fledgling community should reach a consensual public modus operandi is not surprising. Localism and civic autonomy in the end finally predominated over internal divisions. That a
self-consciously working-class party should run such a town, even for a
year, is surely the more incongruous idea and remarkable achievement.

While the two new fragment towns, by one rationale or another,
settled into a relatively quiet resolution of their internal affairs, the
situation in what remained of old Rutland town (roughly two-thirds of
the original population) took on an entirely different complexion. If the
state legislators had meant to wipe out Rutland labor politics by town
division, they failed. Except for the loss of population and taxable
property, the only new political factor in Rutland town after 1886 was the
added stigma of betrayal attached to many of the town's business leaders;
as a result, labor politics enjoyed an unusually long and productive life.
As in West Rutland, the Rutland United Labor party swept the February
1887 town meeting, then fell off the following year. But the circumstances
were quite different. Unlike the situation in the new town to the west, the
underlying social tension separating workers from the Yankee elite did
not evaporate in old Rutland. Its greater size—Rutland was finally incorporated as a city under mayoral-aldermanic government in 1892—and its
more complex economy militated against political manipulation by a few
employers. Finally, there was no shortage of confident young Knights
willing to challenge the older guardians for control of the community's
future. Rutland workingmen thus found it possible to regroup after their

first electoral setbacks and to recapture important positions under United Labor and United Workingmen's banners in 1890; they remained a potent independent force through 1892. Even as the numbers behind the Knights dwindled, the constituency that the Order had created endured. When labor finally transferred its strength to the Democratic party, it infused that party with new prospects and with a new character derived from the workingmen's movement.[20]

Rutland's business leaders at first retreated from the very framework of partisan loyalty to unite behind the widespread contemporary phenomenon of a nonpartisan Citizens party of order. Though the effort initially amounted to little more than dressing up the old ruling Republican faction in new outfits—which got nowhere in 1887—it soon became a more effective counterweight to independent labor politics. Capturing the 1888 town meeting and proclaiming "Rutland Redeemed," the Citizens ticket generally dominated local government until it liquidated itself in 1894. Fear that a loss of business confidence in the town would drive away jobs and investment (a fear seemingly confirmed by the October 1887 announced departure of a local shirt company) no doubt helped the antilabor party. So did two new businessmen's organizations— one a private club, the other a merchants' association—that sought simultaneously to refurbish Rutland's image abroad and to activate "men of education and standing" at home. Though not exactly the association of "Republicans, Democrats, and workingmen joining hands . . . to secure the public good" that it claimed, the Citizens were more than an instrument of middle-class fear and repression. As early as 1888 Rutland Democrats like the attorneys J. D. Spellman and T. W. Maloney, who had joined in the antidivision fight and generally enjoyed good relations with organized labor, were taking an active role in the Citizens activities. Unlike the old party caucuses, a mass public meeting ratified the Citizens slate in 1888; in future elections the candidates themselves were nominated at "open" party caucuses.[21]

The more successful the Citizens phenomenon became (i.e., the more it resembled a truly democratic consensus), the less well it served its originators' purposes. Bipartisan inclusiveness had proved the key to the Citizens winning ways beginning in 1888, but that approach also risked loss of control over the direction of the movement. As early as the 1888 village election, Citizens leaders were expressing fears that the Knights had infiltrated preliminary meetings and secured nomination of some of their men in Citizens costumes. Two years later, Republican and Democratic businessmen opened what they called a Non-Partisan caucus with a pledge of willingness to select men from all competing parties. The organizers withdrew quickly, however, when workingmen allied with a dissident Democratic faction proposed a genuine "unity" slate. The *Herald* described it most coolly "as a whole not the men who naturally would be selected to conduct the business of any corporation equal in importance and with equal interests at stake to the town of Rutland." Again in 1891 workingmen upset the official slate with a caucus victory for an iron molder for street commissioner. Even if steered through the uncertainties of the caucus, business-endorsed candidates still might face a stiff labor challenge on election day. Both in 1890 and 1891, after achieving partial success within the Non-Partisan slate, workingmen won other positions—and even secured a Georgite tax on unoccupied land—on the strength of their own independent tickets.[22]

The Citizens or Non-Partisan approach thus proved an unhappy compromise with the tidy control that the business elite acting through the Republican party had once exercised over local affairs. As early as 1888, J. D. Spellman had ruffled the feathers of the socially homogeneous Republican inner sanctum with whom he was formally cooperating by publicly protesting the exclusion of a Jewish-*Republican* merchant tailor from the Citizen ticket. By substituting personal popularity and skillful campaigning for party loyalty and social standing, the new system allowed maverick Republicans and ambitious Democrats such unwelcome openings. Republican leaders of the antilabor coalition watched helplessly as their Democratic partners wooed the opposition forces, steadily enlisting them under the banner of the minority party. The growing ties between the Democrats and what was left of the labor movement were apparent in the representation of Vermont's District Assembly 200 at the 1890 Denver Knights of Labor convention by the editor of Rutland's new Democratic *Evening Telegram*. In the same year the *Herald* deprecatingly labeled the emerging pattern of electioneering "Spellmanism."[23]

It was not long, therefore, before the same people who had condemned labor's "party politics" in 1886–87 for having "no place" in local affairs summoned it to active duty. By 1894, two years after incorporation, the *Herald* had decided that "non-partisan" city government was proving no better than the "old town meeting mobs." "Narrow ward interests," in the *Herald*'s view, were leading irresponsible Citizens representatives toward unnecessary street and sewer construction, pushing up taxes and the municipal debt. "A Republican town," the paper advised, "should have Republican government." Indeed, once oft-repeated elegies to New England town democracy had given way to a growing pessimism about local self-government. The *Herald* argued in 1895 for the appointment of a professional city engineer and the transfer of "elected committee duties" to "executive [appointed] officers." One could not expect government to improve, this line of logic ran, until the "substantial men of the city—the men with real interests at stake" took charge. To protect the city from the vicissitudes of local politics, the Republican party took structural measures of its own. The party's city committee tightened local organization in 1895 with the formation of a stable executive leadership and permanent ward committees. In addition, the Republicans prepared to operate closed primaries and asserted the right to remove local delegates who flaunted the city committee's authority.[24]

With the dissolution of the Citizens ticket, a competitive two-party system generally reasserted itself over the young city's government. The Republicans, to be sure, remained the majority party, but they frequently faced a stiff challenge from the revitalized Democrats. Heavily working-class Catholic Wards 7 and 8, for example, transferred their bloc-voting support from independent labor to Democratic candidates. The same district that in 1887 elected a United Labor marble worker to the board of selectmen by a vote of 136 to 1 was the single defector in 1904 from Theodore Roosevelt's sweep of the city. An even more direct link was provided in the personage of Thomas H. Brown, the Knights' district master workman; throughout the 1890s Brown secured nearly automatic claim to the seventh ward's Democratic aldermanic seat.[25]

A decade-long political transformation ultimately replaced the clublike atmosphere of old town meeting days with the institutionalization of *two-party pluralism*. The change also roughly coincided with the dissolution of town meeting democracy into the representative structures of city government. If one looked only at the before (say, 1885) and after (say, 1895), Rutland might indeed fit conventional expectations of political modernization and progressive municipal development. Such a view, however, by attending only to certain external benchmarks and neglecting the impact of class conflict and working-class mobilization, would miss the substance of what had happened in Rutland, and why. The social polarization engendered by the Knights of Labor had been responsible for destroying the deferential subparty factionalism in local government. In a period of conflict, two opposing formations, each of which saw itself as outside of or above the bounds of partisanship, had fought for political power. Two-party competition became the norm in local politics only *after* and *as a result of* the storm that had preceded it. Rutland, in short, had not passed inexorably along a linear trail of development. Its entire political edifice had been rendered, sundered, and reconstructed in the face of a radical challenge from below.

Conventional views not only tend to take for granted a political pluralism that the Rutland case suggests was the *product* of a historical struggle shifting the social balance of power; they also present an all-too-sanitized picture of two-party pluralism. A final bit of narrative is in order.

Rutland Democrats, riding the desperation and bitterness of local workingmen in the depression of the mid-1890s (and calling for work relief programs for the unemployed), elected the former Knights of Labor leader T. H. Brown mayor of an otherwise Republican-controlled city government in 1896. Panic again spread through the business establishment. The mayor found himself entirely frustrated. All his appointments were blocked, and government came to a near standstill. Halfway through Brown's term, the banker Percival W. Clement, head of the board of trade, warned that the Howe Scale Company, the town's principal manufacturer, might abandon Rutland unless "confidence" were quickly restored. In the same breath Clement declared his willingness to shoulder the responsibility of city executive if called upon. Brown did step down from office, explaining simply that the opposition could not manage "a Republican town."[26]

Given the active enfranchisement of the lower classes, no one political form, it would seem, was entirely "safe" from popular manipulation. Whatever the forms through which it occurred, a marked disjuncture in *control* between political and civil society signified, for some, a social crisis, one that could not be resolved until power had been reconsolidated on new terms. In this regard it bears reemphasizing that the very social relocation of power as much as the substance of the decisions involved defined the perceived threat. In Rutland such a crisis had twice boiled over, once in 1886, once in 1896. The basic tinder for such a crisis—that is, the discrepancy in control between the political and the economic sphere—has accumulated, albeit in different proportions, on many different occasions in American history. The central crisis (and collapse) of southern Reconstruction, the direction (and limitation) of such New Deal programs as the TVA and WPA, and the 1978–79 showdown over retention of a municipal power company in Cleveland, Ohio, to take three examples, while divorced in all particulars from events in Gilded Age Vermont, share an underlying flashpoint of conflict. If, as in each of these examples, political power tends to gravitate back toward consonance with private power, such a tendency at once reemphasizes the intimate connection between the two spheres of authority and suggests the ultimate reliance of politics on civil organization. A change or sharp break in the nature of political rule (i.e., the political balance of power) is likely to be sustained only if it is accompanied by a successful revision of the lines of force within civil society. In the Rutland case the social tremors reflected in the Knights of Labor toppled one form of elite rule but obviously did not, in the end, topple the elite.

If, in conclusion, we are ultimately stressing the social sources of politics rather than the institutional forms, that is not meant to belittle examination of the forms. In the case of Rutland, after all, it was the forms of politics (i.e., parties, caucuses, governmental divisions), or more precisely the *transition* within those forms, that helped to orient us to and define the limits of the movement from below. The changes in political forms at once reflected and illuminated the complex tensions of the local social reality. The Rutland story provides only one (rather, only three) examples of intimate interaction between working-class social history and the development of American political institutions. It is true, I suppose, that known situations of labor upheaval would prove the most fertile ground for further explorations along these lines. The period of the Great Upheaval, at least, is replete with distinct but related examples. But I think that quite different periods may be susceptible to similar analysis. An examination of Boston's incorporation in the 1820s, for instance, refers to the breakdown of a "deferential pattern of politics. . . . No longer able to agree among themselves, the members of the upper class found it increasingly difficult, as one of them delicately phrased it, 'to manage that class which is acted upon.' " The point of collapse of any existing political form or arrangement may, in fact, be a good place for the social historian to dig in. Giovanni Sartori, a political sociologist, has asserted provocatively, "Whenever conflict means what it says, parties fall into disrepute." Any scholar who chooses to explore this axiom may find the connection between political and social history inextricable.[27]

NOTES

This essay originally appeared in *Social History* 7 (January 1982), 43–58. Reprinted by permission. I am grateful to Donald M. Scott for his searching comments on the manuscript and to Lewis Perry for exercising better judgment than I wanted to admit.

1. Charles Francis Adams, *Three Episodes of Massachusetts History,* 2 vols. (Cambridge, Mass., 1892), 2:965–74; John Gould, *New England Town Meeting: Safeguard of Democracy* (Brattleboro, Vt., 1940), 59–60. See, e.g., John M. Murrin, "Review Essay," *History and Theory* 11 (May 1972), 226–76; Stephan Thernstrom, *Poverty and Progress: Social Mobility in a Nineteenth-Century City* (New York, 1970); Michael H. Frisch, *Town into City: Springfield, Massachusetts, and the Meaning of Community, 1840–1880* (Cambridge, Mass., 1972).

2. For illustrative application of modernization theory, see Robert H. Wiebe, *The Search for Order, 1877–1920* (New York, 1967); Samuel P. Hays, *The Response to Industrialism, 1885–1914* (Chicago, 1957); and Richard D. Brown, *Modernization: The Transformation of American Life, 1600–1865* (New York, 1976).

3. Gerald N. Grob, *Workers and Utopia: A Study of Ideological Conflict in the American Labor Movement, 1865–1900* (Chicago, 1969): Michael J. Cassity, "Modernization and Social Crisis: The Knights of Labor and a Midwest Community, 1885–1886," *Journal of American History* 66 (June 1979), 41–61.

4. For further elaboration of these themes, see Leon Fink, *Workingmen's Democracy: The Knights of Labor and American Politics* (Urbana, Ill., 1983).

5. H. P. Smith and W. S. Rann, *History of Rutland County, Vermont* (Syracuse, N.Y., 1886), 170, 158–59, 161–62; Edward Chase Kirkland, *Men, Cities, and Transportation: A Study in New England History, 1820–1900*, 2 vols. (Cambridge, Mass., 1948), 1:166–67, 229–30; Jim Shaughnessy, *The Rutland Road* (Berkeley, Calif., 1964), 358, 471; U.S. Tenth Census, 1880, *Statistics of the Population* (Washington, D.C., 1883), 1:355; *Rutland County Gazetteer and Business Directory* (Syracuse, N.Y., 1881); U.S. Tenth Census, 1880, *Report on the Building Stones of the U.S. and Statistics of the Quarry Industry* (Washington 1885), 10:109–11; Walter H. Crockett, *Vermont: The Green Mountain State*, 5 vols. (New York, 1921), 4:98–99; Paul A. Gopaul, "A History of the Vermont Marble Company" (ms., St. Michael's College, Winooski, Vt., 1954), 42, 47.

6. Hiram Carleton, *Genealogical and Family History of the State of Vermont* (New York, 1903), 406–7; *Book of Biographies: Biographical Sketches of Leading Citizens of Rutland County, Vermont* (Buffalo, N.Y., 1899), 113–15; Rutland city directories, 1884–85, 1889–90; Smith and Rann, *History of Rutland County*; *Rutland Herald*, 1880–86. On the dominance of the Republican party, see John D. Buenker, "The Politics of Resistance: The Rural-based Yankee Republican Machines of Connecticut and Rhode Island," *New England Quarterly* 47 (June 1974), 212–37.

7. *Rutland Herald*, Jan. 29, Sept. 8, 1886.

8. Ibid., Aug. 27, 1886.

9. Ibid., Feb. 26, 1887; Manuscript Tenth Census, 1880, Rutland County, Vt.

10. Jonathon Garlock and N. C. Builder, "Knights of Labor Data Bank: Users' Manual and Index to Local Assemblies" (ms., University of Rochester, N.Y., 1973); *Rutland Herald*, Sept. 2, 1886.

11. Redfield Proctor to William P. Dillingham, Sept. 14, 1886, Proctor Family Papers, Proctor Free Library, Vt.; *Rutland Herald*, Nov. 1, 3, 1886; "Division of Rutland, Argument of Remonstrators before Committee in Representatives Hall, Nov. 9, 1886," Proctoriana Collection, Vermont State Library, Montpelier.

12. Proctor to Dillingham, Sept. 14, 1886, Proctor Family Papers; *Rutland Herald*, Nov. 4, 1886. The insurance agent L. H. Granger typified middle-class antidivision sentiment in his fear of the power of a man like Proctor. To Granger, twin dangers threatened republican government; one involved "the anarchists who seek to destroy, the other, greater because insidious—the encroachments of great corporations, which seek to control and pervert our political institutions, until we shall live only in their shadow." *Rutland Herald*, Oct. 30, Nov. 20, 1886; *Burlington Free Press*, Nov. 20, 1886.

13. *John Swinton's Paper*, Dec. 5, 1886; *Rutland Herald*, Dec. 7, 1886.

14. *Rutland Herald*, Mar. 2, 1887.

15. David C. Gale, *Proctor: The Story of a Marble Town* (Brattleboro, Vt., 1922), 213; Redfield Proctor to Elizabeth H. Arnot, Dec. 24, 1888, to Emil Oelbermann, Jan. 1, 1887, to Francis B. Riggs, Jan. 5, 1887, to The Cunard Line, Nov. 15, 1887, to F. R. Brainerd, July 8, 1887, to Rev. J. C. McLaughlin, Mar. 12, 1886, Proctor Family Papers; Crockett, *Vermont*, 4:394–95. As late as 1975, Anna McLaughlin, the senior librarian at the Proctor Free Library, recalled how "Miss Emily,"

Redfield's daughter, used to place new pairs of shoes in front of the workers' doors at Christmas; McLaughlin herself had once been sent to a Boston hospital for a checkup at the wish and expense of the Proctor family. Conversation with Anna McLaughlin in October 1975 at the Proctor Free Library, reconfirmed by telephone, Dec. 13, 1976.

16. *Rutland Herald,* Oct. 23, 1886, Mar. 2, Nov. 18, 1887, Mar. 29, 1888.

17. Minutes of the Selectmen, Oct. 22, Nov. 1, 1887, West Rutland town archives; *Rutland Herald,* Feb. 28, 1887.

18. *Rutland Herald,* Feb. 28, 1887; Annual Reports of the Board of Officers, West Rutland town archives; *Rutland Herald,* Oct. 22, 1886, Nov. 7, 1888.

19. T. H. Brown to Terence V. Powderly, June 20, 1887, Terence V. Powderly Papers, Catholic University, Washington, D.C.

20. Postdivision Rutland retained sections of the Vermont Marble Company, a few smaller marble concerns, the Howe Scale Company works, several foundries and machine shops, wood-working establishments, two shirt factories, railroad shops, printshops, and binderies. By 1890 Rutland town's population stood at 11,760, compared to West Rutland (3,680), Proctor (1,758), and the village of Rutland Center (786).

21. On Citizens tickets, see Zane L. Miller, *Boss Cox's Cincinnati: Urban Politics in the Progressive Era* (New York, 1968), 88–89; Cassity, "Modernization," 57; and Cliff Kuhn, " 'Democratic Confusion': Working-Class Politics in 1880s Atlanta" (ms., University of North Carolina at Chapel Hill, 1980).

22. *Rutland Herald,* Mar. 27, 1888, Mar. 3, 4, 1890, Mar. 13, 1891.

23. Ibid., Mar. 27, 1888, Mar. 3, 1890; Knights of Labor, "Proceedings of the General Assembly, 1890," Powderly papers.

24. *Rutland Herald,* Jan. 23, 1894, Jan. 29, 30, 1895.

25. Separated by railroad yards from the rest of the town, Wards 7 and 8 included St. Peter's Roman Catholic Church, parish, and convent house, and both the Irish-Catholic and French-Catholic cemeteries. Ibid., Jan. 21, 1888, Mar. 14, 1892, Mar. 2, Nov. 9, 1904.

26. Ibid., Feb. 19, Mar. 4, 1896, Feb. 10, 15, Mar. 3, 1897.

27. Robert A. McCaughey, "From Town to City: Boston in the 1820s," *Political Science Quarterly* 88 (June 1973), 191–213; Giovanni Sartori, *Parties and Party Systems: A Framework for Analysis* (Cambridge, Mass., 1976), 16. On this use of Sartori, see Leon Fink, "The Italian Connection: An American Historian's Encounter with Political Theory," ms., American History and the Social Sciences Seminar, Rome, Oct. 6–9, 1993. On connecting state and political party formation to changing social structures in the United States, see J. Morgan Kousser, *The Shaping of Southern Politics: Suffrage Restriction and the Establishment of the One-Party South, 1880–1910* (New Haven, Conn., 1974); Stephen Skowronek, *Building a New American State: The Expansion of National Administrative Capacities, 1877–1920* (Cambridge, Mass., 1982); Richard Oestreicher, "Urban Working-Class Political Behavior and Theories of American Electoral Politics, 1870–1940," *Journal of American History* 75 (March 1988), 1257–86; and Richard Franklin Bensel, *Yankee Leviathan: The Origins of Central State Authority in America, 1859–1877* (Cambridge, Mass., 1990).

4

A Labor Crusade behind the Magnolia Curtain: Hospital Workers and the Politics of Race and Class

By 1968, the New York City Retail Drug and Hospital Employees Union, Local 1199, had come a long way. With its roots among Jewish pharmacists and drugstore workers in the left-wing Congress of Industrial Organizations of the 1930s, Local 1199 had, since 1958, successfully ventured into the previously unorganized voluntary hospital field. Combining their own twin commitments to industrial unionism and racial justice with the growing stirrings in the minority community, the ex-Communist union leaders Leon Davis, Elliott Godoff, and Moe Foner had fashioned a veritable crusade for recognition of the industry's low-skilled, black and Hispanic, and overwhelmingly female service workers. Within ten years some thirty thousand hospital workers in the metropolitan area had organized and raised their minimum weekly wage from $28 to $100. Local 1199's achievement relied on three basic ingredients: genuine mobilization of the hospital work force, including preparation for militant strike activity; a political campaign aimed at arousing support from the surrounding community; and expert public relations leading ultimately to the sympathetic intervention of local or state officials. Directly reflecting the rising expectations unleashed by the civil rights movement, union partisans had come by the late sixties to believe that the joining of "union power" and "soul power" had unlocked the secret to a whole new tide of union building among America's poor and unskilled.

Still, there was cause for skepticism. In several respects New York City was particularly well suited to the union's style of crusadelike organizing.

Historically, public officials there had been more liberal, the black community better organized, and the state more willing to subsidize social services than elsewhere in the country. Hospital managements, while not receptive to trade unionism, had at least moderated their antagonism in the face of a political culture long accustomed to collective bargaining. But could lessons learned in New York be applied elsewhere? The first national test of the "union power, soul power" strategy came in 1969 when a group of hospital workers in Charleston, South Carolina, sought 1199's protection. The formula that had begun to pay handsome rewards in the cosmopolitan North suddenly came up against a new antagonist, one equipped with a time-tested record of resistance to social change, and the ensuing confrontation left an ambivalent legacy for all concerned.

Accentuating the general pattern of the twentieth-century South, union organization in South Carolina not only failed to establish a mass base in the 1930s but experienced a precipitous decline following the ill-fated postwar Operation Dixie (1946–53). While the state's urban centers contained a relatively high percentage of manufacturing workers for the region, this did not redound to the benefit of labor organization. Indeed, during the 1960s South Carolina vied with North Carolina for the lowest rate of unionization in the nation. Aside from sizeable concentrations of communications workers, the metal trades council of the navy yard, and papermakers (all overwhelmingly white), the state's 50,000 union members were scattered among black longshoremen, white building trades workers, and small pockets of machinists and clothing, textile, and furniture workers. Antiunionism was one issue that united up-country industrialists, like the J. P. Stevens Company of the Greenville-Spartanburg area, with their traditional low-country political competitors. A statewide business and political consensus reinforced a state right-to-work statute and an official ban on public employee strikes with an extra, unofficial antiunion vigilance.[1]

Viewed against this background, the strike by Charleston hospital workers from March 20 to June 27, 1969, was one of the South's most disruptive and bitter labor confrontations since the 1930s. Less than forty-eight hours after the dismissal of twelve black union activists, 450 workers at the Medical College Hospital (MCH) of the University of South Carolina heeded a strike·call by the newly formed Local 1199B. Eight days later, 60 workers walked out at the smaller Charleston County Hospital. All of the strikers were black; and all but twelve of them were women.

While already an important element of the union's message, the civil rights theme assumed an unprecedented centrality in the Charleston strike. Led by Reverend Ralph Abernathy, the Southern Christian Leadership Conference (SCLC) joined with 1199 in the fight for hospital workers' rights. As a result, a city that had generally escaped the heat of the civil rights movement belatedly experienced a kind of municipal civil war. After four months, nearly 1,000 arrests, and millions of dollars in lost property and boycotted sales, the strikers returned to work with some material gains but without official union recognition. Each side claimed victory, but the fact is that within a year of the strike the union movement among Charleston hospital workers had withered. "Charleston" proved to be more a codeword for what 1199 had become and where it planned to go than for what it had actually accomplished for hospital workers in the southern city.

The labor troubles in Charleston were tied to postwar economic and social changes in the area. Defense spending, commercial trade, and tourist dollars showed signs of awakening Greater Charleston from a long history of economic stagnation. But the fruits of recovery trickled down unevenly to the city's residents. Black citizens who made up nearly half the city's population and a third of the larger metropolitan area experienced little of the "revival of Charleston" after 1950. In 1970, 40 percent of black families lived below the poverty level and another 10 percent subsisted just above it.[2] Black women hospital workers formed the core of a new, low-wage service sector in the Charleston area, drawn from the expanding reserves of domestic and farm-related labor markets. These nonprofessionals worked for a subminimum wage of $1.30 an hour.

For many young women who had grown up on the truck farms of all-black island communities, hospital employment meant a stark encounter with the residual effects of a racial caste system. In 1968–69, the MCH had no black physicians on its staff and no black students in its School of Nursing, yet all low-paid nurse's aides and service workers were black. The same separation sharply distinguished the care offered to private (mainly white) versus public, nonpaying (overwhelmingly black) patients. Bed and waiting room assignments, as well as restroom use, were divided along racial lines, and certain practices seemed openly to reflect assumptions of black racial inferiority—for example, black husbands were not allowed in delivery rooms, yet whites were.[3]

If tradition still weighed heavily in some matters during the 1960s, the MCH was in other respects undergoing changes common to hospitals nationwide. Local modernization efforts took place under the watchful eye of college president and hospital director Dr. William McCord. The son of American missionaries in South Africa, he had served for twenty years as professor and chairman of the department of chemistry before being chosen in 1964 to lead the college through a period of ambitious expansion and upgrading. McCord embarked on a $15 million building plan, securing a $12 million grant in 1969 from the Department of Health, Education, and Welfare ($8 million for physical expansion and $4 million for research). Among other administrative changes, he recruited John E. Wise, a business graduate from the University of Kentucky, as vice president for administration and finance. Wise found the tall, broad-chested, cigar-smoking director "authoritarian" in style but "responsive to new and modern ideas." Wise quickly developed a centralized person-nel policy to uproot old departmental fiefdoms and moved to replace the subsidized employee cafeteria with higher take-home pay.[4]

Racial subordination in the Charleston hospitals reflected the area's long-standing social and political patterns. Although 32 percent of South Carolina was black, not one black state legislator had been elected since Reconstruction; indeed, it was one of only two states in which fewer than six of ten eligible blacks were registered to vote. Charleston, where older black males still doffed their caps to white passersby, seemed to fall well within Robert Coles's characterization of the entire state in 1968: "No southern state can match South Carolina's ability to resist the claims of Black people without becoming the object of national scorn." Not until 1967, for example, did the city have its first black council member, Saint Julian Devine.[5]

Committing few of the rhetorical or physical excesses of a Bull Connor in dealing with rising black expectations, the city's modern-day patri-archs had managed to preserve a relative social calm during the civil rights era. White political leaders (coordinated via the so-called Broad Street Gang of bankers and lawyers) tended to smother dissent with conciliatory gestures and an appeal for civic unity to a black elite of ministers, contractor-realtors, and funeral home directors. Reminiscing in 1985, one local black leader recalled earlier race relations as lacking overt hostility so long as blacks acquiesced in limiting themselves to "a certain place."[6]

During the 1950s the city had largely been spared social unrest as civil rights activists like Esau Jenkins and Septima Clark concentrated on education and voting rights in outlying island communities. Agitation within the city following the Supreme Court's 1954 *Brown* v. *Board of Education* decision was dampened by publication of the names of all integration petitioners in the *News and Courier*, a conservative daily. Charleston's only real trouble came during a 1963 summer desegregation campaign aimed at local merchants. The Charleston Movement led lunch-counter sit-ins, mass demonstrations, and night marches, includ-ing one major confrontation with police, and finally achieved a nondis-criminatory agreement with the city's major stores. Tensions had evi-dently eased in the city the next fall when, without major incident, a successful NAACP suit and court order enabled eleven black children to attend previously all-white public and parochial schools. Peaceful, if still largely symbolic, integration came to the entire city school system the next year.[7]

Advances in Charleston race relations were typically the result of slow but persistent efforts by middle-class white liberals working with a few black activists. Alice Cabaniss, who ran a small bookstore in the parish hall of the Episcopal Cathedral, helped to integrate South Carolina's League of Women Voters and also worked for racial progress through the United Church Women. "It all began," she recalled, "when I discovered, to my chagrin, at the age of fifteen, that my uncle by marriage was the Grand Dragon of the S.C. Ku Klux Klan." Her husband, Joseph, chaired the Charleston Council on Human Relations, "for which we had endured some social ostracism but not too much because both of us were guaranteed Southerners." In addition, he had been instrumental in recruiting the racial moderate John Conroy for Charleston police chief in 1964. Conroy and Cabaniss were old Marine buddies, and Conroy had married one of Mrs. Cabaniss's good friends from high school in North Charleston.[8]

The local style of handling racial tensions led to formation of a community relations committee to deal with the "long hot summers" of 1967 and 1968. The thirty-member committee, comprised of an equal number of blacks and whites, included the banker Hugh Lane, the liberal attorney Gedney Howe, a navy admiral, an air force general, and several older black businessmen as well as a representative of the younger militants in the person of William Saunders. In committee sessions and before groups like the all-white Rotary Club and the Red Carpet Club—the "inner sanctum" of the Charleston Chamber of Commerce—black Episcopal minister Henry Grant tried to "interpret the community one to another." Yet in the end such efforts could not contain the frustrations welling up among younger working-class blacks. The years of talk and symbolic legal and legislative victories only underscored the substantive lack of change in the lives of poorer blacks and their daily domination by a variety of white authorities, as typified by conditions at MCH. In Charleston, "black power" ultimately combined with the long-standing grievances of black workers to break through a decade of containment of social unrest.

Charleston's first hospital organizers reflected the combined impact of the new "black power" impulse and an earlier political education garnered during the Korean War. A small circle of young racial militants formed around their elder statesman, thirty-seven-year-old William Saunders, who in 1968 was working as a foreman in a local mattress factory. Saunders had come out of the army in 1954 determined to change things for his people. His involvement in the Johns Island voter registration and integration fights convinced him that the nonviolent philosophy of the civil rights movement was a "sham," and he openly quarreled with older leaders. The situation became so tense, according to Saunders, that by 1966 the local black leaders interceded to have the governor nullify his election to the Office of Economic Opportunity's War on Poverty commission. Speaking through the *Low Country Newsletter,* Saunders soon voiced the rising anger within the black community. Malcolm X and the Student Non-Violent Coordinating Committee (SNCC) both influenced his sense of political urgency and prompted his hosting a 1967 Christmas visit to the Charleston area by SNCC leader Stokely Carmichael. In Saunders's view, SNCC was "the total black organization." He claimed, "every time that the power-that-be got rid of the person that they thought was bad, the next one was worse. They were structured in a way to dissolve, and that's the way we did the organization that we had." Together with the Black Muslim Otis Robinson, Saunders fashioned a tight-knit, semisecret, self-defense group complete with code names and weapons. To avoid detection, he and his friends held meetings next to a loud jukebox. The level of daily fear reached its height in 1968 after the killings of three students at South Carolina State College in Orangeburg and the assassination of Martin Luther King, Jr. Saunders recalled, "We all planned to die."

Community organizing on Johns Island had put Saunders in touch with several hospital workers at the MCH, including twenty-six-year-old Mary Moultrie, the daughter of a Charleston navy yard worker. Moultrie had recently returned from working in a New York City municipal hospital as a licensed practical nurse, but the MCH would not recognize her New York credentials and slotted her at the less-responsible and lower-paid position of nurse's aide. While she had already done some work with the civil rights crusader Guy Carawan of Tennessee's Highlander Center and with Charleston activist Esau Jenkins, Saunders was waiting for Moultrie and others at the hospital to recognize that "they had a problem" at their own workplace. It did not take long.[9] In February 1968 a white nursing supervisor gave orders to a group of five black nursing assistants without first sharing with them the contents of patient charts. Incensed at this violation of customary respect, the women walked off the job and were summarily fired. Moultrie and her co-workers alerted Saunders. Thanks in part to the intervention of black community leaders, who monitored compliance with Title VII (the employment provision of the 1964 Civil Rights Act), the workers won reinstatement.

This episode triggered a continuous, although still informal, organizing network among Charleston's hospital workers. Saunders, for one, initially "saw very little difference between George Meany and Richard Nixon. . . . I felt labor management was ripping off the workers." Instead, he and his friends at first envisioned a kind of broad-based association of community-owned businesses aimed at getting blacks into the "economic mainstream." Moultrie, who had only distant contact with a New York City Teamsters Union local at Goldwater Memorial, agreed: "At that time we didn't have a union in mind to affiliate with or anything like that. We just knew we had to do something to protect our jobs. We didn't want to be picked off one by one. So we sorta kept it a secret. We'd go around and whisper to people and we'd catch people during break time and on lunch hour. We kept it out of the ears of the whites. After we started having the weekly meetings we used to get community people to come in and meet with us."

Isaiah Bennett, president of Local 15A, Retail, Wholesale, Department Store Union, became a key community contact on the way to formal organization. With roots in the militant 1945–46 strike of the Food, Tobacco, Agriculture, and Allied Workers—in which an old spiritual became the movement song, "We Shall Overcome"—the local still (in 1968) represented a few hundred workers at the American Tobacco Company in Charleston. Bennett provided the hospital workers a meeting hall and lobbied community leaders to establish a representation and grievance system for the MCH employees. As a black trade unionist, he occupied a precarious position within Charleston society: he could talk easily to local officials, yet he exercised little real influence. (So powerless were the black trade unionists, in fact, that the tobacco workers had never made a municipal political endorsement. "Hell," explained Bennett, "we always saw we got a fox and wolf running and both of them, they just alike.") Bennett initially recruited Gedney Howe to represent the hospital workers; he also began meeting with Mayor J. Palmer Gaillard, Jr., and recalled, "I know that many times I go to him . . . you know, he's always sympathetic. But then when the pressure's really got down on him, he turns just like anybody else. He never would make a statement on our behalf on radio or TV or anything."

Bennett and others seeking a compromise settlement got nowhere. From the beginning the hospital turned a deaf ear to all talk of negotiation, referring interested parties to the interpretation of state statutes by Attorney General Daniel MacLeod, who said that without specific enabling legislation public employees had no right to collective bargaining and, further, that no state agency could authorize such discussions. Meanwhile, hospital administrators took countermeasures, hiring Greenville textile counsel and anti-union specialist Knox Haynesworth on an expensive consultancy basis. The MCH offered to discuss work-related problems only with small groups of workers selected at random; administrators promised to use "every legal means at our disposal—make no mistake about that," to resist the union. An early response to the organizing effort came in the form of a crude cartoon picturing a fat white union boss enjoying wine, cigars, and shapely female company at the workers' expense. With nearly 300 workers taking part in organizational meetings and community groups requesting mediation, the one, obviously insulting concession offered by the hospital to the black workers was an extra holiday on Robert E. Lee's birthday.[10]

Informal conciliation efforts were stymied, and union representation beckoned as the only alternative for the aggrieved workers. New York City's Local 1199 received an appeal from Charleston. The workers' organizing leaders had first asked Bennett to enroll them in his tobacco workers' union, but Arthur Osman, international vice president of the RWDSU, suggested instead that they contact the international's appropriate hospital affiliate. In late September or early October 1968, Food, Tobacco, Agriculture, and Allied Workers' member Lillie Mae Doster helped Moultrie draft a letter to Local 1199, which only months before had established a national organizing committee headed by Elliott Godoff, with Henry Nicholas as his top assistant. Staff members had been dispatched to Detroit, Philadelphia, Baltimore, and the New Jersey and Connecticut areas; now, the call from Charleston served to put the union's principles, as well as its national aspirations, to a sudden test.[11]

David White, Brooklyn area director of the hospital union, was sent to scout out the situation in Charleston. He had lived in the New Jersey–New York area since he was nine years old and was particularly uncomfortable about his mission to Charleston:

> I'd heard all these war stories about the South and how it was and I had to take a plane into Columbia, South Carolina, and then had to get a connecting flight to Charleston. When I got there [Columbia] I found that that so-called connecting flight had been canceled a month before. So I said, oh my God, now I got to talk to some of these crackers. There was a Hertz desk in the airport and I told the guy I wanted a car to go to Charleston and I was shocked. He was as courteous to me as he could possibly be and then after we signed the papers for the car, he said to take Route 26 to Charleston. And I said, where do I find 26? So the guy got in the car and drove all the way out of the airport and showed me where Route 26 was and the way to Charleston. I expected to see like in the movies the southern roads with the trees and the vines hanging from the trees [but] then

I came to this big modern six- to eight-lane highway and within an hour or so I was in Charleston. . . . what impressed me was the tremendous spirit of the people there—the determination, you know, to do something to improve themselves; so that I had to come back and report that I thought there was a possibility of organizing the people and I had to give a favorable report.

After other New York leaders confirmed White's impressions, Henry Nicholas was dispatched to Charleston in October 1968 to officially charter Local 1199B, the hospital union's first out-of-state local.[12] Over 400 MCH workers elected Mary Moultrie president; Isaiah Bennett stepped into a senior advisory position and William Saunders remained an important, unofficial presence among the workers. From New York, union officials offered advice to the Charleston workers but left early direction of the campaign in local hands.

Formal union backing quickly raised the stakes of the workers' demands for recognition, and "high noon" rallies demonstrated the solidity of support for 1199B among the black service staff. Delegations besieged local and state lawmakers, vehemently protesting the refusal of McCord to meet with the employees. Gov. Robert McNair and key legislators were courteous, but no progress was made. In response to what Moultrie characterized to Columbia legislators in February 1969 as an "explosive" situation, state officials could only point to plans for a long-term reclassification of all state jobs that might be completed within a year. "We're tired of asking and begging," Moultrie told the legislators. "Now we are demanding. We want union recognition." "We warn you, time is running out," added Bennett.[13]

South Carolina leaders did little to conciliate the hospital workers, despite a self-proclaimed "progressive" attitude. While the legislature had the power, in principle, to envelop the hospitals within the state labor law (as had happened in New York and a few other states), no public representative emerged to champion such an option. Without yielding substantive ground, the state tried to resolve the matter by fostering better communication between workers and administrators. On March 4 McCord unveiled a plan of monthly grievance meetings: one person, selected at random, from each department would represent fellow workers at the meetings. The situation was far beyond such cosmetics.

The rising demand for dignity and respect, which had first set off the worker protests at MCH, led directly to the strike on March 20. Two days earlier, at the urging of Mayor Gaillard, McCord agreed to meet with a workers' delegation that included union members. However, when Moultrie and six other workers arrived for the scheduled morning conference, they found that the director had invited eight "loyalists" to balance out the meeting. Within minutes nearly a hundred protesting prounion workers were packed into the hospital auditorium. An administrative assistant canceled the session and ordered the workers to return to their jobs. They did so, but only after huddling outside the hospital with Bennett. The next day twelve union activists, including Moultrie, were formally dismissed for dereliction of duty. One day later, March 20, after consultations between 1199B leaders and Nicholas, who had flown in from Detroit, the strike began. While the strikers made only two demands— union recognition and the rehiring of the twelve fired workers—McCord was economical in his reply: he was "not about to turn a 25 million dollar complex over to a bunch of people who don't have a grammar school education."[14]

The picketers who gathered in front of the MCH entrance faced the reality that, unlike any other strike in which the union had so far been engaged, they were taking on not only a rigid hospital administration but a city and state power structure that was overtly hostile to the union effort. A temporary state injunction banning all picketing was immediately issued, though on the advice of State Circuit Court Judge Clarence Singletary the order was amended to limit the number of picketers to ten, spaced 20 yards apart over a distance of 200 yards. "According to the injunction," scoffed Moultrie at a football stadium rally, "we could put only five people on this field from goal post to goal post. I think even the governor, as slow as he is, could get through a picket line like that." When union attorneys appealed Singletary's ruling to the federal courts, Judge Charles E. Simons, former law partner of Senator Strom Thurmond, declined jurisdiction in the matter.[15]

Throughout the strike the union was unable to play off competing power centers among state and local political authorities as it had in New York. Governor McNair was shielded from direct contact with the Charleston strike and set the state's overall pattern of response: "No agency of the state can be involved with a union." Perceived from the beginning as a provocation and threat to law and order, the strike led to the deployment of city police, then agents from the State Law Enforcement Division, and finally National Guard troops in full riot gear. Street demonstrations produced hundreds of arrests. The Dunkirk-like stand of state authority before the protesting workers was reflected in the governor's statement before the South Carolina Bar Association on May 10: "In a sense this is not a simple test of will or a test of strength. This is a test of our whole governmental system as we have known it in South Carolina."

Years later Judge Singletary reflected on the larger context of official reactions to the hospital dispute:

In the 1960s South Carolina was among the leaders in the South in attracting industry and our technical education program . . . and our development board had become a model for other southern states. Our governor and officials were going all over the world seeking industries and one of the inducements, obviously, was productive labor without the labor union problems that other areas of the country were experiencing. So I think that that was one of the reasons that we didn't want to give up. When I say "we," I think of the political leadership.

Unintentionally, Singletary's "we" probably also included whomever was involved in the attempted fire bombing of Henry Nicholas's motel room on March 27, an incident that forced the union to scatter its representatives in unannounced lodgings under armed guard for the strike's duration.[16]

In retrospect, one might well wonder why a small outside organization like 1199 would throw itself into the situation in Charleston. "I really don't think they knew what they were getting into," Isaiah Bennett would later suggest. Moe Foner indirectly confirmed that initial support for the Charleston strike was less a careful calculation than a moral and political imperative: "What do you do? You could either walk away from it, in which case you lose, or else you could scruff along. We couldn't walk away." However, the union's Charleston strategy was less naive than it appeared. While responding spontaneously to local developments and without a specific, prior battle plan, 1199 had nevertheless been preparing itself for some time for an escalating civil rights–based struggle. Its ties to the campaigns of Martin Luther King, Jr., and the SCLC, formalized symbolically in Coretta Scott King's honorary chairmanship in 1968 of the union's national organizing committee, now took on critical significance.[17]

The decision to support a strike in Charleston depended directly on the union's confidence in its working relationship with the civil rights organization whose roots lay in the Deep South. As Foner himself allowed, the union faced two decisions in Charleston: "The first key decision is to have a strike; the second decision is that this strike cannot be won in the strike alone, that this has to become a national issue. But before you make it a national issue, the other thing is that this strike can only be won if it's made a labor–civil rights issue. . . . The only way to do that is to convince SCLC to come in." On a personal level the bonds of trust between the civil rights group and the labor organization were secured by the attorney and long-time activist Stanley Levison, a close friend of Foner and a former Communist still shadowed by the FBI who had served for years as a trusted adviser to King and to SCLC lieutenant Andrew Young. With Levison as go-between, the two organizations developed a coordinated strategy for the Charleston strike: the union would remain in charge of the workers' own activities and coordinate national support for the strikers, while the SCLC would direct a community-based campaign of civil disruption.

The Charleston strike, coming a year after King's assassination during the Memphis sanitation workers' strike, offered the SCLC the chance to renew its purpose and strength. Ralph Abernathy's efforts in 1968 to pick up the mantle of King's Poor People's Campaign were seriously hampered by the mud, indiscipline, and generally unfocused strategy of the Resurrection City encampment in Washington, D.C. Organizationally, the SCLC was in disrepair, internally feuding over Abernathy's leadership. Through Levison's mediation, however, the SCLC decided to make Charleston its priority battleground.[18] Andrew Young remembered:

> We began to see that having made significant social and political progress we'd have to take on the economic question of full employment, of the right to organize, of increasing the minimum wage, of guaranteed annual income. . . . Hospital workers came into the category of the working poor. . . . And so the Poor People's Campaign was also the first opportunity we had in a national way to try to reach out, to form a coalition between blacks, Hispanics, native Americans, and American Indians, the trade union movement, and, say, white workers in Appalachia and in the inner cities. It was really an attempt to overcome racial and cultural differences and move into a common economic effort to get our nation to eradicate poverty.

In certain key respects the SCLC approached Charleston as it had Montgomery, Selma, and other towns where it had faced a closed fist of opposition. "When you could not get the government to negotiate, either the state government or the local government," Young recalled, "you had to mobilize the entire community, the churches and the high school students in a total program of noncooperation or economic withdrawal." According to the organization's own pragmatic ground rules, the SCLC's entry into the strike had to be ratified by the local black community, and such assent was by no means assured. Although people like Esau Jenkins and Septima Clark had ties through Highlander to the national civil rights movement, the SCLC had never developed a base in Charleston. The older black community leadership was, in fact, reluctant to involve itself in confrontation tactics, while younger Charleston militants also looked suspiciously at outsiders, particularly those still philosophically wedded to nonviolence.

David White, sent from Brooklyn to serve as community relations liaison, remembered a tense meeting of the citizens' support group sometime during the first two weeks of the strike. Carl Farris was at the meeting representing the SCLC, as were ministers, businessmen, and other black leaders who were trying desperately to negotiate a peaceful resolution to the dispute, several "expressing a very strong feeling against bringing [the SCLC] in" on the grounds that "wherever they go, they cause turmoil." White recalled: "SCLC did not want to come in unless invited by the local citizens ... after all, they needed their cooperation. The meeting went on and on and quite a few people went home and then we—Farris and me—we were really working to delay ... until we could get a yes vote. I didn't even know the guy but I realized immediately what he was doing and he realized what I was doing and together we got an invitation to ask the SCLC to come in and aid the strikers."

The 1199/SCLC collaboration came at a certain cost. More moderate local figures, shy of the projected strategy, separated themselves or were shoved aside from the ensuing events. The white-dominated South Carolina AFL–CIO, for example, effectively turned its back on a struggle waged on civil rights grounds, and even the mostly black Charleston branch of the National Maritime Union distanced itself from the strikers because of "racial overtones which we cannot accept." The escalation of social stakes also alienated the early striker organizer Isaiah Bennett, who openly opposed the strategic arrangement with the SCLC. Bennett's continuing search for compromise through contacts with local authorities was monitored suspiciously by 1199 officials.[19]

The SCLC more than made up for local defections by its full-blown commitment to the Charleston campaign. Abernathy visited the strike-torn city for the first time on March 31 and committed the civil rights organization to an energetic display of "people's power" in the streets of Charleston. Thereafter, Andrew Young and staff members Farris, James Orange, and Hosea Williams made Charleston their second home, while Abernathy spent considerable time there as a lightning rod for mass mobilization, and Coretta Scott King arrived at carefully selected moments for greatest impact. Once involved, the SCLC drew on a network of several hundred contacts gained through what Young called the "underground work" of the state's citizenship or voter education schools.[20] Numerous signs of the spirit of community self-help engendered in other civil rights battles were evident. Surrounding black communities on James, Johns, and Edisto islands—indeed, all the way up to Columbia—expressed support through church donations. Within the city itself strikers received free haircuts, free meals at restaurants, and in some cases even had home and car payments made for them.

Under the SCLC's direction the campaign's physical focus immediately shifted from the union hall to black churches. White recalled:

When they came in the first thing they did was to contact all the ministers in the city and start lining up churches so we could have mass meetings in the evening. They also contacted ministers where they would loan us their churches during the day to organize the young people, kids all the way down to around eight and ten years . . . and they organized activities for these kids, classes where we had lectures on black history. I found out in Charleston, without the church you can't do a fucking thing. And everything we did was through the church, whether you believed in religion or not.

The truth is that the black religious community in Charleston was initially divided on the strike. But when the Interdenominational Ministerial Alliance, a citywide association for the enhancement of black welfare, refused to commit itself, younger black clergy like Z. L. Grady of the Morris Brown AME Church, J. T. Enright of the Plymouth Congregational Church, and Mack Sharpe of the Fourth Baptist Church formed the Committee of Concerned Clergy, which openly sided with the strikers.[21]

The SCLC's strike strategy was ambitious. "It is only when you create the same kind of crisis in the life of the community as you have in the lives of workers," explained Young, "that the community will give in." By activating the local black community and simultaneously evoking the sympathies of an outside, liberal white audience, the SCLC hoped to force through shame, fear, or property loss a retraction of the official line of intransigence toward the strikers. As at Birmingham in 1963, the SCLC expected that disruptive but determinedly nonviolent crowd actions would provoke authorities into a massive counterresponse that would end up paralyzing normal operation of the city. In the end, the "economic power structure" (or self-interested business leaders) would bring the "political power structure" (state and local officials) "in line" (toward a compromise settlement).[22]

The civil rights aspect of the Charleston campaign was evident on April 21 when Abernathy promised to "sock it to Charleston." Demonstrators staged frequent mass marches through the city's central business corridors, past National Guard troops outfitted with rifles, bayonets, and riot visors. Invading the historic Battery district, strike supporters paused symbolically at the Old Slave Mart Museum. Learning from the bitter disarray that had marked the Memphis SCLC campaign, Charleston organizers effectively incorporated black youths into the official protests, even outfitting a young Ranger brigade in colorful costume. One Saturday morning demonstration featured scores of teenagers dribbling basketballs down King Street, the city's main commercial thoroughfare. An affluent local matron recalled the unpleasant disruptions: "It was horrible, absolutely horrible. . . . Why even today when I go downtown I can still see all those colored people marching around and singing and praying and everything." By the end of April the situation had grown tense: ten marches in six days, repeated confrontations with the police, and nearly 500 arrests, including Abernathy and the visiting 1199 president Leon Davis. Abernathy called for a boycott of classes by schoolchildren, declaring; "Jesus said that a little child shall lead them [and] you are a traitor if you go to school." School officials said that attendance immediately dropped by a third.[23]

The nonviolent confrontations engineered by the SCLC required great self-control by both leaders and followers. As happened in other civil rights struggles of the late sixties, tensions developed between movement organizers and a fringe of supporters who wanted to increase the stakes of the conflict. William Saunders's "black power" group, for example, maintained an uneasy but close connection to the official union campaign. As an informal confidant of Moultrie, Saunders dispatched an armed "community militia" to strike meetings and demonstrations; he also functioned as both an ally and a critical observer of the national strike leadership. By his own account he sought to push beyond "the respected black leaders" in this citywide test of wills: "I wanted [to involve] everybody in the community that had been in jail before, that had a record, . . . the people that lived on the street." In Saunders's view the uncontrollable, unpredictable nature of individual acts—no matter how reckless—served as a powerful lever against white authority. "If you feel you have a contribution to offer," he said, "go ahead and offer your contribution [and] the less people that knows about what you're doing, the safer everythings are." Directly or indirectly, such thinking seemed to sanction the firebombings, gunshots, and breaking of windows that occasionally punctuated the Charleston events. Strike organizers took a dim view of these "spontaneous" measures, condemning such acts as the work of "thugs," "hoodlums," and even "agents provocateurs." In fact, at one point they reportedly paid Saunders and his group in an effort to maintain basic compliance with strike discipline.

On May 1, amid planned confrontation and random violence, Governor McNair imposed martial law and a dusk-to-dawn curfew in Charleston. Alice Cabaniss later captured the feel of the disturbed city in a poem called "Strike and Curfew":

> Through the narrow, empty streets,
> trees and bees and birdcall line

the concrete unexpectedly
since fear in black sat down
along the curb to mutter insurrection.

Bivouacked in the suburbs,
mothers mend what they might
yesterday have thrown away,
await the lifting of the curfew,
to replenish larders, resume laughter.

Merchants lounge in doorways
cursing ease, grouping angrily,
hawk-like where their mice have fled
to cooler caves, patrolling windows,
counting guardsmen going by.

That friendly seethe, familiar faces,
melts to vacuum. Denmark Vesey smiles
with pleasure from another century;
black shadows on the empty streets
undo the handshakes of my friends.[24]

Martial law temporarily halted daily demonstrations, but it also attracted nationwide publicity to the strikers' cause. Reproducing in macrocosm the local alliance in Charleston, national civil rights and labor organizations rushed encouragement and tangible expressions of support to the strikers. Led by Abernathy, Davis, Coretta Scott King, and Walter Reuther, president of the United Auto Workers, a Mother's Day march and rally drew 10,000 participants. "You thought we'd just die out after a day or two of marching," Mary Moultrie taunted the governor. "You thought we'd say 'Sorry boss' and put those handkerchiefs back on our heads. Sorry about that governor, but we just had to disappoint you." On May 24 the SCLC called for an economic boycott of King Street businesses and for "shop-ins," whereby demonstrators clogged grocery aisles and cash register lanes, blocking all transactions.[25]

While Moultrie and Abernathy talked of confrontation, Mrs. King underscored the moral claim of the unionizing effort. On April 29 she blessed the women leaders among the Charleston strikers, comparing them to Harriet Tubman, Sojourner Truth, Rosa Parks, and Fannie Lou Hamer. She assured them that "if my husband were alive today he would be right here with you tonight." A week later before a labor banquet honoring A. Philip Randolph, Mrs. King told of being greeted at the Charleston airport by a reporter just back from covering the war in Southeast Asia.

He came up to me and said, "Mrs. King, welcome to Charleston, South Vietnam." The plain truth is that the city of Charleston is an armed camp. More than 1,000 national guardsmen wearing gas masks and flashing bayonets encircle the black community. Armored tanks rumble through the streets. Helmeted state troopers surround Charleston's churches and hospitals. And hundreds of decent men and women, young and old, black and white, have suffered jailings and mass arrests. Why? Simply because a courageous group of terribly exploited hospital workers have dared to stand up and say to the people who run the city of Charleston and the state of South Carolina that they are sick and tired of being sick and tired.[26]

Risking arrest and family hardship day after day, the Charleston hospital workers proved themselves one of the most dedicated groups of union men and women ever encountered in an American labor dispute. Their letters, many written from jail cells during the waning days of the strike, attest to the personal meanings of the struggle. The union was "like an oak tree in a petrified forest," wrote Mrs. D. P. Heyward, "standing with you through trials and tribulations and surrounding you with strength and love." She saw the strike as a matter of getting "all the little people together [to] decide now or forget forever the hope of becoming a real American citizen." Lattie Mae Glover, an aide at the MCH, wrote from jail, "I've seen sometimes in 1199B meetings and on the picket-line Satan comes our way. But it appear to me that whenever Satan comes 1199B has a prepared way to deal with him."[27]

Claire G. Brown, an obstetrics technician at MCH, had five children, some of whom accompanied her to jail. "It was one of the most exciting, hardest, and important periods of my life," she reflected.

The walking, walking, and more walking. The hours and efforts spent trying to get programs together for mass meetings. The sacrifice to my husband and children. Many times my husband performed many of the duties that were mine as a wife and mother, and at times became quite upset, but beared with me.... There were days I wanted to cry, I was so depressed, because it seemed that in spite of all the hard work and sweat, we weren't accomplishing anything, ... but 1199 didn't lie to us, they laid it on the line and let us know just how hard it was going to be.[28]

Vera Smalls, a fourth-generation Charlestonian and the twenty-two-year-old mother of two young daughters, was one of the twelve nurse's aides whose discharge precipitated the strike. Her husband, a Lockheed assembly-line worker, had just returned to work after a layoff of several weeks. Three months into the strike she told a *New York Post* reporter, "I hear from my parents about times being hard, but I never experienced it before." Her living room furnishings (except for a picture of Martin Luther King, Jr., and a Lockheed calendar) were in danger of being repossessed, she had fallen behind on her rent, and she was only barely able to buy milk for her children. The SCLC had given her "the courage to go on," she said. "I need my job so we can live decently. But I won't go back until they realize black people are entitled to have a union too."[29]

The search for public dignity through the union campaign also drew on a private, religiously sanctioned identity. Donna and Virgie Lee Whack, County Hospital ward clerks, and a younger sister still in school together accumulated nearly two months of jail time during the strike. Virgie Lee Whack believed that "South Carolina is a sick society and maybe a strike like ours was God's way of making his people realize that. . . . In Church, the one thing I did learn was that salvation didn't come on a silver platter. There would be suffering and sacrifice like what Jesus spoke of and if [you] wanted victory you had to work for it and hold out to the perfect end."[30]

Many of the strikers sensed a dramatic role reversal as a result of their actions: with outside help the long-suffering acted-upon had become the actors. Donna Whack recalled that "a hidden slogan in my mind" was "if Mr. Charlie can have union representation, Annie Lou can have hers too." "I really enjoyed the hit and run demonstration," wrote Alma Harden, 1199B co-chairperson at County Hospital, "especially blocking traffic on the historic Cooper River Bridge [and] finding out where the Governor was having luncheon, which I think was very funny. Charleston S.C. will never be the same. The historic sights will not be historic any more. The sacrificing Black people in Charleston has been historic." For Rosabelle Deas the strike "let the White men know that slavery is gone forever." The practical nurse Annie G. Fobbs penned this prayer: "O Lord God to whom vengeance belongeth, show thyself, Lift up thyself, Thou Judge of the earth, how long shall the wicked triumph?"[31]

In the 1199/SCLC way of thinking, it was rather the wrath of public opinion that might finally deliver the Charleston strikers from their sufferings. To that end union leaders sought to combine press coverage, financial support, and political intervention at the national level, as it had in New York. If the city and state reactions looked bad to a national audience, the argument ran, then aid to the strikers would pour in from the outside until local authorities were forced into a settlement.

On the surface this strategy spelled success and signaled a new spirit for the American labor movement. Running for weeks as national news,

the Charleston strikers drew support from both expected and unexpected
sources. New York's 1199 members were the first to help, contributing
some $52,000 in emergency funds. A Brooklyn nurse's aide, Annie Scott,
for example, sent $50 to the Charleston struggle "because I remember
ours." The national AFL-CIO and the fledgling UAW–Teamsters Alliance for Labor Action (ALA) competed as benefactors. Walter Reuther
came forward with a $10,000 contribution to 1199 (along with $500 per
week to the SCLC), prompting William Kirchner, the personal representative of George Meany, to show up in Charleston with a check for
$25,000—which the ALA ultimately matched.[32] Moe Foner observed to
Andrew Young, "If the labor movement would only split two more ways,
we'll make a profit here." A wide variety of groups and individuals
responded to full-page newspaper appeals by contributing $13,000, which
included the proceeds from a carnival at the New York City Brearly
School for Girls, a cake sale from the eighth-grade honors English class at
I.S. 70, and a declaration of support from the Psi Upsilon fraternity at the
University of Rochester. In all some $185,000 was raised.[33]

Politically, the strike became a liberal cause célèbre. Twenty-five
congressmen, led by New York's Edward Koch, urged President Richard
Nixon in late April 1969 to appoint a special representative to mediate
the Charleston dispute. The congressional initiative, politely rebuffed by
the White House, likened the actions of the "power structure" in Charleston
to "the kind of treatment that those who make up the great unions of the
country were faced with in 1935." Two weeks later seventeen senators, led
by Jacob Javits of New York and Walter F. Mondale of Minnesota,
appealed for federal mediation in a situation that had become "a test of
the principle of non-violence at a time when many in America are losing
faith in that principle as a strategy for social change."[34] On May 11, in a
show of northern liberal support, Koch attended the Mother's Day demonstration in Charleston, along with John Conyers and Charles Diggs of
Michigan and William F. Ryan and Allard K. Lowenstein of New York.
To a remarkable degree the hospital workers' campaign had revived a
spirit of interracial cooperation at a time of otherwise intense polarization and breakdown of the traditional coalition between liberals (especially
Jewish liberals) and blacks.

Among other impressions of the march, Koch seized on the young
Rangers security guards, outfitted in red Stetsons, white bush boots, and
red and black kerchiefs: "How different they seemed from the Black
Panthers, who, had they been present, would have worn their black
berets, leather jackets and dark glasses. My hostility toward the inflamma-
tory Panthers made me feel an empathy, a rapport with these Rangers
who clearly were capable of defending the march without scaring the

marchers." As he listened to the speeches and a special presentation to
the civil rights heroine Rosa Parks, Koch wondered, "What has happened since the March on Washington? Why is there warmth and brotherhood here in Charleston and coldness and apartheid in New York City?"
Earlier in the day he had been touched by a lunch with Reverend
Abernathy and his ten-year-old son, Ralph Abernathy III. Responding
to a question about what he wanted to be when he grew up, the youngster
answered, "either a minister, an attorney or a freedom fighter." Koch
wrote on his return to New York that he hoped the boy would not have to
choose between his life goals and that, "sophomoric as it may [sound,] I
intend to be a Congressman and a freedom fighter."[35]

Unfortunately, neither the endurance of the strikers nor the array of
outsiders who came to their support swayed the Charleston hospital
administrators or the state's political officials. Six weeks into the conflict
the two sides seemed utterly deadlocked. The union's time-tested formula of confrontation followed by settlement had, in fact, hit some
serious strategic snags, the most important being the ineffectiveness of
the work stoppage itself. From the beginning, the Charleston strike
probably created more trauma for the city than actual dislocation for the
hospitals. Service at both the medical college and county hospitals was
never severely curtailed because the MCH reportedly reduced its patient
load from 450 to 300 beds, while County Hospital cut back by half. Also,
54 new workers had been hired at County Hospital by the end of the first
month of the strike, and the medical college made do with 250 new
employees and a volunteer labor force. Strikers Naomi White and Gloria
Frazier remembered with bitterness the black men who drove their wives
to work, right through the picket lines, some of them visibly armed.
While the union forces were surely correct in claiming some disruption
of normal services, the fact is that when Abernathy was treated in late
May for an ulcer reactivated by a hunger strike, he went to County
Hospital.[36]

Politically, the strike organizers discovered just how far removed they
were from their traditional friends. Governor McNair, originally presumed to be open to compromise, simply would not budge on the issue of
union recognition. Instead, he tried to avoid it by offering new material
benefits to hospital workers. An early June news leak hinted that an
ongoing review of all state employee relations would recommend that
the state minimum wage for public workers be raised from $1.30 per hour
to the federal minimum of $1.60. In addition the review panel promised
to take a serious look at job classifications, holding out the hope of
rational salary readjustment and work descriptions. State legislators registered their opinion of the strike in no uncertain terms, responding to

the SCLC-organized school boycott with a bill that made it unlawful "to encourage or entice a child to stay out of school." First offenders could be fined up to $1,000 and given a prison term of up to two years.[37]

Resistance to union demands at the state level had a counterpart in the corporate consensus among Charleston community leaders. Early in the conflict Judge Singletary had set the mark for successful containment of the civil disturbance by restraining overzealous prosecution of the strikers. A graduate of the College of Charleston, the judge had taken his law degree at the University of Michigan and saw himself as an enlightened moderate on race and labor matters. To his dismay, however, hospital officials (who wanted a total ban on picketing) initially seemed to have "no idea" of the possible violent repercussions of the strike. Singletary had them meet with the mayor's legal counsel, Morris Rosen, Chief of Police John F. Conroy, and a State Law Enforcement Division (SLED, a state investigative unit established in 1947) representative, Leon Gasque, "to make certain that the community understood the potential."

Relying on the city's experience with the 1963 sit-ins, Singletary and law enforcement officials coupled firmness with discretion in limiting violence and property damage. Several times, for example, the judge overlooked or delayed contempt citations; on principle he kept his rulings to a bare minimum. Chief Conroy, an articulate ex-marine from Niagara Falls, New York, complemented the judicial rulings with a cool, patient approach to the demonstrators. He refused to arrest picketers violating an injunction during Coretta Scott King's Mother's Day visit, explaining simply, "We don't want a holocaust." On other occasions SCLC veterans like Abernathy, expectantly equipped with Bible, toothbrush, tube of Crest, and ready-for-jail denims, and James Orange, with fifty-three arrests and ten jail sentences to his credit, were confounded by Conroy's exceptional patience.[38] In fact, white officials of the city and state were so temperate and civilized in their response that the expected crisis atmosphere in the local community was slow to materialize. Charleston's black citizenry, in particular, never fully rallied to the strikers' cause. Moultrie's castigation of the local black elite as "Dr. Thomases and Miss and Mrs. Ann" and Young's characterization of them as people with "black skins and white minds" reflected the strike leaders' own frustrations.[39]

One other aspect of police response to the strike—this one more ambivalent and inconspicuous than the public law enforcement of Chief Conroy—deserves mention: SLED director J. P. "Pete" Strom's subtle help in defusing the union coalition by undermining the mutual trust among its constituent parts. For example, Strom fortified community relations leader Rev. Henry Grant's mistrust of the union and SCLC "outsiders" and encouraged him to play an independent role in settling the strike. Grant recalled Strom telling him, "You know, you don't have to be with [the union]. They don't have the troops. We have the troops."

Even a militant like William Saunders might have been swayed by SLED diplomacy. Saunders remembered times when he expressly resisted entreaties from the governor's office and SLED agents to announce the imminent resolution of strike issues, "when in fact it wasn't going to happen." But he also remembered a meeting with Strom at Dorchester Motor Lodge during a period of tense negotiation and increased street activity:

> When I got to the parking lot where I was supposed to meet him, I went to the trunk of my car. All the SLED agents got out of their cars, and I just stayed in the trunk and messed around for about five minutes and I just knew they didn't know what to do and I finally took my bag out and went over to the chief's car. They didn't know whether to shoot me or what to do then. And then, the chief told me, "You know, Bill, one of the reasons that I'm here is that I feel . . . we got proof that there's a group of people here in Charleston [who want to kill] you, and we want to protect you.

According to Saunders, those reportedly out to get him were "white [craft] union people, who were anti some of the stuff that I was doing here." He believed that Strom was sincere in wanting to protect him but was surprised when, after complaining about petty police harassment—being stopped constantly and ticketed for "bad tires, . . . for lights," and so on—Strom said, "Here, I got a number I'll give you that anytime that you're having problems, the cops stop you, you call this number and then we'll handle it." In the end, said Saunders, "we got to be pretty good friends."[40]

As the forces of resistance gathered against the strike, the union was effectively painted by white Charlestonians as an unwanted intrusion. The county council (which oversaw County Hospital) officially protested "the unwarranted strike and unrest foisted on its citizens by a small group of individuals, many of whom are unrelated to this area, interested only in their own self-seeking ends." Some conservative Charlestonians went further: a paid public announcement signed by prominent businessmen and five clergymen linked the union to a campaign of worldwide Communist insurgency, which "in places like Algeria, China, and Cuba" has sought to divide the people "along racial lines, religious differences, or employer-employee relationships, as in the Medical College case."[41]

For many Charlestonians the assault on their city cut deeper than issues of trade unionism or civil rights. The message of deliverance and freedom carried by the SCLC in its oft-repeated refrain of "We Are

Somebody" implicitly castigated the old ways of a city whose very historic-mindedness was both its pride and its chief economic selling point. In a paid "Letter to Ralph Abernathy," Rev. Leon J. Hubalz, pastor of Blessed Sacrament Church, told readers of the May 7 issue of the *Charleston News and Courier:*

> Remember what you said when you came to Charleston?—about not wanting to see any more historic sites? When you said that I do not think you knew what it could mean to some of our Negro friends. . . . You have heard of the famous Gardens. Do you think any real connoisseur can walk through one of these gardens with-out appreciating the know-how and tender care of the Black man that makes it all possible? Have you ever seen the look of pride on the Black man's face as he watches these tourists admire these gardens? . . . What of the colored Mammy? Could all your speeches and marches ever replace the glow of pride on her face as she watches, day after day, as her little charge grows into a man of importance in the world?

The hospital workers' struggle was thus projected over a wide set of issues and symbols. It stood on one side for a rebellion against years of white domination and black subservience; on the other side it summoned up an almost chauvinistic civic loyalty, an instinctual defense of a way of life. In such a polarized setting, few white-dominated institutions dared break ranks with the antistrike forces. Indeed, those who called for conciliation risked real recrimination. A white Methodist bishop, Paul Hardin, Jr., for instance, forbade support by Methodist ministers for the strike; when three black ministers broke ranks, they were quickly trans-ferred to lesser positions.

The Roman Catholic church was an exception. Since the church hierarchy's opposition to the New York hospital campaign in 1959, both the spirit of Pope John XXIII and a developing engagement with the civil rights movement had affected church responses in important ways. Ernest Unterkoefler, bishop of the Charleston archdiocese, continued the quiet but firm support he had lent to civil rights issues since his arrival in the city in 1965 (including marching at the head of the Poor People's Campaign caravan as it entered Charleston in 1968). He publicly blamed the strike on "constant refusals [of hospital officers] to communicate with the representatives of the non-professional workers in their organizational choice." The Charleston pastorate took an even more active role than the bishop. Rev. William Joyce of the all-black St. Patrick's parish was elected secretary of the prostrike Committee of Concerned Clergy, which com-prised approximately 30 of 265 ministers in Charleston who supported the workers' right to collective bargaining and union recognition. St. Zavier's, a small Catholic hospital, joined the black-owned McLennan-Banks proprietary hospital as the only institutions in the city prepared, if requested, to negotiate with the union. Joyce, Rev. Leo Croghan, a diocesan priest, and Rev. Thomas Duffy, director of Catholic Charities and a prison chaplain, were all arrested during nonviolent demonstrations on behalf of the strikers.[42] On May 15, in a critical commentary rarely heard in Charleston, the weekly *Catholic Banner* castigated city officials and the news media for "pulling a Magnolia Curtain down over their head and eyes," seeing only "what serves their emotional needs." "We have a curfew, militia and policemen making a great show of force, and all kinds of balderdash, to protect us from a few strikers, most of them very mild women indeed. One sometimes wonders whether South Carolina thinks it is a State of the Union or a banana republic."

Catholic support for the strike hardly went unnoticed by white Charlestonians. The popular local columnist F. B. Gilbreth, Jr., using his regular pen name Ashley Cooper, called the church's effective encouragement of illegal demonstrations "absolutely intolerable, unless anarchy is to be adopted as a way of life." Duffy found out that strike support meant a fall from public respectability, as invitations to the local Kiwanis Club and myriad other social organizations and functions were withheld. Moreover, the strike produced severe friction between the church and its wealthier white patrons, benefactors like real estate developer and Port Authority chairman Joseph Riley, who, according to Duffy, "washed their hands" of the church hierarchy. As a result, in 1969—for the first time—the local United Fund deleted Catholic Charities from its list of community service grant recipients.[43]

During the first two weeks of May, 1199 leaders reluctantly (and privately) reached the conclusion that, as Moe Foner puts it, "we just did not have the cards." Relying as they were on daily transfusions of outside aid to maintain their operation, the union forces faced not only the depletion of their resources in Charleston but growing strains on their services to 1199 members in New York. A grim reassessment of the situation brought up the difficult question of how, after focusing so much energy and attention on Charleston, could the union disentangle itself without suffering a humiliating national defeat. Publicly, the first hint of a change in the union's position came on May 15 when Elliott Godoff said that 1199 might compromise its demand for direct recognition in favor of some independent intermediary voice for the hospital workers—a tactical move that directly evoked the union's acquiescence in the face-saving 1959 PAC agreement. While this initiative, in and of itself, produced no sudden shift in the state's hardline position, 1199's flexibility soon combined with the appearance of an unexpected outside force to raise the odds for a compromise solution.[44]

Escalating intervention by the federal government, first evident in a report from the civil rights division of the Department of Health, Education, and Welfare, Atlanta Field Office, transformed the situation in Charleston. Sometime during the latter half of May, through contacts with HEW under secretary (and former CORE leader) James Farmer and former under secretary Ruby Martin, union leaders learned that the Medical College Hospital was being audited under the terms of federal regulations governing millions of dollars in grants going to the medical complex. After informal contacts between 1199 officials and Atlanta Field Office director Hugh S. Brimm, the HEW noncompliance report of June 4, in addition to citing thirty-seven civil rights violations by the MCH administration, formally recommended the rehiring of the twelve union workers whose dismissal had touched off the strike.[45] As might be expected, the financial pressure implied by the HEW findings immediately triggered new moves toward a settlement.

Although the word "negotiation" was not publicly used, Andrew Young decided to make a direct effort to reach the MCH's William McCord. To everyone's surprise McCord took the phone call himself and quickly arranged a meeting. Young recalled: "Frankly we just listened to [McCord] for about two hours, telling us all that he tried to do for these workers and . . . how we were wrecking his hospital and so on. I didn't try to answer him or argue with him. I said, 'But Dr. McCord, what we're interested in is finding a way to go on from here, together.'" Unofficially, McCord agreed to dispatch the hospital's vice president for development, William Huff, for further exploratory talks with Young. (Huff had come to Charleston from New York, where he had worked in an 1199-organized hospital.) What ensued, Young remembered, was a kind of triangulated set of exchanges between the parties: "We began to just explore a kind of agreement. In the meantime we were calling this information to New York and they were calling this back down to the governor's office. And the governor then was calling McCord and the officials in Charleston. So we never really sat down in the same room with the governor or his people."

While the private contacts between Young and hospital administrators produced the outlines of a substantive compromise, another set of meetings took place, the goal being to hammer out an official public agreement. Preferring not to meet publicly with union or SCLC officials, hospital board members (acting for the governor's office) scheduled sessions with strike leaders and designated community representatives, including Reverend Grant and William Saunders. A June 5 meeting at the Santee-

Cooper hydroelectric plant in Monck's Corner, some thirty-five miles north of Charleston, witnessed a significant softening in the board's position.[46] As Saunders remembered, the initial physical encounter of the women strikers with the hospital directors was tense and awkward, but "then the trustee board went and got chairs for the ladies to sit down . . . and the attitude began to change." Within days the basic pieces appeared in place to end the Charleston strike. On June 9, 1969, after cutting the city's curfew hours in half, the governor publicly accepted the state's responsibility to comply with federal guidelines. McCord then announced the hospital's willingness to take back the strikers and to rehire the twelve fired workers. State and hospital officials, anxious to end the unrest in Charleston but politically constrained from appearing to appease the strikers, could now blame Washington for forcing concessions.

As in New York City ten years before, the longer-term issue of union recognition was purposefully left unresolved by the negotiators. However, without any formal reference to recognition or collective bargaining, the hospitals did agree to a new grievance procedure allowing workers to bring one representative to grievance sessions. Hopes were high in the union camp as the informal signing date of June 12 neared for a real agreement.

Then, only hours before the planned meetings, McCord reneged on his promise to rehire the twelve workers, claiming hospital staff opposition to the move. McCord's action, in fact, reflected a shifting of larger political forces. On the morning of the projected settlement-signing date, Congressman L. Mendel Rivers and Senator Strom Thurmond reportedly prevailed upon HEW secretary Robert Finch to postpone his threatened fund cutoff to MCH "pending a personal investigation" after he returned from a planned vacation in the Bahamas. This federal about-face was evidence of a larger conflict within the Nixon administration over civil rights enforcement. Liberal pressure for compromise and settlement of the dispute arose from a committed group of second-level administrative staff in HEW. Politically, however, Nixon's 1968 "southern strategy" had looked to a different constituency and was susceptible to different pressures. In this case the demands of state party leaders and political advisors crucial to Nixon's narrow national electoral victory could not be ignored. State Republican chairman Ray Harris had already placed Governor McNair and his fellow Democrats on notice for any waffling on the hospital issue. Now national Republicans were told to toe the line.[47]

Collapse of the projected settlement set off two more weeks of rising tension, including night marches, fire-bombings, and threats to tie up area telephone lines as well as transportation and major business arteries. Leaders of the International Longshoremen Association dropped hints that their union might close the port of Charleston, while 1199 sympathizers talked of union agitation spreading to the South Carolina textile industry. Pickets appeared overnight at the New York City headquarters of the J. P. Stevens, Deering-Milliken, and Manhattan Shirt companies, and Ralph Abernathy even raised the spectre of a national boycott of specified South Carolina manufactured goods.[48] For their part, strike leaders genuinely feared a breakdown of their whole operation in Charleston. Uncharacteristically, SCLC aide Hosea Williams gave vent to uncontrolled emotions at a June 20 rally at Memorial Baptist Church: "White folks are crazy. White America is insane. We have played around with Charleston long enough. We're going to march in Charleston tonight or we're going to die." Clashes with police and hundreds of arrests over the next few days were reported, along with sporadic gunfire and dozens of suspicious fires. Andrew Young warned of a "violent fringe" within the movement: "They are short of money, it is hot, most have family responsibilities, and they see no relief in sight."[49]

Union leaders had all but exhausted their tactical supplies. Among his calculated leaks to the press and government officials, Moe Foner remembered the ultimate threat to bring Coretta Scott King and her family to Charleston to be arrested; rumor even had it that Joan Kennedy might accompany her. Playing out a final lead on a tip from the *New York Post* writer James Wechsler, Foner called presidential counselor Daniel Patrick Moynihan and said, "Look, I'm not going to be responsible, but I think you have to know, the night marches are going to continue, and this town is going to burn." Moynihan promised to see what he could do.

For a second time the strike's deliverance issued from Washington. This time the White House transferred authority over the Charleston crisis from the vacationing Finch to labor secretary George Shultz. Armed with the renewed threat of a fund cutoff, and with Mayor Gaillard's acquiescence, Shultz sent a federal mediator, William Pierce, to Charleston on June 24. On Friday, June 27, after a call to William McCord from White House aide and former state Republican chairman Harry Dent, invoking the national interest, the hospital director agreed to rehire the twelve fired workers along with the strikers. At the same time Young paid a surprise visit to white nurses at the MCH and convinced them to drop their opposition to the return of the strikers. McCord initialed an agreement late that afternoon, then both sides proceeded to the Frances Marion Motel to announce the settlement. McCord's official statement was terse: "The strike is settled."[50]

Union officials knew that the strike drama was not over yet. As in 1959, they sought to extract a victory or at least a vital "foot in the door" from the strike's apparently stalemated ending. By selectively leaking details of the settlement and putting the best possible interpretation on the official language, 1199 once again finessed a public relations coup. The *New York Times,* for example, noted on June 28 that the settlement, which included wage increases, "appeared to meet the major demands of the hospital workers." Although no mention was made of union recognition or collective bargaining, the union pointed to the grievance procedure and the possibility of a voluntary dues checkoff via the employee credit union (a device that had been used to settle the Memphis sanitation workers' strike in 1968) as indirect evidence of union influence. The strike-ending terms prompted jubilant community celebration at the Zion-Olivet United Presbyterian Church, and to many observers Local 1199B appeared to have broken through the "Magnolia Curtain." Reverend Grant, for one, proclaimed the Charleston settlement "more than a compromise"—"It was a victory."[51]

Years later, black Charlestonians looked back on the tangible, positive changes achieved for the community through the hospital workers' strike. "It was like a revolution," remembered Grant. Black voter registration "shot up like mad," neighborhoods in Charleston County were substantially integrated, and in general "people were forced to take notice of the entire black community." In 1970 Herbert U. Fielding, a Charleston funeral home director, joined the first black delegation to the state legislature since Reconstruction; vocal strike supporter Rev. Robert Woods followed a few years later. Black representation on the city council went from one to six delegates in the ten years following the strike. William Saunders, who chartered a community service and organizing program called COBRA and later ran unsuccessfully for political office, asserted in 1979 that the strike had made whites "respect blacks for having organized. They're a little scared now and will negotiate before they reach that same level of polarization."

Whatever its indirect "community" benefits, talk of "victory" proved premature for hospital workers' Local 1199B. At the time of settlement, many of the second-level 1199 and SCLC staff left the city still convinced that the foundation for a successful union local had indeed been laid. But during the months following the strike the MCH administration not only refused to authorize checkoff through the credit union but undermined the union's authority in the grievance system by limiting the number of times that the same person could serve as a grievant's representative. In addition, local union leaders faced an erosion of both outside support and internal goodwill. When County Hospital followed the MCH settlement with nearly identical strike-ending terms on July

19, outside aid to Charleston workers all but dried up. The money was gone, the issue had lost its national dramatic appeal, and, perhaps most important, the New York union and the SCLC had other priorities. The Charleston hospital workers had no office of their own, and organizers from New York visited only intermittently. The lone SCLC staffer, James Orange, was soon involved in new community campaigns, including a citywide organizing drive by black sanitation workers.

Under these circumstances the local leadership around Mary Moultrie proved unable to sustain difficult grassroots organizing. A national symbol of the Charleston cause who had addressed an AFL-CIO convention and even posed with Hubert Humphrey and Golda Meir during the strike, Moultrie was unprepared for the tasks that greeted her. When the real terms of day-to-day life in the hospitals reasserted themselves, long-simmering mistrust and jealousies among the Charleston activists burst forth in a destructive fury. Jubilation quickly turned to bitter recrimination and accusation against Moultrie, against Saunders, and against the union itself. Henry Nicholas echoed a common view among national union leaders in his assessment that Moultrie's problems revealed a basic tension between the union's metropolitan base and its provincial outpost. "Like the U.S. in foreign countries, we tried to prop up a leader," he explained. "But when you move the prop, the leader falls [and it's] dangerous." Acknowledging that Moultrie was a magnetic "Barbara Jordan type of speaker," Nicholas believed that the union may have pushed her beyond her limits: "She could do all things that had to be done at the moment, but the understanding of what she was really doing was missing."[52]

The poststrike disillusionment among the hospital workers took a heavy personal toll on Mary Moultrie. Her effectiveness as a strike leader had proved personally disorienting, and when she was voted out as chapter president not long after the strike's end, she withdrew from hospital organizing in discouraged confusion. The gap between Moultrie and national union leaders was highlighted in a family trip she took to New York City in 1973. With one of her cousins, an 1199 member in New York, Moultrie paid a visit to the attractive new headquarters of the national hospital workers' union, the Martin Luther King Labor Center. Her cousin led her down one hallway at the end of which she encountered a giant, blown-up photograph of herself marching arm in arm with Walter Reuther. Moultrie left the building without even making her presence known to officials upstairs. In the end she felt "hurt and disappointed with a lot of people" she had been involved with. "If I had it to do again I would. But then I'd be careful," she said.

The strike's failure to produce a solid victory also complicated the future of the southern-based civil rights movement. Tragedy in Memphis, ineptitude in Washington, D.C., chronic financial problems, and divisive internal wrangling raised the stakes for the SCLC's labor- and class-oriented strategy as applied to Charleston. Except for a few headlines, the SCLC could hardly draw strength, let alone a model for further actions, from the Charleston stalemate. In the world of what-might-have-been, Charleston might have served as an effective regenerator of the Poor People's Campaign, an inspiration for the broad labor and civil rights alliance that SCLC founders like Bayard Rustin, Ella Baker, and Stanley Levison had sought for years. Indeed, the possibilities were evident in August 1970 when an interracial group of steelworkers in Georgetown, South Carolina, sixty miles north of Charleston, walked off their jobs after demanding a union contract. Faced with a protracted strike and menacing state police, the strikers called on the SCLC for help. Aided by the showing of the 1199-produced film *I Am Somebody* (drawn from footage of the Charleston events), visits by Mary Moultrie and other hospital workers, and a series of SCLC street demonstrations, the United Steelworkers' local emerged with a solid four-year contract. The experience convinced attending SCLC organizer Carl Farris that "black and white workers across the nation are ready to move together as brothers and sisters in the struggle."[53]

In the end, however, such dreams were not to be. Friction within the organization and failure to score truly dramatic victories with its economic organizing strategy left the SCLC increasingly demoralized. Charleston itself proved to be one more drain on the sinking civil rights organization's resources. By the end of 1969, Andrew Young was already expressing doubts about the viability of an "exhausted organization" and shortly afterward resigned to pursue a political career. Other resignations followed until in 1973 a once robust staff of 125 had been depleted to 17. The SCLC continued to involve itself in community efforts throughout the South, but its nonviolent and largely defensive campaigns failed to attract national attention and support. Surveying the overall civil rights scene in 1970, the *New York Times* reported "very little direct action . . . anywhere in the South today."[54]

Beyond the bittersweet local and regional effects of the Charleston struggle lay its impact on 1199 nationally. Here the returns for the union proved much more tangible. In the course of the Charleston campaign the hospital union, before a nationwide audience, had proved itself willing and able to take on any foe. Particularly for black urban workers the "union power, soul power" crusade broke down barriers separating labor organizing from the community-based black militancy of the era. If such tactics could exact concessions in the heart of the antiunion South, might they not utterly triumph in the urban-industrial North? In the weeks following the Charleston settlement, 1199 organizers confidently set up shop in a half-dozen cities. *I Am Somebody* became a staple in introducing the organized hospital workers to labor and community groups across the country. The mere threat of "pulling another Charleston" even extracted a union recognition agreement from the prestigious Johns Hopkins Hospital.

With the Charleston campaign 1199 had strengthened its image as a "civil rights union." To be sure, the principles of interracial solidarity were evident during the early years of the old drugstore local, and they had been basic to the very creation of an organization among hospital service workers. Now, however, the connection between workers' rights and racial progress had reached a new stage and in the following years would prove both an asset and a liability as the hospital workers reached out across the country. At the end of *I Am Somebody,* the strike steward Claire Brown declares: "If I didn't learn but one thing it was that if you are ready and willing to fight for yourself, other folks will be ready and willing to fight for you." She was right, of course. But, too often, the outcome of a political fight just as surely depends upon timing and location.[55]

NOTES

Excerpted from Leon Fink and Brian Greenberg, *Upheaval in the Quiet Zone: A History of Hospital Workers' Union, Local 1199* (Urbana, Ill., 1989), 129–58. Reprinted with the permission of Brian Greenberg. For their help with key aspects of research in this essay, I would like to thank Steve Hoffius, David Garrow, Jack Bass, and George and Randy Kaiser. In addition, Robert Korstad and Harry Watson provided useful editorial criticisms.

1. *American Statistical Index,* 1976 s.v. "Southeast Regional Reports, 6946-133," "Work Stoppages," "Union Membership and Employment for the Southeast"; "Employment and Economic Growth: Southeast," *Monthly Labor Review* 91 (Mar. 1968), 18–19; telephone interview with George Kaiser, field representative for the AFL-CIO in South Carolina since 1965, Apr. 29, 1963; South Carolina Department of Labor, *Annual Report, 1978–79,* pt. 2: *S.C. State Budget Control Board: Departments and Resolutions,* 77–82.

2. Jamie W. Moore, "The Lowcountry in Economic Transition: Charleston since 1865," *South Carolina Historical Magazine* 80 (Apr. 1979), 156–71; Frederic Cople Jaher, "Antebellum Charleston: Anatomy of Economic Failure," in *Class Conflict and Consensus: Antebellum Southern Community Studies,* ed. Orville Vernon Burton and Robert C. McMath, Jr. (Westport, Conn., 1982), 207–31; *U.S. Census, 1950,* vol. 2: *Population,* pt. 40 (South Carolina), 46, 168–70; *U.S. Census, 1970,* vol. 1: *Population,* pt. 42 (South Carolina), 23, 198, 204, 208.

3. See Kay Day, " 'My Family Is Me': Kin Networks and Social Power in a

Black Sea Island Community" (Ph.D. diss., Rutgers University, 1983); *Washington Post,* June 16, 1969.

4. Sanford Sherman, "The Charleston Strike" (ms. in possession of Moe Foner, n.d.), 7; *Business Week,* Apr. 5, 1969.

5. *Congressional Quarterly Weekly Report* 28, no. 51 (Dec. 11, 1970), 2951–52; Robert Coles and Harry Huge, "The Way It Is in South Carolina," *New Republic* 159 (Nov. 30, 1968), 17, also 17–21.

6. This pattern of racial containment is described by William Chafe, *Civilities and Civil Rights: Greensboro, North Carolina, and the Black Struggle for Freedom* (New York, 1980); Stephen O'Neill, "The Struggle for Black Equality Comes to Charleston: The Hospital Strike of 1969," *Proceedings of the South Carolina Historical Association,* 1986, 83.

7. Interview with Rev. Thomas Duffy, Feb. 18, 1980; *New York Times,* Sept. 3–4, 1963; *New York Times Index,* 1964.

8. Letter, Alice Cabaniss to Leon Fink, Aug. 1, 1983; telephone conversation with Joseph W. Cabaniss, Feb. 13, 1985.

9. *New York Jet,* June 5, 1969.

10. For a more liberal interpretation of public employee law by two legal counselors representing 1199 in Charleston, see Eugene G. Eisner and I. Phillip Sipser, "The Charleston Hospital Dispute: Organizing Public Employees and the Right to Strike," *St. John's Law Review* 45 (Dec. 1970), 254–72; *Los Angeles Times,* Apr. 14, 1969. Haynesworth was a cousin of Clement Haynesworth, a federal judge who later that year was nominated, then contested and defeated, for appointment to the U.S. Supreme Court.

11. "Review of the Union Meeting," July 22, 1968, Davis Correspondence, National Union of Hospital and Health Care Employees Records, 1937–76, Labor-Management Documentation Center, Cornell University, Ithaca, N.Y. (hereafter 1199 Archives).

12. Convincing evidence of the Charleston workers' seriousness was reported by visiting 1199 vice president Doris Turner. She was scheduled to meet with organized workers one evening at the tobacco workers' hall but because of airline delays did not arrive until after midnight. Before she went to the hotel she decided to stop by the meeting hall, just in case someone had waited for her, and found it full of hospital workers.

13. *Charleston News and Courier,* Feb. 27, 1969; *Charleston Evening Post,* Mar. 5, 1968.

14. *Charleston News and Courier,* Mar. 20–21, 1969; *Charlotte Observer,* Apr. 4, 1969; interview with Henry Nicholas, Jan. 11, 1978; "Case Study: The Charleston Hospital Strike," *Southern Hospitals,* Mar. 1971, 16–18; *Business Week,* Apr. 6, 1969.

15. *The Medical College of Charleston* v. *Drug and Hospital Union, Local 1199B,* 52, slip op. at 596 (S.C.C.P. Ninth Judicial Circuit, July 9, 1969); Sherman, "Charleston Strike," 63.

16. *The State* (Columbia, S.C.), May 10, 1969; J. H. O'Dell, "Charleston's Legacy to the Poor People's Campaign," *Freedomways* 9 (Summer 1969), 201; *Charleston News and Courier,* Apr. 9, 1969.

17. See David J. Garrow, *The FBI and Martin Luther King, Jr.* (New York, 1981), esp. chap. 1; Adam Fairclough, *To Redeem the Soul of America: The Southern Christian Leadership Conference and Martin Luther King, Jr.* (Athens, Ga., 1987), 30; interview with Moe Foner, Mar. 9, 1979.

18. Levison's continuing role in strike strategy discussions as well as backbiting and personality conflicts within SCLC were relayed to the FBI through "confidential sources." Memos, Mar. 31 and Apr. 24, 1969, secured through the Freedom of Information Act (File No. 54688 80514 73518) by David Garrow and shared with the authors.

19. *Charleston News and Courier,* Apr. 2, 1969; interview with Henry Nicholas, Apr. 14, 1982.

20. *Charleston News and Courier,* Apr. 25–26, 1969; "Case Study"; *New York Times,* May 30, 1969. An FBI memo, dated May 2, 1969, reported: "Young sees the SCLC capitalizing on a framework they have laid in the citizenship schools and feels it is important, to call in their citizenship contacts from other counties. Young recommended that win, lose, or draw they will mobilize South Carolina politically in the process.... Young mentioned that they have done more underground work in South Carolina than any other state in the South and that the citizenship schools have trained people in every county. He estimated six to seven hundred people have attended these schools in the last five years."

21. O'Neill, "Struggle for Black Equality," 86.

22. *New York Times,* May 4, 1969.

23. *Charleston News and Courier,* Apr. 24–25 and 28, 1969; *New York Times,* Apr. 26 and 29, 1969.

24. Jack Bass, "Strike at Charleston," *New South* (Summer 1969), 35–44. The poem is quoted on p. 44.

25. Moultrie speech, Charleston file, 1199 Archives; *Baltimore Afro-American,* May 31, 1969.

26. *New York Times,* Apr. 30, 1969; Coretta Scott King speech, May 6, 1969, Charleston file, 1199 Archives.

27. Letters from Charleston strikers, Charleston file, 1199 Archives.

28. Ibid.

29. *New York Post,* June 26, 1969.

30. Letters from Charleston strikers.

31. Ibid.

32. Annie Scott to 1199, May 19, 1969; list of monetary contributions to Charleston strike, Aug. 1, 1969, 1199 Archives.

33. Ann Fay (Brearly School) to Mrs. King, June 4, 1969; Eleanore Levenson (I.S. 70) to Mrs. King, May 9, 1969; Charles Serota et al. (University of Rochester) to Mrs. King, May 8, 1969, Charleston file, 1199 Archives.

34. Sherman, "Charleston Strike," 53–54, 60–61.

35. *Park East,* June 12, 1969.

36. Interview with Naomi White and Gloria Frazier, July 25, 1979, by Steve Hoffius (transcript courtesy of interviewer); *Charleston News and Courier,* Apr. 30, 1969; "Case Study."

37. *Business Week,* May 17, 1969. See, e.g., *New York Times,* Apr. 21 and 29, May 14–15, June 6, 12, and 18, 1969; *The State,* May 30, 1969.

38. *New York Times,* Apr. 23, 1969; *Newsweek,* May 5 and 12, 1969.

39. *New York Post,* June 27, 1969; letters from Charleston strikers.

40. While acknowledging in a June 23, 1982, telephone conversation with Leon Fink that he had been on hand for nearly every day of the hospital workers' strike, Chief Strom declined to be interviewed on the subject. Nevertheless, the hints about his role in Charleston seem of a piece with his documented initiatives during other civil disturbances. Strom, who had gained a reputation as "the J. Edgar Hoover of South Carolina," had helped to break up the Ku Klux Klan in the 1950s, and in 1964 he headed off violence when students picketed an appearance by George Wallace in Columbia. For his subtle efforts before the deadly confrontation at Orangeburg, S.C., on February 6, 1968, see Jack Nelson and Jack Bass, *The Orangeburg Massacre* (New York, 1970), 31, 202.

41. County Council Resolution, n.d., Charleston file, 1199 Archives; *Charleston News and Courier,* Apr. 26, 1969.

42. *Charleston News and Courier,* June 3, 1969; *New York Times,* June 4, 1969; statement by Bishop Unterkoefler, n.d., Charleston file, 1199 Archives.

43. *Charleston News and Courier,* May 1, 1969.

44. Sherman, "Charleston Strike," p. 61.

45. *Charleston News and Courier,* May 30, 1969; letters, Hugh S. Brimm to William McCord, Sept. 19, 1968, and June 4, 1969, Charleston file, 1199 Archives.

46. O'Neill, "Struggle for Black Equality," 88.

47. Cf. *Washington Post,* June 16, 1969; *Charleston Evening Post,* June 13, 1969; Bass, "Strike at Charleston," 35–44; Leon E. Panetta and Peter Gall, *Bring Us Together: The Nixon Team and Civil Rights Retreat* (Philadelphia, 1971), 183–87; Harry S. Dent, *The Prodigal South Returns to Power* (New York, 1978), 130–31.

48. *Charleston News and Courier,* June 21, 23, and 26, 1969; *Charleston Evening Post,* June 10, 1969; *New York Times,* June 26, 1969; O'Dell, "Charleston's Legacy," 205–8. The textile trade paper, the *Daily News Record* (June 26, 1969), called the strike "a bombshell set to explode at the back door of the South Carolina textile industry."

49. *Charleston News and Courier,* June 21, 1969; *New York Times,* June 25, 1969.

50. Dent, *Prodigal South,* 130–31; *New York Times,* June 28, 1969; interviews with Moe Foner, Mar. 9, 1979, and Andrew Young, Jan. 31, 1980.

51. *New York Times,* June 28, 1969; *1199 Drug and Hospital News,* July 1969. On the Memphis sanitation workers' settlement the previous year, see Philip S. Foner, *Organized Labor and the Black Worker, 1619–1981* (New York, 1981), 384.

52. On the poststrike unraveling process, see Steve Hoffius, "Charleston Hospital Workers' Strike, 1969," in *Working Lives: The Southern Exposure History of Labor in the South,* ed. Marc S. Miller (New York, 1980), 225–58.

53. Carl E. Farris, "The Steelworkers' Strike in South Carolina," *Freedomways* 11 (2d quart., 1971), 189, also 178–91. The increasing numbers of blacks in the southern industrial labor force likely did create a window of opportunity (at least until the oil shock, stagflation, and textile import crisis of the mid-seventies) for

the wider application of "union power, soul power." The Oneita strike at Andrews, S.C. (1971–73), the J. P. Stevens campaign at Roanoke Rapids, N.C. (1974), and the Farah strike and boycott at El Paso, Tex. (1972–74), also drew heavily on civil rights themes but without the involvement and resuscitation of a national civil rights movement. See Carolyn Ashbaugh and Dan McCurry, "On the Line at Oneita," *Southern Exposure* 4 (1976), 30–37; Bill Finger and Mike Krivosh, "Stevens vs. Justice," ibid., 38–44; Bill Finger, "Victoria Sobre Farah," ibid., 45–49.

54. Fairclough, *To Redeem the Soul*, 11–35, 385–405. In painting the outcome of the Charleston strike as one of undiluted union victory (p. 396), Fairclough himself was apparently misled by the union's and the SCLC's immediate poststrike enthusiasm.

55. A postscript to the 1969 Charleston strike suggests that objective conditions for hospital worker organizing in South Carolina have not improved much. In 1981, following an NLRB election of the previous year, 1199 negotiated a contract in Tuomey, S.C., reportedly the first unionized voluntary hospital in the South. When that contract expired, management proposed to remove both the arbitration-of-grievances clause and the dues checkoff; they also subcontracted out the housekeeping department (where the union had over 95 percent membership) and threatened to do the same with the dietary department. Before the next contract expired in June 1984 the hospital laid off 16 nurse's aides, 14 of them black union members, and replaced them with all-white LPNs who had been told not to join the "Black Union"; other black union members also were replaced with white part-time workers. A one-year contract was signed in September 1984 that called for a meager 2 percent raise for most workers. Then, on October 5 the hospital laid off 53 nurse's aides, most of whom were union members. In four years' time the bargaining unit had dropped from 426 workers to 300, and union membership was down to less than 70 voluntary dues-payers. In January 1985 the hospital filed a decertification petition, and by March the last 30 union dues-payers voted unanimously to officially disavow their representation by the union. In April 1985 Tuomey Hospital hired back many of the aides it had previously laid off—at $3.35 an hour (a $2.00-an-hour wage cut). See *Officers' Report to the Seventh Convention of National Union of Hospital and Health Care Employees (AFL-CIO)*, December 9–12, 1987, Hartford, Conn., 38.

PART THREE

Peculiarities of the Americans

5

The New Labor History and the Powers of Historical Pessimism: Consensus, Hegemony, and the Case of the Knights of Labor

On July 4, 1890, Terence Vincent Powderly, general master workman of the Knights of Labor, addressed a labor picnic of five thousand men, women, and children in the anthracite valley town of Priceburg, Pennsylvania. Carrying a copy of the Declaration of Independence, Powderly determined to make it "the text for my sermon this afternoon."

> Written over a hundred years ago, of a condition which existed then, we wonder on reading it over now, in the closing days of the nineteenth century . . . how it comes that the indictment drawn up against the English king applies with such startling force to the agencies we now find usurping the "divine right of kings" and making slaves of men who proudly, but thoughtlessly, boast of their freedom—that freedom which they claim came down to us from revolutionary sites as a heritage to be enjoyed in the full glare of the sun of universal liberty. Are we the free people that we imagine we are? Do we as fully appreciate the blessings of liberty as we think we do?[1]

How shall we interpret Powderly's remarks at Priceburg? Were his words a meaningful expression of class conflict in America, contesting bourgeois values and politics? Were they on the contrary mere "eulogistic coverings," a rhetorical gesture decorating behavior that was actually anchored in Lockean individualism and "liberal" material self-interest? Alternatively, shall we posit Powderly's sermon on the Declaration of Independence as a kind of halfway house between the two possibilities listed above, the expression of a powerful "movement culture," but one nevertheless weighted down by "divided consciousness" or "contradictory elements" that in the end fatally "promoted internal divisions and pointed toward accommodation as well as resistance"?[2]

Such questions mirror a larger pattern of responses to the abundant literature on nineteenth-century American labor protest. In the community and occupational studies forming the new labor history, a prominent theme has been the discovery of alternative cultural meanings or distinctive subjectivities in working-class expression and behavior.[3] In that context "labor republicanism," or some variation on that term, has served to define the characteristic ideology of the organized labor movement in the nineteenth century. As early as the 1820s workingmen's leaders had self-consciously begun to indict an emergent industrial order by affirming the significance of the nation's political commitment to independent citizenship. The labor reform critique was carried further in the post–Civil War years. A combination of affirmation and negation of American culture was reflected in the eloquence of labor radical George E. McNeill in the late 1870s: "We declare an inevitable and irresistible conflict between the wage-system of labor and the republican system of government."[4]

Recent scholarship on the Knights of Labor has highlighted the cultural theme common to the new labor history. As the largest and most representative labor body until its time—and probably the single largest unionizing movement in the Western world during the 1880s—the Knights appear to most students of their movement as a natural repository of a characteristic and distinctive American labor vision. The new historians of the Knights, in fact, have commonly analyzed the movement as propelled not merely by a set of specific group grievances but, as Susan Levine writes, by a "counter-vision of cooperation, equality, and social responsibility." At its height the Gilded Age labor movement, argues David Scobey, "would pose alternative productive relations to the marketplace, an alternative conception of the republican polity, even an alternative morality to this 'present system of all for self.' "[5]

But how cogent, widespread, and deep-seated was the labor critique of American capitalism? A renewed search for synthesis of social and political history has left many scholars skeptical of the labor historians' claims. To the skeptics the very defeat of opposition movements suggests their internal weakness and inconsistency of purpose. They view the notion of an autonomous "movement culture" distinct from the larger culture of acquisitiveness as so much naive romanticism. Then, too, there is the problem of connecting the past with the present: How can we reconcile alleged nineteenth-century radical traditions (whether among New York artisans, Knights of Labor, or Populist farmers) with America's world-historic conservatism in the twentieth century?[6]

Two critical responses promise some guidance in this area. John Patrick Diggins and T. J. Jackson Lears offer provocative evaluations of labor protest in relation to nineteenth-century political culture. From separate, even opposite, perspectives, these two distinguished intellectual historians deflate what they consider the parochial sentimentality of the new labor history. Diggins dismisses the significance of radical labor rhetoric and professed oppositional values on the basis of the overwhelming orientation to interests in American culture. Lears, on the contrary, takes seriously the language and culture of protest but sees within it the seeds of its own destruction. The analysis Diggins presents leads to the resurrection of a cultural-consensus interpretation of American history; Lears seeks to invigorate Antonio Gramsci's concept of cultural hegemony.

Together, the two contributions offer an excellent opportunity to assess the limits of popular American radicalism and to explore the relationships between power and culture in American history. I argue here that the history of the Knights of Labor demonstrates the existence of a viable labor culture, and I use that history to engage Diggins and Lears on the larger questions. While welcoming the quest for analytic rigor championed by the two authors, I want to challenge Diggins's insistence on the universal saturation of American culture in a dreary liberalism of private accumulation and Lears's overvaluation of intellectual coherence as a test of political and cultural authenticity.

In his biting and ambitious commentary "Comrades and Citizens: New Mythologies in American Historiography," Diggins restates the case for a liberal consensus in American political culture throughout the nineteenth century. Despite claims to the contrary, argues Diggins, nothing has emerged from working-class history (not to mention the histories of slavery and of the American Revolution, which he treats in other sections of the essay) to refute the notion that American workers shared the economic individualism of the middle classes, that they were fundamentally motivated by material self-interest, and that, despite specific complaints and grievances, they embraced no "conscious rejection of capitalism," no "negation of bourgeois society." The newer monographic literature, according to Diggins, has been heavy on behavioral evidence but unconvincing in its projections of worker motivation or its ascriptions of collective consciousness. Of course, an explicit focus on consciousness has emerged through the study of language and rhetoric.

Dismissing the formal "language of labor" as "eulogistic coverings" of more essential motivations, however, he remains doubtful that American workers ever really expressed "thoughts and ideals distinct from the middle class." With the skepticism of a Henry Adams, a Mark Twain, or a Richard Hofstadter toward popular culture, Diggins—implicitly endorsing the assumptions of the earlier Commons-Perlman school of labor history—denies that the presence of republican idealism in labor rhetoric conveyed anything of historical substance. Like professional politicians, representatives of labor were instinctually given to nostalgic flights of fancy. Beyond Diggins's critique of recent trends in social history lies a basic incredulity as to the existence of "alternate" or "autonomous" nonliberal subcultures in the United States. The parts, he seems to be saying, simply do not fit with what we know of the society as a whole. Ipso facto, only a misty-eyed partisan could take such claims seriously.[7]

Unlike Diggins, I find that workers in the Gilded Age really did break away from middle-class values, even as their relation to liberalism might best be considered ambivalent. First, however, there is a problem about the nature of evidence. Diggins seems as dissatisfied with Herbert G. Gutman's "thick descriptions" of workers' behavior as with Sean Wilentz's emphasis on political language.[8] For explanations of groups' real motives and attitudes, it is not exactly clear which kinds of sources—unless one awaits some sort of "spectral" illumination—are to be admitted as evidence. Surely, the sustained coordination of language and social action should be reason enough to credit a distinct set of thought and ideals, a group outlook, at least to the same extent that one would infer an outlook from the language and actions of other groups, like the "liberal middle class."

The argument for a labor-centered cultural alternative in the Gilded Age is, I think, better approached by contrasting evolving conceptions of the public good than by a priori definitions of working-class versus middle-class ideologies, or liberal versus nonliberal worldviews, for the vision expressed in Powderly's speech was the product of an unfolding political process. With a simultaneous appeal to the laboring classes as citizens and as producers, the Knights of Labor effectively reached out in the 1880s from a base among artisans and coal miners to a cross-class constituency, including small shopkeepers, even a few manufacturers, and a growing factory proletariat. The occupational inclusiveness of the Knights—who barred only lawyers, stockbrokers, bankers, and saloonkeepers from membership—also permitted the labor body to extend itself beyond a constituency of old immigrants and old-stock Americans toward new-immigrant, Afro-American, and female recruits. The result was an economic and cultural solidarity extending beyond a given class or corporate interest. Gramsci called such a social formation a "historical bloc." As Gramsci argued of blocs, the very strength of the Knights lay in their ability to tap "bourgeois" as well as "proletarian" segments of society and thus to constitute themselves as a potential sociopolitical alternative to the mass political parties and the corporations.[9]

A moralistic, republican message sealed the unity of the Knights' heterogeneous constituency. To the Knights' partisans, emphasis on the "labor theory of value" and "the producing classes" went hand in hand with commitment to "independence" and "American citizenship." While "liberal" in its continuing respect for private property and fear of concentrated power in public or private hands, popular labor rhetoric appropriated a "republican" emphasis on the public good and individual moral responsibility to promote it. Indeed, to establish a footing for the practice of good citizenship, the Knights wished to encumber the liberal marketplace with a limitation of working hours, recognition of union shops, and a host of legislative reforms, including abolition of the banking system and nationalization of monopoly power. Asserting a direct link between civic virtue, political democracy, and the economic welfare of the laboring classes, the Knights fashioned a social democratic vision—albeit one without the accoutrement of the administrative state.[10]

Rather than the empty posturing that Diggins suggests it was, labor's use of republican rhetoric represented a penetrating grasp of a specific historical juncture. As in their appropriation of the name of a medieval, chivalric order, the Knights of Labor critically juxtaposed faded traditions to the forms of modern life that had denuded older values of their meaning. Workers publicly embraced the "commonwealth" integument of the national political heritage precisely because the dominant social forces in the United States were wrenching the culture in another direction.

In the age of Tom Paine, the advance of democracy and the economic dynamism associated with a free market appeared to most Americans as twin pillars of progress. By the late nineteenth century, however, in middle-class eyes progress was increasingly identified with material innovation and expansion, to the relative neglect of democratic forms and manners. For instance, although Justice Stephen J. Field's precocious 1873 dissent in the Slaughterhouse cases employed language not unlike Powderly's in identifying "equality of right in the pursuit of the ordinary avocations of life" as the "distinguishing privilege of citizens of the United States," it did so only to narrow public decision making over the marketplace. Similarly, when iron master and Democratic party leader Abram Hewitt celebrated the opening of the Brooklyn Bridge in 1883, not the promise of democracy but the "never-ending struggle of man to subdue the forces of nature to his control and use" was uppermost in his mind. Even the "humble [Horatio] Alger citizen" whom Louis Hartz took as emblematic of Gilded Age popular culture betrayed little of the critical democratic rhetoric that Powderly used. His yearnings were different: "he was prepared to wait, save, and work hard, until the million dollars came to him as well." Politically, I would suggest, this capitalistic "locke" on the nineteenth-century inheritance was secured by the "resurgent Republicanism" engineered by Mark Hanna in the 1890s. In 1896 the gathering columns of a new historical bloc achieved more than a symbolic breakthrough.[11]

It is against the background of an existing, official liberalism that the words and deeds of the Knights of Labor must be weighed. In such circumstances we may save Diggins's assertion of common "liberal" values uniting all elements of the public only by an act of intellectual elasticity that effectively masks the historical process at work. To be sure, labor and capital in the Gilded Age shared a common national political tradition to which each had recourse. While demanding obligatory allegiance, however, that political inheritance, which Hartz called the "liberal tradition" and which others insist was at least initially infused with "classical republican" commitments, offered neither a comprehensive description of American social values nor much guidance about future political action. Classical republicanism, for example, Rowland Berthoff observed, "as a static, unitary theory, properly concerned only with maintaining civic virtue, . . . was an awkward basis for a dynamic, expansive economy and ever more plural society." The life breathed into those foundational forms and the doctrines with which they were mixed varied, depending on the actor and the social context. Still clinging to an eighteenth-century security blanket, Gilded Age industrialists made their own ideological adjustments in a new world of corporations, managerial expertise, and international entanglements. Bold departures in theories of economics, law, and governmental administration all offer testimony to elites' adaptation of earlier American values.[12]

The labor movement, likewise, stitched together old and new elements of meaning. The language of labor republicanism itself reflected the internal crisis and attempted restructuring of liberal political ideology. The labor theory of value, for example, underwent a subtle transformation. A mere strand of individualist Jeffersonian thought (and one that disappeared in neoclassical economics), it became a moral pillar of the collective claims of the laboring classes. Similarly, participants in the labor movement used antimonopoly principles, rooted in a free-market critique of mercantilism, to attack the very creations of the marketplace, even as they still attributed the exorbitant powers of banks, railroads, and utilities to governmental favoritism.[13]

Aside from refashioning such bedrock political values, Gilded Age

Figure 1. The Great Seal, official insignia of the Grand Assembly of the Knights of Labor.

labor drew on what Raymond Williams has called "residual" cultural elements: "certain experiences, meanings, and values . . . lived and practiced on the basis of . . . some previous social and cultural institution or formation." In particular, the Knights found ample, if informal, wellsprings of communal solidarity and collective discipline inside a society formally sworn to individual rights and the logic of self-interest. As Gregory Kealey and Bryan Palmer have documented, ethnic traditions, prior workplace cultures, community parades and celebrations, and the mutualism of voluntary societies were among the borrowings that helped animate the move toward a new solidarity among working people in the 1880s. Workers' newer class identity, David Scobey argues, "redefined older communal loyalties" through a variety of instruments: boycotts, sympathy strikes, cooperatives, unions based on class rather than skills, special support for unskilled workers, reading and lodge rooms, gymnasiums, employment bureaus, and finally, independent labor politics.[14]

As evidenced in their order's name, hierarchy of officers, and elaborate ritual, the Knights of Labor were particularly indebted to the larger culture of nineteenth-century Anglo-American fraternalism. Begun as a secret, oath-taking brotherhood (in 1881 the oaths were discontinued to forestall Catholic opposition), the Knights in many respects bear out Charles W. Ferguson's venerable claim that "class-consciousness, American style . . . expressed itself through the characteristic medium of social clubs and secret orders. The native technique of reform is, first of all, to demand three raps and a high sign." If the order's ritual book, the *Adelphon Kruptos,* borrowed heavily from Masonic and Odd Fellows ceremony, however, the emphasis of its own mutualism was original and pointed. Powderly's elucidation of one symbol of the order—the "Great Seal of Knighthood"—is instructive (see figure 1). Looking from the inside out, the equilateral triangle covering the Western Hemisphere was endowed with three layers of meaning—"humanity": or birth, life, and death; the elements of human happiness: land, labor, and love; and the three keys to economics: production, exchange, and consumption (along with the lesson that "no middlemen are necessary to carry on business . . . profits are not a necessity"). The lines of the inner pentagon, representing justice, wisdom, truth, industry, and economy, defined the principles of "Universal Brotherhood," while they also symbolized the five senses, the five elements of nature (land, air, light, heat, and water), and the demand for a five-day work week. Powderly's illumination of the pentagon went further to include five mechanical powers, "the lever, pulley, screw, wedge, and hammer." "Though not, strictly speaking, a mechanical power . . . the hammer was introduced that the member might be instructed how to weld together the various natures, dispositions, sentiments, feelings, and aspirations by which men are actuated in gaining their ends. . . . As improvements are being made every day in the machinery of the world, we assert our right, not alone to these powers, but to the results of man's toil while making use of them."[15]

In addition to reinterpreting contemporary political culture, the Knights *politicized* the culture of civil society and everyday life. Harnessing popular values regarding education, temperance, and family responsibility to a critique of the wage system, the "movement culture" of the Knights contested the implications of the most basic American assumptions. While embracing the principle of self-improvement, for example, the Knights incorporated it into a cooperative ethic. As David Brundage has emphasized, their version of the principle "bore little resemblance to self-improvement as conceptualized by the YMCA and its business supporters." Likewise, the Knights made of "domesticity," the Victorian feminine counterpart to male productive efficiency, a moral and political sword to swing at the factory lords. Equal rights, Susan Levine has demonstrated, commingled with domestic idealism in the critical vision of the Knights. A poem emerging from the national carpet weavers' strike of 1885 suggests the interplay of spheres male and female, past and future.

> We ask not your pity, we charity scorn.
> We ask but the rights to which we were born.
> For the flag of freedom has waved o'er our land,
> We justice and equality claim and demand.
>
> Then strive for your rights, O, sisters dear,
> And ever remember in your own sphere,
> You may aid the cause of all mankind,
> And be the true woman that God designed.[16]

In word and deed, the late nineteenth century thus provided ample evidence of popular opposition to the consolidation of control over economic and political life by a corporate elite. One might still argue that such a contest implied neither conscious rejection of capitalism nor categorical repudiation of liberal values. But if we limit ourselves to the broad antitheses of capitalism versus socialism, liberalism versus communalism, we are likely to miss the real play of historical possibilities at the time. Behind Diggins's dismissal of popular American protest, one senses, as the British historian Robert Gray has noticed in another context, "the straw person model of a class conscious and revolutionary working class, equipped with a rigorous class ideology and theoretical understanding of the capitalist economy." Such cases, Gray declares, are terribly hard to come by. The twentieth-century straitjacket of the why-is-there-no-socialism question masks the more interesting and important question: What would it have taken for America to be different by 1900—or, by extension—today?[17]

I suggest that labor's Gilded Age appropriation of the very "vital center" of American political discourse, rather than a denial of alternative social ends, was a testament to the still undetermined character of that political discussion, a sign of latent possibilities yet unrealized. The case of the Richmond, Virginia, Knights' cooperative building association is instructive. On one level the existence of such an institution reflected the "classless" American search for property and home ownership. From members' weekly dues, a lottery periodically was held and a house and lot awarded to the winner, who, after repaying the association at a rate of ten dollars per month, took title to the property. The lucky worker even had the "choice of several potential lots" and "the right to state the style that he desires the house to be built." However, this institution of "acquisitiveness," as Diggins might call it, was hemmed in by democratic and communal considerations. As Peter Rachleff notes, "the principle of equality—in dues, shares, and opportunity—was itself a critique of standard banking and financial operations." In addition, the association directed that individuals who fell behind in payments be treated as leniently as possible. Even those who could make no more payments would not lose their investment. "The individual was to be bought out, not foreclosed upon because at this time the individual's family would be in its greatest need." In just such ways the workers' movement attempted to sustain individualism in socially responsible forms.[18]

The pattern exemplified above of radical appropriation from dominant or residual cultural forms is not unique to the American working class. The stirrings of revolt among Silesian weavers in 1848, which included songs attacking putting-out bosses as bloodthirsty aristocrats, convinced Barrington Moore, Jr., of the crucial role of "precipitates of past historical experience" in present action. Similarly, the British Chartists, Gareth Stedman Jones has discovered, raised the first modern mass movement of working people on the basis of an eighteenth-century symbolic universe.[19]

Intuitively, the Gilded Age American labor reformer grasped the same truth about the roots of popular mobilization. Powderly's targets that day in Priceburg included anthracite coal owners who, to cut costs, had shut down pits, leaving thousands unemployed the previous winter. "One hundred years ago," declared the general master workman, "we had one king of limited powers.... Now we have a hundred kings, uncrowned ones, it is true, but monarchs of unlimited power, for they rule through the wealth they possess." Powderly sought not only to celebrate but also to transform the nation. Changed circumstances since 1776, his argument went, required that the political and the economic spheres must be fused to preserve justice and civic virtue. Whether that message was a recipe for reform (a new liberalism?) or revolution (incipient socialism?) may be open to dispute. But it is hard to see how it fits Diggins's characterization of American worker protest as "simply a reluctance to undergo the painful ordeal of change."[20]

Those who take the study of working-class culture seriously will probably pay closer attention to Jackson Lears than to John Diggins. If Diggins tends to depreciate the distinctive articulations of labor movements, Lears's essay "The Concept of Cultural Hegemony" pays them considerable respect and attention. Displaying a thorough grasp of recent social history, theoretical insights drawn from cultural anthropology, linguistics, and literary criticism, and Gramscian Marxism, Lears in many respects offers a model synthesis of critical social theory and concrete historical analysis. Indeed, in the end the fault with Lears may lie less in an insensitivity to the logic of popular expression than in a hypersensitivity to language and culture as arenas of social struggle.

Lears endeavors to revive Gramsci's concept of "cultural hegemony" as a starting point for "understanding historiographical problems that have asserted themselves with special force during the last fifteen years [1970–85]." As his primary problem, Lears attempts to reconcile the abundant evidence of worker "resistance" with the persistent failure of workers' movements to change the structure of power in America. Drawing on a host of major works in nineteenth-century labor and social history, Lears posits the emergence of a "historic bloc" of small producers who "shared enough social experience and perceptions of the common interest to develop a coherent world view." The radical edge of that view, agrees Lears, contained "egalitarian and communal currents that challenged developing inequalities of wealth and power." "By the late nineteenth century, the producer ideology animated mass movements from the Knights of Labor to the People's party."[21]

The originality of Lears's argument derives from a critical analysis of that populist formation. To explain the disappointment of opposition culture in America, Lears summons from Gramsci's argument about hegemony (defined as "the 'spontaneous' consent given by the great masses of the population to the general direction imposed on social life by the dominant fundamental group") a subtheme, the notion of "divided" or "contradictory" consciousness: "Consent, for Gramsci, involves a complex mental state, a 'contradictory consciousness' mixing approbation and apathy, resistance and resignation." Cultural hegemony, suggests Lears, may well explain the general incapacity of the lower orders to escape their domination from above: "Subordinate groups may participate in maintaining a symbolic universe, even if it serves to legitimate their domination. In other words they can share a kind of half-conscious complicity in their own victimization." Equipped with an explanation from hegemony, the radical historian may allow for the same paralyzing cultural mimicry among workers as discovered by his liberal counterpart—while pursuing a class analysis. "Unlike liberal notions of consensus," notes Lears, "Gramsci's vision acknowledges the social and economic constraints on the less powerful, then aims to see the ways that culture collaborates with those constraints."[22]

The failure of American popular movements, explains the Gramscian

Lears, derived not only from the force of the opposition ("they had more guns") and strategic mistakes (as when the Populists fused with the Democrats) but also from their own fatal incoherence and ideological ambivalence. "Powerful countertendencies within the producer ideology . . . often subverted its egalitarian and communal aims." In particular, Lears cites entrepreneurial ambition, evangelical religion, and electoral politics as a kind of devil's brew of individualism eroding the communal fiber of movement culture. This partial identity with the dominant culture, suggests Lears, finally undermined a struggle that already faced an imbalance of power and control of coercive force. Lears's account resembles the discussion of Populist culture provided by Alan Trachtenberg. The latter observes that the "underlying 'producers' philosophy' seemed an attack more on the scale of capitalism, on the 'greed' of the already rich and powerful, than on the fundamental relations of production." While crediting the farmers' movement with "a *cultural* campaign of great magnitude," Trachtenberg detects "certain long-standing unresolved ambiguities" within Populist identification with the American nation. From such depictions it may be inferred that divided consciousness led to political confusion and ultimately to acquiescence—in Gramsci's words to "a condition of moral and political passivity."[23]

Before contesting Lears's thesis, I want to admit its superficial appeal. There is much about the Knights of Labor that might fit the notion of a divided consciousness. The Knights' message to the producing classes, while opposing wage labor in the abstract, tended to deemphasize the conflict between wage workers and employers, resist mass strikes, and ignore mounting class antagonism in favor of visions of an arbitrated world of harmony. Likewise, as Trachtenberg has argued regarding the Populists, labor republican identification with "the nation" inevitably caused political confusion: "Constituted in the name of 'the people,' the republican state seemed one with the nation, the society, the culture. Not the state itself, but those who temporarily occupied its sacred corridors and residences, placed themselves in contention in the normal political processes." The "legitimacy and aims" of the federal government thus never became a "national political issue." Although the producer culture possessed a critical, even "utopian," thrust, "the same cultural premises also defined republican forms as the only political means for the freeing of the nation from obstructive selfish interests." Such a stance left considerable room for co-optation of labor's cause by party politicians uninterested in radical reform. The Democratic judge Richard Prendergast, at Chicago's 1886 Labor Day picnic, might draw the crowd's assent to these comments on the "Red, White, and Blue":

Within the pale of the law, over which this flag was placed, there
was abundant opportunity for the industrial population, as well as
every other section of our people, to achieve every legitimate
aspiration ("Hear, Hear"). If the condition of labor up to this time
had not been what it should be, if the laws of our country . . . had
not been what they should be . . . it was not the fault of the Constitution or the spirit and genius of our institutions. It was because the
people had not been educated to know all that could be done
within those laws and by the use of the privileges which those laws
guaranteed (Applause and cries of "That's Right").

Exactly such preachments might attract enough labor votes to elect
figures like Carter Harrison in Chicago, Tom Hannon in Kansas City,
Kansas, or George Sanderson in Lynn, Massachusetts, only to see them
cave into business or partisan imperatives once in office.[24]

If both in the shop and at the ballot box the producer culture of the
Gilded Age stopped short of a frontal assault on corporate power, it
proved susceptible as well to individual entrepreneurial greed and political gain at the expense of the larger community. Kealey and Palmer's
discussion of "unscrupulous rascals and the most infamous damn liars
and tricksters at large" operating among the Ontario Knights reveals the
political hucksterism possible within the marketplace of a mass movement.
The constant appeals for self-discipline in individual conduct and for
workplace unity, beyond the interests of a single trade, perhaps themselves constitute evidence that the Knights' goals were going against their
members' predispositions. When a Union Pacific strike leader, J. N.
Corbin, defined the order as essentially "a school room," which set
rational standards of behavior and enlightenment while teaching workers
to fend off the temptations arising from the saloon, gambling, and the
"debasement of the popular press," he implicitly acknowledged that the
"movement culture," far from being autonomous, was suspended within
a large and powerful set of influences. Did not Powderly's suggestion that
the working classes should follow Ralph Waldo Emerson's advice to
"supersede politics by education" betray the American reformer's impossible desire to be, as Warren Susman put it, "in but not of the world"?[25]

During the years of the Order's demise, moreover, the wolves of
avarice and unbridled individualism clearly feasted on the carcass of a
movement that had once tried to hold them at bay. Racial division,
industrial defeat, and political intrigue, for instance, combined by the
late 1880s to lay ruin to a once-promising coalition of trades in Richmond,
Virginia. By 1895 only three assemblies remained. One reportedly consisted
of scab musicians who had taken the place of the musicians' union during

an 1894 theater strike. A second, a tobacco workers' assembly at the local
J. Wright Company, represented a repudiation of all that the Order had
once stood for. Consisting of twenty-five white men, including the managers and officers of a factory employing over three hundred black men
and forty white women, the assembly served mainly "to boom the sale of
its product among workingmen in other sections of the country" through
display of "Knights of Labor brands and labels." In addition, through
connivance with a high-priced commissary on company property and a
moneylending scheme at astronomical interest rates (15 percent per
week, 780 percent per year) deducted from weekly wages, the assembly
for several years had been "systematically robbing the operatives" according to a local labor investigating committee. Such scandal, combined
with the general disarray and defeat of the movement, provoked a bitter
lament from William Mullen, former district master workman of the
Richmond Knights:

> The growing greed for gain, and the mad rush which men are
> making with the hope of amassing great fortunes, have so hardened
> the conscience of men, and so paralyzed their sense of responsibil-
> ity and justice, that they give no thought as to what suffering their
> course may bring to others, so long as their ambition for gain is
> satisfied.... And there is little doubt but that a thrill of joy passes
> through their unholy frame when one who has grown too old to be
> as valuable as in former years, drops at his post or is ground to
> fragments in the machinery he works—they see a vacancy for a
> stronger, younger man—with stronger muscle to work their purpose,
> from whose healthy veins they can take deeper draughts of blood.[26]

Having acknowledged the lure of acquisitiveness within the workers'
world, we must still question its salience in the movement's decline and
political failure. Was the movement hobbled by cultural and ideological
contradiction? By focusing exclusively on the ambivalence of their
movement's strategy, the porousness of its defenses against bourgeois
values, and the incoherence of its vision of the future, one might per-
ceive the history of the Knights of Labor as an instance of capitulation to
cultural hegemony. At least two serious flaws, however, accompany such a
formulation.

First, engagement and even partial assimilation of the dominant culture by an opposition movement might be a sign of political strength
rather than weakness. Lears forgets that it is not an intellectual alternative for which serious political movements are striving but a social one.
The historical bloc that would supplant the established social-political
matrix must draw in constituencies attached to traditional values. At the

height of their power, in May 1886, leaders from the General Assembly of the Knights of Labor were invited to a special session of the Church Congress, convened coincidentally at the same time in Cleveland, Ohio. Identifying with labor's aims of economic "cooperation" over "laissez-faire," a Baptist minister from Brooklyn, New York, Wayland Hoyt, spoke of "the duty of flushing the cold law of supply and demand with the warm colors of Christ's truth of brotherhood." In return, John Jarrett, former president of the Amalgamated Association of Iron and Steel Workers, the largest trade union in the country, and Henry George, America's leading radical intellectual, testified to the power of Jesus Christ as inner presence and as historical example of the quest for "the kingdom of God on earth." In closing the unity meeting of labor and the Social Gospel, Rev. William Wilberforce Newton, an Episcopalian, exclaimed, "I don't know whether the Knights of Labor have captured us or we the Knights; but thank God we are beside them." Like their adaptation of the nation's political heritage, such an identification with Protestant religious zeal might seem a muddying of class consciousness. But their ability to touch the hearts and minds of the people by invoking cherished values accounted for the Knights' organizing success in the first place. Writing of the English working class, Robert Gray observes that "effective social movements are constructed of alliances . . . in which different languages of mobilization have to be articulated together, very often around some kind of language of popular democracy and radical humanism." Religious visions and middle-class visionaries contributed to the Gilded Age alliance. That the process of movement building also attracted a variety of business and political schemers hardly constitutes evidence of cultural paralysis. Rather, like any bandwagon, the labor movement carried some freeloaders.[27]

Second, it is not clear that the syncretic producers' culture that helped create a mass movement tangibly contributed to the movement's undoing. For all their ambivalences and inner tensions, the Knights of Labor did not capitulate to, nor were they absorbed by, liberal employers, politicians, or opinion makers. It would be more accurate to say that they were defeated by those forces. The yellow-dog contract, criminalization of the boycott, the antistrike injunction, and the gleam of militia bayonets, which by the end of 1886 had broken labor's momentum, were not the tools of consent. In the aftermath of defeat, amid the decline and disintegration of a once-powerful movement, individual workers looked for new strategies and solutions and found them in a variety of forms—in employer-sanctioned self-improvement, in craft unions, in ethnic solidarities, in the urban boss system, and within the refuge of the family. It would be double punishment, however, in the name of a hegemonic "contradictory consciousness" to blame the defeated challengers for the new order that swept over them.

The Knights might well have surmounted the problems of contradictory consciousness were it not for the other obstacles that they faced. To be sure, they showed weaknesses in relation to the larger culture, but not demonstrably fatal ones. In practice, the problem with strikes was less the Knights' unwillingness to countenance class conflict than the outbreak of *too many* strikes that the organization could neither control nor adequately sustain. If they often identified in principle with the republican state (allowing openings for bourgeois politicians), the Knights rarely made politics the center of their activity. When they did, however, they tended to move toward independent labor politics and to develop pragmatically an expansionary use of public authority. As for the cultivation of temperance, self-discipline, education, and the mistrust of popular culture, here the labor reform leaders of the Order placed themselves in the long traditions of republican moralism. Rather than a prescription for hegemony, such asceticism (common to revolutionary movements of all kinds) provided the one chance to draw workers out of a daily absorption in the logic of marketplace values. Finally, the entrepreneurial invasion of the Knights' own ranks was both a sign of weakness and a testament to the ability of the Order to enlist a wide-ranging community of supporters. Moreover, as the case of Richmond suggests, the most parasitic individualism came to the fore only after the movement had lost its capacity to strike out for larger purposes.

Despite his general emphasis on the intellectual limits of radical dissent, Lears himself may agree. Knowing something of the tenacity of labor struggles, he readily acknowledges at one point that it was not labor's "accommodation" but its "resistance" to dominant authority that proved its undoing: "At particular times and places, one can argue that the dominant historical bloc had not established a hegemonic culture and therefore turned to violence to protect its interests. The period from 1877 to 1919, for example, offers abundant evidence that subordinate groups did not consent to the hegemony of industrial capitalism."[28]

But larger theoretical implications surely follow from such a formulation. We can, for example, perhaps make too much of a test for cultural or ideological coherence in assessing groups like the Knights of Labor. If we turned our lens in another direction, say, to historical "winners" (for example, American revolutionaries in 1783, or German fascists in 1933) we would still find black holes of intellectual contradiction and confusion. Lears has elsewhere characterized the hegemonic ideology of the late nineteenth-century American bourgeoisie as one of "evasive banality." Having one's intellectual house in order, for all its intrinsic appeal, is apparently no guarantee or prerequisite of historical significance. Most social movements, like the hegemonic orders they contest, may well turn out to be tinkers, roughly reshaping an inherited set of values, more often than adroit intellectual draftsmen.[29]

Intellectual and cultural historians run the risk of short-circuiting historical development, displacing the complexity of political conflict with a partial "war of ideas." The very notion of contradictory consciousness, after all, implies the possibility of an alternative unified consciousness, presumably from some pure proletarian perspective. We can only wish those who search for such consciousness Godspeed. The possibility of a hegemonic order, like that of a consensual order, of course cannot be dismissed out of hand. There are undoubtedly instances (I have found one case myself in a company town in Vermont) that seem appropriate to such a description. In applying such totalizing terms, however, we should be bound by the warning sign "Limited Access Only." Lears neatly dissects the problems of the consensus paradigm. Diggins raises important doubts about using the hegemony argument for understanding master-slave relationships. But if hegemony theory might best be restricted to a textured civil society (which differs from a slave regime in that consent is a real issue), it also might be better applied to the absence, rather than the presence, of protest. Lears eloquently calls for a historiography that will recover "alternatives that were no less real because they were submerged or silent." "To discover what was left out of public debate and to account historically for those silences" defines a valuable province for hegemonic analysis.[30]

Unfortunately, where one is pursuing the active, organized articulation of popular grievances—as with the producer culture—hegemony theory may itself act as a historical silencer. Only with an imperious and conservative bias can one assert on the basis of selected texts that one knows the limits of a particular insurgent moment, that "muddled subjects" were somehow bound to fail. A reverse effect also operates. Social historians who in reaction to an exaggerated "hegemonic ideology" of the middle class discover its dialectical counterhegemonic counterpart among workers should also take heed; they may exaggerate the intellectual coherence of those opposing the dominant order. In the case of the Knights of Labor, we can demonstrate that the ideological contest with the powers that be was intense. But we ought not read back a post-Leninist version of strategic proletarian thought—as even Gramsci tended to do—into the late nineteenth century. The point for historians is not to enshrine a moment of conflict in a term like "class consciousness" but rather to explore the multiple meanings and intentions to which that moment gave voice.[31]

If labor's defeat in the Gilded Age, for example, was primarily a matter of military, industrial, and strategic setback (rather than co-optation from above), then perhaps our attention ought to focus on the specific political events that shut off one set of historical possibilities in favor of another. Accepting the American *cultural* landscape as a given, might things nevertheless have turned out differently?[32] Imagine, for a moment, that in the absence of the Haymarket bombing, the eight-hour day had been won in North America's leading cities by coordinated work stoppages during the spring of 1886.[33] Rather than beginning a downward slide, the Knights of Labor (as well as the skilled trade unions) thereby drew new confidence in the efficacy of united action across skill lines. A new urban labor electoral coalition likewise received an immediate stimulus. Depending on the sensitivity of their antennae and the openness of their nominating procedures, the major parties (especially the Democrats) won election in some cities as "friends of labor." "I have a suspicion," Judge Prendergast said presciently in his 1886 Labor Day address in Chicago, "that the political parties want to be on the winning side." In other cities from Rutland, Vermont, to New York, New York, to Richmond, Virginia, independent labor forces had by the end of the year consolidated their initial beachheads. From its mixed-trade base in the big cities, a rejuvenated labor movement next laid plans for the mass production industries. With the help of money and muscle from the outside, Chicago's immigrant packers, at the center of America's single biggest industry, secured union recognition by the end of the decade. Garment and textile workers, mostly women, across the Northeast and Midwest quickly followed. Increasingly, in urban factory centers "Americanization" of the new-immigrant arrivals took place in a union context stressing the establishment of an "American Standard of Living."[34]

Employers and their friends in the courts, of course, did not roll over. Labor's urban base was threatened by court decisions declaring the boycott an unfair restraint of trade and invoking automatic injunctions against sympathy strikes. Spreading confrontations on the railroads and in coalfields further polarized laboring communities and the law-and-order alliance of business with state and federal authority. Finally, a brutal setback for the Amalgamated Association of Iron and Steel Workers at Homestead, Pennsylvania, in 1892 offered a catalyst for national political mobilization by the Knights of Labor, now over a million strong. Only with a common, minimal set of rights, local activists realized, could labor survive the corporate reaction. Around the country workers settled on a single national political priority—statutory recognition of labor's rights to organize, strike, and boycott, and crystal-clear prohibition of incursions on those rights by employer police forces, yellow-dog contracts, and injunctions. How to win such protection? By alliance with Populist farmers, who, impressed by labor's political revolt, moved as early as 1890 toward an independent, third-party alternative. Backed by Populist and big-city Democratic votes, labor's "Bill of Rights" thus passed the Congress and was signed hesitatingly by President Grover Cleveland in 1893.

By the early 1890s contemporaries found the American political trajectory increasingly difficult to predict or define. European observers, as well as the new social science professionals, expressed puzzlement at a state of affairs they began to call "American exceptionalism." A labor-Populist alliance was making multiple new demands on government, surrounding the marketplace with a congeries of redistributionist and antimonopoly devices while sustaining the power and legitimacy of the self-activity of workers and farmers in their communities. Threats to the newly dominant historical bloc, particularly given a darkening economy, were rife. What if the Supreme Court should declare the Labor Act unconstitutional? What if newly formed employers' associations, through coordinated national lockouts, should openly challenge labor's community-centered strength? American capitalists were of two minds on the issue of confrontation, given labor's organized strength and political influence. The National Association of Manufacturers was all-out for blood. Many of the larger industrialists, however, hesitated. Would an event such as a national railroad strike ignite the smoldering sentiments for socialism in the workers' ranks? Already, western miners were talking of a direct attack on state power itself. And what would be the consequences of open class warfare for economic productivity? Could they attempt some compromise with the republic of the producing classes? Mark Hanna, the shrewdest political representative of big capital, thus came forward with the idea of a National Civic Federation, a corporativist agreement among industrialists, bankers, labor, and farmers (to be sanctioned by the state) that seemed to offer something to everyone but total victory to no one. In a most messy proposal Hanna accepted trade unionism and the eight-hour day (but only if unions disbanded powerful shop committees controlling production); he accepted government backing of farm cooperatives (but only through government subsidy of private banks). Even with such an olive branch extended to his industrial and political adversaries, however, Hanna remained unsure whether Tom Watson, Samuel Gompers, and Terence Powderly (with Frank Ferrell and Leonora Barry standing behind him) would accept. What, Hanna wondered, would it take to satisfy the American worker?

A hundred years after that pivotal decade set off by the spring of 1886, a new generation of scholars carefully scrutinized the historical record. Among other scraps of material, they came across a speech Powderly delivered at Priceburg, Pennsylvania, in 1890. There Powderly tried to tap the moral passion of the protagonists of the American Revolution to confront the problems of the Industrial Revolution. "Should we not make an effort to dissolve the political bonds which have connected the vital interests of the American people with the trusts, combines, and monopolies of the present age? Is it not high time for us to cast about for a means of separation and should we not declare the causes which impel us to shake off the yoke of monopoly when we seek for the final separation? Is not history repeating itself, is it not time to think of making a new Declaration of Independence?" the general master workman intoned. Among other measures, Powderly advocated government purchase of telephones, telegraphs, railroads, and coalfields, saying he could "see no reason in supporting two governments when one [would] answer all practical purposes." Powderly answered the argument that private ownership of coalfields was vested in Pennsylvania state law with a lesson on the history of the commonwealth of William Penn: "the title we have to these lands . . . had its origin in profligacy and licentiousness. Our state is the price of the drunken revels of a licentious king, who spent his wealth on dissolute women and fawning courtiers who pandered to his lusts. I am not in favor of disturbing vested rights when they are right, but do not believe in a vested wrong."[35]

Twentieth-century labor and cultural historians realized that such thoughts and ideals had had a powerful, transformative effect on the political economy by the turn of the century. To be sure, the Knights of Labor had not stamped the future in their own image. But who ever did? It was enough that their thoughts and deeds, colliding with opposing forces and alternative visions, had shifted the spectrum of twentieth-century possibilities. In the circumstances, therefore, no one looking back thought to attach the concepts of liberal consensus or bourgeois hegemony to their efforts.

In projecting such a counterthrust at the shrewdest of our cultural historians, I do not mean to underrate culture in comparison with politics. My argument is that American popular culture in the late nineteenth century might have contributed to a different set of outcomes than those that occurred. The capacity—the values and ideological commitments—for the counterscenario outlined above already existed. To understand why events took place as they did, and not as we might imagine them, requires the historian's close attention to context. In the case of the Knights of Labor we have some pieces of an explanation. The inability to withstand employer offensives (particularly those of employers like the big packers, railroad corporations, and steel owners) deprived the Knights of much of their magical early luster. In the face of Haymarket and mass strikes, moreover, the Knights' leadership openly winced and took self-protective cover. Skilled workers, who had taken a calculated gamble in merging their craft-based solidarities with the broader goals and inclusive strategy of the Knights of Labor, withdrew from the Order in favor of less risky, more restricted spheres of action. Claiming authentically to speak for a more militant labor movement—but one raised on members' corporate, rather than class, interests—the American Federation of Labor quickly stepped into the breach left by the sagging, internally rent frame of the Knights.[36]

Even after Haymarket one promising option still beckoned the embattled general movement of producers. That was the road of independent labor politics, to try to use state power to change the rules of a game that had begun to go badly. In a remarkable display of the depth of the Gilded Age labor revolt, workingmen's tickets sprang up in 1886–87 in every corner of the country. Yet, although those tickets won in 61 of 189 contested locales, the political moment for united labor power, like the industrial moment that preceded it, soon expired. A declining base of organized constituents, co-optation of labor programs and candidates by the major parties, and the labor culture's own ambivalence toward state action and party formation dulled the edge of the political challenge. Although class issues continued to break into the political discourse, urban workers by the turn of the century generally found enfranchisement within a political system defined by ethnicity rather than class. Powderly's 1890 address to the miners of Priceberg appears in retrospect less a call to arms than a requiem for an expired social movement. Theoretically anticipating the renewed promise of a Populist crusade also wedded to bedrock national values, Powderly's eloquence could not hide the fact that he was playing with an empty hand.[37]

The "cultural" contribution to labor republicanism's real-life denouement cannot be abstracted from the worsening repression, political disunity, and strategic disaster that ensnared the movement. To be sure, arrest of the Knights' forward momentum did bring to the surface a variety of ideological tensions as well as personal animosities. Debate over defense of the Haymarket defendants, the Order's proper relation to independent trade unions (and the question of craft federation versus "mixed" assemblies within the Knights themselves), the temperance issue, and electoral options reflected not only confusion of vision among the Order's leaders, but also a larger uncertainty of purpose among a heterogeneous rank and file. Yes, under the stress of defeat, fear, and the unknown, the edifice of a worker's movement and a labor alternative did crack. Division and contradiction ultimately replaced unity and confident initiative from below. The distance between the historical imbroglios suffered by the labor movement, however, and the intellectual deficiencies deduced from general readings of the larger "liberal" culture or the workers' own "producers' culture" is obvious. Amid the uncoupling of the labor alliance, workers—whether through craft unions, ethnic politics, and fraternal or religious associations—found solace less in individualism than in alternative social solidarities. It was not the self *versus* the group that was at issue for American workers, but which group? One might well debate the relative mix of force, misbegotten strategy, and "co-optation" or "accommodation" involved in this conjuncture of events. But would-be puzzle solvers must recognize the complexity of the problem they are dealing with.[38]

My worry is that a late twentieth-century political pessimism has strained the cultural stew, inadvertently depriving it of its strongest flavorings. A 1950s smugness over "why *they* lost" has been replaced by equally confining 1980s cynicism explaining "why *we* lost." That the ingredients within American popular culture might, from moment to moment, produce contradictory political possibilities, as I have argued above, suggests the need to turn our attention from "mass" values, attitudes, and motivations per se to the manner and moment in which such thoughts were articulated. Who spoke, when, and under what circumstances—not merely what was said—are vital clues to the cultural context. Then, too, if the culture was a mix of varied ingredients, who, one might well ask, stirred the pot? Within the labor world of the 1880s, for example, such an approach would require a closer look at the role of independent newspapers, local labor intellectuals, and the interconnections across the country of self-educated agitators who considered themselves "labor reformers." Just where this leadership class came from, what diverse ethnic and regional configurations it took, what tensions were manifest between it and the rank and file, and what happened to the reformers following the Knights' demise have yet to be studied. More generally, the transformation of communications within the workers' world may hold the clue to many puzzles. A great gulf, for instance, appears to separate the dynamic of labor's advance of the 1880s from that of the 1930s and 1940s. If the legitimating "brainworker" element of the earlier period was lodged within the labor movement itself, the New Deal coalition joined industrial workers with sympathetic academics, politicians, and government administrators. What changes in community structure, socialization, and public authority had intervened?[39] Then, too, as Lears is well aware, there is the issue of language. In particular historians should pursue the decline of the language of labor republicanism. What factors—immigration, changing labor processes, state reform, state repression—weakened its intrinsic explanatory powers? How, following the defeat of the Populists, was it effectively marginalized in public discourse? Among American working people what streams of thought displaced it? By focusing less on changing basic values than on the very processes by which meanings were organized and empowered in American life, a cultural history of labor movements will no doubt continue to have plenty to teach us.

NOTES

This essay originally appeared in the *Journal of American History* 75 (June 1988), 115–36. Reprinted by permission. I dedicate this essay to the memory of Herbert Gutman. For helpful comments and questions along the way I thank Matthew Bewig, Robert Korstad, Susan Levine, Peter Coclanis, Donald Reid, Jacquelyn Dowd Hall, Harry Watson, and especially James Epstein and Paul Krause. I am also indebted to the suggestions and penetrating criticisms of David Thelen, Susan Armeny, and four anonymous reviewers for the *Journal of American History*. An earlier draft was read at the U.S. Working-Class History and Contemporary Labor Movement Symposium, Indiana University of Pennsylvania, October 23–25, 1985.

1. Terence V. Powderly, "Powderly at Priceburg," address, printed July 17, 1890, p. 1, reel 91, Terence V. Powderly Papers, Catholic University of America, Washington, D.C.

2. John Patrick Diggins, "Comrades and Citizens: New Mythologies in American Historiography," *American Historical Review* 90 (June 1985), 614–38, esp. 629; T. J. Jackson Lears, "The Concept of Cultural Hegemony: Problems and Possibilities," ibid., 567–93, esp. 575.

3. As a point of departure, see Herbert G. Gutman, *Work, Culture, and Society in Industrializing America: Essays in American Working-Class and Social History* (New York, 1976), esp. 293–342; and David Montgomery, "Labor and the Republic in Industrial America, 1860–1920," *Le mouvement social* (no. 111, 1980), 201–15.

4. See Sean Wilentz, *Chants Democratic: New York City and the Rise of the American Working Class, 1788–1950* (New York, 1984); Alan Dawley, *Class and Community: The Industrial Revolution in Lynn* (Cambridge, Mass. 1976); David Montgomery, *Beyond Equality: Labor and the Radical Republicans, 1862–1872* (New York, 1967); and for the best treatment connecting the earlier labor reform critique to the Knights of Labor, Richard Schneirov, "The Knights of Labor in the Chicago Labor Movement and in Municipal Politics, 1877–1887" (Ph.D. diss., Northern Illinois University, 1984), 14–68. George E. McNeill, "The Problem of Today," in *The Labor Movement: The Problem of Today,* ed. George E. McNeill (Boston, 1887), 459.

5. My point about the Knights in comparative terms is elaborated in Leon

Fink, "Looking Backward: Reflections on Workers' Culture and the Conceptual Dilemmas of the New Labor History," in *American Labor History: Toward a Synthesis*, ed. Alice Kessler-Harris and J. Carroll Moody (DeKalb, 1988). Susan Levine, *Labor's True Woman: Carpet Weavers, Industrialization, and Labor Reform in the Gilded Age* (Philadelphia, 1984), 103; David Scobey, "Boycotting the Politics Factory: Labor Radicalism and the New York City Mayoral Election of 1886," *Radical History Review* 28-30 (Sept. 1984), 292. See also Gregory S. Kealey and Bryan D. Palmer, *Dreaming of What Might Be: The Knights of Labor in Ontario, 1880–1900* (New York, 1982), 278, 275; Peter Rachleff, *Black Labor in the South: Richmond, Virginia, 1865–1890* (Philadelphia, 1984), 192; Leon Fink, *Workingmen's Democracy: The Knights of Labor and American Politics* (Urbana, Ill., 1983), 219.

6. For an influential use of the term "movement culture," see Lawrence Goodwyn, *Democratic Promise: The Populist Moment in America* (New York, 1976), esp. 713. This argument is placed in sharp relief in an exchange among labor historians beginning with Sean Wilentz, "Against Exceptionalism: Class Consciousness and the American Labor Movement, 1790-1920," *International Labor and Working Class History* (no. 26, 1984), 1-24; Nick Salvatore, "Response," ibid., 25-30; Michael Hanagan, "Response," ibid., 31-36; Steven Sapolsky, "Response," ibid. (no. 27, 1985), 35-38; Sean Wilentz, "A Reply to Criticism," ibid. (no. 28, 1985), 46-55.

7. Diggins, "Comrades and Citizens," 625-29. Diggins addresses primarily the work of Herbert Gutman and a representative set of essays, Michael H. Frisch and Daniel J. Walkowitz, eds. *Working-Class America: Essays on Labor, Community, and American Society* (Urbana, Ill., 1983). For an example of the Commons-Perlman approach to labor history, see Selig Perlman, *A Theory of the Labor Movement* (1928; reprint, New York, 1970).

8. Diggins, "Comrades and Citizens," 625, 628.

9. For helpful elaboration on Antonio Gramsci's terms, see Walter L. Adamson, *Hegemony and Revolution: A Study of Antonio Gramsci's Political and Cultural Theory* (Berkeley, Calif., 1980), 169-201. On the importance of "allied groups," see Chantal Mouffe, "Hegemony and Ideology in Gramsci," in *Gramsci and Marxist Theory*, ed. Chantal Mouffe (London, 1979), 168-204.

10. I am not taking sides here on the historical debate over the timing of republicanism's subordination to liberal individualism in formal American thought and institutions. For a sample of the debate, see J. G. A. Pocock, *The Machiavellian Moment: Florentine Political Thought and the Atlantic Republican Tradition* (Princeton, N.J., 1975); Joyce Appleby, "What Is Still American in the Political Philosophy of Thomas Jefferson?" *William and Mary Quarterly* 19 (April 1982), 287-309; and John Patrick Diggins, *The Lost Soul of American Politics: Virtue, Self-interest, and the Foundations of Liberalism* (New York, 1984). A synthetic and convincing gloss is offered by James T. Kloppenberg, "The Virtues of Liberalism: Christianity, Republicanism, and Ethics in Early American Political Discourse," *Journal of American History* 74 (June 1987), 9-33.

11. Eric Foner, *Tom Paine and Revolutionary America* (New York, 1976); Robert G. McCloskey, *American Conservatism in the Age of Enterprise: A Study of William*

Graham Sumner, Stephen J. Field, and Andrew Carnegie (Cambridge, Mass., 1951), 72-103; Slaughterhouse cases, 16 Wall. 36 (1873); Alan Trachtenberg, *Brooklyn Bridge: Fact and Symbol* (New York, 1965) 8; Louis Hartz, *The Founding of New Societies: Studies in the History of the United States, Latin America, South Africa, Canada, and Australia* (New York, 1964), 105; Clarence Ames Stern, *Resurgent Republicanism: The Handiwork of Hanna* (Ann Arbor, Mich., 1963).

12. The polarization around political traditions suggested here is influenced by the treatment of British Chartism in Gareth Stedman Jones, *Languages of Class: Studies in English Working-Class History, 1832-1982* (Cambridge, Eng., 1983), 90-178. See also, Craig Calhoun, "The Radicalism of Tradition: Community Strength or Venerable Disguise and Borrowed Language," *American Journal of Sociology* 88 (March 1983), 886-914; Louis Hartz, *The Liberal Tradition in America: An Interpretation of American Thought since the Revolution* (New York, 1955); Rowland Berthoff, "Writing a History of Things Left Out," *Reviews in American History* 14 (March 1986), 1-16, esp. 12. Where Berthoff finds great gaps between American's ideological justifications and lived reality, I detect a more continuous, if socially divided, pattern of patchwork intellectual creations. For changing intellectual currents, see James Livingston, "The Social Analysis of Economic History and Theory: Conjectures on Late Nineteenth-Century American Development," *American Historical Review* 92 (Feb. 1987), 69-95; Morton J. Horwitz, *The Transformation of American Law, 1780-1860* (Cambridge, Mass., 1977); Gerald W. McFarland, *Mugwumps, Morals, and Politics, 1884-1920* (Amherst, Mass., 1975); and James Weinstein, *The Corporate Ideal in the Liberal State, 1900-1918* (Boston, 1968).

13. Fink, *Workingmen's Democracy*, 3-17.

14. Raymond Williams, *Marxism and Literature* (New York, 1977), 122-23; Kealey and Palmer, *Dreaming of What Might Be*, 289-92; Scobey, "Boycotting the Politics Factory," 288-90.

15. Norman J. Ware, *The Labor Movement in the United States, 1860-1895: A Study in Democracy* (New York, 1929), 92-93; Charles W. Ferguson, *Fifty Million Brothers: A Panorama of American Lodges and Clubs* (New York, 1937), 173, 175-76; Terence V. Powderly, *The Path I Trod: The Autobiography of Terence V. Powderly*, ed. Harry J. Carman, Henry David, and Paul N. Guthrie (New York, 1968), 438-42. On the Knights' seal, January 1878, marked the founding of the General Assembly, the meeting of national delegates, while "A.K. the 9th" honored the order's founding in 1869.

16. David Brundage, "The Producing Classes and the Saloon: Denver in the 1880s," *Labor History* 26 (Winter 1985), 40; Levine, *Labor's True Woman*, 131.

17. Robert Gray, "The Deconstruction of the English Working Class," *Social History* 11 (Oct. 1986), 373.

18. Rachleff, *Black Labor*, 129-30.

19. Barrington Moore, Jr., *Injustice: The Social Bases of Obedience and Revolt* (White Plains, N.Y., 1978), 141-44; Jones, *Languages of Class*, 102-5.

20. Diggins, "Comrades and Citizens," 625.

21. Lears, "Concept of Cultural Hegemony," 574-76, 569, 577.

22. Antonio Gramsci, *Selections from the Prison Notebooks*, ed. and trans. Quentin

Hoare and Geoffrey Nowell Smith (New York, 1971), 12; Lears, "Concept of Cultural Hegemony," 570, 573, 572.

23. Lears, "Concept of Cultural Hegemony," 575–76; Alan Trechtenberg, *The Incorporation of America: Culture and Society in the Gilded Age* (New York, 1982), 176, 179.

24. Samuel Walker, "Abolish the Wage System: Terence V. Powderly and the Rhetoric of Labor Reform," paper presented at the Knights of Labor Centennial Symposium, Newberry Library, Chicago, May 17–19, 1979 (in Fink's possession); Trachtenberg, *Incorporation of America*, 180–81. For Richard Prendergast's speech, see *Chicago Tribune*, Sept. 7, 1886, 1. See Schneirov, "Knights of Labor," 271–310; Fink, *Workingmen's Democracy*, 112–48; Dawley, *Class and Community*, 215–16.

25. Kealey and Palmer, *Dreaming of What Might Be*, 173–203; Brundage, "Producing Classes and the Saloon," 42–43; Terence V. Powderly, "Address of the Grand Master Workman, Sept. 4, 1883, to the Seventh General Assembly of the Knights of Labor," reel 91, Powderly Papers; Warren Susman, *Culture as History: The Transformation of American Society in the Twentieth Century* (New York, 1984), 86–97, esp. 95.

26. Alex B. McCulloch, "To Organized Labor and Its Friends Everywhere," broadsheet, Aug. 26, 1895, reel 91, Powderly Papers; Rachleff, *Black Labor*, 200. Compare Mullen's lament with the discouragement of Detroit leader Joseph Labadie in 1888: "The point of contest is will the butter come? Can it be we are churning skim milk? Is the virtue gone out of our membership? Has personal ambition and jealousy come in to frustrate our purposes?" Richard Jules Oestreicher, *Solidarity and Fragmentation: Working People and Class Consciousness in Detroit, 1875–1900* (Urbana, Ill., 1986), 211. In his 1982 address to the Organization of American Historians, Herbert G. Gutman emphasized the "central tension in all dependent groups ... between individualist (utilitarian) and collective (mutualist) ways of dealing with, and sometimes overcoming, dependence and inequality." Herbert G. Gutman, *Power and Culture: Essays on the American Working Class*, ed. Ira Berlin (New York, 1987), 404.

27. *Labor, Its Rights and Wrongs* (Westport, Conn., 1975), 244–45, 263–64, 268–69; Henry F. May, *Protestant Churches and Industrial America* (New York, 1949), 183–84. See also George M. Frederickson, "Intellectuals and the Labor Question in Late Nineteenth-Century America," paper delivered at the annual meeting of the American Historical Association, New York, Dec. 1985 (in Fink's possession); Gray, "Deconstruction of the English Working Class," 373.

28. Lears, "Concept of Cultural Hegemony," 579.

29. T. J. Jackson Lears, *No Place of Grace: Antimodernism and the Transformation of American Culture, 1880–1920* (New York, 1981), 7–26.

30. Lears, "Concept of Cultural Hegemony," 572–73, 585–86; Leon Fink, "Politics as Social History: A Case Study of Class Conflict and Political Development in Nineteenth-Century New England," *Social History* 7 (Jan. 1982), 43–58; Diggins, "Comrades and Citizens," 616–22. Even cases of relative "silence," however, will have to be approached carefully. See Jacquelyn Dowd Hall, Robert Korstad, and James Leloudis, "Cotton Mill People: Work, Community, and Protest in the Textile South, 1880–1940," *American Historical Review* 91 (April 1986), 245–86.

31. Lears, "Concept of Cultural Hegemony," 573.

32. On labor's defeat, for example, see James Holt, "Trade Unionism in the British and U.S. Steel Industries, 1888–1912: A Comparative Study," *Labor History* 18 (Winter 1977), 5–35. For the inspiration of counterfactual reasoning, I am indebted to Charles Sabel and Jonathan Zeitlin, "Historical Alternatives to Mass Production," *Past and Present* 108 (Aug. 1985), 133–76. Also suggestive here is Lears, "Concept of Cultural Hegemony," 585.

33. Commenting on the twenty-second anniversary of the hangings of the Haymarket anarchists, a socialist daily in 1909 asserted that "it was not alone these four men that were strangled in Cook county jail yard. The Labor Movement of America was also strangled. The working class of America in 1886 was moving forward as no other working class in the world was moving. It was moving forward as the labor movement of other countries have since moved, only at greater speed, using its political and industrial power at the same time. . . . No more powerful blow was ever struck for capitalism than when that bomb was thrown on Haymarket square." Lucy Parsons, *Famous Speeches of the Eight Chicago Anarchists* (New York, 1969), 37. Although Lucy Parsons herself scored such logic as the chimera of political socialists and although no *single* counterfact may be assumed to reverse the course of history, Haymarket was a seminal event. Combined with already existing tensions (of skill, ethnicity, and strategy) within the labor alliance, Haymarket and its aftermath of antilabor reprisals checked the forward momentum of the Knights of Labor and the hopes for coordinated, national industrial action.

34. On real tendencies toward Americanization in a union context, see James R. Barrett, *Work and Community in the Jungle: Chicago's Packinghouse Workers, 1894–1922* (Urbana, Ill., 1987), 118–53.

35. Powderly, "Powderly at Priceberg," 2, 7, Powderly Papers.

36. For a most perceptive discussion of the "decline of the subculture of opposition," see Oestreicher, *Solidarity and Fragmentation,* 172–221. For a subtle, comparative analysis, see Gerald Friedman, "The State and the Making of a Working Class: The United States and France," paper delivered at the Social Science History Conference, St. Louis, Oct. 1986 (in Fink's possession).

37. On the rise and fall of labor politics, see Steven J. Ross, "The Politicization of the Working Class: Production, Ideology, Culture, and Politics in Late Nineteenth-Century Cincinnati," *Social History* 11 (May 1986), 171–95; and Fink, *Workingmen's Democracy,* 28–29, 219–33.

38. On "competing cultural systems," see Oestreicher, *Solidarity and Fragmentation,* 30–75, 172–79, 222–32.

39. See, for example, Theda Skocpol, "Political Response to Capitalist Crisis: The Case of the New Deal," *Politics and Society* 10 (no. 2, 1980), 155–202.

Power, Culture, and Memory

T. J. Jackson Lears

It is refreshing to find someone with a good word to say for the concept of cultural hegemony. Even though Leon Fink misconstrues my argument in certain ways, he and I share a lot of common ground—more, I think, than he realizes. Certainly he is more sympathetic to Gramscian ideas than some American intellectual historians have been. They have tended to doubt that the concept can be wielded with any precision. In Thomas L. Haskell's wickedly funny formulation, for example, Gramscianism is to Marxism as Unitarianism is to Christianity: a "feather pillow" to catch those falling from the true faith. From this point of view, the concept of cultural hegemony is too soft but also too volatile. "Like dry ice," Haskell writes, "hegemony always tends toward sublimation, becoming merely a diffuse aspect of the human condition rather than a distinct feature of particular societies that one could ever point to in explanation of specific events and actions."[1]

That criticism is accurate but misconceived. As I have already acknowledged, it is probably true that no organized society can exist without governance by a hegemonic group.[2] There is no explanatory power inhering in words or phrases like "hegemony" or "historical bloc"—anymore than in "modernization," "false consciousness," "consensus," or "social system." Gramscian terms provide a theoretical vocabulary that acquires meaning only in specific contexts; the value of that vocabulary is that it highlights the relation between culture and power without reducing mental and emotional life to a mere epiphenomenon of economics or demography. There is little point in asking, Do we see hegemonic processes operating in this or that society? (That is what Aileen Kraditor once referred to as a "yes-type" question.[3]) The more salient questions are: Which groups composed a hegemonic (or counterhegemonic) historical bloc at particular historical moments? How were alliances forged—through what combination of economic interests, moral impulses, ethnic ties, common prejudices, collective fantasies? How were those alliances dissolved or reshaped? Why did some groups peel away and others remain?

Fink's account of the rise and fall of the Knights of Labor poses those questions in provocative ways. He correctly focuses on the "processes by which meanings were organized and empowered in American life," discovering the sources of the Knights' strength in their capacity to mobilize "traditional values" as the cement for a broad-based challenge to concentrated power. He traces the decline of the movement to "a declining base of organized constituents, co-optation of labor programs and candidates by the major parties, and the labor culture's own ambivalence toward state action and party formation," suggesting that "craft unions, ethnic politics, and fraternal or religious association" displaced class issues as the key source of workers' social identity.[4] I am not sure that I can accept the argument in all of its details. Like other labor historians in the Thompsonian mold, Fink sometimes still seems to assume that class consciousness provided the firmest basis for radical politics, even when his own evidence may suggest that local sources of solidarity were more important than the abstract notion of class. Nevertheless, I am impressed with his argument's capacity to illuminate the making and unmaking of a counterhegemonic culture.

Fink and I share the belief that cultural values are critically important in shaping and energizing a labor movement. But what makes an oppositional culture endure? Intellectual coherence? That is what Fink believes I have argued. Maybe I do overvalue clarity and underrate confusion: that is an occupational hazard of philosophers and intellectual historians, who may be seduced by what William James called "the sentiment of rationality" even when they declare themselves opponents of a rationalist worldview.[5] But in this case Fink's complaint is a little misplaced. I cited the confusions in the producer culture primarily to show the limited and ambiguous nature of working-class consent to dominant groups' hegemony. I also observed (as Fink does) that the notion of divided consciousness suggested only a slightly more sophisticated version of false consciousness, that it still implied the existence of an ideologically correct "unified consciousness" to be promoted by a revolutionary vanguard. To overemphasize the importance of intellectual coherence in an oppositional culture is to resurrect the ghost of Lenin, who continued to stalk the pages of Gramsci's prison notebooks.

But if intellectual coherence is not the glue that holds a culture together, what is? Obviously, there can be no single answer to such a sweeping question. But the most comprehensive effort would have to begin by acknowledging that nearly all the most resilient oppositional cultures have been rooted in collective memory, in "precipitates of past historical experience," to use Barrington Moore's language. Such an admission is difficult for modernizers of any political hue, who dismiss any attachment to the past as "nostalgia" (a word that needs a long vacation from contemporary public discourse). In the modernizers' view, anything less than full adjustment to "the painful ordeal of change" constitutes escapism. The passive submission to the allegedly inevitable forces of history involves the sort of deterministic thinking that used to be considered the exclusive property of orthodox Marxists; in fact, it pervades the entire Western liberal tradition.[6]

In recent years, though, social and cultural historians have begun to reshuffle familiar liberal categories. The discovery that radical protest has often had conservative sources is one of the major historiographical advances of the last two decades. Now we need to carry the implications of that discovery into the even more problematic arena of the twentieth century—a period when locally based popular culture has been gradually marginalized by national and later multinational corporations, when collective memory has been devalued by advertising and the mass media, when the pain of separation from the past has been airbrushed from the iconography of "economic development." The closer one gets to the present, the harder it is to find genuinely popular sources of broad-based radical dissent; the vernacular voices of protest are eloquent (in the labor struggles of the 1930s, the civil rights movement, the effort to end the Vietnam war), but they are often difficult to hear above the buzz of background noise—the official version of events provided by the corporate media. So it is perhaps out of desperation that many left academics have begun to look for evidence of popular protest in the very citadels of corporate power: in television, radio, and other mass-marketed forms of culture. Their quest has been inspired by the theoretical work of Mikhail Bakhtin and Frederic Jameson, among others. Following Bakhtin, they have argued that even mass culture is not monological but dialogical, that every utterance is addressed to an audience that may reinterpret or subvert the speaker's intended meaning. Even apparently monological statements, from this view, can imply their opposites. Following Jameson, they have insisted that a dominant culture takes root not by imposing ideology but by addressing utopian longings; and those longings may have subversive implications. Armed with these insights, leftist cultural historians have discovered traces of collective memory in Hollywood films, early network television programs, and other supposed citadels of social amnesia.[7] I am intrigued by these often ingenious arguments and impressed by the variety of forms ordinary people have preserved to express their attachments to the past.

Nevertheless, I think such arguments may exaggerate the significance of the dissent embodied in mass cultural forms. There is too strong a tendency to elevate what is often a univocal, closed system of imagery into an elegant Bakhtinian conversation, where every neofascist utterance by Clint Eastwood implies a counterfascist critique of "late capitalism." Contemporary cultural historians too often forget that the mass media are, among other things, expressions of concentrated power. There are times, in the current cultural atmosphere, when I yearn for a dose of vulgar Marxism. As an attorney friend of mine once told me after handling yet another eviction case for New Haven Legal Aid, from his perspective vulgar Marxism looked like a pretty powerful interpretive tool. Amid brilliantly manipulated images and chants of liberation through consumption, it is easy to forget how systematically our "abundance" is entwined with imperial structures of power.

There may be counterhegemonic tendencies even in the corporate media, but it would be a mistake if in our zeal to uncover them we overlooked the sources of dissent in the interstices of our society, in groups that have been exploited or simply ignored by modernizing elites. I think we should try to distinguish between genuinely popular culture and the corporate-sponsored mass culture that is so often mistaken for it. But we should also acknowledge the capacity of mass culture to shape popular attitudes. This is not to exhume the notion of monolithic social control (the favorite dead horse lashed by contemporary cultural historians), or to deny that twentieth-century people have preserved their dignity and autonomy against the claims of the modern corporation and the bureaucratic nation-state. It is simply to reassert the relevance of Gramscian inquiries into the relations between culture and power. Without pigeonholing every expressive gesture as either "accommodation" or "resistance," we need to continue pondering the connections between the glittering surfaces of mass culture and the mechanisms of coercion they conceal.

NOTES

This commentary originally appeared in *Journal of American History* 75 (June 1988), 137–40. Reprinted by permission. T. J. Jackson Lears is a professor of history at Rutgers University.

1. Thomas L. Haskell, "Convention and Hegemonic Interest in the Debate over Antislavery: A Reply to Davis and Ashworth," *American Historical Review* 92 (Oct. 1987), 829–78, esp. 834, 835.

2. T. J. Jackson Lears, "The Concept of Cultural Hegemony: Problems and Possibilities," *American Historical Review* 90 (June 1985), 567–93, esp. 579n25.

3. Aileen S. Kraditor, "American Radical Historians on Their Heritage," *Past and Present* (no. 56, 1972), 136–53, esp. 137.

4. Leon Fink, "The New Labor History and the Powers of Historical Pessimism: Consensus, Hegemony, and the Case of the Knights of Labor," *Journal of American History,* 75 (June 1988), 115–36.

5. William James, "The Sentiment of Rationality" (1879) in William James, *Collected Essays and Reviews* (New York, 1969), 85.

6. Fink, "New Labor History and the Powers of Historical Pessimism," 128–31, 124.

7. Mikhail Bakhtin, *The Dialogic Imagination: Four Essays,* trans. Michael Holquist

and Caryl Emerson, ed. Michael Holquist (Austin, 1981); Frederic Jameson, *The Political Unconscious: Narrative as a Socially Symbolic Act* (Ithaca, N.Y., 1981), esp. chap. 6. The idea that mass culture promotes a kind of collective amnesia is implicit in many of the writings of the Frankfurt school, notably, Max Horkheimer and T. W. Adorno, *Dialectic of Enlightenment,* trans. John Cumming (New York, 1982).

The Misuses of Gramsci

John P. Diggins

Leon Fink has written a provocative essay. As far as I am aware, it is the most thoughtful defense of the labor historiography produced by his generation of historians, who came of age in the sixties and maintain the perspective they learned from that era's movements. But his essay would have been more telling had it confronted directly my critiques of the new labor history. Thus, of my skepticism about the work of Sean Wilentz and the late Herbert Gutman, Fink writes: "For explanations of real group motives and attitudes, it is not exactly clear what kinds of sources—unless one awaits some sort of 'spectral' illumination—are to be admitted as evidence." In that earlier essay I tried to make it clear that I regard as trustworthy evidence not the objects of working-class leaders' protests and complaints but what they demand and what they do to realize their demands. "What does labor want? We want more school houses and less jails; more books and less arsenals; more learning and less vice; more constant work and less crime; more leisure and less greed; more justice and less revenge."[1] That statement, delivered by Samuel Gompers in 1893, seems to me more admissible as evidence of workers' attitudes than does Terence Powderly's statement of 1890. Fink cites the later document again and again; he also criticizes me for using the term "eulogistic coverings" while at the same time he insists that historians must pay utmost attention to the "context" of a statement or action. Yet Fink himself fails to do what he instructs. The expression "eulogistic coverings" is Kenneth Burke's, and that pioneering linguist and analyst of rhetoric used it to show why public speech is the last place where private interests are openly admitted unless they are presented as representing the general interests of society.[2]

But Fink, Wilentz, and other labor historians seem to have a boy scout's fondness for Fourth of July orations. Yet what is Powderly's reference to the Declaration of Independence in a July Fourth speech supposed to prove? Southern slaveholders invoked the declaration to argue the right of secession, later northern capitalists cited it to defend commerce and profits against government and taxes, and today oil companies take out ads dramatizing "the spirit of '76" to defend the right of offshore drilling. Even its author saw no connection between a written declaration of human equality as a "self-evident" truth and the daily reality of slavery and indentured servitude.

Many labor historians seem to be mesmerized by patriotic rhetoric and the "language of republicanism." Anyone found using such language or that of class conflict is presumed to be outside capitalism's cultural hegemony. Fink cites "the eloquence of labor radical George E. McNeill . . . : 'We declare an inevitable and irresistible conflict between the wage-system of labor and the republican system of government.' "[3] The statement may be eloquent, but is it revelatory of workers' attitudes? My critique asked Marxist historians to be truly Marxist and follow their mentor's advice by attending to deeds and actions rather than speeches and declarations. Aware of the problem of belief and conduct, Marx made practice, not language, the test of truth.

With the "linguistic turn" in intellectual history, it is not surprising that labor historians should adopt the new paradigm and go searching for the evidence of class consciousness that is supposedly to be found in political language. But a protest against unjust conditions carried on solely in speech and rhetoric tells us little about actual attitudes and motives. Political and moral utterances have dubious explanatory content for the historian. "It would have been theoretically satisfactory," observes Jon Elster, "to argue that the grounds on which capitalism is to be condemned are also those that will motivate the struggle to abolish it. Marx, however, does not succeed in showing that this connection obtains."[4] Nor does Fink.

In focusing on words rather than deeds, labor historians have made their work easy, for they do not have to deal with such unmentionable sins as racism, bigotry, racketeering, drunkenness, and wife beating. Fink implies that the Knights of Labor cannot be studied in terms of its actions because its members were inhibited by the union's "inability to withstand employer offensives." But he wants readers to "imagine, for a moment" what the situation might have been like had "garment and textile workers, mostly women" successfully joined with others in winning "statutory recognition of labor's rights to organize, strike, and boycott." Why do we have to "imagine"? In the twentieth century the International Ladies Garment Workers Union won such demands. Once firmly established, garment and textile workers engaged in the same racial and ethnic discrimination and exploitation that a half century earlier the Knights sought to eliminate—now it was Jews and Italians denying equal opportunity to blacks and Puerto Ricans. That a union had radical foundations is no evidence that it lived up to its radical ideals. The teamsters union was founded by Trotskyists.[5]

Fink looks to the language of political ideals as a means of overcoming an older school of thought, specifically the Commons-Perlman school, which had concluded, after a decade of research, that the American working class is in its needs and aspirations essentially conservative. Fink assumes that because historians have shown that labor leaders invoked the declaration and the "language of republicanism" something has been demonstrated about the dissident, radical temperament of American workers. Perhaps. But it should be noted that if labor leaders truly understood the implications of the declaration, on the one hand, and of republicanism, on the other, they would not be able to invoke both simultaneously. The declaration demands that Americans be free of tyranny in the name of liberty; republicanism, that they subordinate their interests to the public good in the name of *civitas*. It is for this reason that political philosophers regard John Locke and Niccolò Machiavelli as incompatible. No doubt labor leaders may exploit both systems of ideas as weapons of protest, just as today a president of the United States can invoke the ideas of John Winthrop and Tom Paine without seeming to realize that what the former wanted to uphold, the latter wanted to destroy. But it is one thing to use political ideas and another thing to abide by them. If labor leaders really understood what was being asked of citizens in civic republicanism, they would have had to agree that work and labor are inferior to politics and statesmanship and that the pursuit of interests is incompatible with the demands of virtue.

It is revealing that Fink seeks to prove his points not by quoting rank-and-file workers but by quoting other historians of his generation and of his persuasion. All of them agree that "ethnic traditions, prior workplace cultures, community parades and celebrations" and other institutions like family and religion created "solidarity" among the workers. Whether or not that was the case, "solidarity" has little to do with the question of labor's political character. The new social historians assume that capitalism is based on atomistic individualism and the pursuit of gain by persons whose idea of getting ahead means leaving others behind. Marxist historians in particular have used the humbug of individualism to try to claim that tightly knit units like the family and community neighborhood remained immune to the culture of capitalism and thus served as counterhegemonic enclaves. The entire edifice of that argument rests on the assumption that capitalism is about individualism. Is it?

It should be noted that the first exponents of capitalism and commercial society—the Scottish philosophers David Hume, Adam Smith, Adam

Ferguson, and others—believed not only that the behavior of economic man is socially determined but also that hegemony, in the form of deference and emulation, meant that the lower classes would strive to imitate the values and behavior of the class strata immediately above. Smith would have had no trouble seeing workers' parades as a collective demand for social recognition as well as political power. As to the family as the bastion of anticapitalism, the Scots would have seen it as the first impression of property as "exclusive possession." Indeed, it is hard to see how labor historians can claim that American workers upheld both familial values and "republican moralism." Alexis de Tocqueville worried that the tendency of the American male to "withdraw" into the privacy of his house and family meant that he had shut the door to the republican world of civic duty. Max Weber esteemed Machiavelli for praising the Florentine citizens who put the interest of their city-state ahead of even the salvation of their souls. American historians praise workers for putting the interests of their families, communities, and ethnic traditions ahead of the nation-state. But the promoting of such interests would please Edmund Burke, not Marx or Machiavelli. It seems labor historians are laboring under a confusion of categories.[6]

The confusions are further compounded when Fink advises readers to turn from my analysis to that of T. J. Jackson Lears and his discussion of Antonio Gramsci. I respect Lears's learned and skeptical treatment of Gramsci's concept of "hegemony." But it is interesting how many American social historians, no matter how much they emphasize the importance of "context," pay little attention to the historical context of Gramsci's prison meditations and as a result misinterpret his ideas. Where social historians continue to do history "from the bottom up," Gramsci believed it more important to study history from the top down in order to penetrate such superstructural phenomena as education, art, and philosophy, as well as popular culture. Where historians have become preoccupied with the language of politics, Gramsci insisted that people's real conception of the world is found not in their verbal affirmations but in their practical activity. And where American historians claim that workers in the past have had the potential for breaking the spell of hegemony, Gramsci saw no such possibility in the history of Italy. Gramsci believed Italy's past failures could be overcome in the future if the nation's intellectuals abandoned their cosmopolitan aloofness and merged with the masses. The American historian's answer to Gramsci is simply to enter the academic profession and rewrite the past. American exceptionalism indeed!

Similarly with the concept of a "historical bloc." Fink uses that Gramscian idea to prove the "very strength of the Knights in their ability to tap 'bourgeois' as well as 'proletarian' segments of the society and thus to constitute themselves as a potential sociopolitical alternative to the mass parties and the corporations." Although Fink must admit that the Knights' efforts petered out and that even Powderly's speech was, in the end, a "requiem," in the early part of his essay he wants readers to believe that the Knights had formed a solid "historical bloc" by relying on political language alone: "A moralistic, republican message sealed the unity that the Knights sought for their heterogeneous constituency. To the Knights' partisans, emphasis on the 'labor theory of value' and 'the producing classes' went hand in hand with commitment to 'independence' and 'American citizenship.' "[7]

Curiously, when it comes to the uses and abuses of political language, Fink becomes not a conflict but a consensus historian. In contrast to many nineteenth-century writers (Tocqueville, Henry David Thoreau, Orestes Brownson, Richard Hildreth, and others), Fink sees no conflict between the labor theory of value and republicanism. Yet the former doctrine, broad enough to encompass Locke and Marx, upholds labor and man as *homo faber;* the latter, from Aristotle to Hannah Arendt, dismisses as debasing the life of labor and production and extols instead the noble life of politics. To describe labor as committed to "independence" tells us nothing about its commitment to something higher than "negative liberty" and resistance to political authority.[8]

Even Gramsci had to face the acute dichotomy between labor and politics when he tried to persuade Italian Marxists that civic life need not be the "sphere of domination." But when Gramsci spoke of "historical blocs" he was honest enough to admit that in the entire two thousand years of Italian history there had been no successful case of such formations arising.[9] Neither in Roman times, nor in the Middle Ages, the Renaissance, and the *Risorgimento* did intellectuals come forward to meet the needs of an ascendant class by establishing and articulating its hegemony. What Fink describes as an exemplary success on the part of the Knights would be judged a naive theoretical failure in Gramsci's analysis, a "passive revolution" that failed to touch the ruling class's hegemonic hold on the social order. The success of a historical bloc requires the total uniformity of culture and power representing a single point of view. Such ideological integration and cohesion hardly describes Fink's inchoate mishmash, an immiscible chorus of political tongues that supposedly "sealed the unity" of liberals, republicans, the bourgeoisie, and even "the proletariat." Gramsci, perhaps the prince of the proletariat, would remind Fink that it is not the incantations of language that prove the existence of radical consciousness and solidarity; it is the imperative of praxis.[10]

NOTES

This commentary originally appeared in *Journal of American History* 75 (June 1988), 141–45. Reprinted by permission. John P. Diggins is a Distinguished Professor of history at the Graduate School, City University of New York.

1. John Patrick Diggins, "Comrades and Citizens: New Mythologies in American Historiography," *American Historical Review* 90 (June 1987), 614–38; Leon Fink, "The New Labor History and the Politics of Historical Pessimism: Consensus, Hegemony, and the Case of the Knights of Labor," *Journal of American History* 75 (June 1988), 115–36; Bernard Mandel, *Samuel Gompers: A Biography* (Yellow Springs, Ohio, 1963), 64.

2. Fink, "New Labor History and the Politics of Historical Pessimism," 118, 134. Kenneth Burke derived the concept from Jeremy Bentham and related it to Karl Marx's idea of "mystification." Kenneth Burke, *A Rhetoric of Motives* (1950; reprint, Berkeley, Calif., 1969), 99–102.

3. Fink, "New Labor History and the Politics of Historical Pessimism," 116.

4. John Elster, *Making Sense of Marx* (New York, 1985), 340.

5. Fink, "New Labor History and the Powers of Historical Pessimism," 134, 132; Herbert Hill, "The ILGWU Today: The Decay of a Labor Union," *New Politics* 1 (no. 4, 1962), 6–17. On the teamsters and longshoremen's unions, see Daniel Bell, *The End of Ideology: On the Exhaustion of Political Ideas in the Fifties* (New York, 1960), 175–209.

6. Adam Ferguson, *An Essay on the History of Civil Society* (New Brunswick, N.J., 1980), 96–107; Alexis de Tocqueville, *Democracy in America*, ed. J. P. Mayer, trans. George Lawrence (New York, 1969), 503–17; Max Weber, "Politics as a Vocation," in *From Max Weber: Essays in Sociology*, ed. H. H. Gerth and C. Wright Mills (New York, 1946), 126.

7. Fink, "New Labor History and the Powers of Historical Pessimism," 119.

8. Hannah Arendt, *The Human Condition: A Study of the Central Dilemmas Facing Modern Man* (Chicago, 1958); Isaiah Berlin, *Four Essays on Liberty* (New York, 1969).

9. The "sphere of domination" is Marx's view of politics, which Gramsci sought to revise in order to appreciate politics as autonomous and independent of economics. See Walter L. Adamson, *Hegemony and Revolution: A Study of Antonio Gramsci's Political and Cultural Theory* (Berkeley, Calif., 1980), 202–7. The failure of Italy to develop "historical blocs" is dealt with in John P. Diggins, "The Curse of Cosmopolitanism: Gramsci's Critique of Italy's Intellectual History," paper delivered at the conference on "Gramsci and the West," Bologna, Sept. 24, 1987 (in Diggins's possession).

10. But praxis, alas, has its price. Without the appearance of a genuine mass of proletarians, that is, Marx's prophetic dream come true, the implication of Gramsci's strategy of forming "historical blocs" can only be conservative. Today the Italian Communist party is reaching out to Italian Yuppies, "i ascensori," those on the rise, which is only in keeping with Gramsci's advice that Communists must always identify with the emergent class. At a 1987 conference in

Bologna, while Communist leaders from all parts of the world were making impassioned speeches, thousands of men, women, and children were strolling in and out of tents that each Communist country had proudly set up to display its products. Surrounded by shining new cars, computers, and other modern conveniences. I asked the Gramscian scholar Walter Adamson what Antonio would make of all this emphasis on consumption. He shrugged his shoulders, laughed, and chortled, "Popular culture!" Those bulging Bologna tents said more about workers' attitudes than anything uttered in political speech.

The Struggle for Hegemony

George Lipsitz

Gramsci . . . has become a fountain from which
everyone takes whatever water they need.
— Massimo Salvadori, 1970

Hegemonizing is hard work.
— Stuart Hall, 1987

In "The New Labor History and the Powers of Historical Pessimism," Leon Fink makes an important contribution to scholarship about American political culture by addressing the debates over the Gramscian categories of domination, resistance, and hegemony. He presents hegemony as something to be struggled *for,* rather than as something imposed *on* inert masses. Fink demonstrates that dominant ideology is contested terrain, involving concessions to aggrieved populations as well as control over them. Finally, Fink insists that power is wielded within the context of historical blocs—temporary and unstable alliances built on combinations of ideology and self-interest that can be both created and destroyed through political struggle.

It is perhaps a measure of the inescapable irony of our time that Antonio Gramsci's ideas have gained popularity among scholars largely as a means of explaining the futility of efforts to change past and present capitalist societies. Above all else, Gramsci was a revolutionary strategist, an individual who instructed others to temper their "pessimism of the intellect" with an "optimism of the will." He knew about defeat and domination from personal experience and systematic study, yet Gramsci still championed a political and ideological struggle *for* hegemony. He called for "a war of position," in which aggrieved populations seek to undermine the legitimacy of dominant ideology, rather than just a "war of maneuver" aimed at seizing state power. To counter the hegemony of ruling historical blocs, Gramsci sought to fashion oppositional coalitions capable of struggling for a world without expolitation and hierarchy. He described traditional intellectuals as "experts in legitimation" but called for the development of "organic intellectuals" able to give voice to the repressed needs and aspirations of oppressed groups.[1]

Yet the Gramsci who appears in much contemporary scholarship is less a strategist of social struggle than a coroner conducting an inquest into the blasted hopes of the past. John Patrick Diggins uses Gramsci's concept of hegemony to explain the seemingly unchallenged primacy of liberal individualism in American political culture, while T. J. Jackson Lears cites Gramsci's work on "contradictory consciousness" as an explanation for how American workers in the nineteenth century exercised a "half-conscious complicity in their own victimization." In their challenging and eloquent analyses, Diggins and Lears focus on the undeniable triumphs of liberal individualism and consumer capitalism over oppositional movements stressing equality, collectivity, and mutuality. But they present hegemony less as something to be struggled *for* than as something imposed *on* society from the top down. Most important, they present the failures of oppositional movements in the war of maneuver as if they were also failures in the ideological and political war of position.[2]

Of course, defeat does matter. Institutional economic and political power means a great deal, and oppositional movements pay a terrible price for failure. But as Stuart Hall, a theorist of British cultural studies, points out, "hegemonizing is hard work." Dominant groups must not only win the war of maneuver—control over resources and institutions—but they must win the war of position as well; they must make their triumphs appear legitimate and necessary in the eyes of the vanquished. That legitimation is hard work. It requires concessions to aggrieved populations. It mandates the construction and maintenance of alliances among antagonistic groups, and it always runs the risk of unraveling when lived experiences conflict with legitimizing ideologies. As Hall observes, it is almost as if the ideological dogcatchers have to be sent out every morning to round up the ideological strays, only to be confronted by a new group of loose mutts the next day. Under those conditions, dominant groups can ill afford to assume their own society is wholly pacified, although of course it is in their interest to have others think that all opposition has been successfully precluded or contained.[3]

One reason for Fink's differences with Diggins and Lears stems from his subject of study. The concrete struggles for power waged by the Knights of Labor in the late nineteenth century displayed an opposition to liberal individualism much greater than Diggins believes was possible, and the self-activity of masses in motion during that era belies the "half-conscious complicity" in their own victimization that Lears alleges to have been characteristic of the American working class. If the power of dominant ideology forced the Knights into addressing demands for individual, private, and material advancement, the lingering legitimacy of republican ideology enabled them to pose credible and popular demands for collective, public, and moral rewards. Dominant ideology imposed costly contradictions on their program, but political activism enabled the Knights to expose and to benefit from contradictions within dominant ideology as well. Even defeat did not mean an end to struggle; the institutional failure of the Knights did not preclude subsequent labor militancy and radical politics. In fact, the lessons of struggle taught by the Knights created the social and individual preconditions for future political contestation by millions of Americans. Fink learns from the people he has chosen to study, and he finds important evidence underscoring the activist implications of Gramsci's writings—about the instability of bourgeois hegemony, the struggle for legitimation essential to all oppositional movements, and the enduring culture of opposition in America that survives any individual episode of struggle.

Yet, in my view, Fink does not go far enough; he does not follow his argument to its logical conclusion. His scenario about how the Knights might have emerged victorious is plausible, and it properly calls attention to one of the many "roads not taken" from the past that continue to illumine possibilities for the present. But it undercuts his earlier insights about the war of position. It places too much reliance on the short-term institutional struggle for power and too little emphasis on the long-term ideological work of constructing counterhegemonic ideas and institutions. By defining victory in terms of specific concessions to be wrested from the ruling class, Fink relegates consciousness to a secondary role as either an obstacle to, or an instrument for, concrete social changes. Yet consciousness is also an end itself. Long traditions of working-class self-activity have properly focused on concrete material gains or desired structures of social organization, but only as instruments for ending alienation and for promoting democracy and justice. We have learned from hard and bitter experience that even the seizure of state power by oppositional movements does not necessarily entail victory for aggrieved populations. No single material or structural improvement has meaning in itself, only as a means toward building a world without exploitation and hierarchy. And building that world is a political process in which people change themselves and others at the same time that they change the social distribution of wealth and power.

Some examples may make the point clearer. In the early stages of the civil rights movement, Malcolm X spoke disparagingly of a process that encouraged black people to risk their lives for the "privilege" of drinking a cup of coffee at a lunch counter next to white people. He argued that such a struggle sought "equality" rather than "justice," pathetically replicating and reinforcing the values of the oppressor within an oppositional struggle. Yet as the movement unfolded, he changed his mind. Malcolm X came to see that the process of self-activity intrinsic to the movement made people take direct action against the conditions that oppressed them and in addition led them to assert the right to act as they chose. The goals of the movement might have been reformist and reflective of bourgeois hegemony, but the process of struggle itself involved a radical reconstruction of both individuals and society. Similarly, in *The Civil War in France,* Karl Marx could write approvingly of the Paris Commune, even though its specific achievements were objectively reformist (the introduction of direct democracy and an end to night work for bakers) and even though it provoked brutal and total repression by the state. Marx could endorse those measures not because they transcended the norms of bourgeois ideology but because they expressed the self-activity of bourgeois citizens transforming themselves and others through mutuality and collective action. To dismiss either the civil rights movement or the Paris Commune as examples of the power of liberal individualism or the workings of contradictory consciousness is to miss their role in the war of position as instances where human self-activity manifested and legitimated the most radical kinds of oppositional thought and action. One need not imagine how those two insurgencies might have succeeded in taking state power to understand how they helped shape a prefigurative counterhegemony with enduring historical and ideological import.[4]

As the examples of the American civil rights movement and the Paris Commune demonstrate, victory and defeat are not mutually exclusive categories. The civil rights activists who waged a reformist struggle for juridical equality also nurtured and sustained more radical possibilities in the processes of struggle. In terms of concrete concessions, they secured little more than the 1964 Civil Rights Act and the 1965 Voting Rights Act. Yet the ideological and political forces set in motion by that movement reverberated to every corner of the world in subsequent years and served as the impetus for oppositional action on innumerable fronts. The Paris Commune failed miserably to achieve its own ends; but it served as an example of what workers could do and as a guide toward the kind of world they might build long after the communards themselves were dead.

Even failure has its uses; it brings to the surface necessary information about the shortcomings and contradictions of oppositional movements. For example, in *Personal Politics,* Sara Evans shows how the male-dominated civil rights movement subverted its own ideals and interests by failing to understand and correct its own sexism. Yet that very failure convinced women that an autonomous struggle over gender issues had to be waged, and their self-activity led to profoundly radical challenges to existing ideology and power. Similarly, Paul Buhle's *Marxism in the United States* explores the ways in which radical political parties and oppositional movements have imperfectly understood organic ethnic and class angers, cultural radicalisms, and utopian aspirations in America. To ask how these parties and movements might have attained power is less important than to ask what they might have done better to understand the grass-roots interests and aspirations on which they relied.[5]

It is also difficult to identify exactly when oppositional ideology and action fails or succeeds. In 1859 it might have seemed that Afro-American resistance to slavery had had little effect. By 1865, when two hundred thousand black soldiers had joined the Union army and when slaves in the South had staged a general strike in the fields, the legacy of Afro-American resistance had taken on a different cast. The differences between 1865 and 1859 did not depend solely on the events of those six years; they also stemmed from the hidden yet enduring consequences of resistance that had been going on for centuries. Likewise, in Jack Conroy's wonderful novel from 1933, *The Disinherited,* the narrator remembers that his father's union lost every strike along the way, but that even as it lost, conditions gradually got better for the workers. Their willingness to strike never seemed to bring any victories in the short run, but it served as a threat to management and consequently as an incentive for concessions that might avoid strikes in the long run. In *The Disinherited* that memory of class struggle informs the self-definition and willingness to take risks that brings Conroy's hero into one of the most important mass mobilizations in history—the union organizing drives of the 1930s. Even in failure, social contestation changes the material and ideological balance of power in society. Conversely, even when social contestation succeeds, it is only setting the stage for future changes.[6]

The literary critic Mikhail Bakhtin tells us that there is no such thing as a pure monologue, that every utterance is part of a dialogue already in progress.[7] As much as anyone, historians know the wisdom of that formulation. We turn to the past to understand the hidden dimensions of current discussions; we enter into dialogue with other historians to build true and useful understandings of events and issues that escape us as individuals. Fink builds on the insights of Lears and Diggins in his understanding of the past, just as those two scholars build on Gramsci and others in their analyses. But the habit of dialogue is not the property of historians alone, or of traditional intellectuals who write books and articles; it is an essential way of understanding the world for historical actors as well. The organic intellectuals engaged in past and present social contestation can never be static entities embodying a pure consciousness. Rather, they are participants in a dialogue, authors of an ongoing narrative whose final chapter is never written.

NOTES

This commentary originally appeared in *Journal of American History* 75 (June 1988), 146–50. Reprinted by permission. George Lipsitz is a professor of ethnic studies at the University of California, San Diego.

1. Antonio Gramsci, *Selections from the Prison Notebooks,* ed. Quintin Hoare and Geoffrey Nowell Smith (New York, 1971), 9–10, 60–61, 173–75.
2. John Patrick Diggins, "Comrades and Citizens: New Mythologies in American Historiography," *American Historical Review* 90 (June 1985), 614–38; T. J. Jackson Lears, "The Concept of Cultural Hegemony: Problems and Possibilities," ibid., 567–93.
3. Stuart Hall, oral presentation, Minneapolis, Minn., April 3, 1987 (notes in Lipsitz's possession).
4. Harvard Sitkoff, *The Struggle for Black Equality, 1954–1980* (New York, 1981), 165, 186; George Breitman, ed., *Malcolm X Speaks* (New York, 1965); Karl Marx, *The Paris Commune* (New York, 1934), 85.
5. Sara Evans, *Personal Politics: The Roots of Women's Liberation in the Civil Rights Movement and the New Left* (New York, 1979); Paul Buhle, *Marxism in the United States: Remapping the History of the American Left* (London, 1987).
6. Jack Conroy, *The Disinherited* (Westport, Conn., 1982).
7. M. M. Bakhtin, *The Dialogic Imagination: Four Essays,* trans. Michael Holquist and Caryl Emerson, ed. Michael Holquist (Austin, 1981), 410.

The New Labor History at the Cultural Crossroads

Mari Jo Buhle and Paul Buhle

The new labor history has reached a crossroads. Perhaps the tragic passing of Herbert Gutman in 1985 marked the end of an era. The years since find practitioners and critics alike taking stock of his scholarship and its influence upon the writing of United States history in general.

The new labor historians faithfully accepted the subjectivity of the working class as their major theme, Leon Fink points out, and directed their research toward evidences of distinctive patterns of behavior. That approach successfully subordinated the conventional narrative of trade union development to the analysis of a less clearly defined subject, class formation.

The pathbreaking scholars redefined class as a cultural, more than an economic, category and class consciousness as a collective expression not necessarily encompassed by such institutions as trade unions or political parties. In E. P. Thompson's much-quoted formulation, class became "an historical phenomenon, unifying a number of disparate and seemingly unconnected events, both in the raw material of experience and in consciousness." Thompson explained class consciousness, then, as "the way these experiences are handled in cultural terms: embodied in traditions, value-systems, ideas, and institutional forms."[1] Under Thompson's aegis, American scholars emphasized the analysis of religion, rituals, kinship, and community. The resulting studies virtually transformed the traditional subjects of labor history—strikes, trade unions, and political movements—into nearly equivalent "cultural terms." Such scholarly strategy, which restructured the relationship between "experience" and "consciousness" to privilege the latter, made possible the field's greatest contributions and also prefigured its current methodological dilemma.

Behind what we now call the "cultural approach" to working-class history stands a long and complex scholarly evolution. Thompson essentially validated and appropriated practices already well underway. The rapid growth of the social sciences in the early decades of the twentieth century prompted a determined and often radical search for synthesis. A "science of society" promised, to many researchers, the liberation of humanity from shackles of ignorance and superstition. By the 1920s groups of anthropologists, psychologists, sociologists, and (belatedly) historians had begun working simultaneously and often cooperatively to enlarge the meaning of "culture" in order to encompass systems of beliefs and behaviors, rather than merely a society's material artifacts and political systems.

As early as 1933 Ruth Benedict formulated a succinct definition: "A culture, like an individual, is a more or less consistent pattern of thought and action." Researchers at first restricted their studies to allegedly simple "primitive" societies, such as Pacific island or native American tribes. Speculative thinkers soon enlarged the investigative terrain to include modern nations. Erich Fromm's *Escape from Freedom* (1941) considered Nazi Germany; Benedict's *The Chrysanthemum and the Sword* (1946) addressed the peculiarities of Japan. Margaret Mead's *And Keep Your Powder Dry* (1942) and Geoffrey Gorer's *The American Character* (1948) won acclaim for bravado in applying the anthropologists' techniques of cultural interpretation to contemporary American society.[2] Although some critics warned against the temptation to reason simplistically from allegedly primitive to complex societies, historians followed the lead of anthropologists and psychologists to gain a fresh perspective on American life. Ironically, this search took definite form as cold war–era Americans proclaimed consensus to be the unique, dominant theme of the civilization. Daniel Boorstin, Louis Hartz, David M. Potter, and Richard Hofstadter, among many others, explored in various ways the "patterns of culture" that seemed to have made America exceptional. Potter, whose very subject (Americans as the *People of Plenty*) appeared to marginalize the gritty reality of non-middle-class America, perhaps most directly placed history in the field of social sciences and for that reason became exemplar of the interdisciplinary promise.[3]

Although the democratic upheavals of the 1960s intensified an assault on consensus history, the most responsive historians did not return to the Progressive emphasis on the institutional and political narrative. "The exact form the new history would take was far from certain," Ira Berlin later concluded; "the absence of a clear agenda sent historians scurrying in all directions, incorporating insights from other disciplines, adopting new methods, and tinkering with new technologies."[4] Scholars such as Gutman thus appropriated the focus on culture and interdisciplinary practices. The strategy offered them the best hope for escaping the dilemmas of previous radical scholars trapped between old-fashioned, abstract, heroic treatments of the working class (or women, or minorities) and no less old-fashioned muckraking of the rich and powerful. It also promised to recuperate culture from the domain of the elite. By restricting fields to manageable size, by adopting techniques of "thick description" and of oral interviews, they in a sense restored the original methods of anthropologists studying discrete cultures. After nearly three decades of a new labor history replete with innumerable community and shop-floor studies, diligent researchers have compiled massive evidence of distinctive working-class "cultural terms," ranging from family structure and sex roles to voting habits and organizational affiliations.

Never before had history focused on the working class offered either methodological or interpretive challenge to the scholarly mainstream. The previous Commons school of labor history, by contrast, had helped to shape consensus history through decades of studies deflating radical claims about American labor, basing its work methodologically on a detailed institutional narration of unions and their leaders. Where Commons scholars quietly obliged their colleagues, the insurgents proposed to rewrite United States history at large.

The Thompsonian pursuit of "cultural terms" has understandably, however, proved far more difficult to systematize than the Commons view, and it has remained more subject to counterattack. No doubt the

Reagan era, like previous conservative times, has had a major effect. The political drift rightward has encouraged a renascent cold war defense of "Western" values, including the vision of a consensual United States past with minimal internal conflict.[5] But even for those most sympathetic to the new labor history, the very conceptual link between "experience" and "consciousness" has begun to look like a bridge too far. Moments of bitter conflict and apparent clarity of expression have been assembled and detailed almost, one would think, beyond refutation. The persistence of class consciousness beyond such moments remains, however, to be seen. In other words, class formation can be amply documented through cultural study; class development, not susceptible to such treatment, cannot. While faithful devotees produce more detailed variations on familiar themes, others respond to a vague sense of crisis by extending their disciplinary range ever further. A few seem to be reassessing the entire project.

Structuralism and poststructuralism play a large role in the refiguration, whether particular historians have turned a page of the formal studies issuing from those movements or not. As when Potter, Gutman, and others turned to interdisciplinary developments thirty years ago, historians of various specialties and ideological persuasions now turn in the direction of the new wave. Linguists, anthropologists, philosophers, literary scholars, and a sprinkling of historians have proposed a fresh questioning of assumptions. The resulting many-sided debates defy summary. For the purposes of historians, the denial of Enlightenment assumptions about historical progress and the interrogation of historical documents as ambiguous links with the past have been the central theoretical developments. Unlike previous species of romanticism, which attempted to throw a wrench into the gears of advancing industrial society, the newer intellectual trends reflect and focus a widespread sense of crisis in the humanities at large.[6]

The great negative contribution of structuralism and poststructuralism has been to strike at the root of earlier assumptions made in studying "patterns of culture." As the purported mediation between experience and consciousness, culture could be analyzed in an almost functionalist manner. But what if the mediation itself had to be broken down in various parts, interpreted as an expression of various subjective responses? What if American historians' working assumptions, for instance, have been limited by an assumed universality of cultural response that turns out to be far more complex, especially in the present century of Western (and incipient American) decline from the imperial center of world civilization? What if the definitions of American "specialness" have for centuries been misconceived by ignoring the effects of America upon the rest of the human equation? And what if modernism, in its sweeping effects and its own internal crisis, has rendered the very meaning of historical development increasingly moot? One consequence of "decentering" familiar assumptions has certainly been the tendency toward a new incoherence, cloaked in esoteric "discourse" accessible only to initiates. But the other possibility is a heuristic and more open approach toward the subjects of history—individuals and groups—and the self-consciousness of their engagement in the historical process.[7]

While historians have once more been slow to respond to a mode that has fairly swept (and, in many cases, invented) sections of the academy, the scholars of gender, race, or class formations have begun to explore the possibilities of the new disciplinary admixture. Such historians have revealed in their very scholarly language a discernible shift in perspective, from the historicity of context toward a study of the processes *by which meaning is created.* Indeed, the very sophistication of the new labor historians has awakened a sensitivity to limits. The retelling of history around the consciousness of the collective subject, however contextualized with details, effectively points up the inaccessibility of the past except as a "story." The dual possibilities, the esoteric and heuristic, emerge simultaneously.

The understanding of culture that Thompson and his disciples inherited from the social scientists of the pre–World War II era no longer dominates the conceptual landscape. Where structuralist anthropology once fostered the historical examination of "cultural terms" as mediators between experience and consciousness, now literary or cultural theory offers a direct entry into subjectivity through a highly theoretical study of language. Here, the earlier privileging of consciousness tends to become absolute. Where structuralism suspected all materialism of an empiricist bias, poststructuralism's bias against experience becomes a way of subsuming it entirely into the realm of consciousness. Joan Scott states this baldly: "There is no social experience apart from people's perception of it."[8] Whereas Thompson differentiated between experience and consciousness and searched for historically defined mediations, poststructuralists seem to assert the futility of attempting to document experience. Language—defined (at times) as not only words or rhetoric but everything in Thompson's list of cultural terms—becomes for many writers the only subject worth pursuing. Noted for its difficulty and specialized vocabulary, poststructuralist theory in this key has often managed to simplify (or, rather, oversimplify) the interpretive equation. Experience appears to vanish. Only consciousness remains accessible.

One can readily imagine the most extreme consequences, some of which show signs of manifestation. Precisely the studies of gender, race, or class, once together known as the new social history, tend to lose their moorings in the social sciences and to become part of the shifting theoretical field of hermeneutics. To some a nightmare, to others this prospect summons up a pleasant dream. In a 1987 essay, John E. Toews welcomed methodological innovation but warned against its worst potentialities: "The history of meaning has successfully asserted the reality and autonomy of its object. At the same time, however, a new form of reductionism has become evident, the reduction of experience to the meanings that shape it. Along with this possibility, a new form of intellectual hubris has emerged, the hubris of word-makers who claim to be makers of reality."[9]

Only partially do the intellectual historians T. J. Lears and John Patrick Diggins appear to grasp the significance of the current discussions about history and meaning. Although warning against endowing language with the power of overdetermination, Lears interprets the processes of cultural hegemony, Fink points out, as a function of the essential authority invested in elegant argument. So eager to interrogate others, he fails to question his own premises. Diggins remains uninterested in the processes of cultural transformation, accepting at face value Alexis de Tocqueville's observations made a century and a half ago. Were he more theoretically attuned, Diggins might address individualism, in the fashion of Michel Foucault, as the dominant discourse. He would then be appropriately equipped to consider, as Joyce W. Warren has, how the ideological concept of bourgeois individualism was constructed in the late eighteenth and early nineteenth century by excluding all but white males, that is, by denying the independent existence of other people. The obviousness of these points is striking, as if the intellectual history of Diggins and Lears had somehow become a backwater to the rapid methodological currents elsewhere in the profession.[10]

Leon Fink, a social historian more actively engaged with the important issues at hand, argues straightforwardly for further work in the direction most neglected, that is, context. He points out that the one-sided emphasis on consciousness *in general* may remove us yet further from an understanding of historical process, and thus from consciousness in its true plurality. We have, according to Fink, an urgent "need to turn our attention from 'mass' values, attitudes and motivations per se to the manner and moment in which such thoughts were articulated." Or again: "Who spoke, when and under what circumstances—not merely what was said." In part, Fink is proposing a return to "History as Past Politics," the philosophy of the preinterdisciplinary age. But he wants past politics with a difference. For the old why-is-there-no-socialism-in-America question that gives rise to both Diggins's and Lears's contemplations, Fink provides a better one: "What would it have taken for America to be different by 1900—or by extension, today?"[11]

Fink's question may have the sound of contrary-to-fact. But Fink is working on fruitful lines close to the heuristic side of the poststructural dynamic. Diggins assumes consensus, and Lears seeks the complexities of acquiescence. Fink asserts the complex *possibilities* alive at any moment of human experience. The question "who spoke . . . not merely what was said" illuminates and contextualizes the newer methodological contributions. We cannot ignore either the subjectivity of the speaker or the specificity of the particular events; to do either imprisons us at a level of generality in which all American history becomes a bland sameness. The identification of the pertinent elements, so far as they can be interpreted from available evidence, likewise demands more than the traditional consensus historian or the new labor historian has been expected to bring to the particulars. It demands, among other things, a consciousness of ourselves as creators of meaning.

The "what if," so well known to the multitudinous utopian writers of the nineteenth century, has in turn a resonance in the Russian linguistic philosopher and literary historian Mikhail Bakhtin's notebooks (which may possibly supply, for the next generation, what Antonio Gramsci's notebooks offered to the last one). Bakhtin cries out against scholarship rendered faulty by its limiting assumptions: "What we foreground is the *ready-made* and *finalized*. . . . Even in antiquity we single out what is ready-made and finalized, and not what has originated and is developing. . . . We have narrowed it [the past] terribly by selecting and modernizing what has been selected. We impoverish the past and do not enrich ourselves. We are suffering in the captivity of narrow and homogeneous interpretations."[12] Bakhtin, the grandfather of poststructuralism, has put the matter clearly. One cannot specify the alternatives for viewing the past, but one can certainly avoid impoverishing it. Those alternatives remain, as Fink would say, to be demonstrated through the use of evidence and the scholarly imagination. We may draw a certain comfort, or encouragement, from the effort of leading biological scientists to meet us halfway. Jerome Bruner, George Herbert Mead Professor of Psychology at the New School for Social Research, offers the provocative hypothesis that "culture" helps *create* the uses of language. To understand the fundamentals of the development of language therefore demands an understanding of social context, as the heterodox Russian linguist (and contemporary of Bakhtin) Lev Vygotsky pointed out long ago. Understanding context, in turn, demands not merely closer factual examination but also a full medley of historical approaches to the multiple realities present at any moment.[13]

Toews evokes the vision of a bridge between memory and hope, its construction the natural task of historians who came of age in the shadow of the 1960s. The "pressing need" now is to reevaluate critically the prevailing assumptions about the relationship between experience and meaning. We might well consider Thompson's and Gutman's own initial purposes, to study class formation as the ultimate political development in modern history. If we look carefully, we can readily see behind those purposes the romantic impulses, the ethnic millenialism and political commitment, that powered those two historians' mighty effort.[14] Their disciples and descendants have in moments of weakness or confusion tended toward a study of subjectivity minus the political subject. Fink directs us to restore the concept of agency to the historical formulation. By an optimistic reading, the exploration of cultural terms—with all the twists and turns of methodological approach—has at last made possible a return to the point of departure and to the familiar "big questions" of American history.

NOTES

This commentary originally appeared in *Journal of American History* 75 (June 1988), 151–57. Reprinted by permission. Mari Jo Buhle teaches American civilization and history at Brown University. Paul Buhle is director of the Oral History of the American Left at Tamiment Library, New York University.

1. E. P. Thompson, *The Making of the English Working Class* (New York, 1963), 9–10.

2. Ruth Benedict, *Patterns of Culture* (New York, 1933), 46; Erich Fromm, *Escape from Freedom* (New York, 1941); Ruth Benedict, *The Chrysanthemum and the Sword: Patterns of Japanese Culture* (Boston, 1946); Margaret Mead, *And Keep Your Powder Dry* (New York, 1942); Geoffrey Gorer, *The American People: A Study in National Character* (New York, 1948).

3. See especially David M. Potter, *People of Plenty: Economic Abundance and the American Character* (Chicago, 1954).

4. Ira Berlin, "Introduction: Herbert G. Gutman and the American Working Class," in Herbert G. Gutman, *Power and Culture: Essays on the American Working Class*, ed. Ira Berlin (New York, 1987), 18.

5. Edward Said, "Intellectuals in the Post-Colonial World," *Salmagundi* (nos. 70–71, 1986), 44–64.

6. John E. Toews, "Intellectual History after the Linguistic Turn: The Autonomy of Meaning and the Irreducibility of Experience," *American Historical Review* 92 (Oct. 1987), 879–907, esp. 906. For a further example, see Anson Rabinbach, "Rationalism and Utopia as Languages of Nature: A Note," *International Labor and Working Class History* (no. 31, 1987), 30–36; from an approach of aesthetics, Andreas Huyssen, "Mapping the Postmodern," *New German Critique* (no. 33, 1984), 5–52; and from literature and history, Frederic Jameson, "Postmodernism, or the Cultural Logic of Late Capitalism," *New Left Review* (no. 146, 1984), 53–92.

7. See, for example, Susan E. Drake, *Wilson Harris and the Modern Tradition: A New Architecture of the World* (New York, 1986), 169–85.

8. Joan Scott, "On Language, Gender, and Working Class History," *International Labor and Working Class History* (no. 32, Fall 1987), 40.

9. Toews, "Intellectual History after the Linguistic Turn," 906.

10. T. J. Jackson Lears, "The Concept of Cultural Hegemony: Problems and Possibilities," *American Historical Review* 90 (June 1985), 567–93; John Patrick Diggins, "Comrades and Citizens: New Mythologies in American Historiography," ibid., 614–38; Joyce W. Warren, *The American Narcissus: Individualism and Women in Nineteenth-Century American Fiction* (New Brunswick, N.J., 1984).

11. Leon Fink, "The New Labor History and the Powers of Historical Pessimism: Consensus, Hegemony, and the Case of the Knights of Labor," *Journal of American History* 75 (June 1988), 115–36. For an example of the political trend in the new labor history, see Nell Irvin Painter, *Standing at Armageddon: The United States, 1877–1919* (New York, 1987).

12. Mikhail Bakhtin, "Extracts from 'Notes' (1970–71)," in *Bakhtin: Essays and Dialogues on His Work,* ed. Gary Saul Morson (Chicago, 1986), 180; Caryl Emerson, "The Outer World and Inner Speech: Bakhtin, Vygotsky, and the Internalization of Language," ibid., 1–19.

13. Jerome Bruner, *Actual Minds, Possible Words* (Cambridge, Mass., 1986).

14. On the romanticism and Jewish radicalism of Thompson and Gutman, respectively, see Paul Buhle, "E. P. Thompson and His Critics," *Telos* (no. 49, 1981), 127–37; and "Herbert G. Gutman: Learning about America," *Radical History Review* (no. 36, 1986), 103–6.

Relocating the Vital Center

Leon Fink

I am indebted to all five commentators for deepening and extending the issues raised in my essay. I express particular appreciation to Professors Diggins and Lears for their willingness to hear me out, then to respond, each in his own thoughtful way. There are only a few matters that require further ink on my part.

Jackson Lears possesses a powerful capacity to envelop diverse elements within his own original synthesis. In his article on cultural hegemony, arguments for and against use of that concept are presented in a delicate pas de deux. Perhaps, as he suggests, I stumbled at one point on his fancy footwork. In any case, I think we do share a sense of what the big problems are. He is right, for example, to identify oppositional culture in the twentieth century as a topic that desperately needs further analysis. While not entirely disagreeing with his initial skepticism regarding the potentialities of mass culture, I have wondered (elsewhere) whether

part of our problem in the search for "modern" resistance does not arise
from a recent tendency among social and cultural historians to over-
dramatize the traditionalism of earlier protest, thus leaving the modern
era denuded of all capacity for radical transformation.[1]

The feisty reply of John Patrick Diggins, my favorite pessimist, requires
a bit more intervention. In my view his learned, if somewhat dyspeptic,
commentary contains two very helpful points. First, those of us who
invoke labor republicanism as a category of nineteenth-century analysis
must more carefully distinguish it from the more formal tradition of
classical, civic republicanism from which it derives. Whether the vulgar-
ity of the laborite version—nineteenth-century workers did not, after all,
have the advantage of reading Hannah Arendt, Adam Ferguson, J. G. A.
Pocock, or Diggins on the subject—really detracted from their political
message is, of course, another question. Second, Diggins's questioning of
the assumed ties between individualism and capitalist culture is provocative. No doubt he is right for the long haul, but I would suggest that
there are moments, such as the late nineteenth century, where capitalist
and individualist logic appear to coincide. In such moments, otherwise
disparate brakes on possessive individualism—the nation, the workers,
the community, the ethnic group, the family—may be summoned into
service by the political opposition. In the case of the Knights of Labor,
the family, for example, was heralded less as an inherent "bastion of
anticapitalism" than as a source of moral values on which an economic
and political opposition might form. Surely the political function of
those social entities is not fixed but enjoys a history of its own. Still,
Diggins has raised an important question.[2]

It is not when he contests my interpretation of labor-populist culture
but when he disdains the entire enterprise that I must take most serious
issue with Diggins. His own original argument rested on intellectual
constructs in portraying an America of universal, consensus liberal values.
Now, rather than confront another interpretation of those constructs, he
prefers to deny their significance altogether. It is curious that I should
find him wanting when he seeks to become the "vulgar Marxist" for
whom Jackson Lears occasionally yearns, that is, when he disdains
expressed beliefs and ideology altogether in favor of his own brand of a
utilitarian, interest theory of motivations. Surely the millennium (or at
least the next synthesis) is near when the intellectual historian wants acts,
not words, while the labor historian appeals to the power of ideas?
Fourth of July rhetoric, I insist, offers a clue to a large yet discrete set of
popular political understandings. In a rich disquisition on "everyday"
forms of resistance among Malaysian peasants, the political scientist
James C. Scott similarly urges us to pay close attention to the articulated

thought of the powerless: "Gramsci is, I believe, misled when he claims that the radicalism of subordinate classes is to be found more in their acts than in their beliefs. It is more nearly the reverse. The realm of behavior—particularly in power-laden situations—is precisely where dominated classes are most constrained. And it is at the level of beliefs and interpretations—where they can safely be ventured—that subordinate classes are least trammeled."[3] As for the Knights of Labor, I do not want to enter Terence Powderly in a pissing contest with Samuel Gompers or even Antonio Gramsci. Serious discussion of opposition culture cannot rest, as Diggins implies, solely on a scale of outcomes: by that test, all too convenient for academic historians, history is only a story of winners. For our purposes it does not matter that Friedrich Engels recognized in the Knights "an immense association spread over an immense extent of country . . . held together . . . by the instinctive feeling that the very fact of their clubbing together for their common aspiration makes them a great power in the country."[4] All I would insist here is that we are dealing not just with the rhetoric of a few leaders but with the expressed aims of a mass movement, one that had repercussions both in its immediate successes (the United States Bureau of Labor, the extension of the eight-hour day, labor leverage on the political parties) and as a standing example of the power of solidarities across skill, race, and gender divisions. The professed aims and ideals of such a movement, as articulated by both leaders and rank and file (increasingly well documented by historians) cannot be lightly dismissed.

The first generation of Progressive intellectuals, including the economists-cum-historians Richard Ely and John R. Commons, were among those influenced by the Gilded Age revolt among American workers. If that protest is now to be called "a naive theoretical failure," I think we could use a few more such failures. In our own day, such a "passive revolution" might not only do the workers some good but even relieve some historians of their post-1960s ennui.[5]

The impassioned eloquence of George Lipsitz demonstrates that not only Mikhail Bakhtin's dialogue but also Gramsci's war of position extends itself into academic debates. Generally, I cheer his amplification of the power of consciousness as it echoes through partial political victories and even outright defeats. Admittedly, however, I am not quite so bullish on America or so whiggish on oppositional culture as he seems to be. Despite his rhetorical allowance for the price of failure, Lipsitz may underestimate the fragility, and overestimate the integrity, of consciousness as an end in itself. Absent the political movement and institutional supports, there is no telling where an idea might stray. Defeat of the Knights of Labor, for example, led to a subsequent demeaning as "middle-class reformism" of efforts to combine within the same labor movement tangible material gains and a countermorality of daily community life. I am also prepared to believe that elements of the late nineteenth-century Populist critique—monetarist radicalism, the cult of independence, and community morality—could later be harnessed to right-wing, as well as left-wing, movements. Nor can victories always be counted on to generate a sustaining vision of the future. The self-activity of the civil rights movement, for instance, may also be said to have ended in a most demobilizing reliance on the courts and executive orders rather than on a democratic strategy for change. Particularly in pluralistic, bourgeois-democratic cultures—where the dynamic is probably somewhat different than in the castelike isolation of peasant cultivators that Scott explores—we must keep a close eye on the shifting kaleidoscope of consciousness and social forms. Neither pessimist nor Pangloss, having rejected a conservative essentialism, I am not inclined to adopt a more radical one.

While I am happy to be subsumed by Mari Jo Buhle and Paul Buhle into the poststructural dynamic, I must admit that if I am a poststructuralist it is of the ex post facto kind. Perhaps more historians would hearken to this "new wave" of scholarship were its theoretical claims more amply backed by the propaganda of the deed. I certainly agree with the Buhles on the importance of combining structural analysis—be it cultural, social, or economic in emphasis—with attention to political agency. I think that is what Herbert Gutman was trying to do in his work. He was a seeker after hidden worlds and unknown acts. Freeing himself of disciplinary shackles, he defined culture broadly: "The ideals workers expressed in prose and poetry were more than rhetoric. They were the outcropping of a complex system of social values, itself resting on the bedrock of a distinctive social structure. Work patterns, leisure habits, a network of voluntary associations, and much else knit together a common culture. Devices for self-protection were important, but by themselves did not give coherence to life."[6] Whether in an immigrant letter, a local election or strike report, or a slave register, Gutman sought in addition to accounts of acts and events the set of meanings through which largely unremembered people understood their times. Rediscovering the language, as well as the deeds, of his many subjects was a part of this process. At its best, I think, such social history also makes a political contribution, not only expanding our curiosity about the past, but also firing our imagination of the future. I would hope to frame my essay in that image.

NOTES

This response originally appeared in *Journal of American History* 75 (June 1988), 158–61. Reprinted by permission.

1. Leon Fink, "Looking Backward: Reflections on Workers' Culture and the Conceptual Dilemmas of the New Labor History," in *American Labor History: Toward a Synthesis*, ed. Alice Kessler-Harris and J. Carroll Moody (DeKalb, Ill., 1988).

2. I have argued elsewhere that the American legal system, in particular, accentuated the identification of individualism with capitalist interests. Leon Fink, "Labor, Liberty, and the Law: Trade Unionism and the Problem of the American Constitutional Order," *Journal of American History* 74 (Dec. 1987), 904–25. John P. Diggins, "The Misuses of Gramsci," ibid., 75 (June 1988), 141–45, esp. 143. The genealogy of the labor historian's appropriation of the "republicanist" concept is well-treated in Daniel T. Rodgers, "Republicanism: The Career of a Concept," *Journal of American History* 79 (June 1992), 11–38.

3. James C. Scott, *Weapons of the Weak: Everyday Forms of Peasant Resistance* (New Haven, Conn., 1985), 322. Scott's work, which I have only recently discovered, merits further attention. See especially "Hegemony and Consciousness: Everyday Forms of Ideological Struggle," in ibid., 304–50.

4. Gregory S. Kealey and Bryan D. Palmer, *Dreaming of What Might Be: The Knights of Labor in Ontario, 1880–1900* (New York, 1982), 2.

5. Diggins, "Misuses of Gramsci," 145. See Benjamin G. Rader, *The Academic Mind and Reform: The Influence of Richard T. Ely in American Life* (Lexington, Ky., 1966), 66–69; Lafayette G. Harter, Jr., *John R. Commons: His Assault on Laissez-Faire* (Corvallis, Oreg., 1962), 18.

6. Herbert G. Gutman, *Power and Culture: Essays on the American Working Class*, ed. Ira Berlin (New York, 1987), 131.

6

Labor, Liberty, and the Law:
Trade Unionism and the Problem of the
American Constitutional Order

In 1958, American workers—who had first given May Day political currency in 1886—saw the holiday officially assigned a new, public meaning: Law Day. Responding to a spirited campaign by the American Bar Association (ABA), President Dwight D. Eisenhower, in words that would soon be repeated in joint resolutions of Congress, declared that "freedom under law is like the air we breathe. People take it for granted and are unaware of it—until they are deprived of it." Even in the proclamation of Law Day, however, the president tacitly acknowledged other associations with the day. Immediately identifying the canons of jurisprudence with the welfare of the American worker, the proclamation quoted the famous lines of Edmund Burke: "The poorest man may, in his cottage, bid defiance to all the forces of the Crown. . . . the storms may enter; the rain may enter—but the King of England cannot enter: all his forces dare not cross the threshold of that ruined tenement!" Beyond protecting rich and poor alike from its own wrath, the state, affirmed the Republican president, had also entered into a new social compact with American working people.

> It has moved to meet the needs of the times. True, it is good that the King cannot enter unbidden into the ruined cottage. But it is not good that men should live in ruined cottages. The law in our times also does its part to build a society in which the homes of workers will be invaded neither by the sovereign's troops nor by the storms and winds of insecurity and poverty. It does this not by paternalism,

welfarism and hand-outs, but by creating a framework of fair play within which conscientious, hard-working men and women can freely obtain a just return for their efforts.[1]

While organized labor was not a prime mover in the creation of Law Day, it certainly did not stand in the way. Respect for, even sanctification of, the law and legal procedure had in fact already become incorporated into the public posture of the postwar, newly united American Federation of Labor and Congress of Industrial Organizations (AFL-CIO). Indeed, a year before the ABA went into action, the *American Federationist* dedicated its May 1957 issue to the theme "Respect for the Law," and prominently quoted from Abraham Lincoln's "Lyceum Speech" of 1838:

> Let every American, every lover of liberty, every well-wisher to his posterity swear by the blood of the Revolution never to violate in the least particular the laws of the country and never to tolerate their violation by others. As the patriots of '76 did to the support of the Declaration of Independence, so to the support of the Constitution and laws let every American pledge his life, his property and his sacred honor. Let every man remember that to violate the law is to trample on the blood of his father and to tear the charter of his own and his children's liberty.[2]

President Eisenhower and the AFL-CIO did indeed seem to be breathing the same air. But like much else about the postwar cultural consensus, the celebration of American law covered over a much more complicated historical relationship between workers and the Constitution as interpreted through the legal system. On the one hand, American trade unions had early and persistently celebrated, adopted, and identified with the charter of American liberty as the basis of their own aims and ambitions. On the other hand, unions ran into repeated, and often dire, friction with the law as actually administered. How to capture the constitutionalist idiom without being swallowed up by it? How to honor the national political inheritance without being destroyed by it? Those are questions that have bedeviled and continue to bedevil American social movements.

The law, as E. P. Thompson concluded in *Whigs and Hunters,* functions as both institution (courts, statutes) and ideology (a set of rules and norms "tenaciously transmitted through the community"). Through its dual incarnations, Thompson observed, eighteenth-century English law "in most respects" served and legitimized class power. At the same time the very centrality of the law as a force of order and legitimation made it "a place, not of consensus, but of conflict." From within the legal tradition, for example, the plebeian classes erected "alternative norms," demanding the extension of principles of equity. Over time, noted Thompson, the law thus served at once as a powerful hegemonic force for the established order and as a progressive brake on the naked self-interest of the ruling classes.[3]

In American labor history the law has yet to be fully explored in Thompson's terms as a restricting, yet dynamic, force within the workers' world.[4] To be sure, a great deal of useful attention has focused on the connections between working-class social movements and national political culture. What has been described as "labor republican," "equal rights," or "commonwealth" ideology has been identified with the central tenets of nineteenth-century American workers' movements. Such labor variants of the national political inheritance have been distinguished from the radically bourgeois, entrepreneurial, "law and order," or property-centered variants that usually prevailed in government and industry. These investigations have rightly helped rejoin American social and political history, clarifying the conflicting meanings and uses of a republican political tradition. While reaching varying conclusions—for example, seeing different mixtures of authentic radicalism and liberal hegemony in labor activity—most studies have approached political culture primarily as an arena of consciousness and worldview.[5]

The case of the law and the Constitution, however, presents a distinct problem for labor historians. While equipped with their own perspectives and aspirations, workers, of course, did not live in a world shaped according to their preferred version of Americanism. They had not only to deal with their direct economic antagonists; in addition, they often had to deal with encumbrances or even repression imposed by the state. To be sure, with widespread suffrage, workers were sometimes able to mitigate the terms of state intervention through legislative action. They had far less capacity to intervene in the interpretations of the laws. Whatever their own ideals and whatever their political influence, they were subject in the end to the Constitution and the laws as interpreted by the courts.

How workers' movements responded to the bourgeois command over the interpretation and instruments of law is the problem I wish to explore here. How, for example, was a collective movement to justify itself in a land that offered legal sanction only to individual rights? How did unions defend themselves against recurrent charges of conspiracy and restraint of trade? Did an era of injunctions and a crushing legal offensive erode labor's "republican" faith? If so, what assumptions took its place? Finally, to what extent did New Deal reforms reconcile labor idealism with the instrument of the state and (to use Ronald Dworkin's term) the "law's empire"?[6]

Within a broad chronological sweep, this essay will concentrate on the
labor movement during the generalship of Samuel Gompers. At the
height of what many historians have recognized as the "exceptionalist"
drift of American labor history—away from class economic and political
strategies, toward a homegrown conservative pragmatism—legal issues
then took on their most determining historical role. While arguing for
the significance of the legal order in American labor history, however, I
do not wish to suggest that the outcome was delimited in advance or
entirely "from above." The case of Britain, which shared fundamental
legal forms and jurisprudential concepts with the United States but
nonetheless departed decisively from American industrial relations practice in the twentieth century, will prove particularly instructive on this
point.

Workers in the Republic

Throughout American history, workers, perhaps more or less sincerely,
have sought to identify their interests and actions directly with national
governmental institutions and political principles. This was especially so
in the first century of the new republic, when the contested civic concepts
of "independence," "equality," "free labor," and "commonwealth" carried a discrete social, as well as a political, meaning. None, for example,
were more zealous than the artisan classes in seeking ratification of the
United States Constitution. Similarly, as early as 1810 the Declaration of
Independence was used to justify a strike. More generally, worker ideology in the antebellum decades has been defined in many studies as
"artisanal republicanism." Even disfranchised female workers at Lowell
found political sustenance as "daughters of free men."[7] Protests at
midcentury in New England's shoe factories likewise appealed directly to
a political tradition of "equal rights"; not coincidentally, the greatest
strike up to 1860 occurred on Washington's birthday. Following the Civil
War, a gathering working-class movement again chose the symbols of the
Republic as the basis for its critique of corporate capitalism. The nation,
argued a prominent spokesman for the Knights of Labor, must choose
between "the wage system of labor" and "the republican system of
government." The written constitutions of the national trade unions also
borrowed from the structure and procedure of the nation's federal
institutions.[8]

Labor's connection to state-related values appears particularly defini-
tive when other intellectual sources to which the movement might have
turned are considered. Republicanism, after all, was not the only political ideal available to justify labor solidarity. One of the most significant
alternatives was the tradition of craft and occupational culture. In their

classic study of British trade-union development, for example, Beatrice Webb and Sidney Webb cited initial attempts by the skilled crafts to seek guildlike protection of their existing stake in society through "the doctrine of vested interests." Thus, in 1845 the British Amalgamated Society of Engineers (ASE) compared its members to physicians who held diplomas or to authors who were protected by copyright. Arguments from "vested interest" or corporate occupational communities, however, succumbed to legal and philosophical attack and soon disappeared from labor's public political identity even in Britain. The group discipline and avowed regulatory purpose of the older "combination" quickly gave way, at least rhetorically, to the more voluntaristic intentions of the "union." "United to protect, not combined to injure," proclaimed the British brush makers in 1840. While the Webbs suggested that the argument of vested interests was succeeded by pragmatic arguments based on middle-class political economy ("the doctrine of supply and demand"), more recent historiography points to an intervening middle passage in which British workers rested their claims on political arguments drawn from a radical reading of eighteenth-century constitutionalism ("the rights of freeborn Englishmen").[9]

In their reliance on broader national political assumptions, British and American workers seem to have had much in common. Very early in the course of industrial development both groups detached themselves from economic theories that explicitly justified the use of collective action to control or govern the marketplace. Instead, they placed their faith in a looser tradition of individual "rights" that linked their interests and freedom of maneuver to those of the citizenry at large. American workers, generally benefiting from the breakdown of the British mercantile order, were rarely tempted to resurrect a corporatist or guildlike justification of their activities. Instead, they looked confidently to the principles of the new nation itself to safeguard and justify their legitimate interests.[10] For both British and American workers such a claim on the central political culture of the nation reflected their real gains and felt promise. On the other hand, identification with the constitutional order also posed risks. Could labor defend its version of the legal-political order in the face of adversity? If not, might it not lose a sense of purpose, its vision of the future, as well as its capacity to persuade others to its side?

To be sure, American trade unionists occasionally called upon certain currents of collective reasoning. Commitment to the "working class" of classical socialist theory offered an alternative to republicanism, as in German Marxism, or a collectivist fusion with it, as in French socialist-republicanism or American Debsian socialism. The former was evident, for example, in Samuel Gompers's initial exposition of the "principles of trade unionism" in 1888, which, without any republican reference, appealed to "the natural law of collective action" and "working-class unity" as the "germ of the future state." Likewise, the fraternalism of voluntary societies and varieties of Christian communalism influenced American trade unionism in ways that ignored or extended the boundary of "rights" consciousness. While not insignificant, however, such currents remained for the most part subordinate to the more common theme of workers as American citizens, at once pursuing their interests, defending their rights, and safeguarding the Republic.[11]

Problems of Republicanism

Unfortunately, workers' understanding of republican rights often differed from that of those officially entrusted with the interpretation of the Constitution. Together, a residual animus of the common law and a developing "moral authority" granted, in American jurisprudence, to the "force of liberated individuality" posed a frontal legal challenge to labor's freedom of maneuver. As J. R. Pole concluded in his study of constitutional equality, "It is the individual whose rights are the object of the special solicitude of the Constitution and for whose protection the Republic had originally justified its claim to independent existence." From the sanctity of the individual, moreover, as Morton Horwitz has indicated, it was not far to the sanctity of the entrepreneur.[12]

In the first decade of the nineteenth century, the conspiracy and restraint-of-trade verdicts against journeymen's associations indicated that workers' collective endeavors would have to be weighed against the right of individuals to pursue their interests freely in the marketplace. The journeymen's groups hailed before the courts in those early skirmishes had assumed that American justice would simply throw out the common law inhibitions on worker activity as so much "superstitious idolatry" of the Old World.[13]

They would have no such luck, however, for the restrictive conspiracy and restraint-of-trade doctrines, even when divorced from British master-and-servant acts and Combination Laws, remained embedded in American jurisprudence. Thus, as early as 1837, inaugurating nearly a century of similar vain appeals, the artisan-linked Locofocos of New York City made a demand for judicial restraint part of their party platform. To be sure, there was some improvement for workers in the precedent-setting *Commonwealth* v. *Hunt* decision of 1842, which treated the formation of trade unions as a justifiable exercise of rights of voluntary association, rather than as an illegal conspiracy. The right of freely contracting individuals to form unions, however, still did not clarify unions' rights of action as representative bodies. "The authority of the union to make and enforce rules as an embodiment of the aggregated free wills of its members," observes Christopher Tomlins, "remained illegitimate and open to prosecution as criminal conspiracy." A predilection to view control as an essential condition of property ownership, faith in a free marketplace as a precondition for economic well-being, and a fear of factions operating outside the constituted sovereignty of public authority all figured in the early judicial suspicion of trade-union activities. To a remarkable extent, the basic issues identified in the conspiracy cases would continue to pose problems for labor through the twentieth century.[14]

During the renewed labor conflict of the Gilded Age, the conspiracy doctrine reemerged as an inviting tool for legal actions against organized workers. After 1880 employers increasingly brought suits for damages and sought injunctive relief from strikes or boycotts; such actions usually rested on an initial charge of conspiracy. In all such cases the courts began by assuming the existence of a free, unobstructed marketplace, an assumption that cast suspicion on trade union–inspired "disruptions." An occasional finding that workers were exercising rights superior to those they were violating (as in Justice Oliver Wendell Holmes's "just cause" doctrine of 1894) depended, as Holmes noted, on the rare "economic sympathies" of the judge. The main current of justice was indicated in a single statistic: between 1880 and 1931 more than eighteen hundred injunctions were issued against strikes. In that period, a 1945 study concluded, "The power of the courts was invoked to assist in defeating most of the more important strikes . . . and only a smaller proportion of the relatively less important ones." By 1910 the most elemental forms of trade-union response to corporate power, the strike and boycott, were either (in the latter case) effectively curtailed or (in the former case) severely handicapped by judicial censure. Legislative attempts to redress the balance proved all but useless. While the scale of the legal impediment varied over time and place, the basic problem remained the same: the suasion that an organized body of workers might exercise over their workmates, as well as their potential replacements, contradicted the voluntaristic assumptions, individual sovereignty, and respect for property embedded in the law.[15]

Experience with the law and with ineffectual legislative remedies placed the American labor movement in a strategic and an intellectual quandary. Even as an industrial economy placed new pressures on workers, stimulating the impulse to organize, the Republic to which they looked for ultimate protection bristled with hostility. From the 1880s through the 1920s organized labor recurringly puzzled over the problem of its relation to state authority. Two broad lines of response, neither in the end very successful, were adopted.

The first impulse, most effectively represented by the Knights of
Labor, stretched republican idealism to new political limits. Their rhetoric suffused with appeals to community and nation, the Knights sought
to regenerate American life and institutions through a radical activation
of citizenship. By defining their contemporary enemies as a new "slave
power" (thus invoking both the recent Civil War and instinctual American hatred of feudal serfdom), the Knights cast themselves as the last,
best defenders of a true republic of individual liberties. As the labor
editor John Swinton characteristically put it, the United States had been
blessed with perfect institutions until "the robbers got into our country"
and "shattered its grand constitution. Out with the piratical crew!" Typical of the Knights' self-image was their 1886 message of support to the
Ohio Woman's Suffrage Association, which defined the Knights' aims
entirely within the tradition of natural rights and human liberty. The
"real mission" of their order, affirmed the General Assembly, "is the
complete emancipation and enfranchisement of all those who labor. It is
imbued with the lofty spirit of the Declaration of Independence."[16]

An implicit preference for the Declaration of Independence over the
Constitution allowed Gilded Age labor at once to identify with the
national purpose and to invoke transcendent "rights" beyond the reach
of complicated, ambivalent, or hostile judicial interpretation. Even
Gompers (who normally rested his claims on other grounds) caught the
fever of "aroused republican citizenship" while campaigning for Henry
George in 1886. Responding to his opponents' charges of anarchism,
Gompers lashed back: "If they tell us to appeal to the ballot-box and
when we do so they call us Anarchists, then anarchy is not wrong. . . . We
have yet left to us certain inalienable rights."[17]

Stirred by the appeal to equal rights, the Knights, perhaps not surprisingly for an organization that denied lawyers membership, generally
held the courts and their intricate legal reasoning in righteous, if
somewhat ignorant, disdain. Even when attempting a serious defense
of the legitimacy of the boycott in 1886, for example, Knights' executive
officer George McNeill showed little patience for fine points of legal
doctrine:

> Recent decisions of judges upon the question of conspiracy and
> boycotting are new revelations of an old fact, that the interpretation
> of law rests largely upon the public sentiment of the wealthy part of
> the community. The Dred-Scott decision was declared infamous by
> those who were lifted to the level of the spirit of our institutions;
> yet, nevertheless, that decision was a confession that the controlling
> classes were under the subtle influence of the slave-power. . . . So,

too, the attempts now made to prevent the working people from using the great power of the boycott will be found to be in contradiction, not only of individual, but of constitutional rights. A man has not only the right to buy where he pleases, but has the right to advise another man to buy or not to buy of friend or enemy; *and whether the exercise of the boycott is judicious or injudicious, justifiable or unjustifiable in certain instances,* the innate right of man to the privilege of exercising his moral power and social influence in the direction of trade, or to withhold trade, cannot be safely denied.[18]

By the 1890s radical reform zeal, whether exercised at the workplace or at the ballot box, had run into a virtual stone wall of judicial interference. Renunciation of fraudulently inflated railroad bonds by state legislatures, the regulation of working hours and conditions, and progressive income taxes had all been ruled unconstitutional. State laws intended to limit applications of the conspiracy doctrine in labor disputes had likewise failed to elicit respect from the bench. Beginning with the Debs case growing out of the Pullman strike of 1894, the United States Supreme Court helped redirect the animus of the Sherman Antitrust Act from business monopolies to the actions of labor unions. In important respects, the pivotal presidential campaign of 1896 pitted the forces of producer republicanism against a Supreme Court mindful of the security of corporate and finance capital. Indeed, perhaps more radical than any economic changes that William Jennings Bryan's Populist-Democratic forces proposed were the Democrats' platform commitments promising an end to "government by injunction," proposing jury trials in all contempt cases, opposing life tenure for federal officials, and even suggesting "reconstituting" (adding new members to) the Supreme Court. As Texas governor J. S. Hogg explained, "This protected class of Republicans proposes now to destroy labor organizations . . . proposes through Federal courts, in the exercise of unconstitutional writs, to strike down, to suppress and overawe these organizations."[19]

The collapse of the political initiatives launched during labor's great upheaval of the 1880s and the Populist crusade of the 1890s raised the ante for those who clung to the republican tradition. The old forms had become so thoroughly compromised that they would require structural, and not merely moral, renovation. As the Western Federation of Miners (WFM) complained in 1902, "The document of national liberty, the federal Constitution and the organic law of every state of the Union seem to be helpless in placing the strong arm of protection around the rights and liberties of that army of men and women who are camped on the industrial field." For Eugene Debs and others on labor's left flank in the

1890s, a new, socialist, constitutionalist departure was in order. "Socialism," declared one WFM delegate, "has written a declaration of independence which will gather together the scattered shreds of liberty." Invoking a similar vision of social democracy for the twentieth century, Henry Demarest Lloyd called before the 1893 AFL convention for a "grand international constitutional convention in which a new magna charta, a new declaration of independence, a new bill of rights shall be proclaimed to guide and inspire those who wish to live the life of the commonwealth."[20]

But while political adversity carried some to a more radical elaboration of labor republicanism, it left others disillusioned and groping for alternative visions. Terence Powderly, former leader of the Knights of Labor, for example, was one of the tired ones. After the turn of the century, he looked back on the Knights' republican enthusiasm as a form of innocent naïveté: "Maybe we placed a too implicit faith in what the Declaration of Independence held out to us. Perhaps some lingering, belated wind from the scenes of the early days of the French Revolution carried to our minds the thought that equality could be won, so far as rights and duties went, without reddening our record with a single drop of human blood."[21]

The AFL and the "British" Road to Legitimacy

The young American Federation of Labor disengaged from the tradition of labor republicanism that had identified workers' interests with the rights and welfare of American citizens in general. Ronald L. Filippelli has summarized this development: "Gompers saw that individual freedoms were meaningless in a society consisting of powerful interest groups. . . . To Gompers, individual freedom had no meaning unless protected by collective power."[22]

Both German and British examples nourished the more self-sufficient, politically detached perspective of the new American labor federation. AFL founders, true to their ideological roots in the First International, emphasized working-class organization at the expense of legislative or electoral initiatives. The constituent unions of the Federation of Organized Trades and Labor Unions—which in 1886 became the AFL—meanwhile took their organizational cue from the businesslike, new-model British bodies like the Amalgamated Engineers and the British Trades Union Council. Gompers called the British labor movement "the only one with traditions and historical development." The survival and stability of the trade unions as organizations were the first great accomplishments of the British movement (well before the new political departure of a Labour party), and the example was one that the AFL would struggle to replicate with "pure and simple" priorities. Disillusioned with the political option in America, Gompers and the national AFL leadership had by the 1890s effectively detached labor's agenda from any vision of change for the nation as a whole.[23]

Paradoxically, the AFL's resistance to a transformative political strategy led it to an intimate and unparalleled involvement with American constitutional and legal questions. Seeking to win a place within the established social order, the labor federation was forced to pay close attention to the inner workings and assumptions of a legal and political system skillfully appropriated by employers. Thus, regardless of Gompers's personal dismissal of individual rights, his AFL representatives nevertheless constructed the first serious defense of American trade unionism based on the acceptance of individualist and market-oriented assumptions. In the AFL years the rhetoric and public posture of the labor movement became stamped more than ever before with the imprint of legal entitlement.

The search for an acceptable constitutionalist idiom and a more carefully crafted legal footing for organized labor was already under way in the 1890s. While condemning the prevailing "corruption" of the judiciary, AFL editorialists in 1895 predicted that "courts are to have something to do with solving the labor question, whether the toilers like it or not." A memo from the New York attorney George H. Hart to Gompers in 1896 briefed the federation president on the proper defense of unions from yellow-dog contracts and other intimidating measures. "Today," Hart explained, "the rule is that it is legal to unite and combine with the purpose on the part of the employee to advance his wages and on the part of the employer to reduce the price of wages." The First Amendment, moreover, clearly "secures the right to every individual 'to peaceably assemble' " and thereby renders attempts to prevent employees from assembling a violation of the Constitution. The operating "rule" between disputants, Hart emphasized, was freedom from coercion: "neither must coerce or attempt to coerce or intimidate or injure the other." Citing the authority of the Fourteenth Amendment (otherwise a notorious obstacle to labor interests), the AFL counsel defended the right to organize from any attempt "to deprive a person of his civil rights, his individual liberty and freedom of action."[24]

Hart's message was part of a growing trend toward ideological moderation within the trade-union leadership. Instead of fleeing from the common law with ringing invocations of the Declaration of Independence or other appeals to natural-rights doctrine, labor at the turn of the century painstakingly sought to turn inherited legal doctrine to practical advantage. As early as 1893 the AFL gave wide circulation to an essay by the abolitionist-turned-anarchist Dyer Lum, which viewed human history as one great progression from "compulsion" to "voluntary cooperation." Trade unionism, according to this formulation, fit neatly into broader economic and social development toward "free association." As a collection of the voluntary wills of freely participating individuals, organized labor, argued the new AFL line, was perfectly compatible with the dominant doctrines of American jurisprudence. What labor wanted was not to transform or to regenerate the commonwealth but just to be let alone to go about its business. Thus the American labor leadership came to embrace a version of what British analysts have dubbed "collective laissez-faire."[25]

The likeness was more than coincidental. The British system, which effectively allowed distinct industrial groups to contend for power without the state's interference, had evolved through the parliamentary system of the late nineteenth and early twentieth centuries in recognition of the need for order in industrial relations and in deference to the unions' growing influence in political affairs. Facing similar threats of conspiracy prosecution and civil damages via injunction from strike-related activities, the British trade-union movement had by 1906 scored a series of legislative victories. Following the statutory legalization of unions themselves in 1871, the Conspiracy and Protection of Property Act of 1875 formally exempted trade disputes from criminal conspiracy charges. Although the breakthrough to legal immunity was narrowed in the 1880s and 1890s by a reassertion of coercive judicial power—a trend capped by the Taff Vale decision of 1901—it set a happy precedent for the future. Backed by a Liberal government seeking trade-union votes, the Trade Disputes Act of 1906 granted the unions immunity from civil law prosecutions just as the 1875 statute had from criminal law prosecutions. As a general rule this legislation and surrounding measures (combined with the customary deference of the British courts toward statutory intent) set the foundation for a judicially insulated industrial relations system that lasted until 1971.[26]

AFL leaders watched the British developments with envy. While advocating anticonspiracy legislation before the New York State Assembly in 1887, Gompers appealed directly to British precedent of the previous decade: "Surely if monarchial England can afford to expunge obnoxious laws from her statutes, the Empire State of the Union can." At the national level labor's commitment to a British-style theory of "judicial abstention" (in equity as well as criminal conspiracy cases) was reflected in the AFL's protracted campaign for congressional relief from the act of injunction. Indeed, from 1894 to 1914 the unions and their friends offered bills to curb equity jurisdiction in every congressional session but one. In testimony in 1904 and 1908, for example, Gompers appealed directly to British example to defend the protected realm of employee activity. John P. Frey, editor of the official journal of the Iron Molders' Union of North America, relying on the research of AFL attorney W. B. Rubin, later summarized the labor federation's view that "American courts of equity, in the matter of labor disputes, have set aside the basic rules of equity as they were recognized and applied in Great Britain and observed by equity courts in this country until 1888." In the Pearre Bill of 1907, the Wilson Bill of 1912, and, in somewhat diluted form, the Clayton Act of 1914, organized labor sought, albeit unsuccessfully, an outright proscription on legal intervention in peaceful labor disputes. In 1908 Gompers collaborated in vain with railroad owners, International Harvester, and the National Civic Federation to ease Sherman Act restrictions on business concentration in exchange for exemption of labor from antimonopoly legislation (in the Hepburn Bill).[27]

Labor's more active "political" posture in the first decade of the twentieth century, adopted in the face of hostile state intervention, amounted less to abandonment of the self-help doctrine of "voluntarism" than to a search for an officially recognized state neutrality in industrial conflict. In congressional testimony in 1906, for example, AFL counsel Thomas Spelling began by accepting the inevitability of marketplace conflict, both between capitalists for control of the volume of trade and between capitalists and labor for control of wages. But just as capital was left free to resort to "the legitimate and recognized methods of warfare" in the "conflicts of capital against capital," so should labor be allowed its methods of warfare "in its hard and unequal struggle against capital." Discountenancing all meddling by the courts in industrial disputes, Spelling retracted any special claim by labor on the state: "Workingmen are not in the habit of trying to get some court to exceed its jurisdiction. They are fighting this battle between capital and labor bravely—fighting it in the open." The arbitrary and interventionist nature of the injunction, according to this argument, unfairly disrupted the normal and healthy combat of the marketplace. As exercised by American judges, injunctions thus "usurp the legislative power and make an *ex post facto* law and crush and destroy one side in a labor dispute."[28]

A world of organized interests had, in the AFL's reasoning, outmoded an argument built on a vision of commonwealth or public interests. Spelling's argument contained only a fleeting reference to an older republican view. Concluding his opening remarks with an emotional appeal, he warned Congress that "when a crisis arises . . . it is not the sons of the steel-trust magnates, or the coal barons, or the Wall Street kings of finance that fight our battles. These fighting men must be drawn from the great mass of the common people, and in that mass labor largely preponderates." Yet, even here, identifying itself as a preponderant interest group distinct from the "mass of the common people," labor sought less to stamp its vision on the Republic than to be allowed its own, self-limited jurisdiction.[29]

Labor's cherished freedom of action in American society received its ultimate formulation in the famous "voluntarism" speech delivered for Gompers by Vice-President William Green in 1924 only months before the AFL founder's death. "I want to urge devotion to the fundamentals of human liberty," wrote Gompers, "the principles of voluntarism. No lasting gain has ever come from compulsion. If we seek to force, we but tear apart that which, united, is invincible." Gompers's penultimate doctrine for American labor should be interpreted not merely as a counterweight to socialist agitation in labor circles but also as a shrewd, if all too tardily crafted, response to American legal and constitutional restraints.[30]

Into the Wilderness

Despite the wishes of the AFL, American trade unionists in the era of industrial consolidation, unlike their British counterparts, never got to experience true voluntarism or "collective laissez-faire." Statutory restraints on judicial authority proved either internally faulty or were effectively annulled by the power of judicial reinterpretation (witness the fate of the Sherman and Clayton antitrust acts). Attempts to grant trade unions an implied statutory immunity from legal intervention repeatedly failed as a result of the American (but not English) practice of judicial review. Indeed, Gompers's address of 1924 on voluntarism appeared against the backdrop of the fiercest judicial volleys yet fired at the trade-union movement. During the decade of the twenties, injunctions rose to a new peak—in the pivotal 1922 railroad shop craft strike alone some three hundred restrictive injunctions were issued. In addition, the injunction power was extended to yellow-dog contracts (in *Hitchman Coal Company* v. *Mitchell,* 1917), picketing was often judicially restricted, and even the Clayton Act, labor's hoped-for "Magna Carta," was interpreted to deny the legitimacy of the secondary boycott (*Duplex Printing Press Co.* v. *Deering,* 1921). "By the end of the 1920s," notes Filippelli, "it was difficult to say with any certainty just what was legal for unions to do."[31]

Lack of immunity placed the AFL in a most exposed position, both politically and intellectually. Having committed itself to work within the framework of American laws and economic institutions, the trade-union federation left itself with little strategic recourse in the face of overwhelming adversity. AFL leaders seethed with resentment against the treatment of unions by the courts. Gompers and John Mitchell almost went to jail for breaking a 1909 injunction in the *Buck's Stove and Range* case. Union meetings rang with militant tones and defiant gestures toward the judiciary. The federation's convention of 1919, for example, declared: "We shall stand firmly and conscientiously on our rights as free men and treat all injunctive decrees that invade our personal liberties as unwarranted in fact, unjustified in law and illegal as being in violation of our constitutional safeguards, and accept whatever consequences may follow."[32] AFL sentiments were rapidly approaching those of the western Industrial Workers of the World (IWW) leader who, when charged with judicial contempt, reportedly responded, "To hell with the court and the judge." Various political responses were contemplated. Challenging antagonistic judges in reelection fights, drafting legislation to permit the recall of judges, and, if necessary, preferring "impeachment against every law-breaking judge" received consideration in 1916.[33]

Criticism, indeed, quickly turned from the evil perpetrated by specific judges to the power of the courts as a whole over the American Constitution. In 1922 the AFL attorney W. B. Rubin spoke of John Marshall's original "usurpation" of the Constitution. By overturning child labor laws ("a blow to the very law of nature, the protection of the dependent offspring") and imposing contempt citations without a jury trial, argued Rubin, the courts had vitiated intended constitutional safeguards: "Our Constitution is a wall to protect us against our enemy from without, not a wall to immure us in submission." Believing that the "separation of powers" had already been "torn to shreds," AFL representatives demanded constitutional amendments providing for periodic election of all judges and, drawing on British practice, for restrictions on the courts' powers of statutory review. Unconnected to any larger strategy of working-class organization or political action, however, all such talk, while comforting in principle, was totally ineffectual.[34]

Given the unreceptive climate for voluntarist collective bargaining, it is not surprising that early twentieth-century trade unions in practice sought other means to advance their interests. Even as the national AFL leadership (together with the labor economists around John R. Commons) were placing exalted faith in private collective bargaining contracts as "constitutions for industry," many of their affiliates were advancing more state-oriented strategies of protection. In Illinois, for example, the labor lobby secured a miners' qualification law (ostensibly a safety device, it prevented importation of strikebreakers) and pro-union licensing acts for elevator operators, plumbers, stationary engineers, boiler tenders, and barbers; teamsters sought legislation on the size of wagon loads, railway unions demanded full crews on trains, and glass bottle blowers tried to prevent the resale of old bottles from junk heaps (they were opposed by milk wagon drivers); even the Egg Inspectors' Union helped to secure their social function with the help of an egg inspection law in 1919. Although such efforts did not transform labor strategy and ideology overnight, they did indicate that the failure or impossibility of self-reliant solutions to labor's plight would ultimately lead back to a reembrace of government and a stronger public role in labor conflict.[35]

Industrial Democracy and the
Legacy of the Wagner Act

In the end, national emergency proved the most skillful midwife to changes in American industrial relations. Drawing on ideas propounded by the Industrial Relations Commissions of 1898–1902 and 1913–15, the federal government moved during World War I and, more permanently, during the Great Depression to accept responsibility for the stability of collective bargaining, union rights, and worker welfare. Influenced less by labor's traditional rights and self-help rhetoric than by appeals to governmental efficiency, economic rationality, and a social gospel morality, as well as labor's political influence, President Wilson's National War Labor Board promised federal protection for the right to organize as well as standards of wages, hours, and pay. What Milton Derber has called the "American idea of industrial democracy," lost during the 1920s, again found favor during the New Deal and World War II.[36]

In the eyes of reformers, the New Deal initiatives heralded a new state-protected "industrial democracy" alongside American "political democracy." During World War II, the National Labor Relations Act (NLRA, 1935), the Fair Labor Standards Act (1938), wartime contracts, and War Labor Board policies created a continuing mechanism of federal enforcement for the Progressive reform doctrines first exercised during World War I. Governmental administration in industrial relations, moreover, promised more than initial aid in stabilizing collective bargaining practices. The New Deal and World War II developments, according to their chief advocates, would inevitably spark further demands for social democratic changes in American life. The vision of a progressive industrial democracy probably reached its apogee in the liberal formulation of a government-backed "right to employment," a decade after the passage of the National Labor Relations Act sponsored by Robert F. Wagner. Counseling action beyond the NLRA's collective bargaining guarantees, Senator Wagner in 1945 proclaimed:

> America faces a future of infinite possibility. . . . This legislation would put all the power of the Government—which means the power of the people—in back of the proposition that every person

able to work and desirous of working shall have the right to useful, remunerative, full-time employment. The actualization of this right will carry with it more than jobs in a limited sense. It will bring, also, all the good things that jobs involve—expanding markets for the products of agriculture and industry; stable legitimate profits for those who invest; more leisure to contemplate the finer things of life; and more resources available for devotion to better education, better housing, better health and better social security.

Not surprisingly, in that moment of optimistic legislative expectation by the New Deal forces, the labor law itself (interpreted by the War Labor Board and a newly sympathetic Supreme Court) was dealing unions an unprecedented hand in economic disputes. Critics charged the government with "widening as far as possible the immunity for striking" and threatening "a climate of economic absolutism similar—but converse—to that experienced a generation ago."[37]

Such worries, of course, proved unfounded. Justified less as an act of emancipation for unions than as an economic policy yielding "greater economic stability through better economic balance," the Wagner Act placed the politically defined public interest ahead of any inherent rights of labor. Not only political considerations (the prolabor forces were in no position to dictate their own terms) but also constitutional ones (the Supreme Court reaction following the 1935 decision in *Schechter Poultry Corporation* v. *United States,* which invalidated the National Industrial Recovery Act, was uncertain) doubtless lay behind the legislative strategy. The theme of economic democracy (as an alternative to totalitarianism) also emerged in the Wagner Act's justification, but such concerns consistently took second place to economic considerations and, even when acknowledged, assumed a peculiarly restricted form. Thus, the law's chief architect, Wagner aide Leon H. Keyserling, reduced the lessons of American labor history to "labor's long struggle for the right to organize and bargain collectively." Other struggles—for a universal eight-hour day, nationalization of the railroads, cooperative forms of production, in short, for a redistribution of power within the Republic—were conveniently forgotten. At best, the new and more favorable legal environment for unionism protected certain activities of the labor movement; it legitimated contract bargaining and immediate economic pressures by specific occupational groups. That even labor radicals generally confined their efforts to the same terrain testifies to the power of state action in shaping popular concepts of freedom and rights in American life.[38]

The Recurrent Dilemma

While temporarily prospering under the new social contract of the thirties, labor never fully escaped its earlier political—and intellectual—conundrum. In the long run, especially given the collapse of the postwar boom, mere immunity from old-fashioned legal harassment together with the machinery of the NLRB has proven wholly insufficient to sustain Eisenhower's vaunted "arena of fair play" for labor. For years historians treated the Wagner Act as something of a Rock of Gibraltar for American trade unionism. But in light of the sharp contemporary decline in union power and influence—a decline significantly exacerbated by perversions of worker protection supposedly guaranteed in the National Labor Relations Act—a number of commentaries question once again the foundations upon which modern-day American industrial relations have been built.[39]

Nelson Lichtenstein and Christopher Tomlins, for example, have emphasized that federally chartered industrial relations, from early on, had a restraining character on rank-and-file activity. The seeds of the legalistic and bureaucratic "insurance agent" unionism of the postwar period thus appear to have been sown amid the very cheering for labor's arrival as a permanent institutional force in American society. By 1947, the Taft-Hartley Act even more clearly demonstrated that what government granted on the grounds of economic sufficiency, government might also take away. Emancipation through the state, concludes Tomlins, proved a "counterfeit liberty."[40]

More than a third of a century elapsed between the AFL's angry renunciation of the Supreme Court's authority in the 1920s and its seemingly happy reconciliation with legal institutions in the 1950s. The turning of another thirty years, however, finds American labor again weakened and marginalized as a political force. Instead of singing the praises of Anglo-American liberties, even the extraordinarily cautious AFL-CIO president Lane Kirkland was by 1983 castigating "laws selectively enforced, in a style that gives a new and bitter relevance to a verse . . . from a savage period of England's distant history: 'The law locks up both man and woman / Who steals the goose from off the common, But lets the greater felon loose / Who steals the common from the goose.' "[41] The very uncertainty of its place in American law and civil society has left labor at the mercy of other, more strongly endowed, institutions. Unable to stand on their own, unions in the 1970s and 1980s have relied on powerful friends whose affections have proven more temporal than constitutional.

The picture of an era of repressive conspiracy indictments followed by an era of equally demobilizing dependency on government by labor leaves one wondering about possible alternatives. In the current stasis of the labor movement, one ironic solution beckons for attention. We are recalled to that brief, but seminal, half decade in American labor history when industrial relations were governed by the principles of collective laissez-faire for which the AFL unions had so long striven. Perhaps the greatest advances in the autonomous organization of American working people took place between 1932 and 1937, after injunction law had finally been struck down by the Norris-LaGuardia Act (1932) but before the decision (*National Labor Relations Board* v. *Jones and Laughlin Steel Corporation*, 1937) validating the role of Wagner Act labor boards. In that period of mass strikes, sit-downs, and armed employer resistance, a new labor movement and perhaps even a new culture based on class identity was born. Might a prolabor political bloc, given a second chance, have opted for an extension of legal immunity rather than a government-defined and government-administered list of industrial rights and wrongs?[42]

Unfortunately, even with the gift of hindsight, no such simple judgment can confidently be made. It is not merely that the rank-and-file uprising of the midthirties might have left little lasting imprint without the Wagner Act and subsequent War Labor Board measures.[43] The problem is more systematic. For the highly integrated industrial economies of the twentieth century, the historical question is not whether the state would intervene in industrial relations but how and to what effect. In comparative perspective, the British case, with its statutory insulation of labor conflict, offers a singular exception among Western states. In France, Germany, and Scandinavia, government long played a more intrusive role in industrial relations than in the United States. Even countries partaking of the British colonial inheritance—Canada, Australia, New Zealand—instituted a more interventionist compulsory arbitration or mediation of disputes.[44] In mass democracies possessing coercive power, notions of collective laissez-faire and judicial abstinence are probably no more realizable than a return to a nineteenth-century producers' republic. Politics—the application of organized social power—will inevitably have a bearing on social conflicts. Even the relative "immunity" conferred by the Norris-LaGuardia Act was a political expression of a depression-induced decline of faith in corporate welfarism. Such immunity, it is worth noting, still stopped short of recognizing solidaristic actions like the secondary boycott. Overall, it makes sense to assume that labor, like other organized parties, will exact as much influence as the moment allows in using the state to meet its needs. From such a reading, at least, the proper critique of modern-day American labor would seem to lie less in its acceptance of the state labor regulation than in its weakness in adapting to a terrain where labor's political muscle would matter more than ever before.

How to take advantage of the law and the opportunities available through the political structure has long remained a puzzle for the American labor movement. Argument and strategic shifts on these issues have proliferated since the early nineteenth century, when the gap between what workers expected and what they received from the constitutional order first became apparent. Hypothetically, as was noted early on, workers might have gone about their business without concentrating on such matters. But "legal fictions" in fact played a vital role in the real world of American workers. Subject to numerous reformulations, the constitutional order has served—and appeared to serve—labor variously as a lifeline or a hangman's rope. Just as in eighteenth-century England, in the United States law certainly "served and legitimated class power." Similarly, it was "a place not of consensus but of conflict." But there is something more. Thompson suggests that the preeminence of the law as a "central legitimizing ideology" was a temporary thing in England, giving way in the nineteenth century to the ideology of the free market and political liberalism. In the United States, despite numerous changes of substance and interpretation, the political and cultural centrality of the law has hardly diminished with time. Perhaps because American national identity itself is drawn so largely from political and constitutional wellsprings, subaltern social groups have sought to orient themselves according to constitutional principles. For good or ill, legal and constitutional principles have long served as the starting point of labor's public self-definition. As the chastened socialist William English Walling wrote in 1926, "We must not think of the American labor movement as existing independently of America's past or present. Our labor movement is not an importation or the result of a theory: it is a typical and representative product of American history. Organized labor has always regarded itself as a product of American democracy." The nature of that democracy, its customs, laws, and capacity to change (as well as to resist change), offers an inviting subject to students of American labor.[45]

NOTES

This essay originally appeared in the *Journal of American History* 74 (December 1987), 904–25. Reprinted by permission. I am particularly indebted to the research assistance of Matthew Bewig, employed with aid provided by a University Faculty Research Grant, who identified helpful primary sources. For offering ideas and useful bibliographic suggestions, I should also like to thank: John Orth, Stuart Kaufman, Kenneth Fones-Wolf, Patricia Greenfield, Cynthia Herrup, David

Brody, William Leuchtenburg, James Epstein, Robert Korstad, Peter Coclanis, Craig Calhoun, and Staughton Lynd. An earlier draft of this essay received a stimulating reading from participants in a colloquium held at the University of Massachusetts, Amherst, in November 1986; in October 1986 I also benefited from comments received at the "In the Shadow of the Statue of Liberty" conference, University of Paris, France. Finally, I am grateful to Susan Levine for general criticisms and for editing out some of my most egregious violations of the English language.

1. *Public Papers of the Presidents of the United States, Dwight D. Eisenhower: Containing the Public Messages, Speeches, and Statements of the President, Jan. 1 to Dec. 31, 1958* (Washington, 1959), 362–63. Within two years of its creation, more than seventy-five thousand official observances of Law Day—in schools, churches, and courthouses—were reported across the nation. In 1970 the chief justice of the United States inaugurated an annual "state of the judiciary" address. *The Guide to American Law, Everyone's Legal Encyclopedia* (12 vols., St. Paul, 1983–85), 1:211–12. On the relation of Law Day to the "end of ideology" theme of the 1950s, see Grant Gilmore, *Ages of American Law* (New Haven, Conn., 1977), 105.

2. "Respect for the Law," *American Federationist* 64 (May 1957), 1. See Philip Van Doren Stern, ed., *The Life and Writings of Abraham Lincoln* (New York, 1940), 231–41.

3. E. P. Thompson, *Whigs and Hunters: The Origin of the Black Act* (New York, 1975), 258–69.

4. For the most penetrating account of the evolving assumptions in American labor law and industrial relations, see Christopher L. Tomlins, *The State and the Unions: Labor Relations, Law, and the Organized Labor Movement in America, 1880–1960* (New York, 1985). Tomlins's insights establish the point of departure for my own approach to those issues. For pioneering research from which I have benefited, see Victoria Charlotte Hattam, "Unions and Politics: The Courts and American Labor, 1806–1896" (Ph.D. diss., Massachusetts Institute of Technology, 1987).

5. For Britain, see Gareth Stedman Jones, *Languages of Class: Studies in English Working-Class History, 1832–1982* (Cambridge, Eng., 1983); for France, see William H. Sewell, Jr., *Work and Revolution in France: The Language of Labor from the Old Regime to 1848* (Cambridge, Eng., 1980); and Maurice Agulhon, *La Republique au village* (Paris, 1970). For the U.S., see Herbert G. Gutman, *Work, Culture, and Society in Industrializing America: Essays in American Working-Class and Social History* (New York, 1976); Alan Dawley, *Class and Community: The Industrial Revolution in Lynn* (Cambridge, Mass., 1979); Sean Wilentz, *Chants Democratic: New York City and the Rise of the American Working Class, 1788–1850* (New York, 1984); Steven J. Ross, *Workers on the Edge: Work, Leisure, and Politics in Industrializing Cincinnati* (New York, 1985); Susan Levine, *Labor's True Woman: Carpet Weavers, Industrialization, and Labor Reform in the Gilded Age* (Philadelphia, 1984), 129–53; and Leon Fink, *Workingmen's Democracy: The Knights of Labor and American Politics* (Urbana, Ill., 1983).

6. Ronald Dworkin, *Law's Empire* (Cambridge, Mass., 1986).

7. Eric Foner, *Tom Paine and Revolutionary America* (New York, 1976); Charles

G. Steffen, *The Mechanics of Baltimore: Workers and Politics in the Age of Revolution, 1763–1812* (Urbana, Ill., 1984), 81–101; Wilentz, *Chants Democratic,* 61–103; Thomas Dublin, *Women at Work: The Transformation of Work and Community at Lowell, Massachusetts, 1826–1860* (New York, 1979).

8. Dawley, *Class and Community,* 80; George E. McNeill, "The Problem of Today," in *The Labor Movement: The Problem of Today,* ed. George E. McNeill (Boston, 1887), 459; Theodore W. Glocker, *The Government of American Trade Unions* (Baltimore, 1913), 140–41, 197, 236–37. Although trade-union constitutionalism may have paralleled, rather than copied, governmental constitutionalism, there were also direct influences, although not entirely one way. Glocker, for example, saw the influence of national political traditions in trade-union respect for representative forms of government and in a "federal" approach to national associations, that is, "federations" of labor. The internal judicial systems of the unions mirrored the hierarchical appeals process from lower to higher authority found in the national institutions. American unions more zealously guarded local sovereignty than their British counterparts. However, American unions experimented with the secret ballot system before its adoption by state and municipal governments, and at the turn of the century, labor unions were among the most active advocates of direct-government reforms such as referendum and recall.

9. Lloyd Ulman, *The Rise of the National Trade Union: The Development and Significance of Its Structure, Governing Institutions, and Economic Policies* (Cambridge, Mass., 1955), 586; Sidney Webb and Beatrice Webb, *Industrial Democracy* (London, 1920), 559–99; John V. Orth, "English Combination Acts of the Eighteenth Century," *Law and History Reviews* 5 (Spring 1987), 175. Jones, *Languages of Class,* 90–178; James Epstein, "The Constitutionalist Idiom: Radical Reasoning, Rhetoric, and Action, 1790–1850," paper delivered to the National Humanities Center, Research Triangle Park, N.C., Sept. 1986 (in Fink's possession). See also E. P. Thompson, *The Making of the English Working Class* (New York, 1964).

10. See Wilentz, *Chants Democratic,* 61–103.

11. Tomlins, *State and the Unions,* 32–33. Nineteenth-century British trade-union structures derived, according to Sidney and Beatrice Webb, directly from friendly societies, which probably borrowed the "spirit of association, clothing itself in more or less similar picturesque forms" from the Freemasons and the Odd Fellows. In the post–Civil War era in the United States, the Noble and Holy Order of the Knights of Labor was only the most successful of numerous secret labor societies that appropriated the structure and ritual of the fraternal orders. Sidney Webb and Beatrice Webb, *The History of Trade Unionism* (London, 1920), 19–20; Charles W. Ferguson, *Fifty Million Brothers: A Panorama of American Lodges and Clubs* (New York, 1937), 175–76. See also, Gutman, *Work, Culture, and Society,* 79–117.

12. J. R. Pole, *The Pursuit of Equality in American History* (Berkeley, Calif., 1978), 147, 358; Morton J. Horwitz, *The Transformation of American Law, 1780–1860* (Cambridge, Mass., 1977).

13. For a review of the early regulation of English labor, see Orth, "English Combination Acts," 176–211. On "idolatry," see Wilentz, *Chants Democratic,* 98.

The case of the New York journeymen cordwainers, 1809, offers an eloquent example of the early skirmishing over core legal and philosophical concepts. The city's master shoe workers had charged trade-union leaders with conspiracy for their part in a general strike aimed at increasing piece rates and controlling access to the trade. The defendants' lawyer, William Sampson, raised the case to epic political principles: "Those who framed the constitution under which we live . . . abrogated all of the common law that should prove in contrariety with the constitution they established. . . . the constitution of this state is founded on the equal rights of man, and whatever is an attack upon those rights is contrary to the constitution. Whether it is or is not an attack upon the rights of man, is, therefore, more fitting to be inquired into, than whether or not it is conformable to the usages of Picts, Romans, Britons, Danes, Jutes, Angles, Saxons, Normans, or other barbarians, who lived in the night of human intelligence." Insisting on a close analysis of the events at hand, the prosecution turned aside the defendants' ideological attack: "certainly, the restriction of illegal combinations to raise the price of articles of necessity, is as congenial to our constitution as any other parts of the common law."

The verdict offered a political victory and a constitutional defeat for the journeymen. They were found guilty of having violated the rights of others but fined only one dollar plus court costs. John R. Commons et al., eds., *A Documentary History of American Industrial Society* (3 vols., Cleveland, 1910), 3:278–79, 318.

14. The Locofocos proposed electing judges for fixed terms and limiting the use of common law precedents in American cases. See Hattam, "Unions and Politics," 109; Tomlins, *State and the Unions*, 43–44. In *Commonwealth* v. *Hunt*, defense counsel Robert Rantoul, Jr., appealed—in the tradition of the early conspiracy cases—for a renunciation of common law labor doctrines: "We might as well be governed by England as to adopt blindly in mass her laws which grow out of her institutions and state of society. Her government is founded upon property. Her laws restraining laborers from interfering with trade sacrificed them to the ruling classes. They are repugnant to the Constitution and to the first principles of freedom." Judge Lemuel Shaw's appeals court decision threw out the defendants' original conviction on conspiracy grounds. While adopting much of Rantoul's argument, Shaw did not preclude further legal action against effective labor organizations. *Commonwealth* v. *Hunt*, 4 Metcalf 111 (Mass., 1842). Walter Nelles, "Commonwealth v. Hunt," *Columbia Law Review* 32 (Nov. 1932), 1145, 1151; Harry H. Wellington, *Labor and the Legal Process* (New Haven, Conn., 1968), 7–13. See also Leonard Williams Levy, *The Law of the Commonwealth and Chief Justice Shaw* (Cambridge, Mass., 1957). William E. Forbath, "The Ambiguities of Free Labor: Labor and the Law in the Gilded Age," *Wisconsin Law Review* (no. 4, 1985), 767–817, esp. 799, elaborates on the intellectual and judicial foundations of the dominant Gilded Age ethic that "individual ownership—of one's capacity to labor in the worker's case, of the (putative) fruits of one's industry in the capitalist's—was the essence of personal right and freedom." On the ambivalence of free-labor ideology embedded in nineteenth-century legal doctrines, see also Brian Greenberg, *Worker and Community: Response to Industrialization in a Nineteenth-Century American City* (Albany, N.Y., 1985), 25–41.

15. On the use of the courts against strikes, see Harry A. Millis and Royal E. Montgomery, *Organized Labor* (New York, 1945), 505–6, 630–31. Both the substance and the procedure of injunction law were stacked against labor. In 118 labor injunction cases in the federal courts between 1901 and 1928, 70 restraining orders were granted on the basis of *ex parte* proceedings, i.e., affidavits from one side without notice to the defendants or even the opportunity to be heard. Wellington, *Labor and the Legal Process,* 39. See ibid., 568–70 on the relative uselessness, or even hostility, to labor of the Sherman and Clayton antitrust acts and the draconian implications of *Loewe* v. *Lawlor* (the Danbury hatters' case), 208 U.S. 274 (1908).

16. For elaboration of the theme of the Knights' republicanism, see Fink, *Workingmen's Democracy,* 3–37. See also Barry H. Goldberg, "Beyond Free Labor: Labor, Socialism, and the Idea of Wage Slavery" (Ph.D. diss., Columbia University, 1979). John Swinton, *Striking for Life: or Labor's Side of the Labor Question* (n.p., 1894), 296. On the changing dimensions of post–Civil War worker republicanism, see Forbath, "Ambiguities of Free Labor," 800–814. *Labor, Its Rights and Wrongs* (Washington, 1886), 204–6.

17. Stuart Bruce Kaufman, "Haymarket and the Federation of Labor," in *Haymarket Scrapbook: A Centennial Anthology, 1886–1986,* ed. Dave Roediger and Franklin Rosemont (Chicago, 1986), 134.

18. George E. McNeill, "Declaration of Principles of the Knights of Labor," in *Labor Movement,* 488–89 (italics added).

19. On the courts' role in Pennsylvania and New York, see Hattam, "Unions and Politics," 133–68. As Hattam demonstrates, such frustration at the hands of the judiciary directly encouraged development of Samuel Gompers's antipolitical, "voluntarist" position. See ibid., 193–201. *In re Debs,* 158 U.S. 564 (1895). Alan Westin, "The Supreme Court, the Populist Movement and the Campaign of 1896," *Journal of Politics* 15 (Feb. 1953), 3–41, esp. 33.

20. Alan Derickson, "Health Programs of the Hard-Rock Miners' Unions, 1891–1925" (Ph.D. diss., University of California, San Francisco, 1986), 36, 37; Henry Demarest Lloyd, "The Safety of the Future Lies in Organised Labor," 13th Convention, AFL, Dec. 1893, *AFL and CIO Pamphlets, 1889–1955* (Westport, Conn., 1977, microfilm), reel 1, item 13.

21. Terence Powderly, *The Path I Trod* (New York, 1968), 55.

22. Ronald L. Filippelli, *Labor in the USA: A History* (New York, 1984), 95.

23. Samuel Gompers, *Seventy Years of Life and Labor: An Autobiography,* ed. Philip Taft and John A. Sessions (New York, 1957), 132. To be sure, in the years after the Danbury hatters' and Buck's Stove cases, the AFL broke with tradition and adopted an energetic legislative program in order to defend its collective bargaining gains from judicial setbacks. Nick Salvatore, "Introduction," in Samuel Gompers, *Seventy Years of Life and Labor: An Autobiography,* ed. Nick Salvatore (Ithaca, N.Y., 1984), xxxiv–xxxvii; *The Buck's Stove and Range Company* v. *The American Federation of Labor,* 36 Washington Law Reporter 822 (1908).

24. James Duncan, "To Purify Our Courts," *American Federationist* 2 (March 1895), 14; George H. Hart to Samuel Gompers, April 16, 1894, *American Federation*

of Labor Records: The Samuel Gompers Era (Sanford, N.C., 1979, microfilm), reel 59, frames 150–59. The reference is courtesy of Stuart Kaufman.

25. Dyer Lum, "Philosophy of Trade Unionism," 1892, *AFL and CIO Pamphlets,* reel 1, item 13; Ken Coates and Tony Topham, *Trade Unions in Britain* (Nottingham, Eng., 1980), 265.

26. Coates and Topham, *Trade Unions in Britain,* 264–91; W. Hamish Fraser, *Trade Unions and Society: Struggle for Acceptance, 1850–1880* (London, 1974), 185–97; Dominic Strinati, *Capitalism: The State and Industrial Relations* (London, 1982), 32–56. The Trade Disputes Act stated categorically: "An action against a trade-union, whether of workmen or masters, or against any members or officials thereof on behalf of themselves and all other members of the trade-union in respect of any tortious act alleged to have been committed by or on behalf of the trade-union shall not be entertained by any court." John P. Frey, *The Labor Injunction: An Exposition of Government by Judicial Conscience and Its Menace* (Cincinnati, [1923]), 24. The problems with legal "immunity" were recognized by some British contemporaries. An official of the Amalgamated Society of Engineers wrote to Sidney Webb in 1903: "Are we to try to get back to ante-Taff Vale [legal immunity]? . . . The best thing for propaganda purposes at present is ante-Taff Vale. But . . . it seems to me that ante-Taff Vale is after all anti-social and but glorified individualism, inasmuch as it seeks to get for groups of men anti-social rights." Some have argued that a tension between trade-union interests and a larger strategy of popular mobilization, a tension reflected in this early legal issue, endured for decades within the British labor movement and is in part to blame for its current crisis. Henry Pelling, *Popular Politics and Society in Late Victorian Britain* (London, 1968), 80–81; see Jones, *Languages of Class,* 239–56.

27. Gompers in 1887 spoke as president of the politically oriented New York State Workingmen's Assembly. Hattam, "Unions and Politics," 168–85. The term "judicial abstention" is drawn from Wellington, *Labor and the Legal Process,* 13–26; Frey, *Labor Injunction,* vii, 21. Gompers favorably cited the British statutes of the 1870s and 1906 before Congress. U.S. Congress, House, Committee on the Judiciary, *Hearing on H.R. 89, A Bill to Limit the Meaning of the Word "Conspiracy" and the Use of Restraining Orders and Injunctions in Certain Cases,* 58 Cong., 2 sess., Jan. 13–March 22, 1904, p. 14; U.S. Congress, House, Committee on the Judiciary, *Hearings on the Pearre Anti-Injunction Bill,* 60 Cong., 1 sess., Feb. 5, 1908, p. 45. Assuming that the civil or equity courts operated to protect property rights, both the Pearre and Wilson bills defined "property" to exclude employer-employee relations—in addition to forbidding the use of the injunction except to prevent irreparable injury to property. The Clayton Act carried no such definition of property. (Section 6 of the act, declaring that "the labor of a human being is not a commodity or article of commerce," proved innocuous in the hands of congressional and judicial interpreters.) While cataloging specific acts immune to injunctions (section 20), it left broad interpretive and definitional powers in the hands of unsympathetic jurists. Thus, in ten of thirteen federal court cases between 1916 and 1920 applying section 20, an injunction was still held a legal remedy. Felix Frankfurter and

Nathan Greene commented on the Clayton Act: "The result justifies an application of a familiar bit of French cynicism: the more things are legislatively changed, the more they remain the same judicially." Felix Frankfurter and Nathan Greene, *The Labor Injunction* (1930; reprint, Gloucester, Mass., 1963), 142–76; James Weinstein, *The Corporate Ideal in the Liberal State, 1900–1918* (Boston, 1968), 78–82.

28. "Legal Rights of Working Men," Opening and Closing Arguments of Thomas Carl Spelling, before the Judiciary Committee of the House of Representatives of the 59th Congress, April 12, May 2, 1906, in *AFL and CIO Pamphlets*, reel 1, item 34, pp. 5, 7, 9–10, 15, 21.

29. Ibid., 28–29.

30. William Green, *Labor and Democracy* (Princeton, N.J., 1939), 96–97; Louis S. Reed, *The Labor Philosophy of Samuel Gompers* (New York, 1968), 96.

31. Frankfurter and Greene, *Labor Injunction,* 52; "Labor and the Courts," statement adopted by the El Paso convention, 1924, *AFL and CIO Pamphlets,* reel 3, item 137; Samuel Gompers, "The Supreme Court at It Again," *American Federationist* 29 (Jan. 1922), 44–48; Samuel Gompers, "Forward, Onward and Upward in 1922," ibid., 44. *Hitchman Coal Company* v. *Mitchell,* 245 U.S. 229 (1917); *Duplex Printing Co.* v. *Deering,* 254 U.S. 443 (1921); Filippelli, *Labor in the USA,* 162.

32. Gompers, "Supreme Court at It Again," 47. See also Samuel Gompers, "5 to 4 on Slavery," *American Federationist* 24 (April 1917), 290.

33. Harry F. Ward, *The Labor Movement: From the Standpoint of Religious Values* (New York, 1917), 170–71; W. B. Rubin, "What Shall Be Done with Judges Who Violate the Constitutional Rights of Labor?" *American Federationist* 23 (Aug. 1916), 664–68.

34. W. B. Rubin, "The Constitution and the Supreme Court," *American Federationist* 29 (Sept. 1922), 675–80; Ernest Crosby, "Jerome and the Judges," ibid., 13 (Feb. 1906), 81. For suggested remedies to judicial antagonism, see Jackson H. Ralston, "Judicial Control over Legislatures as to Constitutional Questions," 1919, *AFL and CIO Pamphlets,* reel 2, item 87. Not surprisingly, organized labor leaped to advocate and defend Franklin D. Roosevelt's court-packing plans in the 1930s. See, for example, William Green "Will Our Constitution Bend—Or Break?" *American Federationist* 43 (Feb. 1936), 135; Victor S. Yarros, "Progress and the Supreme Court," ibid., (June 1936), 616–19; and William Green, "Supreme Court," ibid., 44 (April 1937), 353–54.

35. Tomlins, *State and the Unions,* 77–79; John Mitchell, *Organized Labor: Its Problems, Purposes, and Ideals and the Present and Future of American Wage Earners* (Philadelphia, 1903), 82; Eugene Staley, *History of the Illinois State Federation of Labor* (Chicago, 1930), 268, 281–83, 504.

36. Milton Derber, *The American Idea of Industrial Democracy, 1865–1965* (Urbana, Ill., 1970), 10, 75, 82, 87–91, 118–21; see also Valerie Jean Conner, *The National War Labor Board: Stability, Social Justice, and the Voluntary State in World War I* (Chapel Hill, N.C., 1983).

37. *Schechter Poultry Corporation* v. *United States,* 295 U.S. 495 (1935). Robert F. Wagner, "Introduction," in *The Wagner Act: After Ten Years,* ed. Louis G. Silverberg

(Washington, 1945), 1–2. By reinvigorating section 20 of the Clayton Act in light of the Norris-LaGuardia Act, the Supreme Court effectively cancelled the application of the Sherman Act to trade unions, assuring them an unprecedented immunity from prosecution under the conspiracy and restraint-of-trade doctrines in the course of their normal activities. See *Apex Hosiery Co.* v. *William Leader and American Federation of Full-Fashioned Hosiery Workers,* 310 U.S. 469 (1940) and *Thornhill* v. *Alabama,* 310 U.S. 88 (1940). Irving Bernstein, *The Turbulent Years: A History of the American Worker, 1933–1941* (Boston, 1970), 671–78; Theodore R. Iserman, *Industrial Peace and the Wagner Act: How the Act Works and What to Do about It* (New York, 1947), 20; Charles O. Gregory, *Labor and the Law* (New York, 1946), 376.

38. To escape the fate of the National Industrial Recovery Act, Wagner tied the Wagner Act (NLRA) to the interstate commerce clause of the Constitution, declaring that collective bargaining "promotes the flow of commerce by removing certain recognized sources of industrial strife and unrest." Iserman, *Industrial Peace,* 7–10. In a more recent commentary, Daniel R. Ernst subtly explores the political and legal logic of the framers of key New Deal measures like the Norris-LaGuardia Act and NLRA. Avoiding the formalism of rights rhetoric, already captured by the judicial conservatives, prolabor "legal realists" like Donald Richberg and David Lilienthal opted for sociological and public policy arguments. In effect, they tried a new approach to rescue the public interest from the strangulation of republican rhetoric. Daniel R. Ernst, "His Master's Voice? The Yellow Dog Contract and the League for Industrial Rights," Institute for Legal Studies, University of Wisconsin–Madison, June 1987 (in Fink's possession). Leon H. Keyserling, "Why the Wagner Act," in *Wagner Act,* 5.

39. By 1980, for example, it had become more cost-effective for business to break the law and fire union organizers (paying meager penalties years later) than to respect the legal right to union organizing. Statistically, one in twenty workers who voted (in a National Labor Relations Board election) for a union was fired. Thomas Byrne Edsall, *The New Politics of Inequality* (New York, 1984), 152.

40. Nelson Lichtenstein, *Labor's War at Home: The CIO in World War II* (Cambridge, Eng., 1982), esp. 178–202, 233–45; Tomlins, *State and the Unions,* 99–328, esp. 328. On the enduring intellectual problems entailed in assimilating labor relations to the laws of contract or association, see Philip Selznick, *Law, Society, and Industrial Justice* (New York, 1969), 137–82.

41. *John Herling's Labor Letter,* Oct. 8, 1983 (in Fink's possession).

42. *National Labor Relations Board* v. *Jones and Laughlin Steel Corporation,* 301 U.S. 1 (1937). Such a scenario is implicitly urged by Staughton Lynd, "Beyond 'Labor Relations': 14 Theses on the History of the N.L.R.A. and the Future of the Labor Movement," draft presented at the workshop on Critical Perspectives on the History of American Labor Law, June 10, 1987, Georgetown Law School, Washington, D.C. (in Fink's possession).

43. Unionization rates in metal manufacturing are suggestive here. In 1935, 10.2 percent of production workers were organized; in 1939, 51 percent. David Brody, *Workers in Industrial America: Essays on the Twentieth-Century Struggle* (New York, 1980), 139.

44. For an introduction to the regulation of industrial relations, see the seminal collection by Walter Galenson, ed., *Comparative Labor Movements* (New York, 1952), 378–80, 393–99 (on France); ibid., 284–88, 298–312 (on Germany); ibid., 137–44 (on Scandinavia). See also Gerald Friedman, "The State and the Making of a Working Class: The U.S. and France," paper delivered at the Social Science History Conference, St. Louis, Oct. 1986 (in Fink's possession). H. D. Woods, *Labour Policy in Canada* (New York, 1973), 19–99; F. J. L. Young, ed., *Three Views of the New Zealand System of Industrial Relations: Papers Presented to Members of the American Association of Arbitrators* (Wellington, New Zealand, 1982). If anything, state intervention has been even more automatic in Greece, Italy, Portugal, and Spain; see Howard J. Wiarda, *From Corporatism to Neo-Syndicalism: The State, Organized Labor, and the Changing Industrial Relations Systems of Southern Europe* (Cambridge, Mass., 1981).

45. Thompson, *Whigs and Hunters,* 263; William English Walling, *American Labor and American Democracy* (New York, 1926), 7. Investigations of labor and legal history have, in fact, proved one of the most fertile areas of scholarship. Particularly noteworthy works include the following: William E. Forbath, *Law and the Shaping of the American Labor Movement* (Cambridge, Mass., 1991); Victoria Charlotte Hattam, *Labor Visions and State Power: The Origins of Business Unionism in the United States* (Princeton, N.J., 1993). For overviews of a rich periodical literature, especially that emanating from law journals, see Raymond L. Hogler, "Labor History and Critical Labor Law: An Interdisciplinary Approach to Workers' Control," *Labor History* (Spring 1989), 185–92; and Wythe Holt, "The New American Labor Law History," ibid., 275–93. Were I to seriously rework this essay, I would particularly need to take into account the work of Daniel Ernst, whose investigations of organized employers and labor law tend to challenge the image of the "semi-outlawry" of organized labor by the 1920s presented in my (and Forbath's) work. See, e.g., Ernst, "The Labor Exemption, 1908–1914," *Iowa Law Review* 74 (July 1989), 1151–73; and "Free Labor, the Consumer Interest, and the Law of Industrial Disputes, 1885–1900," *American Journal of Legal History* 36 (January 1992), 19–37.

PART FOUR

Strategic Reinventions
of the American Worker

7

Looking Backward: Reflections on Workers' Culture and Certain Conceptual Dilemmas within Labor History

Strikingly similar themes dominate recent studies of working people on both sides of the Atlantic. Although framed necessarily within a specific national, regional, and local context, labor history scholarship increasingly reveals a common understanding of the logic of collective action, particularly of the cultural currents of working-class life that have operated to sustain or inhibit organized protest. For United States labor historians, recognition of this transatlantic congruence has had a particularly buoyant and liberating effect. The burden of American exceptionalism—the idea that U.S. history was relatively unmarked by the class conflict and class consciousness manifest in Europe, an assumption that tended to belittle the significance of American labor history—has been considerably lightened. The Social Question has been restored to center stage of nineteenth-century American historical investigations, and workers' distinct responses—manifest in community, organization, ideology, or politics—treated with a new subtlety and respect. Such reevaluation of American workers' history has taken place against the backdrop of a conscious if vague awareness that the definitions of European workers' histories were also changing. The new literature, while acknowledging diversity in economic development and political situation, has, in fact, discovered remarkable parallels in labor movements, worker culture, and popular aspirations otherwise separated by geographical distance, national identity, and political autonomy.

It is this common cultural paradigm in the new labor history that I explore here. The triumph of a shared perspective has offered promising opportunities to recast traditionally more insular assumptions within a comparative framework. At the same time, the discipline internationally may now confront both the strengths and weaknesses of its common models of explanation. Some of the most fertile of these basic concepts, for example, hatched as they have been in nineteenth-century studies, are particularly troublesome in dealing with the twentieth century.

One sign of the developing integration of U.S. labor history with trends in Europe is the effective breakdown of any notion of a "regular" or "normal" path of class conflict from which the Americans strayed. Indeed, one might even suggest that as the trumpets of American exceptionalism have been muted, evidences of individual British, German, and French historical exceptionalism or "peculiarities" are flourishing. To be sure, the question of why the United States did not develop a mass labor-based or socialist-oriented political party still provokes scholarly argument. However, in place of Werner Sombart's (or Louis Hartz's or Seymour Martin Lipset's) assumptions about an ideologically concili- ated working class with a consensus culture based on "roast beef and apple pie," speculation today is more likely to turn either on structural anomalies of American business, government, and labor markets or on the difficulties of mobilizing a disaffected but fragmented working class. To put it differently, the question for historians is less why there has been no socialism or class consciousness—questions of political culture—in America than why the considerable labor conflict that took place did not assume a lasting, institutionalized form.[1]

At the same time, the "politicization" (or perhaps more accurately, "state orientation") of the German working classes from which Sombart drew his normative base has, for some time now, drawn historical scru- tiny as the product of peculiarly German (indeed, perhaps more accurately, Prussian) circumstances. Historians now, for example, attribute the early split-off of labor-based radicals from middle-class liberal connections less to natural or inevitable class formation than to the weakness of German liberals, the dependence of German industrial capitalism on state funding, the retardation of national integration, the lack of parliamentary sov- ereignty, and, finally, as a logical response to Bismarck's antisocialist persecutions. German workers (and their unions), ghettoized by a state system but also dependent upon that system for a broad program of social insurance, in the context of the German *Sonderweg*, turned peculiarly but logically to a statist strategy, whether reformist or revolutionary, to deal with their problems.[2]

If the United States and Germany somehow constitute the opposite extremes of political development in the world's Gilded Age, the other two of the big four industrial powers seem hardly to constitute a golden mean. England, the classic first site of the Industrial Revolution, of course, never provided much of a textbook political model. While Chartism, as the world's first mass working-class movement once seemed roughly correlated to socioeconomic development, connections always broke down after the 1840s. One had to wait another half-century for a labor movement with a radical political form and, indeed, considerably longer before one could speak confidently of the Labour party as a major political force. Even such episodic demonstration of class conflict and consciousness, however, draws a skeptical eye from a number of British commentators. Chartism, to begin with, according to Gareth Stedman Jones's reevaluation, was less a class movement than the culmination of eighteenth-century radical political dissent. The very constitutionalist ideals that infused this "people's" movement, according to Jones, obstructed its capacity to confront the industrialist and to take advantage of the positive uses of state power. Patrick Joyce, who focuses explicitly on the factory districts of the later nineteenth century, moreover, finds industrial "paternalism," rather than autonomous worker culture, the norm. He speaks of the "ambivalence of the worker-employer relationship," 1880–1920, rooted in the belief of most workers that the employment situation should be "consensual" in form. The analytic retreat from ascriptions of class solidarity perhaps reaches its apotheosis in Alastair Reid's warning against the notion of any naturally revolutionary working class: "On the contrary defeat is the normal not the abnormal condition of the working class under capitalism, for in the absence of consciously formulated politics and carefully constructed alliances, it is only able spontaneously to sustain temporary sectional revolts." It is seemingly against this sober if not downright pessimistic portrayal of the British working class that Richard Price issued his reemphasis on continuing historical struggles over the labor process and protested the "tendency nowadays to emphasize the internal weaknesses and fractures that make it [i.e., the working class] ultimately impotent against a dominant capital."[3]

Might France then at least qualify as the point of departure for studies of class-based labor movements? Perhaps. France certainly provided the standard scale of European political values in the nineteenth century, offering an ideological identity to conservatives, moderates, and left radicals alike. As Eric Hobsbawm put it, "A tricolor of some kind became the emblem of virtually every emerging nation, and European (or indeed world) politics between 1789 and 1917 were largely the struggle for and against the principles of 1789 or the even more incendiary ones of 1793." The revolutionary consolidation of the French bourgeoisie, unlike the British and German, also self-consciously crystallized political oppositions along lines of social class. Following the Revolution of 1830, according to William Sewell, "the workers created a new type of opposition to the dominant state and society, an opposition that proclaimed the workers' specific identity as laborers, opposed individualism with an ideal of fraternal solidarity, promised an end to the tyranny of private property, and implied the legitimacy of a revolution to achieve these ends. They created, in other words, what would today be called a class-conscious workers' movement." Focusing on the mass strikes of 1890–1914, Michael Hanagan suggests that "there were more politicized worker-militants in France than in either England or the United States."[4]

The problem with the French experience as a way of saving some notion of expected political-ideological response to the Industrial Revolution is that the latter was, in comparative terms, missing. Indeed, E. P. Thompson's categorization of certain eighteenth-century English events as "class struggle without class" might also apply to nineteenth-century French radicalism. France was by far the slowest of the four great Western powers to industrialize (Hanagan called the nineteenth-century economy one of "substantial growth but little fundamental transformation") and remained, according to Bernard Moss, mostly a nation of small workshops until 1900. This paradox of the least industrially developed nation setting the terms of political discourse for "modern industrial" societies generally wreaks havoc with the entire edifice of classical expectation in the relationship of economics and politics, or society and culture. When France is the norm, then not only the Sombartian answer but the question itself is thrown into doubt.[5]

While undermining a pseudocomparative history of national "outcomes," labor history scholarship nevertheless points to some congruities that, more often than not, link North American and European developments. This is particularly true with regard to the sociology and ideology, broadly speaking, of worker movements. By the end of the nineteenth century, for example, Western working-class movements seemed to have passed through two phases of development. The first rested on the organization of skilled workers, artisanal values of production, and republican (or democratic-nationalist) political ideals; the second, on an accommodation to industrial production, recruitment of factory workers, and a break—whether conservative or radical—with republican political tradition. In the United States, I would argue, the first phase spanned roughly the years 1830–90, with a break appearing by the mid-1890s. The 1880s and 1890s, by this schema played out both the highest phase and the disintegration of a social and intellectual formation rooted in the pre–Civil War decades.

In the United States, the coherence of the first phase may be seen to rest on several measures, but the ideological unity of the period is perhaps the most obvious. From journeymen's protests of the 1830s through the Eight-Hour Workday campaigns of 1886, the labor movement made resonant appeal to republican values vested in the American revolutionary settlement itself. These values included an explicit small-producer work ethic, the combination of claims of citizenship and economic value, and an identity of social worth with social utility. Fending off the advocates of unrestricted industrialization in the United States, the Massachusetts shoeworkers' leader Seth Luther, in 1832, was determined "no longer to be deceived by the cry of those who produce *nothing* and who enjoy *all,* and who insultingly term us—the farmers, the mechanics and labourers, the Lower Orders—and exultingly claim our homage for themselves as the Higher Orders—while the Declaration of Independence asserts that 'All Men Are Created Equal.'" William Sylvis, architect and leader of the first national amalgamation of trade unions in the 1860s, would reassert the first principles of a commonsense labor theory of value: "[Labor is] the foundation of the entire political, social, and commercial structure. . . . It is the base upon which the proudest structure of art rests—the leverage which enables man to carry out God's wise purposes." George McNeill, who would draft the preamble to the Knights of Labor constitution, declared "an inevitable and irresistible conflict between the wage system of labor and the republican system of government." As late as 1890, Edward Bellamy spoke for the vast mainstream of labor reform thought in America when he identified himself with the "true conservative party . . . because we are devoted to the maintenance of republican institutions against the revolution now being effected by the money power. We propose no revolution, but that the people shall resist a revolution. We oppose those who are overthrowing the republic. Let no mistake be made here. We are not revolutionists but counter-revolutionists."[6]

Such moral-philosophical claims, to be sure, carried an ambivalent political message, particularly with regard to the operation of markets and the role of government in the regulation of marketplace activity. By defining workers at their existing work as the sinews rather than the victims of society, labor republicanism implied a somewhat restricted, self-administered remedy to be all that was necessary for contemporary social ills. Give workers the minimal resources necessary to sustain their productive activities (e.g., credit, land, the ballot, and cooperatives) and control those parasitic or monopolistic elements that would destroy or hoard society's resources, then civil society could carry on with a minimal state.[7]

The twin emphases on national political traditions and economic associationalism (or workers' self-organization with a minimum of state intervention) were by no means a peculiarly American phenomenon in the nineteenth century. British Chartism's political critique of social problems combined with a minimalist view of government responsibility seems in important respects to have foreshadowed the movement around the Knights of Labor a few decades later. French labor and socialist movements, perhaps as late as 1914, likewise combined elements of republicanism with a social critique based on artisanal craft solidarity and protectiveness. "Trade socialism" or the socialism of skilled workers, which Moss argues defined the nineteenth-century French labor movement, centered on "the belief that workers could only end their exploitation through their acquisition of the means of production and that the form or unit of such acquisition should be the organized body of the trade." Their ideal, argues Moss, represented a "transitional phase" in the history of socialism. "If they accepted some features of industrialism—the concentration of capital, the use of power tools, an increased division of labor—they were aiming to stop the process midway before it destroyed the remaining privileges of the craft." Maurice Agulhon, in his influential study of the Var, first highlighted the integration of artisanal cooperative values and republican thought as the building blocks of French socialism.[8]

It was perhaps not so much the organizational base nor the core ideology of French labor radicals that distinguished them from their American contemporaries but rather a changing *strategy* toward those ends borne of *political* events beyond their control. Thus, a cooperative strategy toward a "social republic," uniting workers with progressive middle-class allies, collapsed, argues Moss, in the open betrayal of labor forces by the "opportunist republicans" of the Third Republic. One result was the revolutionary socialism of Jules Guesde's Parti Ouvrier formed in 1879, a more class-conscious adaptation of the trade socialist idealism and skilled trade constituency of earlier years. Not until the rise of a united Socialist party (SFIO) did political socialism win mass support from French workers, however, and even then, according to Yves Lequin's majesterial work on Lyon, the underlying democratic-nationalist proclivities of the French working class prevailed: "The republican reflex remained the dominant motif of political conduct, in 1914 as in 1848: has it ever ceased to be?"[9]

The German movement, as well, emerged from guild centers of artisans and skilled industrial workers. Even the "German model" of an early and clear split between middle-class and working-class organization and ideology, recent scholarship suggests, was less a function of a radically different consciousness than of national and even regional variations in economic development and state influence. Thus, although the Rheinland, characterized by a relatively early, intense industrialization as well as an authoritarian Prussian state administration, seems to "fit" the national image of class polarization and political socialism (it was here that Ferdinand Lassalle's Allgemeine Deutsche Arbeiter Verein arose in the 1860s), a state like Wurttemburg (or German-Austria as well), with slower economic transformation and a more liberal-democratic constitutional regime, tended to persist in the more republican-oriented labor politics common to France, Britain, Canada, and the United States. It is noteworthy that in his synthetic review of European labor protest, 1848–1939, Dick Geary settled on structural political factors (over cultural or even economic differences) to account for the variations in labor radicalism: "Differing degrees of governmental repression do seem to correlate with levels of working-class radicalism: autocratic Russia produced an unambiguously revolutionary movement, liberal England witnessed strongly reformist labor politics, whilst semi-autocratic Germany gave birth to a working class which was neither uniformly revolutionary nor reformist."[10]

Despite variations in form and strategy, the first phase of modern labor movements was characterized by simultaneous assertion of citizenship rights and of attempts to defend or reassert claims to control over the labor process. Internationally, workers laid claim to the "democratic promise" (whether or not their own governments had democracy in mind) and to a measure of economic and social recognition accruing to their skills (whether or not the marketplace still respected or required their abilities). Such workers, one knows, were not the only ones to take part in contemporary protest, but they stamped the struggle in their image. In their worldview, the self-activity of workers as both producers and citizens was not only important, it was *all* that mattered to set the world right. Hobsbawm has noted that by the mid-nineteenth century, the contending ideologies of social change—liberalism, socialism, communism, anarchism—all posited a kind of "gentle anarchy" as their utopian end. If both aspects of this utopia appeared increasingly irrelevant to labor movements by the turn of the century, traces of the core beliefs remained, perhaps nowhere more steadfast than in the United States.[11]

Within the broad outline of common, Western labor developments, a few assertions about the peculiar strengths and weaknesses of the American movement, at least for discussion's sake, are worth advancing. On the plus side, one wonders whether, within the limits of the first phase of labor movements generally, working-class organization in the United States did not advance further than in any other nation. In particular, a republican aversion to all vested interests and social privilege (as well as awareness of pragmatic necessity in a nation of many peoples) seems to have engendered in the United States a comparatively early and even crusading *universalism* in labor organizing. From the Lynn shoeworkers through the Knights of Labor, *inclusiveness* characterized not only labor ideology but organizing practice during decades in which European movements, by custom if not principle, were still more restricted to craft workers. Jurgen Kocka, for example, has drawn our attention to the hold of *handwerk* (craft) and "journeymen" identity over "class" identity in mid-nineteenth-century Germany. Sewell's study, likewise, suggests the persistency of the older craft estates as both the radical core and the social boundary of the nineteenth-century French movement. My initial reading of the literature suggests no ready European equivalent to the ideological and organizational dynamic that would hoist blacks, women, and the unskilled into the main body of the American labor movement in the 1880s. As a direct consequence, perhaps, no contemporary European labor organization approached the size or influence of the Knights of Labor.[12]

To the extent that this argument is valid, doubt immediately envelops the claim that American society, by its very nature, was peculiarly unsusceptible to polarization by social class. Indeed, it would tend to stand the argument made most clearly by Lipset and Hartz on its head. Instead of "depriving" the culture of a clear-cut model of social divisions (i.e., one that could be readily updated into worker vs. bourgeois antagonisms), the very absence of feudal *staende* (estates) in the United States may have left fewer barriers to organization among the nation's working people.[13]

But the weaknesses of the American republican political culture in building a workers' movement should also be taken into account. Republican ideology offered not only a potentially radical social-political critique but also a badge of merit to be hallowed rather than contested. The eagerness with which immigrant workers, for example, seized on the symbols of the American revolutionary past may have had not only to do with the consonance between U.S. ideals and their own, all-too-often frustrated hopes for democratic self-rule in their home countries but also with the functional uses of republicanism as a ticket of acceptance and legitimacy in their adopted land. Thus, although republicanism undoubtedly possessed a radical cutting edge, it likely acted also as a "civil religion," or form of nationworship, cloaking established political institutions with a sacrosanct untouchability. Of the two (or more) "uses" of republican faith, a number of labor historians (myself included) have been more successful in exploring the radical than the conservative side.

A most useful study, for example, would focus on the successful appeal, circa 1880–1920, of the two major political parties to urban workers; in particular, with what ideological message as well as organizational strategy did the Republican party win the masses away from radical alternatives? One would want to explore, for example, as Nick Salvatore has done so well, not only the roots of Eugene Debs's socialist republicanism but also the limits of its appeal.[14]

One might well recognize the need for a more "Gramscian" (or in American terms, perhaps, "Genovesian") approach to working-class culture; that is, one that seeks a clearer and more careful reading of the distinctions and commonalities of working-class and elite meanings. The extent, as well as the limits, of hegemony might be imaginatively probed not only in studies of politics but also in examinations of popular leisure, religious life, educational experience, and familial expectations. Certainly at the workplace, what Price has called the "relationship between resistance and subordination" might also be more assiduously cultivated.[15]

Despite such deficiencies the new labor history of the nineteenth century has registered one stunning achievement: successfully projecting heretofore invisible working people as conscious historical actors. Evident in a variety of national literatures, this "culturist" thrust has newly defined the ideas, attitudes, and motivation within workers' movements and laboring communities.[16] In generalizing from the literature, one finds two themes paramount in the explanation of workers' collective action: the vanguard role of the craft sector within industrial settings; and, closely related, the "autonomy" of the workers' community. So thoroughly have the twin currents of the defense-of-labor-process and defense-of-community been driven home in studies of labor protest that they may well be said to constitute the central paradigm of the discipline.

In an important sense both aspects of the prevailing wisdom rest on a single insight about the subjectivity of worker movements. Namely, both angles of explanation converge on the *residual* nature of collective action, the ability to draw on the past in confronting the present and future. Thus, skilled workers, or "industrial artisans," when attacked from above, drew on "residual" strengths in the protection of craft or industrial skill and in their inheritance (familial, communal, or intellectual) of a tradition of political activism. This same set of resources seems also to figure in (if only by transference) politicization of semiskilled workers. To take a few prominent examples, just as Alan Dawley's early shoe artisans handed on traditions of equal rights to semiskilled, heavily Irish factory workers, and Yankee farmers passed on notions of independence to their daughters in Thomas Dublin's Lowell mills, so do Daniel Walkowitz's Troy iron molders set the pace for local shirt collar makers and Hanagan's glassworkers in Rive-de-Gier provide the critical sustenance for the town's metalworkers. In each case, skill or the independence of the artisan tradition offer the sources of pride, group identity, and, ultimately, politicization. Artisanal and industrial skill constitute politicization, a kind of lifeline to working-class mobilization, in the sense that those who lose contact with it are likely to perish. Thus, in their comparative community approach, the relatively isolated factory workers in Walkowitz's Cohoes and Hanagan's Saint-Chamond do not generate or sustain the effectiveness of protest evident in settings still influenced by the organizing skills of "threatened artisans."[17]

A similar picture (often linked to the skilled worker paradigm) emerges with respect to community autonomy and labor protest. Organization, the literature suggests, is likely to be strongest where the workers' community attained the most autonomy or relinquished the least control to industrialists. Herbert Gutman's early study of the Tioga and Johnstown County lockouts of 1873–74 perhaps first set the terms for such discussion. The pivotal distinction between the Johnstown workers' defeat and the Tioga workers' successful resistance, according to Gutman, "was neither the stand of the miners nor that of the operators." Rather, "it was the behavior of the non-mining population of Tioga County." An already established community, in short, effectively blocked the path to hegemonic control from above. Since Gutman's seminal local studies, the community as the fulcrum of labor struggles has received heavy emphasis. Two tendencies in this evolving work are worth noting. One is the general tendency to see strength in community autonomy and tradition. Autonomy is often implicitly defined in terms of *distance* from the capitalistic-modernizing "center," whether physical distance, as in Gutman's initial but later-rejected emphasis on the small town, or cultural distance, as in Gutman's analysis of the slave family or others' emphasis on the tenacity of ethnic communalism. The second general tendency is the obverse of the first; that is, to analyze the collapse of mass movements in terms of the destruction of earlier community environments and cultural traditions. The received community, like the traditions of the skilled worker, appears as a lifeline without which labor is unlikely to stir itself. In such terms, for example, John Cumbler contrasted labor strength in Lynn and Fall River, Massachusetts. To quote the reviewer Mike Davis, Lynn's "working class was unified by a highly integrated relationship between leisure, work, and the home. Fall River, on the other hand, lacked such cohesive class-based community institutions, and its workforce was decentralized among relatively isolated work and residential areas." In similar terms, Joyce, in his study of late-Victorian British workers, explains greater radicalization of West Riding versus Lancashire in part on the basis of less-disrupted traditions and community in West Riding, a less pervasive "culture of the factory."[18]

Closely related to the residualist explanations of the capacity of nineteenth-century workers is the theme of the "breakdown" of that capacity. One finds the common threads of this analysis applied first to the turn-of-the-century period but then, episodically, to later decades as well. The break with nineteenth-century conceptualization is ordered on at least two counts. First, the variously labeled ideology of the social republic, labor republicanism, and associationalism universally lost its ability to inspire and direct mass labor movements. In Europe, class-conscious socialism or a more inwardly turned laborism replaced the cross-class peoplehood of an earlier era. Equally, in the United States, the simultaneous rise of big-city political machines (ethnic politics) and business unionism, on the one hand, and a socialist movement, on the other, suggested the passing of labor's identity with radical republicanism or, as older labor historians called it, "reform-minded unionism." In part, this loss of faith in the older message was likely due to the crushing defeats dealt to the instruments that had carried the message forward. It is more than coincidence, I suspect, that the time between the collapse of Chartism and the remobilization of British workers in the New Unionism and Independent Labour politics approximately equals the time span between the disintegration of the Knights of Labor and the rise of successful industrial unionism in the 1930s. Social movements and their regeneration, one might speculate, have a life cycle of their own. As it happens, another analytic thread also seems to connect post-Chartist and post–Knights of Labor eras. The essential critique that each movement made—resting in both cases on ideals of individual rights, artisanal pride in productive work, and attacks on upper-class corruption of the social and political order—must, as Stedman Jones has suggested, have lost a degree of forcefulness over time. If Chartism failed to address the plight of the permanent factory worker, the Knights equally ignored market tendencies toward oligopoly as well as the emergent "managerial revolution." The socialism of the European workers' parties, whatever its intellectual deficiencies, at least took as a starting point the class division (and consequent subordination of labor) that labor republicanism had struggled vainly to transcend. In the United States, disillusionment with the older nobility-of-toil ethic was equally evident in Wobbly "Big Bill" Haywood's admonition "the less work the better" and in Samuel Gompers' advice that "the way out of the wage system is through higher wages."[19]

Ironically, the social changes that accounted for the declining capacities of nineteenth-century workers, resources upon which much labor history has concentrated, also gave birth to the modern industrial working class. Increasingly, we know something of the conditions, the outer trappings, the environment in which that process occurred. Richard Johnson has drawn our attention to the homogeneity and distinctiveness of international working-class culture, "more so 1880–1930 than [in] any period before or after." To the extent that there was ever a classic era of the industrial proletariat, this was it, throwing together (sometimes uniting) skilled industrial tradesmen, semiskilled operatives, and congeries of laborers as well as penny-ante, neighborhood entrepreneurs in concentrated urban-commercial settings. Indeed, the settings themselves (i.e., the spatial and functional differentiation of specific industrial cities) often take on explanatory power of their own for historians of the period. In the United States, social historians have fruitfully concentrated on this changing material environment and on the aggregate profile of an urban working class shaped through a complicated combination of immigrant acculturation, mobility, and labor force segmentation. The work of Harry Braverman, David Montgomery, and David Noble, moreover, has focused attention on the radical redesign of work process undertaken by modern management and workers' efforts by the mass strike to resist or transcend corporate discipline. In the United States, as in Europe, the political chapters of the era—the institutionalization of workers' political parties and national trade unions and the rise of government-sponsored welfare and regulatory measures, followed (selectively) by insurrectionary conflagrations during the war years—are due for more serious historical attention. Forming part of the heritage out of (and to some extent against) which the new labor history took wing, the political history of the "classic" proletariat has yet to undergo systematic reinterpretation.[20]

Whereas the changing parameters of this second (in the United States, post-1890) phase of labor history have not gone unexplored, a peculiar lacuna nevertheless separates twentieth-century studies from those of the earlier period. In particular, the culturalist synthesis exploring the subjectivity of labor mobilization so fertile in nineteenth-century research is largely missing in work on the twentieth century. Indeed, many of the most conceptually arresting works ignore, or at least downplay, worker culture in favor of other emphases, especially the state, legal-administrative forms, economic cycles, and managerial ideology. When invoked at all, reference to a workers' culture in the recent period, so unlike the references to the nineteenth- (or even eighteenth-) century past, is used less to account for *capacity* or *empowerment* than for *somnolence* or *passivity*. Perhaps precisely because of the seeming correspondence of new cultural forces with the absence of a politicized labor movement, the cultural "taming" of the working class carries a long thematic pedigree in the United States. The classic formulation was perhaps that of Robert and Helen Lynds' *Middletown*, which tells us that over the period 1890–1925, a vibrant associational life resting on artisan republican ideals and giving rise to strong Knights of Labor locals succumbed to a consumerism, where "people don't have to think too much" and were satisfied to remain in "the thick blubber of custom that envelops the city's life." Whether the emphasis be on consumerism (as with the Lynds), consumption tied to labor control (as in Antonio Gramsci's notion of "Fordism"), the success of welfare capitalism (David Brody), Americanization from above (Steven Meyer), the "urban trenches" separating work and community experience (Ira Katznelson), community fragmentation (John Cumbler's Fall River; Richard Oestreicher's Detroit), or skill, ethnic, and gender divisions (David Gordon, Richard Edwards, and Michael Reich), the cultural situation of twentieth-century American workers seems to take a sharply downward slide. To be sure, Americans do not suffer alone from this encumbrance: Stedman Jones, likewise, has stressed the privatizing, deradicalizing impact of commercial leisure on late-nineteenth-century London workingmen, and Lequin refers to the "banality of political life and union struggles" in the twentieth-century industrial suburb.[21]

It is ironic, to say the least, that a historiographic tendency that began in the 1960s with great hope of exploring "alternative" and "oppositional" cultural forms should end up in something of a tunnel of twentieth-century pessimism. At one level, of course, the analysis reflects the political realities of the current century against the rosier expectations once projected by some for the working classes. At the same time, the climate of the immediate present likely helps frame the interpretation of the past. Just as the hopes of the later 1960s encouraged the discovery of a "new America" buried in the old, so, perhaps, does the reigning conservatism of the present day produce resignation before the process of cultural "incorporation of America." In Europe, one suspects, a similar gloom gathers around the eclipse of social democratic and laborist experiments.[22]

Aside from such extra-academic influences, however, I suggest that a certain analytic hurdle also bars the path to a cultural explanation of modern worker movements. In one sense the very insights of the residualist perspective as applied to the earlier period may be part of the problem. An overemphasis on roots, sources, and tradition blinds us to the dynamic and creative contributions within worker culture. Looking backward for the cultural bases of collective action, we tend to enshrine a preindustrial, artisanal, worker-controlled, or community-centered past and villify the impact of cultural as well as economic disruptions.

There is, in short, a danger of a blanket antimodernism in our approach as labor historians to cultural process. By focusing on workers' culture almost exclusively through traditions, origins, and inheritances, workers themselves become "traditionalists," threatened by what is new and changing around them. On balance, it is not surprising that at least two attempts to generalize from the new labor history build their arguments (albeit from quite different political angles) around the virtues of tradition. Craig Calhoun (who might be considered a "left" residualist) makes use of the concepts of the "radicalism of tradition" and "reactionary radicals" to account for capacities of mobilization among artisans and peasants that seem to have dried up in modern times. In a thoughtful review of the literature on collective action, he concludes that "traditional communities" "give their members the social strength with which to wage protracted battles, the 'selective inducements' with which to ensure full collective participation, and a sense of what to fight for that is at once shared and radical. This sets traditional communities apart from the modern working class." If Calhoun's conclusions point to what he considers the inevitably changed forms of working-class movements (i.e., from popular insurgency to organized, bureaucratic reformism), Aileen Kraditor (by contrast, a "right" residualist) views much of the same literature in *The Radical Persuasion* as proof of the irrelevance altogether for workers of radical social movements. Celebrating the traditional, familial, and ethnic-centered communities she finds described in the literature, Kraditor sees little indigenous impetus (or need) for change. Socialist agitation, in particular, is presented as an alien, unwelcome, and unnecessary incursion on traditional norms. If few labor historians would adopt either generalization, they should perhaps be more aware of the logical implications of their arguments.[23]

Current working assumptions leave us with no satisfactory view of workers' consciousness and culture in an age of mass production and mass consumption, except for what we can borrow from earlier constellations. There exists, to be sure, a suggestive literature on "mass culture," but it is far stronger as social critique than as social history. Without exploration of popular responses to centrally produced products and images or of the relation of social movements to mass commercial culture, we are prone to fall back on rather schematic generalizations. Stuart Hall has offered a pointed comment on the problem in relation to modern British history:

> One of the main differences standing in the way of a proper periodisation of popular culture is the profound transformation in the culture of the popular classes which occurs between the 1880s and the 1920s.... Without in any way casting aspersions on the important historical work which has been done and remains to do on earlier periods, I do believe that many of the real difficulties

(theoretical as well as empirical) will only be confronted when we begin to examine closely popular culture in a period which begins to resemble our own. . . . I am dubious about that kind of interest in "popular culture" which comes to a sudden and unexpected halt at roughly the same point as the decline of Chartism. It isn't by chance that very few of us are working in popular culture in the 1930s. . . . From the viewpoint of a purely "heroic" or "autonomous" popular culture, the 1930s is a pretty barren period.[24]

It is no wonder that labor historians, who dispatch with early nineteenth-century and even eighteenth-century lower-class worlds with increasing confidence, seem positively uncomfortable in pushing cultural analysis, except most selectively, past the late nineteenth century. The most subtle studies of twentieth-century American workers (e.g., Montgomery, Brody, Ronald Schatz, and Nelson Lichtenstein) largely eschew the cultural interests in consciousness, community, and identity of much of "first phase" labor history. Exceptions like John Bodnar's *Immigration and Industrialization* and David Corbin's *Life, Work, and Rebellion in the Coal Fields* choose subjects where the strengths of the residual perspective continue to be applied with skill. The difficulties inherent in transporting the standing culturalist categories forward in time, however, are evident in one of the few "new histories" of the 1930s. Although providing a fascinating description of rank-and-file mobilization, Peter Friedlander's *Emergence of a UAW Local, 1936–1939* is hobbled by its explanatory reduction of culture to ethnic origins and of actors to character types. Why, in principle, is it easier for us to assess the world of the New York journeyman mechanic in 1830 than that of the Schenectady electrical worker or the Detroit wildcat striker of the 1940s? Can it be in part that the cultural apparatus at our disposal—with its tight-knit communities, ethnic neighborhoods, moral codes, and skilled-worker republicanism—no longer fits but, except for notions of mass embourgeoisement and depoliticization, we have little to put in its place?[25]

A residualist focus on traditional culture at odds with a modernizing reordering of daily life will no doubt continue to offer a useful framework for the study of working-class collective action. So, too, the critique of mass culture may continue to guide us toward some of the explanations for popular apathy and inertia in our century. At the same time, a few straws in the wind (and others waiting to be rustled) point in another direction. It is the direction of culture (and consciousness) in the making rather than on the run. The objects of possible focus, either in a national or a comparative context, are numerous. One obvious subject is the rise of mass leisure, the historical concomitants of which surely are not restricted to social control, general stupefaction, and the evaporation of class consciousness. Another subject surely in need of revision is an assessment of government's expanded role in industrial relations and social welfare. The reigning paradigm, concentrating on an era of comparative workers' autonomy, tends to stop at the water's edge of "state" intervention. While seizing readily on the grim consequences of state reform for plebeian culture and labor's general room to maneuver, we have not gone far toward exploring the inner tensions within and between politics, government administration, the labor movement, and workers' culture. Institutions of mass socialization—including schooling, military service, and public health programs—likely also deserve fresh scrutiny. Even the skilled male worker, whose "demise" forms the backdrop to so much discussion of twentieth-century labor history, might reenter the picture from new angles. As Bernard Sternsher suggests in a review essay, skilled workers have too often been placed in a backward-looking framework, linking them to their artisan antecedents, summoning up the "deskilling" paradigm of the skilled worker as dying breed, and reinforcing the resistance-followed-by-decline-and-fall plot structure of labor history. He suggests that by the training involved in the mastery of their craft, skilled industrial workers possessed not only economic ancestors but progeny among a latter-day educated, technical elite. One might ask, as well, whether the artisanal work ethic had any historical relationship to the "culture of professionalism" and "middle-class" occupational self-definitions of the twentieth century's rising white-collar sectors, which are normally treated as entirely distinct subjects.[26]

As a sign of the interpretive possibilities available within a more modernist framework, let us concentrate on the rise of commercial mass culture. Joyce offers some tantalizing leads in referring (at the very end of his book) to a transformation from "status" to "class" politics (including the emergence of the Labour party). The breakdown of factory, paternal culture he attributes in part to the fact that the "scope of peoples' lives grew larger." Commercialization pierced an old order of ritual life and set expectations. Not only the growth of cities but travel through and out of them affected worker consciousness. So, too, did the breakup of family firms and often sudden imposition of more instrumental management. Finally, the rise of women's employment outside the home, argues Joyce, also helped to erode an earlier nexus of authority relations that ran from community patriarchs down through workers' families. If Joyce points to the liberating influence of late-nineteenth-century commercial forms on earlier provincial and status divisions among workers, two essays by Hobsbawm set further guideposts toward understanding modern working-class culture. Although continually disappointing Labour's "elite of militants," the discreet way of life that developed between the 1880s and the early 1950s was rooted in "us" versus "them" antimonies generated both at work and away from work. One reading of Hobsbawm's material analysis of working-class life would stress the very *imperfect* absorbtion of workers into consumer capitalism as an essential starting point for under-standing twentieth-century class conflicts.[27]

That the radical political edge of working-class life depended as much on the forces of cultural modernism and breakdown as on instincts toward tradition and preservation is apparent in other ways in the literature. Bob Holton's work on British syndicalism, for example, stresses the seeds of foreign ideas planted among the miners of South Wales, as when James Connolly returned from the United States by 1910 a sworn Wobbly. Schatz's emphasis on a vanguard of families possessing "union traditions" in the organization of American electrical workers in the 1930s and 1940s is also relevant. Although mostly "highly skilled men . . . who were in their forties and fifties, had families, and were well-established in the community," this unionizing leadership, as secularists or Catholic anti-clericalists who "nearly all belonged to the C.P. or the International Workers Order" were also cultural nonconformists. Moreover, as Alice Kessler-Harris suggests for an earlier period, the women among unioniz-ing pioneers openly broke with their families, came from nontraditional families (e.g., were divorced, lived with an aunt, etc.), or grew up in the special "union tradition," minority cohort.[28]

The invocation of women's roles in the labor movement, in fact, more generally summons up an alternative approach to cultural process than the one most commonly adopted by labor historians. In women's history, it appears, the cultural focus has often been inverse to that of the new labor history. Because the traditional, autonomous ideals of male culture (including but not limited to the working class) served to mask and mystify the reality of female experience, feminist historians have long adopted a more ambivalent and skeptical attitude toward the received culture and likewise a more optimistic view of post-Victorian possibility. A classic work like Sara Evans's *Personal Politics,* for example, sets for its task the exploration of "new" consciousness and how such cultural trans-formation occurs in the course of a specific set of lived experiences.[29]

Much research on working-class women likewise tends to challenge assumptions within traditional worker culture and to welcome evidence of cultural reordering from modernist impulses. While Mary H. Blewett's study of New England shoemakers, for instance, argues that gender-based divisions within artisan ideology effectively "cut women off" from traditions of collective action, other studies by Susan Porter Benson, Patricia A. Cooper, and Dorothy Sue Cobble point to the mutability of concepts like "skill" and "work culture." In the latter works, women workers in new or traditionally "unskilled" jobs are seen to create parallel mechanisms of craft control and group pride to those of traditionally skilled male workers. Women's historians have also explored cultural change beyond the workplace. Despite the harshness of industrial New York in the antebellum years, Christine Stansell discovers a "dialectic of female vice and female virtue," where in the "ebb and flow of large oppressions and small freedoms, poor women traced out unforeseen possibilities for their sex." Likewise, exploring the impact of commercial culture on the once "homosocial" world of working-class leisure, Kathy Peiss leaves open the question of whether consumerism "diverted working women from their class interests or heightened expectations of the 'good life' in such a way as to encourage collective action and unionization." Perhaps Jacquelyn Hall's study of the 1929 Elizabethton strike offers the most subtle accounting to date of traditionalist and modernist influences on an episode of labor protest. On the one hand, old communities of creek-bed farmers stood fast behind the strikers. On the other hand, young women were particularly prominent in the disturbances "perhaps because the peer culture and increased independence encouraged by factory labor stirred boldness and inspired experimentation." Emphasizing the "dynamic quality of working-class women's culture," Hall characterizes the Elizabethton stalwarts as " 'new women,' making their way in a world their mothers could not have known but carrying with them values handed down through the female line."[30]

While not yet fully integrating workers' industrial and political history with the worlds of popular culture and leisure, several works in twentieth-century American cultural history suggest some revisionist openings. While Pittsburgh's passage from the nineteenth-century Craftsmen's Empire to the early-twentieth-century Steel City clearly represents for the historian Francis Couvares a loss of working-class power and control, it is not an unambivalent descent into doom. Couvares describes a dignity carved out in the midst of an "unconsolidated" mass culture, a way of life created "by alternately retreating into ethnic enclaves and foraying into the still-marginal world of the free and easy." Coping as best they could amid "the massed power of corporate capital," the pre-1919 worker generation is usefully located by Couvares between their "plebeian predecessors" who "could . . . count on the [integrating] power of a local culture" and their "successors in the thirties" who partook in a "wider culture" that could affirm "a pluralistic version of American nationality." It was during this difficult interlude, notes Couvares, that "the terse aggressiveness of a Honus Wagner [Pittsburgh Pirate baseball star of immigrant origins] and subversive autonomy of a Charlie Chaplin" came to mean "something special to their working-class audiences," and when, "cultivating a realm of spontaneity and drama within a framework of subordination and tedium, . . . commercial amusements won mass audiences before they won the compliment of elite criticism."[31]

If American workers through the 1920s made use of mass culture largely in a defensive and nonpolitical way, their very assimilation of common forms of communication, socialization, and technological innovation may ultimately have carried considerable political meaning. Roy Rosenzweig notes that the rise of dance halls and amusement places led in the 1920s both to "embourgeoisement" and to "countervailing forces" catalyzed by the breakdown of an inwardly turned, ethnic workers' culture: "Workers who had spent their time in the movie theater in the 1920s might find their way to the union hall in the 1930s and 1940s, as they sought to achieve what the movies promised but the larger society failed to deliver and as they became increasingly able to make common cause with workers from different ethnic and religious groups." Labor activists in the Southern Piedmont similarly took hope from the cultural changes of the 1920s. Hall, Robert Korstad, and James Leloudis, in a sweeping restatement of southern textile workers' history, acknowledge a cultural component behind the strike wave of the late 1920s and early 1930s. Higher wages, greater literacy tied to compulsory education, newspapers and magazines, and, "perhaps most important," the advent of radio and its projection of their own popular music instilled pride and the expectation of "better times ahead" within a generation that came of age after World War I. The pent-up hopes and aspirations of this regional culture were ultimately manifest in mass strikes and demonstrations, campaigns in which "automobile caravans" spread walkouts from town to town.[32]

The accent laid here on the positive potential for labor of twentieth-century cultural change is offered in a provisional and tentative way. I mean neither to discount the "degradation of labor" thesis nor to deny the relevancy of other, equally sobering and "critical" interpretations of cultural transformation. I certainly do not want to initiate a new labor history whiggism based on workers' expanded access to technology, prosperity, and Mickey Mouse. I do think that investigations of the carving out of room to maneuver in "modern" times, however halting and defused such efforts may have been, require a closer and more nuanced look than we have seen to date. Whether out of such efforts anything like a revised culturalist synthesis will emerge, and whether any such approach could offer a useful comparative index for workers' history across the dislocations of depression, war, and the determinacy of political events, are questions for the future.

If I have raised an implicit criticism of the so-called culturist thrust in recent labor history it is obviously from a different basis than that of several other critics. The return to an institutional or economic focus counseled by some, and the search for a more thorough-going class analysis encompassing the study of domination as well as resistance advanced by others, strike me as healthy signs of pluralism within the field. I should hope, however, that in this unquiet young adulthood of the new labor history we will not fail to advance our work in areas that have already seen major breakthroughs. It is worth remembering, as Johnson has noted, that the "second great era of working-class history" (an era highlighted by Thompson's work in Britain and Gutman's in America) constituted a "rediscovery of class through culture."[33] In North America, consensus history was punctured by the study of consciousness, and from consciousness and revised understandings of a diverse culture, conflict in American history was given new meaning. Far from a flight from class analysis, the so-called culturalists threw open a door nailed shut by conservatives, consensus liberals, and corporate liberal critics alike, making class conflict (as well as other social divisions) again worthy of study. Based on this foundation, there are now real opportunities for comparative studies of class formation, labor movements, and popular cultures. For labor historians, the study of culture always begins with the study of possibility, with the assumption that there is "life below." Rather than bring down the final curtain on culturalism, let us instead have the second act.

NOTES

This essay originally appeared in Alice Kessler-Harris and J. Carroll Moody, eds., *Perspectives on American Labor History: The Problem of Synthesis* (DeKalb, Ill., 1989), 5–29. The ideas for this essay emerged from a Fulbright year of teaching at the Amerika-Institut of the University of Munich, West Germany. I should like in particular to acknowledge the influence of two seminars in which I collaborated with German colleagues: one on the rise of mass culture, with Berndt Ostendorf, director of the Amerika-Institut; the other on comparative labor history, with Irmgaard Steinisch of the Institut für Neurere Geschichte. An early version of the essay was presented as a comment at the International Conference on Critical Theories of Society and Culture, Center for North American Studies and Research, University of Frankfurt (Main), June 18–23, 1984. For helpful comments and suggestions along the way to the DeKalb conference, I would like to thank Hartmut Keil, Daniel Rodgers, Susan Levine, James Epstein, and Donald Reid. In revising the DeKalb draft of the essay, I have profited especially from the counsel of Geoff Eley, James Epstein, James Leloudis, and Donald Reid, and also from the encouragement, just before his untimely death, of Warren Susman. In preparing the essay, I am aware that the literature has proceeded beyond issues I discussed at the conference. The central challenge of my remarks, however, I believe is still relevant. With one exception, therefore, I have maintained the basic integrity of the original presentation, while offering a few historiographic updates in the notes.

1. John H. M. Laslett and Seymour Martin Lipset, *Failure of a Dream? Essays in the History of American Socialism* (Berkeley, Calif., 1984); Louis Hartz, *The Liberal Tradition in America* (New York, 1955); see, e.g., David Montgomery's report on the Why No Socialism in America Conference, *International Labor and Working-Class History* 24 (Fall 1983), 67–70; Eric Foner, "Why Is There No Socialism in the US?" *History Workshop* 17 (Spring 1984), 57–80; and Sean Wilentz, "Against Exceptionalism: Class Consciousness and the American Labor Movement, 1790–1920," *International Labor and Working-Class History* 26 (Fall 1984), 1–24.

2. Jurgen Kocka, "Die Trennung von burgerlicher und proletarischer Demokratie im europaischen Vergleich. Fragestellungen und Ergebnisse," in Kocka, ed., *Europaische Arbeiterbewegungen im 19. Jahrhundert* (Gottingen, 1983), 5–20. David Blackbourn and Geoff Eley's revisionist *The Peculiarities of the German History: Bourgeois Society and Politics in Nineteenth-Century Germany* (Oxford, 1984), while challenging the conventional *Sonderweg* thesis, does so, it is worth noting, not in the name of establishing a new model of social-political development but rather by exploring expectations for historical ideal types upon which exceptionalism or *Sonderweg* theories are built: "In order to have an aberration, it is clearly necessary to have a norm. . . . [Historians] should not speak of German peculiarity but of British, French, and German *particularities*" (pp. 10, 154).

3. Gareth Stedman Jones, *Languages of Class: Studies in English Working-Class History, 1832–1982* (Cambridge, Eng., 1983), 90–178; Patrick Joyce, *Work, Society and Politics: The Culture of the Factory in Late Victorian England* (New Brunswick, N.J., 1980); "Labour, Capital, and Compromise: A Response to Richard Price," *Social History* 9 (January 1984), 70–71; Alastair Reid, "Politics and Economics in the Formation of the British Working Class: A Response to H. F. Moorhouse," *Social History* 3 (October 1978), 361; Richard Price, "The Labour Process and Labour History," *Social History* 8 (January 1983), 72. See also Sidney Pollard, "England: Der unrevolutionare Pionier," in Kocka, *Europaische Arbeiterbewegungen,* 21–38; and Ross McKibbin, "Why Was There No Marxism in Great Britain?" *English Historical Review* 99 (1984), 297–331. On Jones's thesis, see also the provocative critique by James Epstein, "Rethinking the Categories of Working-Class History," *Labour/Le Travail* 18 (Fall 1986), 195–208.

4. Eric Hobsbawm, *Age of Revolution* (London, 1975), 53; William Sewell, *Work and Revolution in France: The Language of Labor From the Old Regime to 1848* (New York, 1980), 282. Michael P. Hanagan, *The Logic of Solidarity: Artisans and Industrial Workers in Three French Towns, 1871–1914* (Urbana, Ill., 1983), 24–25.

5. Edward P. Thompson, "Eighteenth-Century English Society: Class Struggle without Class?" *Social History* 3 (May 1978), 133–65, esp. 148–49; Hanagan, *Logic of Solidarity,* p. 6; Bernard Moss, *The Origins of the French Labor Movement 1830–1914: The Socialism of Skilled Workers* (Berkeley, Calif., 1976), 156–58; see also Ronald Aminzade, "Reinterpreting Capitalist Industrialization: A Study of

Nineteenth-Century France," *Social History* 9 (October 1984), 329–50. For an exemplary, and reinforcing, treatment of this general theme, see Aristide R. Zolberg, "How Many Exceptionalisms?" in Ira Katznelson and Zolberg, eds., *Working-Class Formation* (Princeton, N.J., 1986), 397–456.

6. "An Address to the Working-Men of New England . . . " Boston, 1832 (unpublished document, courtesy Herbert Gutman); Daniel T. Rodgers, *The Work Ethic in Industrial America* (Chicago, 1978), 175; George McNeill, *The Labor Movement: The Problem of Today* (Boston, 1887), 459; John L. Thomas, *Alternative America: Henry George, Edward Bellamy, Henry Demarest Lloyd and the Adversary Tradition* (Cambridge, Mass., 1983), 274–75.

7. See, generally, Leon Fink, *Workingmen's Democracy* (Urbana, Ill., 1983), 18–37.

8. Moss, *Origins of the French Labor Movement,* 156, 160; Maurice Agulhon, *Une Ville ouvriere au temps du socialisme Utopicque: Toulon de 1815 a 1851* (Paris, 1970). For his overview of French historiography, I am indebted to Donald Reid's paper "Local History and Labor History in France," Southern Historical Association meeting, Houston, November 1985.

9. Moss, *Origins of the French Labor Movement,* 73; Dick Geary, *European Labour Protest, 1848–1939* (London, 1981), 48; Yves Lequin, *Les Ouvriers de la région lyonnaise (1848–1914)* (Lyon, 1977).

10. See Dieter Dowe, "Deutschland: Das Rheinland und Wurttemberg im Vergleich," in Kocka, *Europaische Arbeitbewegungen,* 77–105; Helmut Konrad, "Deutsch-Osterreich: Gebremste Klassenbildung und importierte Arbeiterbewegung im Vielvolkerstaat," in ibid., 106–28; Geary, *European Labor Protest,* 63.

11. Lawrence Goodwyn, *Democratic Promise: The Populist Moment in America* (New York, 1976); Geary, *European Labor Protest,* 70–80; Hobsbawm, *Age of Revolution,* 243.

12. See Alan Dawley, *Class and Community* (Cambridge, Eng., 1976); Paul Faler, *Mechanics and Manufacturers in the Early Industrial Revolution* (Albany, N.Y., 1981); Geary, *European Labor Protest;* Jurgen Kocka, *Lohnarbeit und Klassenbildung: Arbeiter und Arbeiterbewegung in Deutschland, 1800–1875* (Berlin and Bonn, 1983), 134–37. See also, Barrington Moore, Jr., *Injustice, the Social Bases of Obedience and Revolt* (New York, 1978), esp. 185–90; Sewell, 154–61, 211–18. Cf., e.g., Fink, *Workingmen's Democracy* (Urbana, Ill., 1983), 220–25; Richmond, Virginia, Knights' call for a movement "irrespective of party, color or social standing," p. 157; Paul Krause, "Labor Republicanism and 'Za Chlebom': Anglo-American and Slavic Solidarity in Homestead," in Dirk Hoerder, ed., *"Struggle a Hard Battle": Essays on Working-Class Immigrants* (DeKalb, Ill., 1986), 143–69, esp. the call for an "amalgamation" of laborers regardless of "creed, color or race"; and Susan B. Levine, *Labor's True Woman: Carpet Weavers, Industrialization, and Labor Reform in the Gilded Age* (Philadelphia, 1984).

13. See, e.g., Seymour Martin Lipset, "Radicalism or Reformism: The Sources of Working Class Politics," *American Political Science Review* 77 (1983), 1–18; Hartz, *Liberal Tradition.*

14. Cf., e.g., Bruce Carlan Levine, "Free Soil, Free Labor, and Freimanner:

German Chicago in the Civil War Era," in Hartmut Keil and John Jentz, eds., *German Workers in Industrial Chicago, 1850–1910* (DeKalb, Ill., 1983), 163–82; Elise Marienstras, "State-building and Civil Religion in the Revolutionary Era" (ms., 1984); Nick Salvatore, *Eugene V. Debs: Citizens and Socialist* (Urbana, Ill., 1982).

15. See esp. Eugene D. Genovese, *Roll, Jordan, Roll: The World the Slaves Made* (New York, 1976). Cf. Geoff Eley and Keith Nield, "Why Does Social History Ignore Politics?" *Social History* 5 (May 1980), 249–71; Bryan Palmer's review of *Eight Hours for What We Will* and *The Remaking of Pittsburgh* in *Social History* 10 (October 1985), 400–404; Price, "Labour Process," 62. For illustrative histories of education, see David John Hogan, *Class and Reform: School and Society in Chicago, 1880–1930* (Philadelphia, 1985), and Julia Wrigley, *Class Politics and Public Schools: Chicago, 1900–1950* (New Brunswick, N.J., 1982).

16. I am adopting Richard Johnson's term here but "Americanizing" it, giving it a looser, more pluralistic set of references. See "Edward Thompson, Eugene Genovese, and Socialist-Humanist History," *History Workshop* 6 (Autumn 1978), 79–100.

17. Dawley, *Class and Community*, 148, 177, 248–49; Thomas Dublin, *Women at Work: The Transformation of Work and Community in Lowell, Massachusetts, 1826–1860* (New York, 1979), 86–107; Daniel Walkowitz, *Worker City, Company Town: Iron and Cotton-Worker Protest in Troy and Cohoes, New York, 1855–84* (Urbana, Ill., 1978), 249–50, 252; Hanagan, *Logic of Solidarity*, 209–17.

18. *Work, Culture and Society in Industrializing America* (New York, 1976), 321–43, quotation 340; "The Worker's Search for Power: Labor in the Gilded Age," in H. Wayne Morgan, ed., *The Gilded Age: A Reappraisal* (Syracuse, N.Y., 1963), 38–68; *The Black Family in Slavery and Freedom, 1750–1925* (New York, 1976). Cf. the author's comments in "A Symposium on Gutman's *The Black Family*," in *Radical History Review* 4 (Spring-Summer 1977), 77. Reference to Cumbler's *Working-Class Community in Industrial America* in "Why the U.S. Working Class Is Different?" *New Left Review* 123 (September-October 1980), 3–44; Joyce, *Work, Society, and Politics*, esp. 201–39, 331.

19. See Gerald N. Grob, *Workers and Utopia* (Chicago, 1969), 3–10; Stedman Jones, *Languages of Class;* Joyce, *Work, Society, and Politics*, 313–14; Rodgers, *Work Ethic*, 156; Alan Trachtenberg, *The Incorporation of America: Culture and Society in the Gilded Age* (New York, 1982), 95.

20. John Clarke, Charles Critcher, and Richard Johnson, eds., *Working-Class Culture: Studies in History and Theory* (London, 1979), 235. On U.S. workers in the industrial city, see, e.g., Keil and Jentz, *German Workers*, 163–82, and Oliver Zunz, *The Changing Face of Inequality: Urbanization, Industrial Development, and Immigrants in Detroit, 1890–1920* (Chicago, 1982). For a comparative perspective on urban community and worker protest, see James E. Cronin, "Labor Insurgency and Class Formation," in Cronin and Carmen Sirianni, eds., *Work, Community, and Power* (Philadelphia, 1983); Harry Braverman, *Labor and Monopoly Capital* (New York, 1974); David Montgomery, *Workers' Control in America: Studies in the History of Work, Technology and Labor Struggles* (New York, 1979); David Noble, *America by Design* (New York, 1977). Cf. Geoff Eley, "Combining Two Histories: The SPD

and the German Working Class Before 1914," *Radical History Review* 28–30 (1984), 13–44.

Fortunately, several contributions have substantially enhanced our understanding of workers' social and political history for this period. For the United States the most important is David Montgomery, *The Fall of the House of Labor: The Workplace, the State, and American Labor Activism, 1865–1925* (New York, 1987). For Britain, see David Howell, *British Workers and the Independent Labour Party, 1888–1906* (Dover, N.H., 1984); Richard Price, *Labour in British Society: An Interpretive History* (Dover, N.H., 1986); and James E. Cronin, *Labour and Society in Britain, 1918–1979* (London, 1984). For rare comparative insight, see Jeffrey Haydu, *Between Craft and Class: Skilled Workers and Factory Politics in the United States and Britain, 1890–1922* (Berkeley, Calif., 1988). For France, a major work establishing the twentieth-century terrain is Lenard R. Berlanstein, *The Working People of Paris, 1871–1914* (Baltimore, 1985). On the "re-making" of the French working class, see Gerard Noiriel, *Longwy: Immigrés et Prolétaires, 1880–1980* (Paris, 1984). Among German labor-political studies, Mary Nolan, *Social Democracy and Society: Working Class Radicalism in Dusseldorf, 1890–1920* (New York, 1981), is exemplary.

21. *Middletown* quotation in Richard Wightman Fox, "Epitaph for Middletown," in Fox and T. Jackson Lears, eds., *The Culture of Consumption* (New York, 1983), 103–41, esp. 135; Antonio Gramsci, *Selections from the Prison Notebooks* (New York, 1972); David Brody, *Workers in Industrial America: Essays on the Twentieth-Century Struggle* (New York, 1980); Steven Meyer, *The Five-Dollar Day: Labor, Management and Social Control in the Ford Motor Company, 1908–1921* (Albany, N.Y., 1981); Ira Katznelson, *City Trenches: Urban Politics and the Patterning of Class in the United States* (New York, 1981); Richard Oestreicher, "Industrialization, Class, and Competing Cultural Systems: Detroit Workers, 1875–1900," in Keil and Jentz, *German Workers*, 52–69; John Cumbler, *Working Class Community in Industrial America* (Westport, Conn., 1979); David Gordon, Richard Edwards, and Michael Reich, *Segmented Work, Divided Workers* (New York, 1982). See Geary, *European Labor Protest*, 111–15; Gareth Stedman Jones, "Working-Class Culture and Working-Class Politics in London, 1870–1900: Notes on the Remaking of a Working Class," *Journal of Social History* 7 (Summer 1974), 460–508. Yves Lequin, "Social Structures and Shared Beliefs . . ." *International Labor and Working-Class History* 22 (Fall 1982), 8–12. Among the most stimulating (but non-culture-centered) works are: Gordon, Edwards, and Reich, *Segmented Work, Divided Workers;* Christopher L. Tomlins, *The State and the Unions: Labor Relations, Law, and the Organized Labor Movement in America, 1880–1960* (New York, 1985); Victoria C. Hattam, "Unions and Politics: The Courts and American Labor, 1806–1896," (Ph.D. diss., MIT, 1987); Sanford M. Jacoby, *Employing Bureaucracy: Managers, Unions, and the Transformation of Work in American Industry, 1900–1945* (New York, 1985). Similarly, for France, see Donald Reid, *The Miners of Decazeville: A Genealogy of Deindustrialization* (Cambridge, Mass., 1985) and Luc Bultanski, *Les Cadres: La formation d'un groupe sociale* (Paris, 1982). In contrast to the prevailing trends, one work is noteworthy for addressing the culture question in a "positive" way: Vernon L. Lidtke, *The Alternative Culture: Socialist Labor in Imperial Germany* (New York, 1985).

22. James Weinstein and David W. Eakins, eds., *For a New America* (New York, 1970); Trachtenberg, *Incorporation of America*. See also the Perry Anderson–Marshall Berman encounter, "Modernity and Revolution" and "The Signs in the Streets," *New Left Review* 144 (March-April 1984), 96–123.

23. Craig Calhoun, "The Radicalism of Tradition," *American Journal of Sociology* 88 (March 1983), 886–914, quotation 900. See also *The Question of Class Struggle* (Chicago, 1981); Aileen Kraditor *The Radical Persuasion, 1890–1917: Aspects of the Intellectual History and the Historiography of Three American Radical Organizations* (Baton Rouge, 1981), esp. 55–85. See also Fink, "My Dinner with Aileen," *The Nation* 236 (June 18, 1983), 770–73. For distinct and original variations on the theme of tradition within workers' culture and (at least implicitly) its juxtaposition to socialist-rationalist radicalism, see John E. Bodnar, *Immigration and Industrialization: Community and Protest in an Industrial Society, 1900–1940* (Baltimore, 1982) and William M. Reddy, *The Rise of Market Culture* (New York, 1984).

24. The canonical and formulaic wisdom is evident in the following passage on working-class life in the post–World War II period: "First, there had been a pronounced tendency under the impact of social and technological change for the traditional institutions of private life, especially the traditional working class family, to disintegrate. . . . This, in turn, is related to a second tendency, toward the replacement of all the traditional forms of proletarian culture and everyday life—which gave working class communities their coherence and provided the underpinnings for the traditional forms of proletarian class-consciousness—with a new, manipulated consumer culture which for convenience's sake we will call mass culture." Stanley Aronowitz, *False Promises: The Shaping of American Working Class Consciousness* (New York, 1973), 95; Stuart Hall, "Notes on Deconstructing the 'Popular'," in Raphael Samuel, ed., *People's History and Socialist Theory* (London, 1981), 229, 231.

25. Montgomery, *Workers' Control in America*. Montgomery's studies, which run from skilled nineteenth-century workers through an analysis of New Deal unionism, in and of themselves suggest the changing first-stage–second-stage change of emphasis. The "cultural" characterization of workers'—work ethic, sense of respectability, male identity, and "ethical code" that appears in the seminal first chapter on the industrial craftsman is never reexamined in the light of twentieth-century experiences. Brody, *Workers in Industrial America;* Ronald Schatz, *The Electrical Workers: A History of Labor at General Electric and Westinghouse, 1923–60* (Urbana, Ill., 1983); Nelson Lichtenstein, *Labor's War at Home: The CIO in World War II* (New York, 1982); Peter Friedlander, *Emergence of a UAW Local, 1936–1939* (Pittsburgh, 1975).

26. For a renewed focus on the state, see Geary, *European Labor Protest;* Cronin and Sirianni, *Work, Community, and Power;* Bernard Sternsher, "Great Depression Labor Historiography in the 1970s: Middle Range Questions, Ethnocultures and Levels of Generalization," *Reviews in American History* (June 1983), 300–19, esp. 304.

27. Joyce, *Work, Society, and Politics,* 337–40; Eric Hobsbawm, *Workers: Worlds of Labor* (New York, 1984), 176–214, esp. 190–92.

28. Bob Holton, *British Syndicalism, 1900–1914: Myths and Realities* (London, 1976), 50; Schatz, *Electrical Workers*, 36–37, 80–101; Alice Kessler-Harris, "Organizing the Unorganizable: Three Jewish Women and Their Union," *Labor History* 17 (Winter 1976), 5–23.

29. Sara Evans, *Personal Politics: The Roots of Women's Liberation in the Civil Rights Movement and the New Left* (New York, 1979).

30. Mary H. Blewett, "Work, Gender, and the Artisan Tradition in New England Shoemaking, 1780–1860," *Journal of Social History* 17 (Winter 1983), 221–48. See also the excellent discussion of the development of the male as breadwinner in Sonya O. Rose, "Gender Antagonism and Class Conflict: Exclusionary Strategies of Male Trade Unionists in Nineteenth-Century Britain," *Social History* 13 (May 1988), 191–208; Susan Porter Benson, *Counter Cultures: Saleswomen, Managers, and Customers in American Department Stores, 1890–1940* (Urbana, Ill., 1986); Patricia A. Cooper, *Once a Cigar Maker: Men, Women, and Work Culture in American Cigar Factories, 1900–1919* (Urbana, Ill., 1987); Dorothy Sue Cobble, "Craft Unionism Revisited: The Case of the Waitress Locals," paper delivered to the American Historical Association, Cincinnati, Ohio, Dec. 27–30, 1988; Christine Stansell, *City of Women: Sex and Class in New York, 1789–1860* (Urbana, Ill., 1987), quotation 221; Kathy Peiss, *Cheap Amusements: Working Women and Leisure in Turn-of-the-Century New York* (Philadelphia, 1986), quotation 188; Jacquelyn Dowd Hall, "Disorderly Women: Gender and Labor Militancy in the Appalachian South," *Journal of American History* 73 (September 1986), 354–82, quotations 372, 379.

31. Francis G. Couvares, *The Remaking of Pittsburgh* (Albany, N.Y., 1984), 126; "The Triumph of Commerce: Class Culture and Mass Culture in Pittsburgh," in Michael Frisch and Daniel Walkowitz, eds., *Working-Class America* (Urbana, Ill., 1983), p. 142.

32. Roy Rosenzweig, *Eight Hours for What We Will: Workers and Leisure in an Industrial City, 1870–1920* (New York, 1983), 227–28; Jacquelyn Hall, Robert Korstad, and James Leloudis, "Cotton Mill People: Work, Community, and Protest in the Textile South, 1880–1940," *American Historical Review* 91 (April 1986), 245–86. For an example of a positive reevaluation of working-class creativity within a modern setting, see George Lipsitz, *Rainbow at Midnight: Labor and Culture in the 1940s* (Urbana, Ill., 1994). For a striking fulfillment of this line of thinking, see Lizabeth Cohen, *Making a New Deal: Industrial Workers in Chicago, 1919–1939* (New York, 1990).

33. Richard Johnson, "Culture and the Historians," in Clarke, Critcher, and Johnson, *Working-Class Culture*, 65. See, e.g., David Brody, "The Old Labor History and the New: In Search of an American Working Class," *Labor History* 20 (Winter 1979), 111–26; Elizabeth Fox-Genovese and Eugene D. Genovese, "The Political Crisis of Social History," *Journal of Social History* 10 (Winter 1976), 205–20; and Lawrence T. McDonnell, " 'You Are Too Sentimental': Problems and Suggestions for a New Labor History," *Journal of Social History* 17 (Summer 1984), 629–54.

8

"Intellectuals" versus "Workers": Academic Requirements and the Creation of Labor History

The educated man should not become linked to an aristocracy of intellect, but should be a guide the army of discontented may trust and follow.

John R. Commons, 1888

So long as the intellectual is investigating specific subjects, which have definite and calculable bearings upon the workers' welfare,—for instance, industrial accidents, unemployment, wage trends, and the like, his tendency to reduce labor in the concrete to an abstraction is restrained. But let the intellectual's thought turn from relatively prosaic matters like the above mentioned to the infinitely more soul-stirring one of "labor and the social order," and it is the rare intellectual who is able to withstand an onrush of overpowering social mysticism.

Selig Perlman, 1928

Despite its limitations, "The Workers' Search for Power" suggested how labor history could be transformed into a history of the working class . . . It shifted attention from trade unions, secret societies, and emigre intellectuals. Instead, it stressed what Gutman had come to believe was the real business of labor history, "the workers themselves, their communities, and the day-to-day occurrences that shaped their outlook."

Ira Berlin, 1987[1]

Both intellectual and political circumstances have put American historians in a peculiarly self-reflective mood of late. While Peter Novick's excavation of the historiographical rock of "objectivity" is the most

celebrated application of a radical skepticism toward the working categories and assumptions of an inherited literature, it fits a larger temper of
the times.[2] The "linguistic turn" within postmodernist thought, pushed
to historical center stage by the gender analysis of feminist historians, in
itself offers a challenge to an empirically minded profession more used to
weighing other peoples' thoughts and deeds than their own.

Yet, even while contending with these intellectual flood waters, historians have been besieged from another quarter. Both on the left and the
right, they are included as targets in searching, if conflicting, critiques of
the American academic's contemporary social function. While the Right
hammers variously at a cult of relativism, ideological conformism, and
sacrifice of teaching to professional prestige, the Left mourns the monopoly of professional academic culture on scholarly work and the resulting
impoverishment of broader intellectual discussion. For both groups, a
basic question arises as to the existence and quality of academics' contact
with a meaningful public.[3]

The bevy of criticism is enough to excite a reexamination of origins
and purpose in every scholarly pursuit but perhaps nowhere more so
than in the subfields of history most closely linked to the political climate
of the 1960s. Indeed, at one level, both postmodernism and the debate
over the academy bespeak a disillusioned (if not vengeful) response to
the heady expectations of committed or "engaged" scholars emerging
from the student New Left.[4] American labor history was one such field,
although its "politicization" has much deeper roots. More than in most
academic units, the practitioners of labor history have long enjoyed a
special sense of social purpose as well as intellectual direction. Interpreting
experience far removed from the pathways of the university campus,
scholars of the labor movement have exhibited a sympathy bordering on
missionary zeal for their subjects. But how, exactly, have academics
conceived of their own relation to working people as objects of study?
How has such self-consciousness (or lack of it) affected past labor history
scholarship? What effect has the academy itself had in shaping the
"public" or "political" role of the labor historian? And with what legacy
for the present day?

The early writing of labor history offers a revealing chapter in paradigm formation as well as political activism within American intellectual
life. In significant ways, those academics who first documented the struggles of American trade unionism were themselves part of the action.
Writing during a time of tremendous ferment within the labor movement,
the intellectuals inhabited an academic world in complex and problematic historical motion, one that placed substantial pressure on political
and intellectual self-definitions. Offering a kind of sociology of knowl-

edge for the most important of these pioneering labor historians, I argue that the intellectuals' personal experience materially shaped a conception of worker and labor union interests with long-term repercussions for public policy as well as scholarship. While the assumptions of these "founders" differ significantly from the repertoire of today's practitioners, exposure of their dilemmas, I suggest, may help us to recognize our own. Or, to put it more provocatively, when "intellectuals" propose to speak for "workers" (as most labor historians do), their own self-image plays a large (and usually unexplored) role in the histories the intellectuals "discover."

The first treatises on workers' organized activity appeared in the 1880s, an era that the economic historian Mark Perlman has aptly titled "The Awakening."[5] On the one hand, the term evokes the clamor of the decade's Great Upheaval, the tide of strikes, protest, and national organizing activity by workers in the exploding ranks of the Knights of Labor and emerging federation of skilled trades, each challenging the power of capital to dictate the terms of an industrial future. But the term applies equally well to those who were doing the writing: reform-minded intellectuals, especially political economists, who experienced the social crisis of industrialism and the advance of specialized knowledge as not merely coincident but connected events. Indeed, the first commentators on the labor movement included some of the most brilliant lights of a new generation of educated Americans, individuals who went on to make their mark within, and in several cases to dominate, their chosen academic or professional fields.

Products of an unprecedented expansion of university enrollments and, particularly, the development of postgraduate programs at several elite schools, the pioneer scholars were men (and a few exceptional women) who generally had inherited a religiously derived moral sensibility for which the poverty as well as the unrest of the industrial city was a new and troubling experience.[6] If American social problems pricked their Christian social conscience, their diagnosis was in turn filtered through a strong European, especially German, intellectual lens. Experience for many in research universities abroad not only offered a model for future American higher education but also exposed these young Americans to a more historical, contingent, and pluralistic view of the world than that suggested by an unbending faith in individualism and the iron laws of classical political economy.[7]

To be sure, prior to the "awakening" of academic intellectuals, there had been no dearth of intellectual interest in radical social reform and improvement in the lives of working people. Political-intellectual "advocates" such as Ira Steward, John Swinton, Henry George, Edward Bellamy, and later Henry Demarest Lloyd and Clarence Darrow had each articulated a prolabor and indigenous American radicalism.[8] But a gulf separated them from the new academic generation. These men lived outside the university setting; their findings were less self-consciously connected to an "objective," scientific, or scholarly quest for truth. They were, generally speaking, citizen-activists appealing to a broad "republican" audience as writers, editors, and attorneys—and, as such, throwbacks to a preindustrial world with a less searing division of professional labor. A few among them, including Steward, William Sylvis, and later Terence Powderly, Edward King, and George McNeill were in fact worker-intellectuals who slid comfortably into prominent roles within the unions and labor reform organizations.

The labor agitators listed above had also been aided by a few "professionals" working more quietly for workers' welfare. Important work, for example, had been accomplished since the late 1860s in the way of collecting information and statistics on wage rates and working conditions, particularly through a growing circuit of state labor bureaus. The most prominent center for such work had been Massachusetts, where the irrepressible advocate George McNeill had served as state labor commissioner (until forced to resign for political reasons) in 1873. McNeill's less obstreperous and more painstakingly professional successor, Carroll Wright, established the basis for a permanent government role in monitoring the national labor force, heading the first federal labor bureau (within the Department of the Interior) in 1884. Although relatively spare in his social judgments, Wright (and a few other empiricists like him) gave vent to a growing economic revisionism, referring scornfully, for example, to the "hard, unsympathetic nature" of the "so-called science of political economy."[9]

What pushed the new economists of the 1880s forward, however, was not only religious sympathy and educational pedigree but also the visible mobilization of the workers themselves. A movement of unions, cooperatives, and political action, loosely grouped around the sprawling presence of the Knights of Labor, initially presented itself as a possible engine of fundamental social change. Willingly dissolving the barrier between campus and community, the young academic radicals saluted the arrival of this rational yet morally charged and broad-gauged social movement. Like breathless late arrivals onto a departing train, the academics threw caution to the winds; saluting the movement for labor reform, they openly identified with its aims and principles while implicitly casting themselves as its chief interpreters abroad and its tutors at home.

The first and clearest exemplar of this trend was Richard T. Ely, perhaps the most influential academic reformer of his generation. Ely, the son of a well-read but struggling Presbyterian farmer from western New York, had secured a position at Johns Hopkins after imbibing the social gospel at Columbia and pursuing a graduate degree at Heidelberg under the historicist economist Karl Knies.[10] Ely wrote *The Labor Movement in America* in 1886 at the height of both academic and political radicalism of the Gilded Age. Decrying the extremes of the old-school "conservative trade unionist" who accepts the "fixed bounds" of "natural laws" as well as the revolutionary socialist, Ely identified a "midway" position that "begins within the framework of present industrial society, but proposes to transform it gradually and peacefully, but completely, by abolishing a distinct capitalist class of employers." The labor movement was to play the leading role in this process.[11] Gradually replacing the formal church as a source of human brotherhood, the Knights of Labor, proclaimed Ely, was "preparing the way for a moral regeneration of the American industrial system and for the establishment of the 'ideal' system, the union of capital and labor in the same hands, in grand, wide-reaching co-operative enterprises."[12] Rather than promoting social divisions, the Knights promised an inclusive moral unity with which even the academic might identify: the Knights of Labor "did not emphasize class war; in fact in certain instances they would admit teachers, preachers, other intellectuals and even employers."[13] Amazed at the integration within the Knights' ranks of diverse occupational groups (and even groups of Confederate and Union Civil War veterans), Ely romanticized the order as the practical working out of a Hegelian Unity of Opposites and invested in it his hopes not only for domestic progress but, ultimately, for ending wars through international parliaments.[14]

To be sure, even in his rhetorical swoon before the movement of the masses, Ely did not surrender a constructive social role for people like himself. His own genteel manners and even a measure of cultural condescension shone through his egalitarian sympathies. To assuage a skeptical middle-class readership, Ely acknowledged the apparent illogic of a political enlightenment arising from "below." "Strange is it not! that the despised trades-union and labor organizations should have been chosen to perform this high duty of conciliation! But hath not God ever called the lowly to the most exalted missions, and hath he not ever called the foolish to confound the wise?" Ely's personal contact with Powderly likewise inverted the normal condescension bestowed by the leader of more than a half-million citizens on a private petitioner. Honored to meet with the university professor, the general master workman humbly addressed his correspondence to "Richard T. Ely, PhD," closed it "Very Respectfully Yours," and readily apologized for his own inattention to economic literature: "I am so busy I seldom get the chance to read the daily papers. I know that this is wrong and that a man in my position ought to have the time to scan the doings of the day . . . but our members do not think that way and I must keep at the drudgery of letter writing and reading all the time."[15]

Ely set an example that others quickly followed. Next to him in the front ranks of the labor-oriented intellectual awakening was Henry Carter Adams, perhaps best known as an early theorist of the regulatory state and a moderate reformist within the academic economics establishment.[16] But Adams's earliest contributions, like Ely's, reflect a more radical cast of mind. Another rebel from midwestern small towns and theological orthodoxy, Adams completed his doctorate at Johns Hopkins in 1878, headed for Germany, and returned to juggle part-time teaching positions at Cornell and the University of Michigan.[17]

Adams's views on the labor problem were distinguished not only by an original elaboration of a worker's property rights in a job but by his public exploration of such issues in the midst of a charged political climate. In Cornell's Sibley College Lectures delivered during the Knights' violence-plagued Southwest Strike in April 1886, Adams resolutely and passionately defended organized labor as "the greatest and characteristic movement of the present century." While censoring the disorder accompanying the strike, Adams accepted the basic logic of strikers who had walked off their jobs to protest the arbitrary dismissal of union members: "What the Knights of Labor say is, that they desire to exercise some of the rights of proprietorship over the industry to which they give their skill and their time. And it's certainly true that concession to their demands would deprive men now controlling industries of the right to control and operate their property 'under well defined rules of law'; but we will not add '[under] common sense,' for that is the question at issue."[18]

Ely and Adams may have been the most intellectually precocious of the Young Turk economists, but both their sympathies and broad analysis of the labor problem were shared in the mid-1880s by colleagues who later elaborated the more conservative principles of twentieth-century economic thought. Perhaps the most prominent was John Bates Clark, the father of modern marginal utility theory.[19] When he was called home from Amherst College to take over his ailing father's plow manufacturing business in Minnesota, Clark witnessed the hard times of surrounding farmers. He passed up a career in the ministry after graduation and turned to economics. Following study in Germany, Clark taught part-time at Smith College, then divided his time between Amherst and Columbia before securing a permanent position at Columbia in 1895. In his early scholarship, Clark tried to combine the moral ends of Christian social reform with the workings of the competitive marketplace, an effort crowned by the publication in 1886 of *The Philosophy of Wealth: Economic Principles Newly Formulated.*

Clark was convinced that "individual competition," which had regulated an earlier era, was now "incapable of working justice," and he looked to new forms of "solidarity" by employers, government, workers, and the church for "the beginnings of a reign of law." In his defense of labor unions and even the boycott as commensurable resources against an unjust distribution of the economic product, and an identification of the Knights of Labor as the chief hope for the unskilled, Clark hoped to contain social conflict by a new institutionalization of economic interests. Beginning with arbitration, then advancing to profit-sharing and ultimately to the "full cooperation" preached by English Christian socialists, society would be "redeemed" when men voluntarily accepted the fraternal principle. "Christian socialism," declared Clark, "is economic republicanism; and it can come no sooner, stay no longer, and rise, in quality, no higher than intelligence and virtue among the people."[20]

The distinguished later career of another Columbia economist, E. R. A. Seligman (who made his reputation in the field of public finance), likewise overshadowed his earlier enthusiasms. While no refugee from the Christian hinterlands (his father was a wealthy German-Jewish businessman), Seligman nevertheless shared much with his generational peers. Following European study and completion of a doctoral dissertation on medieval guilds, Seligman in 1885 helped Ely found the American Economics Association (AEA). "The paramount question of political economy," the young Seligman argued, "is the question of distribution and in it the social problem (the question of labor, of the laborer),—how, consistently with a healthy development on the lines of moderate progress, social reform may be accomplished."[21]

In a celebrated parlay over Henry George's proposed Single Tax before the American Association for Social Science in 1890, Seligman well reflected the simultaneous identification of the New Economists with academic objectivity and social reform. Declaring that there was "not a single man with a thorough training" in economics who advocated the Single Tax, Seligman complained that, while the specialist was universally respected in the natural sciences, "every man whose knowledge of economics or the science of finance is derived from the daily papers or one or two books with lopsided ideas, thinks he is a full-fledged scientist, able to instruct the closest students of the markets or of the political and social organism." George responded energetically to Seligman's attack, at once linking academic economists to the exploiting classes and condemning Seligman's claim to expertise as insidious elitism ("if we cannot all study political economy . . . then democratic republican government is doomed to failure, and the quicker we surrender ourselves to the government of the rich and learned, the better"). Most interesting for our purposes is that Seligman, in final rebuttal, chose to stand not merely on scientific grounds but to argue, pointedly, "It is grossly unjust to ascribe to professors of political economy a truckling or even an unconscious subservience to the powers that be." Indeed, not without a degree of hyperbole, Seligman further insisted that "in the United States, to mention only one instance, almost the entire support which the labor-unions receive is at the hands of the college professors,—a course which has drawn on them not a little opprobrium."[22]

Even in his early, "radical" phase, however, Seligman undoubtedly seemed tame compared to the firebrands around him. Edmund J. James and Simon Nelson Patten, for example, who had helped reorient Ely during his first European trip, also led the fight for a reform-oriented professional association. As director of the Wharton School of Finance in 1886, James, who shortly thereafter was to turn away from social issues toward a career in commercial education and administration (he ended up as president of Northwestern University and then the University of Illinois), vigorously endorsed labor unions and attacked ruthless owners for producing mass discontent.[23]

We may well take the creation of the American Economics Association in 1885 as the first official recognition of an intellectual-labor entente in American public life.[24] For a brief moment, at least, the possibility of what many of the organizers called a "Christian social science" seemed the obvious intellectual corollary of a social and political movement seeking to redefine the political economy on moral principles.[25] The first volume of AEA *Publications* in 1886, for example, included an argument by James for municipal ownership of utilities, Albert Shaw on associations among the Minneapolis Knights of Labor, Edward W. Bemis on producer and consumer cooperatives in New England, and Henry C. Adams's classic justification for government control of monopoly in "The Relation of the State to Industrial Action."

Exactly this juncture between critical scholarship and the social gospel attracted Oberlin College senior John R. Commons to begin a lifelong path of labor studies. Another midwestern refugee from ministerial ambitions, Commons, even as an undergraduate, had decided that "the educated man should . . . be a guide the army of discontented may trust and follow."[26] Following Ely to Hopkins in 1888 and soon helping his mentor to found the reformist Institute for Christian Sociology, Commons quickly emerged as the most determined, as well as the most talented, representative of the new economic thinking.[27] In the 1890s, even as other colleagues turned away from philosophical and political issues, Commons maintained a reputation as an academic "hothead."[28]

A characteristic outburst occurred during a public exchange with the conservative Yale economist Arthur T. Hadley in 1899. In his presidential address to the AEA, Hadley, a defender of the liberal marketplace as an instrument of the common good, urged economists to function above the din of political and social conflict as a kind of farseeing policy elite—"representatives," as Hadley put it, "of nothing less than the whole truth." In rebuttal, Commons, who was speaking without an academic position of his own, caustically dismissed Hadley's presumptions as a mask for bourgeois privilege by denying the fundamental nature of social antagonisms: "As economists I believe we would stand on safer ground if, when our conclusions lead us to champion the cause of a class . . . or to expose another class, we should come squarely out and admit that it is so; not because the class interest is foremost in our minds, but because the class is the temporary means of bringing about the permanent welfare of all."[29]

Of course, the impact of the stirrings of the reform-minded academics should not be exaggerated. Youthfully confident and enthusiastic, they were a distinct and finite subset of social science–oriented professionals. In the circumstances of widespread labor unrest and an organized mass movement, however, when both serious social reforms and more apocalyptic transformations of the social order appeared possible, the visions of the radical idealists left an impression even on more traditionally conservative colleagues. For example, the older economist, federal census superintendent, and president of the Massachusetts Institute of Technology, Francis A. Walker, initially reacted violently against the labor upheavals of the 1880s, heaping abuse equally on strikers, foreign laborers, and radical dreamers like George and Bellamy.[30] Walker's election as president of the AEA in 1887 has been cited as evidence of the organization's budding emphasis on public respectability at the expense of radical reform. But it is worth noting that Walker, a moderate critic of laissez-faire dogma who had years before attacked the Malthusian wages-fund doctrine, took pains to conciliate the labor movement (and thus also to reassure his professional left flank) in his presidential address of 1888. In "Efforts of the Manual Laboring Class to Better Their Condition," Walker joined his colleagues in a remarkably even-handed treatment of the rise of the Knights of Labor and its social implications. He referred to the "revolution" in economic thought that had followed the revolution in political thought during the preceding one hundred years. He saw a shift from a "general consent of economic opinion that all distinct efforts of the laboring class, directed to the advancement of their own interest, must at the best be useless" to "the present time when . . . it is fully recognized that the self-assertion of the laboring class importantly contributes to the equitable and beneficial distribution of wealth; and that such self-assertion, within proper limits and by proper agencies, is not more for the interest of the laboring class than of the employing class, or of the community as a whole." Obliquely, Walker even buttressed the case for direct intellectual-worker contacts by implying that the insights on wage theory of the British economist Henry Fawcett were due in part to the fact that "one-half of his actual intimate daily companions were laboring men."[31]

The "Awakening" period offers ample testimony to the quality of labor-oriented engagement by a generation of socially conscious intellectuals. Whether by joining in forums with labor leaders and social reformers, establishing professional associations through which to maximize their influence on public opinion, or training a younger generation of citizens and scholars in their own classrooms, the new-school economists etched in the possibility for a formal intellectual counterpart to labor-populist currents in workplaces and electoral politics. Perhaps most significantly, these intellectuals imagined that the "scientific" development of their own field of knowledge was intimately bound up with the welfare of working people themselves. As Richard Hofstadter and Walter P. Metzger concluded, "the strategies of the new political economy and of organized labor . . . seemed to coincide."[32]

Yet, overall, between 1890 and 1910, the ardor of the labor-oriented academics perceptibly cooled. In place of public identification with workers' aspirations and open advocacy of social transformation, the young social scientists either withdrew from advocacy altogether or channeled their reform energies into more publicly acceptable roles as policy "experts"—a process that Mary Furner labeled "practical research."[33]

Suspension of a politically engaged, anticapitalist critique by the labor economists likely had several causes and reflected changes within as well as outside the academy. Part of the problem was intellectual. Lacking a developed social theory (while generally disdaining revolutionary socialist models as well as the "amateurish" heterodoxy of a Henry George), the academic radicals faced difficulty in establishing their social claims on anything but subjective moral foundations.[34] "Scientific" integrity as well as the demands of academic respectability thus impelled many of the new economists toward accommodation with the developing marginalist revolution in economic thought, a theoretical universe in which workers appeared less as visionary citizens than as integers of material self-interest.[35] Marginalist theory, moreover, carried a persuasive descriptive brief in an economic world where corporate capital had secured its institutional and legal moorings. In this respect, the collapse of the Knights of Labor by the end of the 1880s and the defeat of subsequent labor-populist political challenges in the early 1890s left few options for theorists who had seriously contemplated a different political economy.

A more immediately revisionist goad to erstwhile academic radicals, however, was supplied by university administrators. Four of the most prominent of the labor-oriented economists—Adams, Ely and his students, Bemis, and Commons—faced the threat or fact of dismissal for their intellectual commitments. These actions were part of a larger house-cleaning of heterodoxy in the universities that climaxed in the mid-1890s, and the survivors of this "intellectual Haymarket" learned the contemporary limits of academic freedom each in his own way.[36]

Adams was dismissed in 1886 from his half-time position at Cornell, following publication of his Sibley College lecture "The Labor Problem." He had been unlucky enough to have as official commentators on his talk both the university president, Charles Kendall Adams, and the president of the board of trustees, the lumber millionaire Henry Sage. While the university president publicly offered his understanding that labor troubles "partly arise from the old familiar weakness of human nature which inclines every man to get all that he can . . . and from the inclination to get large pay for little work," Sage declared emphatically that strikes derived "mainly from our foreign population" who "neither believe in God nor government." Sometime following the debate, Sage reportedly marched into the president's office and declared, "This man must go, he is sapping the foundations of our society."[37]

With his career saved by a full-time, tenured appointment at the University of Michigan, Adams maintained a lower public profile even as he continued to elaborate a defense of collectivist, democratic regulation of the marketplace. It was not through association with popular movements that he subsequently advanced his ideas, however, but through state administrative agencies. Chief statistician in the late 1880s for the Interstate Commerce Commission, Adams pushed for expansive investigatory and regulatory powers and against restrictions increasingly imposed by the courts. While his intellectual curiosity alone may have steered him from the labor question toward other issues, his career suggests a more general gravitation among the new economists away from controversy and toward applied expertise.[38]

In any case, the Adams experience proved a harbinger of the troubles the more outspoken "Elyites" would face in the following decade. In 1894, amid the nationwide railroad strike precipitated by the Pullman boycott, Ely himself, now a well-established full professor at Wisconsin, endured a "trial" before the Board of Regents for alleged support of local strikers as well as for theories that supposedly undermined a society based on private property. To prove his innocence, Ely presented himself as a "conservative" and a "scientist" with no interest in public agitation or even direct contacts with the working class.[39] His case ended in his exoneration and a ringing endorsement of the principle of free inquiry by the university trustees. Although personally vindicated, Ely apparently was deeply wounded.[40] He effectively withdrew from all reform activity for the next five years. In 1902, facing financial stress from his wife's illness, Ely sold his magnificent labor history collection and used the proceeds to invest in real estate. Although he did reassert his reform credentials during the Progressive Era (chartering the American Association of Labor Legislation in 1906), his biographer located a passion for respectability in his actions well before his open political "souring" in the 1920s, when he campaigned against public utilities while maintaining extensive industry connections.[41]

Bemis fared less well. He was forced out of a tenured position at the University of Chicago in 1894 on formal grounds of incompetent teaching, an excuse for the pressures brought to bear on President William Rainey Harper by Bemis's call for municipally owned utilities and criticism of railroad owners. Except for a short stint at a Populist-dominated college in Kansas, Bemis did not regain academic employment.[42]

The pressure on Commons was more subtle. In 1895, Indiana University authorities, having impatiently borne his heresies for three years, "urged" him to take a full professorship extended by Syracuse University. In 1899, however, the same propensities led to outright unemployment when Syracuse eliminated his position. There followed five years of academic unemployment; in 1903, Ely referred to Commons as having been "practically blacklisted." When he finally found a position at Wisconsin, Commons likened the feeling to being "born again . . . after five years of incubation."[43]

Commons's rebirth also occasioned the flowering of the "Wisconsin school" of labor history that culminated in the monumental ten-volume *Documentary History of American Industrial Society* (1910–12) and four-volume *History of Labour in the United States* (1918, 1935). Combining research on labor history, industrial relations, and economic theory with an active concern for public policy, Commons and his students at Madison significantly contributed to the Progressive political thrust of the state in the LaFollette years and beyond. In addition to the industrial relations field, the areas of civil service law, utility regulation, workmen's compensation, unemployment, and monetary policy all received sustained, creative attention from the "Wisconsin crowd."

It is worth noting, however, that in order to rescue institutional labor studies from academic oblivion, Commons had to reposition himself as both scholar and thinker. In Commons's case, the shift from academic bad boy to the mature and influential professional involved a gradual evolution of perspective and a self-conscious learning experience. Commons retrospectively acknowledged a causative link between academic deprivation and his personal and intellectual development. His dismissal at Syracuse, for example, helped reorient his theoretical focus from "abundance" to "scarcity": "I figured that a 'chair' in political economy was not physically pulled out from under you, it was economically pulled out by withholding the funds. . . . At least, I knew, after 1899 at Syracuse, that holding and withholding were not the same, and the latter was more important."[44] The stress on the scarcity value of labor and property as key determinants of economic behavior became a hallmark of Commons's labor history as well as his more theoretical writings. In his view, skilled trade unionists, for example, sought above all to restrict entry into the labor market—an idealism of the job rights of the individual worker and occupational interest group—rather than a larger class-wide solidarity.[45]

Commons's move to Wisconsin also reflected new political understandings. Beginning with a diplomatic leave-taking at Syracuse, Commons, in his writing and in his personal decorum, increasingly earned the respect of colleagues for assimilating professional mores. Endorsing Commons's fitness for an academic appointment, the conservative Harvard economist T. N. Carver insisted, "Whatever may in the past have been said against his so-called indiscreet utterances can not now be said because he has published nothing for a number of years so far as I have learned, which would not stand the severest scientific criticism."[46]

Commons, in fact, had learned more than a lesson in academic manners. Thanks to connections with a few self-made men of broad social vision, his academic hiatus proved a most productive and intellectually creative period.[47] A series of contract research assignments—with the Democratic National Committee, the Industrial Commission of 1900, and the National Civic Federation (NCF)—laid the groundwork for continuous ties to public research projects. From his campus base in Madison, he spearheaded drives in the state for expansive civil service reform, an industrial commission, and workmen's compensation laws; while, through the Commission on Industrial Relations (1912–15), the American Association for Labor Law Reform, and informal networks, he remained for years a signal national influence for labor law reform and social welfare legislation.[48] Like Adams, Commons illustrates the turn among social scientists from the moral and agitational stance of the critical outsider toward technical expertise and influence among policy-making elites.[49]

His growing contact with institutions of social mediation—both government bureaus and the "tri-partite" bodies of business, labor, and public representatives that he long favored—led Commons to a revised understanding of the relationship, and boundaries, between "intellectuals" and "workers." A necessary reliance on the "public interest" (those "two-thirds of the voting population" who were but "spectators" to the inevitable industrial disputes), in particular, required disciplined self-restraint by the labor-oriented intellectual.[50] At the NCF, in personal contacts with United Mine Workers president John Mitchell and American Federation of Labor president Samuel Gompers, Commons learned that the "place of the economist was that of adviser to the [trade union] leaders, if they wanted him, and not that of propagandist to the masses."[51] Disinterested, empirical investigation rather than open advocacy was the intellectual's modern weapon.[52]

Commons's approach accorded well with the dominant tenor of the contemporary labor movement. Out of the nadir of the 1890s depression, labor unions had revived, not on the basis of the inclusive, antimonopoly platform of the Knights of Labor but through the self-protective and politically conservative craft unionism of the AFL. Its leaders, Gompers and Adolph Strasser, who themselves enjoyed a grounding in European Marxism, chose early to present themselves as "practical men" "opposed to theorists" or "fool friends" of labor. Inherently inhospitable to rabble-rousing reformers, trade unions, declared Gompers characteristically in 1898, "are not the creation of any man's brain" but rather "organizations of necessity . . . of the working class, for the working class, by the working class."[53] On the one hand, a unionism oriented toward bread-and-butter issues fit both a legally and a politically defensible image, which facilitated an expansion of collective bargaining. On the other hand, the same tenets provided internal ideological protection from the advocates of independent labor or socialist political initiatives both within and outside the labor federation. Whereas experts might still be sought (and needed) for specific functions (legal defense, bill drafting, and public relations, for example), the AFL, unlike the Knights of Labor, sought no broader alliance with men and women of letters. AFL secretary-treasurer Matthew Woll, in 1919, characteristically responded to criticism from an intellectual "friend of labor": "The AFofL does not take its inspiration from those who sit and peer at it through microscopes in contemplation, nor yet from those who pick and pull at its being with scalpel and forceps in heavy-browed analysis. The AFofL takes its inspiration from the needs of the men and women who toil."[54] Indeed, John Frey, the self-taught editor of the *Iron-Molders' Journal* and trade-union conservative, happily quoted Gompers to the effect that "God save us from our intellectual friends. All I ask is that they get off our backs."[55]

In ways he doubtlessly did not anticipate, Gompers found ready acceptance in the academic world for his formulation of workers' psychology and interests. The postulation of the labor movement as a force born of economic necessity rather than "man's brain" or moral vision justified a stance of scholarly "objectivity" (as opposed to overt union "advocacy") by the academics, which was in any case a political imperative within the university. The twin doctrines of the sovereignty of the labor leader and autonomy of the academic serendipitously fulfilled the needs of both parties.[56]

Together, the contemporary academic and political contexts help explain the special self-consciousness on the part of the Wisconsin school economists about the relationship of intellectuals to the labor movement. In the introduction to his *History of Labour*, for example, Commons identified the intellectuals as "a miscellaneous class of men and women, taking more or less part in labour movements, yet distinct from manual workers." He readily allowed that this group had played a major role in the development of the American labor movement—from Frances Wright and Robert Dale Owen to Horace Greeley, Henry George, John Swinton, Henry D. Lloyd, and George McNeill. But, by a kind of unspoken evolutionary process, the influence of such people was sharply reduced within "the organization or management of the 'wage-conscious' trade unions."[57]

Commons sharpened his argument in an entry in the *Encyclopaedia of the Social Sciences* (1935). There he integrated American developments into larger trends, identifying the "intelligentsia" as the "natural leaders" of the first "desperate" stage of labor movements, "the stage of Marx, Lassalle, Lenin, Powderly, Louis Blanc or Proudhon." "They have a formulated social philosophy and an ability to articulate what the others feel but cannot tell." Then, as the possibility of stable and successful organization develops, new "rank and file" leaders ("a Gompers, an Applegarth, a Legien, a Jouhaux") take over. In Commons's view, such a development was natural and fitting. The intellectual's "proper place" was "not as a leader in forming policies" but "as a technician in details and adviser against mistakes."[58] This prescription set Commons apart from the more doctrinaire stance of socialist and communist intellectuals. By the time he wrote his autobiography in 1934, Commons had lost all patience with a social class he now identified with the extreme political left: "I always look for them [intellectuals] and try to clear them out from all negotiations between capital and labor, and from the councils of labor."[59]

If his own accommodation to the realities of academic and trade union politics inclined the mature Commons to a dim view of the critical intellectual, he left the further elaboration of this perspective to his student, Selig Perlman. Perlman, far more than Commons, integrated the issue of the intellectual's role into the very heart of the Wisconsin view of labor history.

Perlman's first account of the subject, as presented in Commons et al., *History of Labour,* ventured little beyond Commons's own assertion that intellectuals tended "to direct the manual workers away from the strict and narrow interest of wage-earners as a class, and to lead them towards affiliation with other classes."[60] Perlman applied this dictum, in particular, to the Knights of Labor's infatuation with the "panacea" of cooperation—the very topic that had attracted economists of an earlier generation to the labor movement—distinguishing the "middle-class psychology" of the Knights' leaders from the more down-to-earth "wage-consciousness" of the trade unions.[61]

Even more pointedly, Perlman's magnum opus of 1928 defined the continual struggle of "organic labor" against "dominance by the intellectuals."[62] Instead of an "American exceptionalism" à la Werner Sombart, Perlman's intellectual-versus-worker paradigm implied a "Soviet" exceptionalism, with "backward" Russia the one country where the "will to power" of intellectuals within the workers' movement had prevailed. Outside the Soviet Union, argued Perlman, built-in tensions between the two social groups persisted (with the intellectuals weakest of all in the United States), but the trade unionists, mature and well-organized, tended increasingly to shape both industrial and political action in their own pragmatic, nonrevolutionary image.[63] Published as *A Theory of the Labor Movement,* Perlman's work was as much an analysis of intellectuals as of workers. He himself noted to a friend that the "Macmillan people . . . made me . . . abandon my more laborious title of 'Capitalism, Labor, and Intellectuals.' "[64]

Like the work of Ely and Commons, Perlman's masterpiece reflected an implicit commentary on his own relation to his subject. A member of what might heuristically be considered the "third generation" of labor historians, Perlman represented an important departure from his predecessors in one vital respect: he was an immigrant Jew in a non-Jewish and often anti-Semitic academic world. Born in 1888 to a small merchant family in the Russian town of Bialystok, Perlman, a shy child afflicted with a stutter, threw himself into his studies at the *cheder,* or the local Jewish day school. He won a scholarship to the city's science-oriented gymnasium, where an influential teacher introduced him to Georgii

Plekhanov and a new world of intellectual and political radicalism. Perlman followed other Russian émigrés to Italy, studying medicine at the University of Naples.[65]

A fortuitous set of events brought Perlman to the United States in January 1908 at age nineteen. The radical bohemian poet Anna Strunsky was gathering a new wardrobe in New York in anticipation of a European trip with her future husband, the wealthy American socialist William English Walling. Her seamstress turned out to be Perlman's aunt, and talk eventually turned to her brilliant young nephew who read Karl Marx. Subsequent to a personal meeting in Naples, Perlman accepted Walling's invitation to come to New York to do translations; and, when the young immigrant grew tired of office work, Walling kindly agreed to send him to the University of Wisconsin to work with Walling's friends, Ely and Commons.[66]

At Wisconsin, Perlman quickly emerged as a brilliant, uncommonly cosmopolitan student. His undergraduate thesis, "History of Socialism in Milwaukee," completed after one year of coursework, reflected an initial continuity of intellectual and political commitments. Espousing the revisionist "opportunism" of Eduard Bernstein, Perlman extolled Victor Berger and the Milwaukee socialists for the triumph of "realism" over "revolutionism" in labor and political circles.[67]

Even as he imbibed the heady new intellectual influences of his Wisconsin mentors, Perlman, just as at gymnasium, never lost the self-consciousness of being an outsider. Much of this feeling was connected to his Jewishness. Nor was his alienation limited to common, upper midwestern reference to his kind as "sheenies." On a formal level, and by any contemporary comparative measure, Commons's approach to his students was uncommonly tolerant and inclusive. In a later reminiscence for the State Historical Society, Perlman called his adviser "a formal man, rather difficult to get acquainted with . . . [but] exceedingly generous in his intellectual life. . . . I have always maintained that I owe everything to Professor Commons."[68] Yet according to his son, Perlman privately expressed frustration at what he experienced as Commons's residual, cultural anti-Semitism, an attitude that limited the depth of their friendship.[69] One of Perlman's most embarrassing moments came when he brought his parents to live in Madison, after their economic position in Russia had collapsed. Now he was revealed before his mentor not only as a "Jew," not only an "immigrant with a Yiddish accent," but worst of all as a "poor Russian Jew."[70] Moreover, it pained Perlman that the dedication of *A Theory* ("To J. R. C. and N. D. C. [Mrs. Commons]") never received an acknowledgment from his mentor. The worst moment came in 1931 when, before the usual crowd of Friday Nighters gathered at the Commonses' house, Commons declared that Edwin Witte had been named his successor at Wisconsin and openly expressed relief at not having to place Perlman in that position. Perlman did not get out of bed for days after this slight and broke off contact with Commons for an extended period.[71]

For all his accomplishments, Selig Perlman often experienced the academic profession—at least outside his own classroom—as a cold, unrewarding, and inhospitable one. Both by temperament and for lack of invitations, Perlman rarely left Madison. Unlike other Wisconsin colleagues, he did almost no direct public service work and had little contact with labor leaders, public figures, or, outside Madison, even policy-oriented academics.[72] It is noteworthy that the man who produced the most influential picture of twentieth-century labor ideology—the basic common sense of the working-class Tom, Dick, and Harry—never met Samuel Gompers, Matthew Woll, William Green, or John L. Lewis and never addressed a national union meeting or convention.[73]

Perlman's brief but demanding venture beyond the university's walls— field work in 1913–14 for the U.S. Commission on Industrial Relations— offers a revealing glimpse of his imaginative yet limited contact with American workers. The young Perlman was dispatched to New England textile towns that were gripped by fear and repression following a wave of organizing drives inspired by the radical syndicalist Industrial Workers of the World. Traveling incognito in order not to arouse employer suspicions, Perlman carefully sought to gather evidence of industrial conditions and popular feelings.[74] Though unable to gain entrée to workers' homes, he devised an ingenious strategy for acquiring candid and spontaneous opinion: he relied on local Jewish storeowners ("they are as a rule excellent observers of men and conditions and coming into very intimate contact with the laboring people . . . they are in a position to form correct opinions of the manner of thinking of the various elements of the population") and casually chatted with customers in their stores.[75]

Aside from empirical observation and political context, contemporary philosophy seems also to account for the dualism separating Perlman's workers and intellectuals. We might well read Perlman's work as a creative adaptation of the philosophy and social psychology of Deweyan Pragmatism. Perlman's attack on the leftist intellectual's "social mysticism," the reduction of human goals and destiny to a matter of abstract faith, for example, bears close resemblance to the turn-of-the-century pragmatic critique of religious idealism and its ultimate replacement by the scientific study of human experience.[76] Similarly, the "organic" psychology (or "job consciousness") attributed to the worker enjoys the essential qualities of problem solving, instrumental learning favored by the pragmatists.[77]

A further clue to Perlman's broader philosophical bent derives from his close friendship with Max Kadushin, the famous Hebrew scholar who served as Hillel rabbi in Madison from 1931 to 1942. Kadushin's early works, including *The Theology of Seder Eliahu: A Study in Organic Thinking* (1932) and *Organic Thinking* (1938), make explicit reference to an "organismic approach to social science," associating concepts drawn from John Dewey, Alfred North Whitehead, and the anthropologist Lucien Lévy-Bruhl with the logic of rabbinic theology. In particular, the complementarity Kadushin found between "logical" (abstract and systemic) and "organic" (essentially context-related) thought closely corresponds to Perlman's basic dualism, which suggests a common contemporary climate of intellectual discourse.[78]

But Perlman's argument may also be open to a deeper, more personal reading. It is likely that his experiences in Russia and the United States led him not only to a clear delineation of the intellectuals as a separate social group but to a deep ambivalence, connected to his own bittersweet fortunes, about the intellectual's social role. Dating from his early education, Perlman framed the concept of the heroic intelligentsia and offered a moral but politically ineffectual critique of worldly power. He himself more closely fit the modern image of the intellectual as college professor—a humane and philosophical man of letters with many well-formed opinions about the world but totally ill-equipped to act within it or upon it. The social gap suggested in *A Theory* between workers and intellectuals accurately reflected the world Perlman had known in Europe; it was reproduced on the Madison campus, where few manual laborers could be found. Yet, as thoroughly socialized as he was into the intellectual world, the marginalism he felt as a Jewish academic made it difficult for him to feel comfortable with this identity.[79] Unlike many of his more technocratic-minded contemporaries to his right and left, Perlman had no reason to entrust the world to intellectuals.

If fertilized by intimate and even idiosyncratic circumstances, the labor economists' distinction between "workers" and "intellectuals" was nevertheless broadcast over a wide field. On the whole, it met political as well as academic requirements. The historic preponderance of employer power together with an inherent antagonism to collective economic action in American law had sent defenders of workers' welfare searching for a durable shelter.[80] Wisconsin school reformers believed they had found a defensible home for organized labor in the theory of labor relations later known as "industrial pluralism." Connecting collective bargaining not to the destruction of the capitalist order but to its reinvigoration, industrial pluralists pressed for legally sanctioned mechanisms of managed conflict between employers and workers. A champion of the doctrines of his mentor John R. Commons, William M. Leiserson noted as early as 1926 the difference between the relatively new terms "labor relations" and "industrial relations" (implying "mutual accommodation and adjustment") and turn-of-the-century discussion of the "labor problem" or the "labor question," which implied "a solution" in terms of rights and wrongs. The change, in Leiserson's view, had by no means banished ethics from the considerations of reformers; rather, the frozen mentality of Labor versus Capital had been replaced by appeal to "an awakened social conscience" and a larger "public mind," and "new moral tests are [henceforth] applied to both management and workers."[81] A shrewd political and social compromise, the model of collective bargaining sanctioned by industrial pluralism depended on the rational accommodation of conflicting but equally legitimate interest claims. Even as union rights, therefore, were defended on grounds of "public interest" (that favorite resort of the Progressive generation), they would also be subject to the limitations that that interest might impose.

The Wisconsin scholars' ideal of the "pragmatic" worker—self-interested, self-protective, and essentially incrementalist in orientation—indeed helped define the regulated freedom ultimately accorded labor unions in the era of the Wagner Act. Not only did the National Labor Relations Board (NLRB) draw in its very inspiration on Commons's own efforts for the prewar Commission on Industrial Relations but Commons's students Leiserson and Harry A. Millis personally presided over the administrative consolidation of the board beginning in 1939. Not surprisingly, Leiserson analyzed the problem of leftist influence within the newly founded Congress of Industrial Organizations (CIO) and the resultant political backlash against the NLRB within the classic terms of the "intellectual" problem: "Communists and social reformers of various kinds [who] have attempted to capture the movement, control its policies, and divert the power of organized labor into social politics or revolutionary channels and away from collective bargaining and the institutions of stable industrial government which are its normal aims."[82] An early application of the Leiserson-Millis doctrine of administrative objectivity, accordingly, was the dismissal of NLRB secretary and alleged Communist party member Nathan Witt. Secretary of Labor Frances Perkins captured the prevailing view that Witt represented "one of those intellectuals who was in love with labor, who thought that labor was always right and never could be wrong."[83] The comments of these policymakers recall the story of another Wisconsin labor historian, Philip Taft, about his teacher Selig Perlman, for whom " 'intellectual' . . . became a pejorative label for anyone whose views he did not share": "When I taught summer school in 1949 at Madison, there was a meeting of the School for Workers at which the Secretary-Treasurer of the UAW, Emil Mazey, spoke, advocating the formation of a labor party. Going home Professor Perlman asked me, 'Who was that intellectual?' I had to tell him that this was a man who participated in the sit-down strikes, who was one of the finest of the new trade unionists, and who defied the Detroit gangsters who sought to interfere with the union."[84]

Intellectual prescription and government action thus ultimately joined hands. Altogether, the political triumph of labor reform thought must rank as one of the most impressive examples of social change ever emanating from academe. While banishing the disabling injunction and unmitigated employer authority as the modus operandi of American industrial relations, public policy, by the 1940s, formally accepted the "pragmatic" trade unionist (focused on acts of immediate, incremental material improvement) as a worthy industrial citizen, even while barring his "intellectual" counterpart (liable to the delusions of political radicalism or solidaristic acts like sympathy strikes and secondary boycotts) from the door.[85]

However politically efficacious, preoccupation with the "intellectual" as a threatening outsider and factional foe occasioned a notable blind spot. For all their voluminous and monumental exploration of American labor relations, the Wisconsin scholars avoided self-scrutiny. The industrial relations model discountenanced the meddling radical and restricted business and labor to horizons of commonsense materialism. It offered little analysis of its own mediating figures or sources of intentionality. Without apparent irony, some of the best scholars, the most subtle ideologists, and most effective social reformers of the early twentieth century categorically wrote themselves out of their own history.

It is a long way from the labor economists who began the academic study of American labor history to the social historians who dominate the field today. The "new labor history," which first emerged in the late 1960s, arose as much in defiance of as in continuity with the Commons-Perlman tradition. In addition to the disciplinary differences in research methods that conditioned the two perspectives, the newer work, stimulated in part by the political culture of the New Left, challenged the old in its basic ideological perspective. Class conflict replaced industrial pluralism as a central motif; workplace cultures other than those of skilled white males became objects of study; and workers' agency or subjectivity was extended beyond the workplace to encompass familial, ethnic, and community settings. In ways yet to be fully explored, present-day labor historians have also taken advantage of historiographic traditions (developed by African-American historians, women "social investigators," and leftist scholar-activists) outside the academic mainstream.[86]

Curiously, while generally expanding or contesting the findings of their academic forebears, present-day scholars have largely avoided the self-conscious preoccupation that earlier scholarly generations had with the relationship of the intellectual to the worker. To be sure, this issue might be written off as a "nonproblem." Most labor historians, unlike the earlier labor economists, are not rubbing shoulders with the people or events they are interpreting, perhaps reducing the earlier source of tension. Moreover, freed from both the AFL's self-protective autonomism and a classical Marxist concern about "petit bourgeois" influences within a proletarian movement, today's historians are not instinctively affronted by the presence of non–wage earners in movements that often spoke broadly in the name of all "producing classes" or the "republican" majority. Nor, of course, with the collapse of an organized political left, do present-day practitioners contend with the choice of relating to organized labor as expert/technician versus vanguard intellectual.

In all these respects, the intellectual as such has not only slipped from the noose of controversy but lost allure as a worthy scholarly subject. While the autodidact intellectuals common to the Jacksonian workingmen's movement or the Gilded Age labor-political tradition are rather easily assimilated into the multiple community and occupational studies of recent vintage, little interest is shown in comparative "outsiders" whose political, philosophical, or economic analyses may have had less impact on the workers' own movement than on the larger political climate in which labor operated.[87] For the late nineteenth century, to take a prime example, the last serious exploration of worker-reformer relationships, David Montgomery's *Beyond Equality* (1967), appeared just before the impact of the dominant recent trends in the field. It is noteworthy that the only modern study of seminal radical reform figures Henry George, Henry Demarest Lloyd, and Edward Bellamy derives from an intellectual historian. Likewise, with the exception of its bearing on women's history, the close association of leading Progressive intellectual figures with labor circles (including Jane Addams, Florence Kelley, John Dewey, Louis Brandeis, Clarence Darrow, and Frank Walsh, not to mention the Wisconsin labor economists) has gone largely unexplored.[88]

This indifference to the intellectual and professional classes may well reflect the unintended consequences of the best scholarship of the past twenty-five years. Effectively enunciating a new interpretive agenda for the field, Herbert Gutman, as early as 1963, pulled away from "struggling craft unions ... and assorted reformers and radicals" in favor of "the workers themselves, their communities, and the day-to-day occurrences that shaped their outlook."[89] The New Labor historians justly undertook to restore to center stage what E. P. Thompson called the "agency of working people, the degree to which they contributed, by conscious efforts, to the making of history." In practice, rescuing the common people from "the enormous condescension of posterity" inevitably obscured the role of individuals from middle-class backgrounds.[90] More precisely, the transformation of "labor" history (with its economic and institutional bias) into "workers'" history (with its emphasis on initiative "from the bottom up") left little room for the intellectual either as historical figure or self-conscious scholarly interpreter. Overcoming the restrictions, in turn, of Commons-Perlman institutionalism, the consensus assumptions of political historians, and the economic determinism of earlier Marxists, the new paradigm tended toward a kind of cognitive "workerism" or unmediated reconstruction of the workers' own world. Like the "participatory democracy" of the New Left in the political realm, the new labor history assumed a basic cultural integrity among its selected public, who neither intellectually required nor historically desired direction from "above."[91]

But the issue goes beyond a mere redress of scholarly imbalances. Just as the attitude of earlier labor historians toward the "abstract" intellectual was a product (at least in part) of their own academic and political experience, so we might ask if social context is not also a factor in recent interpretations. For even as scholars now openly challenge the circumscribed mental world of the worker as painted by their Wisconsin forebears, they run the risk of validating a deeper, if unspoken, dichotomy between "worker" and "intellectual." Identifying vicariously with the eras of insurgency in American workers' past, while living amid a bureaucratic, defensive, and increasingly powerless labor union present, today's labor historians have not, in any institutionally creative sense, discovered a way to connect personally or politically to their subject matter.[92] The conceptual void regarding the intellectual's historical role thus parallels the relatively isolated state of today's academic denizens.[93] Indeed, the most serious manifestation of the "intellectuals versus workers" problem may well lie in the yawning gap between the scholarly community and the world it presumes to describe. Attacked from the right for partisanship, assailed from the left for irrelevance, today's labor scholar reaches uncertainly for a role that is at once intellectually and politically meaningful.

The contemporary situation eerily recalls the little-noticed conclusion to Thompson's classic work. Even if a "working-class consciousness" among radical artisans had, in his terms, been "made" by the 1830s, Thompson nevertheless pointed to an ominous social cleavage. In the same years as the working-class revolt, the Romantic poets had equally "opposed the annunciation of Acquisitive Man." But the critiques evident within the workers' and the intellectuals' culture had, in Thompson's words, run a "parallel but altogether separate course. . . . In the failure of the two traditions to come to a point of junction, something was lost. How much we cannot be sure, for we are the losers."[94] Win or lose, the dichotomy between scholar (intellectual) and scholarly object (worker) has long played a constitutive role in the writing of labor history. To insist on a "relational" reading of the field's seminal texts is not a means of dismissing their authors, be they young or old.[95] It is rather meant to remind us of our own constant and inevitable presence in what we write.

NOTES

This essay originally appeared in *American Historical Review* 96 (April 1991), 395–421. Reprinted by permission. Initial research for this essay was completed under an arts and humanities fellowship from the University of North Carolina at Chapel Hill and a summer fellowship from the National Endowment for the Humanities. I offered earlier versions to the Perspectives on Labor History Conference, State Historical Society of Wisconsin, March 9–10, 1990, and to the annual meeting of the Organization of American Historians, March 1990. For their suggestions, comments, and criticisms, I am especially indebted to Peter Coclanis, Melvyn Dubofsky, Ellen Fitzpatrick, Mary Furner, Julia Greene, James Leloudis, Philip Scranton, and Joe Trotter. In addition, Harold L. Miller, reference archivist at the State Historical Society of Wisconsin, extended very special assistance. A distinct note of thanks is due Mark Perlman for his willing cooperation in painstakingly reconstructing his father's career. For more on the subject, see Leon Fink, "A Memoir of Selig Perlman and His Life at the University of Wisconsin: Based on an Interview with Mark Perlman," *Labor History* 32 (Fall 1991), 503–25. Finally, appreciation is extended to the anonymous readers of the *AHR* as well as Susan Levine for steady editorial guidance. For elaboration on the themes of gender and ideology in this essay, see Ellen Fitzpatrick, "Rethinking the Intellectual Origins of American Labor History," and my response, *American Historical Review* 96 (April 1991), 422–31.

1. John R. Commons, "Abstract Studies and the Real World," *Oberlin Review* (February 7, 1888), quoted in Roger D. Horne, "John R. Commons and the Climate of Progressivism" (Ph.D. dissertation, University of Oklahoma, 1989), 57; Selig Perlman, *A Theory of the Labor Movement* (New York, 1928), 280–81; Ira Berlin, "Herbert G. Gutman and the American Working Class," in Gutman, *Power and Culture: Essays on the American Working Class* (New York, 1987), 17.

2. Joan Wallach Scott, *Gender and the Politics of History* (New York, 1988); Peter

Novick, *That Noble Dream: The "Objectivity Question" and the American Historical Profession* (New York, 1988).

3. See, for example, Allan Bloom, *The Closing of the American Mind* (New York, 1987); Roger Kimball, *Tenured Radicals: How Politics Has Corrupted Higher Education* (New York, 1990); Charles J. Sykes, *ProfScam: Professors and the Demise of Higher Education* (New York, 1988). Compare Russell Jacoby, *The Last Intellectuals: American Culture in the Age of Academe* (New York, 1987); Tim Luke, Paul Piccone, Fred Siegel, and Michael Taves, "Roundtable on Intellectuals and the Academy," *Telos* 71 (Spring 1987), 5–35; Bryan D. Palmer, *Descent into Discourse: The Reification of Language and the Writing of Social History* (Philadelphia, 1990).

4. See Paul Berman, "Intellectuals after the Revolution: What's Happened since the Sixties?" and Todd Gitlin, "Postmodernism: Roots and Politics," *Dissent* (Winter 1989), 86–93, 100–108.

5. Mark Perlman, *Labor Union Theories in America: Background and Development* (Evanston, Ill., 1958), 1.

6. From 1870 to 1910, the number of university and college students rose four times as fast as the country's population. The change was especially dramatic at the postgraduate level. By 1900, the number of graduate students had increased from fewer than 50 to 6,000, with 90 percent of Ph.D.s awarded by fourteen institutions, and a full 55 percent from "a big five" of California, Chicago, Columbia, Harvard, and Johns Hopkins. The social sciences formed a part of this wave, with history, economics, anthropology, and political science creating graduate departments and journals in the 1880s and sociology following in the 1890s. Within economics, or political economy as it was then called, 3 Ph.D.s were awarded in the 1870s, 11 in the 1880s, and 95 in the 1890s. A total of 228 American women received doctoral degrees prior to 1900; of these, 66 were in the social sciences and only 5 in economics. A. W. Coats, "The Educational Revolution and the Professionalization of American Economics," in William J. Barber, ed., *Breaking the Academic Mould: Economists and American Higher Learning in the Nineteenth Century* (Middletown, Conn., 1988), 344–45; Alexandra Oleson and John Voss, "Introduction," xii, and Dorothy Ross, "The Development of the Social Sciences," 108, in Oleson and Voss, eds., *The Organization of Knowledge in Modern America, 1860–1920* (Baltimore, 1979); Walter Crosby Eells, "Earned Doctorates for Women in the Nineteenth Century," *AAUP Bulletin* 42 (1956), 646, 648. For the best elaboration on women's distinct experience in the emerging world of social science research, see Ellen Fitzpatrick, *Endless Crusade: Women Social Scientists and Progressive Reform* (New York, 1990).

7. Four of the most prominent young scholars to engage the labor question in the late 1880s—Richard T. Ely, Edmund J. James, Simon Nelson Patten, and Henry Carter Adams—had each been influenced by evangelical religious backgrounds as well as graduate work in Germany. The German graduate education model was already being adapted to American circumstances, beginning with Johns Hopkins University, by the late 1870s. Mary O. Furner, *Advocacy and Objectivity: A Crisis in the Professionalization of American Social Science, 1865–1905* (Lexington, 1975), 35–58; Paul J. McNulty, *The Origins and Development of Labor*

Economics: A Chapter in the History of Social Thought (Cambridge, Mass., 1980), 127–40.

8. John L. Thomas, *Alternative America: Henry George, Edward Bellamy, Henry Demarest Lloyd, and the Adversary Tradition* (Cambridge, Mass., 1983).

9. Bruno Cartosio, "Strikes and Economics: Working-Class Insurgency and the Birth of Labor Historiography in the 1880s," in *American Labor and Immigration History, 1870–1920: Recent European Research* (Urbana, Ill., 1983), 23–25, 27. By 1886, fifteen states, following Massachusetts' lead in 1869, had organized bureaus of labor statistics.

10. Benjamin G. Rader, *The Academic Mind and Reform: The Influence of Richard T. Ely in American Life* (Lexington, 1966), 2–27, 54, 56.

11. Richard T. Ely, *The Labor Movement in America* (New York, 1886), 5–6.

12. Rader, *Academic Mind,* 83.

13. Quoted in George M. Fredrickson, "Intellectuals and the Labor Question in Late Nineteenth-Century America," paper presented to the AHA annual meeting, New York City, December 1985.

14. Ely, *Labor Movement,* 75; Rader, *Academic Mind,* 82.

15. Rader, *Academic Mind,* 82; Ely, *Labor Movement,* ix, xi; Terence Powderly to Richard T. Ely, June 6, 1885; December 22, 1886, reel 1, Richard T. Ely Papers, State Historical Society of Wisconsin, Madison.

16. Joseph Dorfman, *The Economic Mind in American Civilization,* vol. 3 (New York, 1949), 164–74.

17. Cornell trustees were skeptical enough of evolving currents in professional economics that they "balanced" Adams's appointment with that of a nonprofessional high-tariff advocate, a humiliating arrangement that *The Nation* called the "Duplex Professorship." Furner, *Advocacy,* 130; Ross, "Development," 38–40.

18. Henry Carter Adams, "The Labor Problem," *Scientific American Supplement* 22 (August 21, 1886), 8861–63.

19. Dorfman, *Economic Mind,* 188–205; see also Franek Rozwadowski, "From Recitation Room to Research Seminar: Political Economy at Columbia University," in Barber, *Breaking the Academic Mould,* 199–200. On the political significance of Clark's "marginalism" (particularly as elaborated in *Distribution of Wealth,* 1899), see James Livingston, "The Social Analysis of Economic History and Theory: Conjectures on Late Nineteenth-Century American Development," *AHR* 92 (February 1987), 69–95.

20. John B. Clark, *The Philosophy of Wealth: Economic Principles Newly Formulated* (1886; rpt. ed., Boston, 1894), 126–48, 174–202.

21. Rozwadowski, "From Recitation Room," 196–97; Furner, *Advocacy,* 98–99.

22. *Journal of Social Science* 27 (October 1890), 44, 84–85, 87–88. Compare Rhoda Hellman, *Henry George Reconsidered* (New York, 1987), 70–73.

23. Dorfman, *Economic Mind,* 160–61.

24. The dominant impetus behind establishment of the AEA is still debated by historians of American social science. Viewed across even a ten-year time frame, tendencies toward professional group promotion seem to have been inextricably mixed with tendencies toward radical social reform. Compare Furner,

Advocacy; and Thomas L. Haskell, *The Emergence of Professional Social Science: The American Social Science Association and the Nineteenth-Century Crisis of Authority* (Urbana, Ill., 1977). While Haskell is generally convincing in stressing the quick transformation of rhetorical "radicalism" into a self-protective posture of professional expertise among the new-school economists who created the AEA, he may have underestimated the impact of outside forces (for instance, those beyond the academics' own career aims) in deflecting the intellectuals' initial reform enthusiasms. On the centrality of the labor problem to the early professional economists, see McNulty, *Origins,* 142–51.

25. *Labor: Its Rights and Wrongs* (Westport, Conn., 1975 [1886]), 30. Of fifty chartering members of the AEA, twenty-three were ministers or ex-ministers. Coats, "Educational Revolution and the Professionalization of American Economics," 358.

26. Horne, "John R. Commons and the Climate of Progressivism," 57.

27. Lafayette G. Harter, Jr., *John R. Commons: His Assault on Laissez-Faire* (Corvallis, Oreg., 1962), 13–19. Commons was attracted to Johns Hopkins precisely by the radical notoriety of Ely, choosing his college after reading a nasty review in *The Nation* of Ely's *Studies in the Evolution of Industrial Society.* Ely to Robert Hunter, October 21, 1903, reel 27, Richard T. Ely Papers. A baseball aficionado (and pretty fair pitcher in his Oberlin college days), Commons dated his conversion to an overall "economic sceptic" to his personal refutation in 1885–86 of Herbert Spencer's casual claim that a curve ball defied the laws of physics: "he knew not the seams on the ball and forgot the friction of the air." John R. Commons, *Myself: The Autobiography of John R. Commons* (Madison, Wis., 1963), 28.

28. Dorfman, *Economic Mind,* 285. Commons confessed to one such warning from Ely in 1895: "I recognize that on some occasions I may have seemed needlessly to have aroused antagonism. It is difficult to combine opportuneness with exposures of injustice, but I believe I am getting more cautious." Furner, *Advocacy,* 200–202.

29. Arthur T. Hadley, "Economic Theory and Political Morality"; and "Comment" by John R. Commons in *Publications of the AEA: Papers and Proceedings of the Twelfth Annual Meeting* (New York, 1900), 45–88, quotations 61, 65, 69, 77, 79. Compare Furner, *Advocacy,* 273–77. Some analysts, in my view, go too far in attributing class-conciliatory corporatist notions to Commons's earliest writings. See, for example, Andy Dawson, "History and Ideology: Fifty Years of 'Job Consciousness,'" *Literature and History* 8 (Autumn 1978), 223–41; and Ronald W. Schatz, "From Commons to Dunlop and Kerr: Rethinking the Field and Theory of Industrial Relations," paper presented at the Industrial Democracy Conference, Woodrow Wilson International Center for Scholars, Washington, D.C., March 28–30, 1988.

30. Dorfman, *Economic Mind,* 101–10.

31. *Publications of the American Economic Association,* vol. 3 (Baltimore, 1889), 162. For a similar turn by the Sumnerian Franklin H. Giddings, see Ross, "Development," 43–44.

32. Richard Hofstadter and Walter P. Metzger, *The Development of Academic Freedom in the United States* (New York, 1955), 31.

33. Furner, *Advocacy,* 271–72.

34. On the problem of contemporary intellectual authority, see ibid, 81–106; Hofstadter and Metzger, *Development,* 401–2; and Haskell, *Emergence,* 190–210. Having dislodged natural law, the radical economists faced the problem of what authority to turn to, other than arbitrary moral claims or public opinion, neither of which proved satisfactory as a basis for "expertise" by the academic class. Academic professionalism, reigning in its political judgments and public interventions, proved one enduring "solution."

35. Livingston, "Social Analysis of Economic History," 69–95.

36. Related cases of political discrimination involved the economist E. Benjamin Andrews at Brown and the sociologist E. A. Ross at Stanford. Dorfman, *Economic Mind,* 240; Hofstadter and Metzger, *Development* 420–23. While Hofstadter and Metzger's long view of free-speech conflicts in American academe remains a most valuable basic work, it seems flawed in serious ways by their own ideological blinders. So concerned were they in the early 1950s to ward off totalitarianism (and intellectual intolerance) from the left and right extremes, especially the resort to irrational "conspiracy" theories, that they were inclined to miss the debilitating effects of bureaucratically imposed norms of academic behavior by the "liberal" center. By identifying the philosophical "empiricist" and "commonsense" traditions of American thought as the chief source of the relative political "neutrality" of American academics, the authors underestimated their own evidence for the political limits imposed on the universities by the turn of the century. See esp. 400–403, 450–51, 506.

37. Adams, "Labor Problem," 8863, 8877–78; A. W. Coats, "Henry Carter Adams: A Case Study in the Emergence of the Social Sciences in the United States, 1850–1900," *American Studies* 2 (October 1968), 189.

38. Furner, *Advocacy,* 115–24, 139–42, 277; Coats, "Henry Carter Adams," 195; Dorfman, *Economic Mind,* 171–72; Coats, "Educational Revolution," 365; Haskell, *Emergence,* 187; Ross, "Development," 47–48, 56–59, 77.

39. Furner, *Advocacy,* 147–58; Rader, *Academic Mind,* 152–54. Excusing his apparent hypocrisy, Ely explained to the associate editor of the *Outlook:* "Suppose if you should become known as a radical you would lose your position on the 'Outlook,' and on account of alleged radicalism you could never secure any other position. Would you not under these circumstances feel a little sensitive about the epithet 'radical'? You see what it can do in the case of Professor Bemis." Rader, *Academic Mind,* 153.

40. Seven years after his trial, Ely confessed that he had still not "gotten over" it. Rader, *Academic Mind,* 152–54.

41. Rader, *Academic Mind,* 192–222, 224–27, 236.

42. Hofstadter and Metzger, *Development,* 427–28; Furner, *Advocacy,* 168–98. For a careful assessment of the Bemis case, see Harold E. Bergquist, Jr., "The Edward W. Bemis Controversy at the University of Chicago," *AAUP Bulletin* 58 (Winter 1972), 384–93; Furner, *Advocacy,* 196–98.

43. Commons, *Myself,* 52; Furner, *Advocacy,* 202; Ely to Hunter, April 26, 1903, reel 25, Richard T. Ely Papers; Commons, *Myself,* 95.

44. Commons, *Myself,* 58–59.

45. See M. Perlman, *Labor Union Theories,* on Commons's four "phases" of trade union analysis, 176–90, esp. 180, 182.

46. Pressed by reporters to explain his departure from Syracuse, Commons kept mum. "He [the chancellor] gave me a rousing send-off. Speaking to a general University convocation, he bewailed the loss of one of their ablest and most popular professors. . . . And there I was sitting on the platform beside him. So I learned the virtue of silence. It makes eulogists instead of avengers." *Myself,* 60–61; T. N. Carver to Ely, December 20, 1903, reel 27, Richard T. Ely Papers.

47. As he explained in his autobiography, "My dismissal turned out to be a fortunate happening. It drove me out for five years to live in the struggles of human beings." Commons, *Myself,* 60.

48. Harter, *John R. Commons,* 89–129.

49. Furner, *Advocacy,* 271–72. This is not to say that respectable, reformist intentions assured academic "immunity" from outside pressures. In 1910, for example, a visit by Emma Goldman to Madison triggered charges of "socialist teaching" on campus and a Board of Visitors investigation centered on Edward A. Ross and the economics department of which he (as a sociologist) was a member. Among graduate students called to testify, Selig Perlman was asked, "Do you think Sociology and Socialism are identical?" Perlman, who had sworn to his mentor Commons, "Brother, they will not fire you on *my* testimony," took pride in an official exoneration of the faculty, especially reference to "striking instances of foreigners who have come to the university as students believing in anarchism and violence, who have been led to discard such beliefs through the instruction given in the university." Merle Curti and Vernon Carstensen, *The University of Wisconsin: A History, 1848–1925* (Madison, Wis., 1949), 2:63–67; Selig Perlman interview, April 13, 1950, State Historical Society of Wisconsin.

50. John R. Commons, *Labor and Administration* (New York, 1923), 72, 78–79, 83. These comments, published in the *American Journal of Sociology,* were first enunciated in a discussion before the American Sociological Society in 1906.

51. Commons, *Myself,* 88.

52. A hard-headed acquaintance with industrial realities, not "the assumptions of natural equality of the Declaration of Independence, or of Adam Smith," would equip the intellectual for a useful role. Ibid., 89.

53. U.S. Senate Committee on Education and Labor, *Report upon the Relations between Labor and Capital and Testimony* (Washington, D.C., 1885), 1:460; Gompers, quoted by Commons, *Myself,* 87; AFL Proceedings of the 18th Annual Convention, 1898, 5.

54. Matthew Woll, "Labor Will Lead," *American Federationist* (June 1919), 513. See also Lyle Cooper, "The AFL and the Intellectuals," *Political Science Quarterly* 43 (1928), 388–407.

55. John Frey to W. A. Appleton, December 21, 1928, John Frey Papers, Library of Congress.

56. For elaboration on some of the intellectual and political differences between Gompers and Commons, see Leon Fink, "The Intellectual as Quarterback: Charles McCarthy and the Debacle of the U.S. Industrial Relations Commission, 1912-1915," in *Intellectuals and Political Life*, ed. Judith B. Farquhar, Leon Fink, Stephen T. Leonard, and Donald M. Reid (Ithaca, N.Y., 1992).

57. John R. Commons, Davis J. Saposs, Helen L. Sumner et al., *History of Labour in the United States* (New York, 1946 [1918]), 1:18-19. In an intriguing aside, Commons noted that "the 'rule' regarding intellectuals and unions is violated" in unions organizing women workers "where intellectuals [presumably a reference to clothing workers' leaders, Hillman and Dubinsky, as well perhaps to Women's Trade Union League figures] have been actual leaders." Commons, 1:18-19. For an arresting commentary on intellectual-labor relations in Europe during the same period, see David Beetham, "Reformism and the 'Bourgeoisification' of the Labour Movement," in Carl Levy, ed., *Socialism and the Intelligentsia, 1880-1914* (London, 1987), 106-34.

58. *Encyclopaedia of the Social Sciences* 8 (New York, 1935), 685-86.

59. Commons, *Myself*, 86-87. Commons traced his first encounter with a destructive intellectual type to T. A. Schaffer, the "unsuccessful or dismissed minister," whose apparent misguided militancy led the steelworkers to disaster in 1902. Ibid., 86.

60. Commons, *History of Labour*, 1:19.

61. Ibid., 2:438. The theme is reiterated in Selig Perlman and Philip Taft, *History of Labour*, vol. 4 (New York, 1935), 4-5. Perlman's emphasis on the worker's psychology of job scarcity soon led him to abandon Commons's term "wage-consciousness," in favor of "job consciousness." Harter, *John R. Commons*, 196.

62. Perlman, *Theory*, 5-6.

63. Ibid., 13-233.

64. Selig Perlman to William M. Leiserson, January 28, 1928, William Morris Leiserson Papers, State Historical Society of Wisconsin.

65. Selig Perlman left no papers, and remarkably little biographical information about him survives in published form. Most of the following portrait is drawn from an interview with his son, Mark Perlman, conducted by the author, January 19, 1989, in Pittsburgh. Although the relationship of father to son was marked by a classical, European-style formality, Mark Perlman recalled that his father talked to him daily about many matters, including his work. That Mark Perlman followed his father into labor economics seems also to have sharpened his understanding and his recollection of his father's words.

66. Reminiscence of Selig Perlman, recorded April 13, 1950, State Historical Society of Wisconsin.

67. Selig Perlman, "History of Socialism in Milwaukee, 1893-1910," unpublished manuscript, University of Wisconsin, Madison, 1910, copy in author's possession courtesy of Mark Perlman.

68. Reminiscence of Selig Perlman, recorded April 13, 1950, State Historical Society of Wisconsin.

69. Ibid. For evidence of Commons's stereotypes of Jews, typical for his time,

see John R. Commons, *Races and Immigrants in America* (New York, 1930), 88–95, 132, 152–53. Mark Perlman noted that two other Jewish students, David Saposs and William Leiserson, were both considerably more "Americanized" and secularized than Selig Perlman—Leiserson came to the United States in 1890, Saposs in 1895—and thereby avoided some of the cultural disdain felt by Selig Perlman. While Saposs, for example, entirely disavowed Jewish religious practice, Perlman rather uncomfortably interrupted his family's Sabbath celebration for Commons's famous Friday Nighter home seminars. And, whenever Leiserson married a non-Jewish woman, Mrs. Commons, according to Mark Perlman's recollection, noticeably took offense. Saposs also displaced the blame for his own personal estrangement from John R. on Mrs. Commons, for example: "Mrs. Commons indirectly hated Jews. Commons never did." Interview with David Saposs by William C. Haygood and Theron Schlabach, September 8, 1964, State Historical Society of Wisconsin. The extensive nature of anti-Semitism in American academe is amply documented in Novick, *That Noble Dream,* 172–74.

70. Commons acknowledged this incident in his autobiography, referring to his wife's help with Perlman's "English composition and desperate family affairs" (*Myself,* 81). According to Mark Perlman, Selig Perlman always felt more readily and warmly received by Ella (Mrs. Commons) than by John R. Yet even Mrs. Commons apparently showed little respect for the religiosity of his wife, Eva, whom he had married in 1918 (Perlman interview). The rebuke of condescension that Perlman felt from Commons was, in part, self-made. Perlman raised the issue of his parents' desperate financial position (factory production of textiles had effectively squeezed out "middle men" like his father) with Commons, and his teacher responded with a substantial raise in his student's stipend. Through the early 1920s, when Perlman found it impossible to secure a regular university position, Commons helped him with grants and fellowships, even intervening when the cantankerous Ely moved to dismiss Perlman after a difference of opinion. When Ely left Wisconsin for Northwestern University in 1925, Perlman finally succeeded to a permanent appointment, assuming much of Commons's old undergraduate teaching load. Helen Sumner to Commons, June 10, 1915, Commons to H. W. Farnam, October 12, 1915, John R. Commons Papers, reel 2; Mark Perlman interview.

71. Mark Perlman recalls the break with Commons as lasting for "several years," but this recollection appears contradicted by the timing of reconciliation, namely, the suicide of Commons's daughter, Rachel, in the early 1930s. Mark Perlman remembers answering a distressful call from Commons in which Commons pleaded, "I want Selig" and "I must have Selig." Selig Perlman spent the evening trying to comfort his former teacher, who had already been doubly wounded by the death of his devoted wife Ella (Nel) in 1928 and the tragic disappearance of his son Jack (after abandoning his wife and child, Jack was found fourteen years later driving a milk truck in Hartford, Connecticut, the apparent victim of a combination of mental illness and amnesia). Commons and Perlman seem to have remained on good terms after this. In a 1950 protest against anti-Semitism within the Wisconsin history department, Perlman extolled his

former teacher for a "liberality not to be found anywhere else in the world." Seven years later, Perlman was appointed the first John R. Commons Professor of Political Economy. Harter, *John R. Commons,* 83; Mark Perlman interview; Commons, *Myself,* 81, 87; Selig Perlman to Merle Curti, May 6, 1950, Merle Curti Papers, State Historical Society of Wisconsin; Dorfman, *Economic Mind,* 4, 395.

72. His only professionally connected government service was the early work for the Commission on Industrial Relations in 1913–14, arranged by Commons, and later consultancy on a history of the World War II War Labor Board; in addition, he had one unsatisfying experience as a labor arbitrator. Mark Perlman, "The Jewish Contribution as Distinct from the Contribution of Jews to Economics," Selig Perlman Memorial Lecture presented April 14, 1981, State Historical Society of Wisconsin (copy in possession of author); Witte, "Selig Perlman," *Industrial and Labor Relations Review* 13 (April 1960), 335–37. Mark Perlman notes that his father felt some disappointment that he was not approached more often by academic, political, or labor leaders for advice. His first invitation to Harvard, for example, did not come until 1948.

73. Nor was the lack of contact a mere matter of physical distance from the leading labor figures. Samuel Gompers's official correspondence, a voluminous exchange with thousands of contemporaries inside and outside the labor movement, contains not a single letter to or from Selig Perlman. American Federation of Labor Records: The Samuel Gompers Era (microfilm edition), reel 58, finding aids. Outside Wisconsin, the one labor leader whose company Perlman did enjoy was David Dubinsky; the two spoke Yiddish together. Telephone interview with Mark Perlman, February 14, 1989; "Perlman's Interpretation of History," A. L. Riesch Owen, ed., *Selig Perlman's Lectures on Capitalism and Socialism* (Madison, Wis., 1976), 47–51.

74. Perlman reported to his research supervisor that, had it not been for an envelope addressed to William English Walling found on his person, a group of suspicious Wobblies in Lawrence, Massachusetts, might well have thrown him out a window. Perlman to Basil M. Manly, December 4, 1913, Commission on Industrial Relations, Record Group 174, National Archives (courtesy of Philip Scranton) (hereafter CIR, RG 174, NA).

75. Selig Perlman, "Preliminary Report of an Investigation of the Relations between Labor and Capital in the Textile Industry in New England," July 24, 1914, CIR, RG 174, NA (courtesy of Philip Scranton).

76. Perlman, *Theory,* 281: "Yet, at bottom, the intellectual's conviction that labor must espouse the 'new social order' rests neither on statistically demonstrable trends in conditions nor on labor's stirrings for the sort of liberty expressed through the control of the job, which any one who knows workingmen will recognize and appreciate, but on a deeply rooted faith that labor is somehow the 'chosen vessel' of whatever may be the power which shapes the destiny of society." On Deweyan Pragmatism and its relation to reform thought, see Andrew Feffer, "Between Head and Hand: Chicago Pragmatism and Social Reform, 1886 to 1919" (Ph.D. dissertation, University of Pennsylvania, 1987), esp. 23–75.

77. Riesch Owen, *Selig Perlman's Lectures,* 127. On the Pragmatists' educational

philosophy, see Frank C. Wegener, *The Organic Philosophy of Education* (Dubuque, Iowa, 1957), 26–48, 209–22; and Feffer, "Between Head and Hand," 113–71, 267–316. For Commons's version of this dualism, see "Utilitarian Idealism" and "Horace Greeley and the Working Class Origins of the Republican Party," in Commons, *Labor and Administration,* 1–6, 33, 49–50.

78. Max Kadushin, *Organic Thinking* (New York, 1976), 247–61, and esp. v–vii. For further reflections on intellectual similarities between Perlman and Kadushin, see Mark Perlman, "Jewish Contribution," 20–21.

79. Beginning in the late 1920s, Perlman did have regular contact with trade unionists as one of the directors of the Wisconsin School for Workers. The interaction was very much on his terms, however. Perlman enjoyed a reputation as "a spell-binding lecturer . . . [who] looked at the ceiling all the time." Mark Perlman interview; telephone interview with Robert W. Ozanne, January 4, 1991. For a political-psychological profile of Perlman, see Benjamin Stolberg, "An Intellectual Afraid," *The Nation* 128 (June 26, 1929), 769–70.

80. Leon Fink, "Labor, Liberty, and the Law: Trade Unionism and the Problem of the American Constitutional Order," *Journal of American History* 74 (December 1987), 904–25.

81. Christopher L. Tomlins, *The State and the Unions: Labor Relations, Law, and the Organized Labor Movement in America, 1880–1960* (New York, 1985), xi–xiv. Leiserson's thoughts were later codified in William M. Leiserson, *Right and Wrong in Labor Relations* (Berkeley, Calif., 1938), 7–12.

82. J. Michael Eisner, *William Morris Leiserson: A Biography* (Madison, Wis., 1967), 41.

83. James A. Gross, *The Reshaping of the National Labor Relations Board* (Albany, N.Y., 1981), 113.

84. Philip Taft, "Reflections on Selig Perlman as a Teacher and Writer," *Industrial and Labor Relations Review* 29 (January 1976), 250. Taft's rather grudging praise for Perlman may have dated to their argument over the authorship of volume 4 of the *History of Labour in the United States.* Taft wanted it to read "Taft and Perlman," but Perlman (perhaps reflecting a continuing sense of slight for his own omission from authorship of volume 1) insisted on "Perlman and Taft." "Reflections," 257; Mark Perlman interview, January 19, 1989. On Taft, see David Brody, "Philip Taft: Labor Scholar," *Labor History* 19 (Winter 1978), 9–22.

85. Tomlins, *State,* 80–82, 241–43; Gross, *Reshaping of the National Labor Relations Board,* 112–30, 239.

86. The pantheon of largely unsung heroes here would include Vera Shlakman, Edith Abbott, Caroline Ware, Norman Ware, Charles Wesley, Sterling Spero, Abram Harris, Samuel Yellen, Sidney Lens, and, more recently, Philip Foner. For a clairvoyant forecast of historiographic trends, see Caroline F. Ware, "Introduction," *The Cultural Approach to History* (New York, 1940), 3–16. For pathbreaking discussion of these countercurrents, see Fitzpatrick, *Endless Crusade;* and Francille Rusan Wilson, "Black Workers, Segregated Scholars: The Origins of Black Labor History, 1895–1920," paper presented to the Perspectives on Labor History Conference, March 9, 1990, State Historical Society of Wisconsin, Madison.

87. Sean Wilentz, *Chants Democratic: New York City and the Rise of the American Working Class, 1788–1850* (New York, 1984), 145–216; Gregory S. Kealey and Bryan D. Palmer, *Dreaming of What Might Be: The Knights of Labor in Ontario, 1880–1900* (New York, 1982), 301–11; Richard Oestreicher, *Solidarity and Fragmentation: Working People and Class Consciousness in Detroit, 1875–1900* (Urbana, Ill., 1986); Leon Fink, "The New Labor History and the Powers of Historical Pessimism: Consensus, Hegemony, and the Case of the Knights of Labor," *Journal of American History* 75 (June 1988), 115–36, esp. 136.

88. David Montgomery, *Beyond Equality: Labor and the Radical Republicans, 1862–1872* (New York, 1967), esp. 387–424. And indeed, "beyond Montgomery," the search for intellectual influences within Gilded Age labor culture passes almost uninterruptedly back to Chester McArthur Destler's classic, *American Radicalism* (Chicago, 1946); John L. Thomas, *Alternative America: Henry George, Edward Bellamy, Henry Demarest Lloyd and the Adversary Tradition* (Cambridge, Mass., 1983); Katherine Kish Sklar, "Hull House in the 1890s: A Community of Women Reformers," *Signs* 10 (Summer 1985), 658–77; Elizabeth Anne Payne, *Reform, Labor, and Feminism: Margaret Dreier Robins and the Women's Trade Union League* (Urbana, Ill., 1988). An exception for the Progressive Era (and again, a volume uninfluenced by the New Labor history) is Irwin Yellowitz, *Labor and the Progressive Movement in New York State, 1897–1916* (Ithaca, N.Y., 1965). A renewed concern for the relations of labor and the state (and consequently state-oriented reformers) may help to bridge the aforementioned gaps. See Steve Fraser, "The 'Labor Question,'" in Steve Fraser and Gary Gerstle, *The Rise and Fall of the New Deal Order, 1930–1980* (Princeton, N.J., 1989); and Christopher H. Johnson, *Maurice Sugar: Law, Labor, and the Left in Detroit, 1912–1950* (Detroit, 1988).

89. Herbert G. Gutman, "The Worker's Search for Power: Labor in the Gilded Age," rpt. in *Power and Culture: Essays on the American Working Class,* ed. Ira Berlin (New York, 1987), 70.

90. E. P. Thompson, *The Making of the English Working Class* (New York, 1963), 12.

91. On the underlying philosophical assumptions of "history from the bottom up" and other tendencies associated with New Left historians, see Novick, *That Noble Dream,* 438–57. Discomfort in identifying oneself fully as an "intellectual" was endemic to the New Left sensibility of the 1960s. As former SDS (Students for a Democratic Society) leader Richard Flacks noted: "Most New Leftists adamantly refused to adopt this label [intellectual]. The word connoted the very things that they were trying to overcome in themselves. For "intellectual" conveys a separation from action, from material reality, from struggle, from whole-hearted commitment. Moreover, not only do "intellectuals" inhabit "ivory towers," but they do so in privilege, claiming exemption from physical labor, claiming also a capacity for understanding the world superior to that of the unlettered, demanding deference even though refusing to share the deprivations and sacrifices of the common folk." Flacks, *Making History: The Radical Tradition in American Life* (New York, 1988), 281.

92. Lack of a conceptualized path for the contemporary labor intellectual is

not to imply that the new labor historians, as individuals, have not conscientiously engaged the larger world around them. They have: witness David Montgomery's consistent activism in strike support in Pittsburgh and New Haven, Herbert Gutman's outreach to working-class audiences for a new social history, Peter Rachleff's public defense of the Local P-9 Hormel workers, or Alice Kessler-Harris's testimony on behalf of affirmative-action hiring in the *Sears* case, not to mention others employed in worker-education programs. But the issue is seldom considered in a strategic sense or taken up as any self-conscious group responsibility.

93. For a provocative elaboration on this theme, see Jacoby, *Last Intellectuals.*

94. Thompson, *Making of the English Working Class,* 832.

95. "Relationism" was Karl Mannheim's term for a non-evaluative cognitive relativism: "relationism signifies merely that all of the elements of meaning in a given situation have reference to one another and derive their significance from this reciprocal interrelationship in a given frame of thought." Mannheim, *Ideology and Utopia: An Introduction to the Sociology of Knowledge* (New York, 1970), 85–86. Compare Novick, *That Noble Dream,* 159–61.

9

Culture's Last Stand?
Gender and the Search for Synthesis
in American Labor History

The call to which these remarks respond asks at once "how gender contributes to ... our understanding of labor history" and whether it "helps us to conceptualize a new synthesis in the field."[1] These two phrases, it seems to me, connect two important but often unrelated discussions in labor historiography, and it is therefore to that relationship—between gender-related issues on the one hand and synthesis on the other—that I here direct my attention. In addressing this topic, I shall necessarily rely less on a private treasure of insights than on the mounting bounty of other practitioners; moreover, if I invoke certain works critically, it is because those works themselves stimulate further questions.

The call for synthesis diplomatically invokes one of the more vexing debates among labor historians over the past fifteen years. Roughly since David Brody first articulated a discontent with the new labor history of the 1970s, a seed of doubt has grown into a field of dismay about the lack of clarity, direction, and ultimate explanations in the study of American working people.[2] The 1984 labor history conference at Northern Illinois University in DeKalb seemed only to highlight tensions within the field; in its aftermath, commentators have tended to unify around a culprit for the collective confusion: culturalism. Initially, and perhaps erroneously employed as a descriptive shorthand for the most original currents in the field, the moniker is now most often employed as a term of abuse, as in Howard Kimeldorf's "tyranny of culturalism" or Daniel Nelson's "faddish 'culturalism.' "[3] In her published afterthought to the DeKalb papers, Alice Kessler-Harris defines the tendency. "Labor historians," she summarizes,

> focused heavily on local history and adopted new quantitative and anthropological methods that attempted to reconstruct the lives and self-experiences of workers in their communities. In this "culturalist" approach, power was intrinsic in the capacity of workers to retain customs, values, language, and traditions in the face of a destructive capitalism. Workers' power resided in their capacity to use these indigenous attributes of their lives to confront, even to stave off, the initiatives of a dominant industrial elite and to shape the future of an industrial society. The search for workers' resistance, wherever and however it appeared and whether in formal or informal institutions, replaced the history of structures.[4]

Synthesis from a culturalist approach appeared wanting, generally speaking, on two alternate, or overlapping, grounds: the case studies, largely concentrated on the nineteenth century, so splintered the forces of cultural formation as to render inscrutable an "identifiable working class"; and they presented a "romantic" portrait of autonomy and empowerment that could not be squared with the obvious weaknesses of the labor movement in the twentieth century.[5] If DeKalb represented the last hurrah of a literature that offered a hopeful reconstruction of a historical counterculture to acquisitive capitalism ("Kaddish for the sixties," Jesse Lemisch called it), the mood quickly shifted toward a sober, neorealism on the limits of the American labor tradition. As a group, in traveling from DeKalb to Detroit, we have passed through the valley of Debunk. It is not so much the possibilities latent in discreet places and moments that attract us now but an urge to get to the bottom of things. In place of the shifting, subjectivist sands of culture as an orienting field, labor historians are determined to locate a structural rock upon which they can hang a more solid synthesis. Within recent literature, such calls have taken diverse incarnations. Harkening back to Brody (and most recently reechoed by Kimeldorf), one tendency would restore an institutionalist emphasis to the field, that is, a work-centered study of organized labor or, perhaps more broadly, a history of industrial relations. A second trend, the province of Marxist social historians like Bryan D. Palmer and social science theorists like Ira Katznelson and Aristide R. Zolberg, speaks in the name of "materialist analysis" for more systematic attention to class formation within comparative capitalist development.[6]

Both of these synthetic alternatives tend to collide directly with our first order of business, the integration of gender into labor history. Not only will neither approach likely refute Ava Baron's judgment that working-class history is "still a preserve of male workers," but their very working assumptions provoke Baron to warn of the "dangers of synthesizing a history that has yet to integrate gender fully."[7] The institutional and class-formation stories of labor history are narratives of power, conceived in a formal and public sense, and rooted, as Elizabeth Faue has observed, "in workplace structure and political participation."[8] To be sure, in a larger sense, labor history is a *counternarrative* to the history of bosses and of the dominant classes, and we should recognize that it is the excavation of that very public contest with the rulers that has delivered so much energy to the field over the past thirty years. What has sustained labor history is the same battle line that Antonio Gramsci described to his son from a fascist prison in 1937: "I think you must like history, as I liked it when I was your age, because it deals with living men, and everything that concerns men, as many men as possible, all the men in the world in so far as they unite together in society, and work and struggle and make a bid for a better life. All that can't fail to please you more than anything else. Isn't that right?"[9]

That men have historically led and dominated the "armies" of the labor movement, of course, does not in itself interfere with a gendered analysis of the subject. It is rather that the *important* contest, in the eyes of most labor historians, lay in the struggle for *power* or *control* at work and the public spaces beyond the workplace. Pursuing these priorities tends to subordinate gender relations to class relations even when discussing a female-majority workforce (like hospital workers), let alone all-male occupations. Thus, Marcus Rediker's brilliant book on eighteenth-century sailors might have speculated on the relations of this first class-conscious work crew with wives and family at home, with prostitution in ports of call, or even with a sexual dynamic in an isolated all-male environment. Such questions might have introduced additional explanations of motivation and behavior into an already rich narrative. A labor-conflict or class-centered agenda, however, carried the author in another direction.[10]

If, in institutional and work-centered labor history narratives, questions of gender relations are likely to be forsaken for more publicly dramatic points of conflict, the materialist class-formation approach is unlikely to do better. The problem, as most of those who have looked closely at the issue know, lies in the *conceptual* inequality of class and gender in the discipline's paradigm building. To put it simply, class always comes first. As Richard Oestreicher explains, "Labor history is about class formation, about the development of class-based institutions and cultural practices, and about the collective efforts of the working class to alter the relations of production, the rules about who does what, and how the product gets allocated." Despite a considerable broadening of themes by the "new labor history"—particularly with regard to experience beyond work—"labor history is still ultimately about workers, and what defines people as workers is their economic activity."[11]

As if to confirm Oestreicher's warning, Bryan Palmer confidently assures us that "class *is,* in the first instance and at its most basic, an objective, structurally determined relationship to the means of production. . . . Status differences and self-identification, however contradictory, are nevertheless irrelevant in this generalized class system, determined first and foremost by the homogenizing tendencies (never absolute) of modern industry and its master, capital." Palmer offers a compelling "aerial photograph" of mid-nineteenth-century social relations; he sees "factories, mills, mines, and construction sites . . . neighborhoods, families, and taverns . . . a myriad of struggles." But the telos of the search for Palmer, however muffled or invisible it is under most climactic conditions, is "class consciousness itself." Palmer's exposé of the depredations of discourse theory upon the recent practice of social history includes an entire (and informative) chapter on the feminist-theoretical treatment of "gender." It is noteworthy, however, that the subject of gender does not intrude on the labor history–centered chapters devoted to "class" and "politics." When one descends from the air to the ground, it appears, the basic questions of historical development fracture into separate fields of vision.[12]

Another serious attempt to rehabilitate a "theory of class formation" is provided in the anthology *Working-Class Formation,* edited by Ira Katznelson and Aristide R. Zolberg. A sense of "vexation" with "the unsorted kitbag of findings" from the "new social history" drives the editors toward a nuanced definition of class as a supple interaction of four discreet levels of analysis. Despite its comparative scope and conceptual rigor, however, the volume suffers, as acknowledged by Katznelson, "from a lack of consideration of the significance of family and gender relations." After all the fine-tuning, we end up with a volume "principally about men in the working class." Why should this be? The problem, he allows, may arise from "distorted portraits of bases of exploitation."[13] It is consistent with the class-formation model that Katznelson should look for a new "level" of class formation for a solution. With a bow to feminist theory, he suggests that the solution will be found in opening the analytic door onto the structure of patriarchy.

Trust in a theory of patriarchy as the key to integrating gender relations into labor history is, indeed, widespread. "Most women's historians," Mari Jo Buhle reports, accept the idea of "two sets of social relations," the productive system of "capitalism" and the sex-gender system of "patriarchy."[14] As Linda Gordon, among others, has emphasized, a system of "reproduction" centered in sexual and familial relationships has equal historical claim to the capitalist system of "production."[15] To the extent that class is rooted in the material reality of the workplace, gender, as Kessler-Harris has noted, "is rooted in the material reality and social relations of the household."[16]

Yet this dual systems approach—often little more than rhetorically embellished into a "gender, race, and class" triad—has already excited criticism. Ava Baron, for example, notes that in treating economic relations as gender-neutral, or even in treating gender strictly as a direct power relationship between men and women, the dual systems approach allows "conventional" labor historians (i.e., those focusing on male actors in male-dominated public settings) to pretty much forego gender analysis.[17] "Some kind of integrationist approach to the class-gender dualism," Baron suggests, is clearly needed, but exactly how one "dissolves the hyphen between capitalism and patriarchy is not self-evident."[18] To make matters more complicated, Baron invokes the historian Elizabeth Fox-Genovese and the anthropologist Gayle Rubin in questioning the very integrity of class and gender as distinct systems. "Categorical theories," she quotes Rubin, "are not concerned with the process by which gender categories are constructed and do not consider why sexual difference is important in the first place. But the significance of sexual difference is precisely what needs to be explained."[19]

Kessler-Harris likewise insists that gender and class be treated as integrated "process": "Since neither household nor wage work is independent of the other, gender participates in class formation just as wage work participates in gender formation." But if this interaction is, as she maintains, a "historical phenomenon"—open to constant shifts of movement—where does this leave *either* class formation or patriarchal structures as heuristic tools for historical synthesis? Rather than a track, a level, or an analytic system, the problem seems to demand a close empirical investigation of developing consciousness, that realm between structure and agency. Dare I suggest that we are returned, in effect, to the doorstep of culturalism?

The true conceptual coordinates of the gender-class question are more apparent when we take a closer look at some of the critical issues addressed within labor history literature. The first concerns the role of the household in structuring labor conflict and protest. In one of the most interesting recent treatments of gender relations at work, Mary H. Blewett discovers a three-cornered contest among Lynn shoeworkers in the famous strike of 1860, with the interests of young women factory workers set off against a "traditionalist" coalition of male artisans and home-based female binders. In Blewett's treatment, "liberation" from the home seems to offer the factory women a significant break from a family-wage-centered, male-dominated calculation of justice and worker welfare, whereas the home-workers still fundamentally identify as helpmates to "fathers, husbands and brothers." Overall, concludes Blewett, "gender-based ideology and work experience cut women off from the most vital tradition of collective resistance in the early nineteenth century."[20]

While Blewett's analysis radically transforms an artisan-centered, male-only literature on the shoe industry, her basic assumption about work versus home as a source of the women's class consciousness fits a rather conventional cultural model. That is, by associating the women's militancy with their *distance* from the household, Blewett tends to confirm the classic assumption that class consciousness is derived fundamentally from *workplace* relations and that the household as both a preindustrial and a patriarchal remnant acts as a drag on class demands.

Other historians, however, have emphasized the *continuities* between the domestic and neighborhood associations of "women's culture" and capacities for political and workplace organization. The Lowell mill girls, for example, derived part of their sustenance for protest from family relationships as "daughters of free men."[21] Similarly, housewives and factory women in the Knights of Labor appear to have actively identified with the "producing classes" from a communal critique of capitalism drawn from nurturant family roles.[22] Even within the hegemony of the American Federation of Labor, consumer-based organizing, as Dana Frank has emphasized, linked women's sphere in important ways to class organization.[23] Finally, the rich literature on women's work culture has consistently added the domain of the family to that of workplace relations as a historical source of working women's resistance to managerial logic.[24] Perhaps the ultimate extension of this revisionist interpretation of the culture of the home occurs in Eileen Boris's attack on the classic image of tenement cigarmakers as female victims incapable of effective organization. Ignoring an earlier history of struggle that had once united tenement and factory producers, both craft unionists and Progressive reformers collaborated in espousing the innocent sanctity of domestic life. The feminist Rheta Childe Dorr, for example, self-consciously justified the use of this "fiction" on grounds that it "sways legislatures and the courts, which, being composed entirely men ... have no more than a theoretical knowledge of Home."[25]

The new "culture of the home" portrayed in women's labor history, to be sure, carries its own theoretical liabilities. David Montgomery, for example, plausibly synthesizes recent work into a two-track approach to class consciousness, broadly defined. While "working men's experience introduced them to class first and foremost through conflict at the workplace," Montgomery says, for women, interdependence within the home and among neighbors turned "the nineteenth-century family" into "a nursery of class consciousness."[26] While ably encompassing female actors within the main labor history narrative, such a formulation remains unduly restrictive. First, the parallel paths are too gender-exclusive, unable to accommodate evidence from studies like that of Blewett and, more recently, of Kessler-Harris and Dorothy Sue Cobble on women's work-centered motivations or the likely ways (much less well studied) that male workers, too, were shaped by domestic and neighborhood-centered experience. Patricia Cooper's open-ended interviews with Philco workers in the 1930s, including testimony in which male aspirations were deflected by family demands, are particularly relevant here.[27]

Despite his sensitive reach for inclusiveness, Montgomery still privileges the workplace as the primary site of class conflict. As if backing away from the comparative messiness of other social arenas, and under pressure to define an overarching thesis, he insists that "the relations of production are the fibers which give coherence to the web of modern social interactions."[28] By again detaching the spheres of reproduction, community, and politics from the industrial worksite, Montgomery indirectly, and perhaps unintentionally, concurs with a basic principle not only of classic Marxism but of the mainstream American labor movement at least since the founding of the AFL.

To integrate gender issues into their central focus, labor historians, as Mari Jo Buhle implies, will need to "reconceptualize basic categories of analysis to include the processes of class formation *outside* capitalist production, as traditionally defined."[29] Two recent works, coincidentally both about Chicago but more than coincidentally both case studies of a rich empirical nature, suggest the possibilities of this broader view of class formation. James R. Barrett's study of packinghouse workers notably blends close examination of the workers' family economy (including the institutions of boarding and child labor) with treatment of union demands for an "American Standard of Living."[30] Implicitly, he locates the generation of "class" consciousness in a plurality of spaces. Lizabeth Cohen strays even further from a work-relations model in assessing labor's changing consciousness in the 1920s and 1930s. Focusing on distinct class appropriations of company welfarism and the instruments of mass commercial culture, she makes a multiform working-class culture a dynamic and discernible historical force.[31]

Beyond offering new explanations for workers' past behavior and consciousness, a gendered cultural history may provide much-needed critical ballast for assessing alternative strategies available to labor movements. Harold Benenson, for instance, calls our attention to an important historic divide in the early nineteenth century prior to which both explanations and forms of class conflict were less male-defined and workplace-centered than afterward: the male breadwinner argument, first enunciated by British artisans in the 1820s and 1830s, he suggests, actually "incorporated the biases of the middle-class gender ideology." By historicizing the cultural conservatism inherent in the Marxist "producerist" orientation, Benenson implicitly draws our attention to more feminist radicalisms (e.g., early nineteenth-century utopian socialism) and more inclusive class strategies (e.g., crowd actions, riots, boycotts) that were plowed under by the dominant tradition.[32] In U.S. labor history, of course, community-centered studies of the labor movement have abounded since the work of Herbert Gutman, and fascination with "buried" traditions like that of the Knights of Labor in part flourished because of the broad, relatively egalitarian spectrum of activity associated with that Order.

Elizabeth Faue's reexamination of the Minneapolis Congress of Industrial Organizations undoubtedly offers the clearest example thus far of a gendered class perspective on movement building. Within the decade of the thirties, she suggests, "men and women workers . . . went beyond the exclusive craft orientation of the AFL and the corporate unionism of the later years of the [CIO]. They rooted unions in the community and directed their attention to what can be described as the reproductive sphere—specifically, consumer concerns, family and community networks, and education."[33]

In several key respects, this revisionist literature on domestic culture and community unionism flows directly, it seems to me, from the legacy of "culturalism." It was E. P. Thompson, of course, who insisted that class consciousness be read as "the way in which [class] experiences are handled in cultural terms: embodied in traditions, value-systems, ideas, and institutional forms." Drawing on anthropological models, Gutman proposed to interpret "culture" as a set of "resources" through which working people addressed their structural or "social" situation.[34] The cultural impulse within labor history has, from the beginning, emphasized the generative power, the creative capacity evident in both organized movements and the daily life of the common people. "Indigenous conceptions of justice or dignity," as Kessler-Harris has observed, have predominated in this analysis over theoretical models or abstractions of consciousness imposed from without. Notwithstanding the gendered boundaries (inherited from Marxist definitions of class) of the "founding fathers" of the new labor history, their very mode of analysis practically encouraged an ever-widening search for lived experience and effectively invited a redrawing of boundaries so long as the new configurations respected indigenous voices.[35]

To be sure, situating gendered labor history in larger relation to working-class cultural analysis is also to identify certain unresolved problems within the literature. For one, gendered labor history may be susceptible to the familiar bugaboo of the culturalists, the charge of romanticism. Those who have read Katznelson, Amy Bridges, or Martin Shefter, for example, might well greet Faue's community model of class consciousness with a cry of "Not so fast!" The community beyond the work site, after all, still carries for them the burden of American exceptionalism, or, as they prefer it now, "incorporation on a reformist and nonmilitant basis."[36] Party and ethnic identity, they suggest, generally overwhelmed class-based organization outside the workplace. What is more, they might add, these forms of community organization were no more open to women than the trade unions.[37] Alternatively, John Bodnar posits the household and community as a key source for the labor upheaval of the thirties, yet outside the parameters of "class consciousness" versus "incorporation." For Bodnar, the search by the immigrant working class for "job security" and "family stability" overrode concern for class "power relationships."[38] Which community traditions and domestic values, in short, are we privileging? Why do the women's work-culture scholars choose only the ingeniously combative resources from the domestic sphere rather than more pacifying traits learned there? It is not to discredit the theses of Faue and others to point out that they have not really addressed such questions.

Another problem for a gendered history might derive from the very fruits of the recent trend toward discourse analysis. The deconstructionist insights evident, for example, in Joan W. Scott's emphasis on the "gendered 'coding' of certain terms" and the "naturaliz[ation of] their meanings" add up to a sober counterpart to the "culture as a resource" school of interpretation.[39] Rather than taking the culture at its face value and respecting its "indigenous conceptions," deconstructionist analysis exposes the ideological construction of all linguistic systems of meaning. Dualisms commonly employed in labor history literature such as men's work/women's work, work/home, skilled/unskilled come quickly unglued under such gender-sensitive scrutiny; moreover, such staples of political-cultural analysis as "republicanism," "autonomy," "control," and "citizenship" also teeter from their virtuous perches. But how might a gendered labor history reconstruct analytic categories once the one-sidedness of both indigenous and historiographic lay-ons has been exposed?

The question is not merely theoretical. In accounting for the militant women weavers of Fall River in the 1870s, Blewett, for example, suggests that "memories of the activities of their own mothers and grandmothers in support of radical politics and the Chartist movement may have inspired some of these Lancashire women."[40] But while for Blewett, Chartism offers a historical vessel of women's empowerment, Anna Clark's close study of women in that movement stresses "the contradictions between Chartism's egalitarian principles and its domestic rhetoric."[41] Thus, one historian's "culturalist" resource is another historian's "deconstructionist" target. Ava Baron struggles mightily to overcome this tension in introducing her recent anthology: "These essays provide new ways to understand how men and women workers attempted to construct and to defend a gendered identity in the context of the many discourses on gender and work simultaneously put forth by employers, unions, reformers, journalists, and others. In these studies we see workers as agents embattled, seeking to gain control over the discourse and the material conditions that defined their identities as men and women, as workers, and as family and community members."[42] But what precisely does it mean to gain *control* over the discourse and the material conditions that defined their identities? How *do* contemporaries break through the indigenous conceptions that bind their culture and language systems? In challenging indigenous discourse as ideologically freighted, do we not risk a return to mere interest theory as an explanation of ultimate ends? Here is a puzzle surely worth further clarification.

In sum, I have mixed feelings about the preoccupation with synthesis within labor history. The advantages of connectedness, I fear, will come at the expense of conceptual fields missing altogether from the main narrative. To be sure, such studies have their uses. Whether focused on organizational, economic, social-cultural, or state-centered foundations, synthetic treatments will prove mutually reinforcing so long as we recognize their boundaries. On the other hand, the gendering of labor history, thus far best expressed within carefully defined moments and locales, bears an uncertain relation to full-blown synthesis.[43] In drawing from the field's culturalist current—with its emphasis on workers' own categories of understanding and action—gendered histories also endow that current with a tougher, more self-critical angle of analysis. Eight years ago, in my contribution to the DeKalb labor history conference, I ended my remarks by calling for "the second act" of culture-centered studies within labor history. The 1991 North American Labor History Conference, a testament to the richest arena of recent work in the field, provided a new answer to my request. To my surprise and delight, the curtain on that act was lifted in Detroit, and its central theme was gender.

NOTES

This essay originally appeared in *Labor History* 34 (Fall, 1993), 178–89. Reprinted by permission. For helpful suggestions—but without complicity—in the preparation of this essay, I wish to thank Susan Levine, Nancy Gabin, and the students in my History 267 graduate colloquium, especially Mary Jane Aldrich-Moody.

1. Letter from Elizabeth Faue to potential contributors to the 1991 North American Labor History Conference, Detroit, Mich., Dec. 20, 1990.

2. Brody's paper "The Old Labor History and the New" was read at the OAH meetings in 1978 and subsequently published in *Labor History* 20 (1979), 111–26.

3. The first reference I know for the term is Richard Johnson, "Edward Thompson, Eugene Genovese, and Socialist-Humanist History," *History Workshop* 6 (Autumn 1978), 79–100, which laments an apparent flight from "theory" and "abstraction" to "authenticity" within neo-Marxist thought. I applied the term more positively at DeKalb, but the negative spin doctors have prevailed ever since. See Fink, "Looking Backward: Reflections on Workers' Culture and Certain Conceptual Dilemmas within Labor History," in J. Carroll Moody and Alice Kessler-Harris, *Perspectives on American Labor History: The Problems of Synthesis* (DeKalb, Ill., 1989), 5–29; Howard Kimeldorf, "Bringing Unions Back In (Or Why We Need a New Old Labor History)," *Labor History* 32 (Winter 1991), 91–103; Daniel Nelson, "Response," ibid., 125.

4. Alice Kessler-Harris, "A New Agenda for American Labor History: A Gendered Analysis and the Question of Class," in Moody and Kessler-Harris, *Perspectives on American Labor History*, 218–19. On culturalism as a synonym for the new labor history, see also Mari Jo Buhle, "Gender and Labor History," in ibid., 58; and Michael Kazin, review of Stephen H. Norwood's *Labor's Flaming Youth*, in *American History Review* 96 (Oct. 1991), 1308–9.

5. Kessler-Harris, "A New Agenda," 219, 221.

6. Bryan D. Palmer, *Descent into Discourse: The Reification of Language and the Writing of Social History* (Philadelphia, 1990); Ira Katznelson and Aristide R. Zolberg, eds., *Working-Class Formation: Nineteenth-Century Patterns in Western Europe and the United States* (Princeton, N.J., 1986).

7. Ava Baron, "Gender and Labor History: Learning from the Past, Looking to the Future," in Baron, ed., *Work Engendered: Toward a New History of American Labor* (Ithaca, N.Y., 1991), 4–5.

8. Elizabeth Faue, *Community of Suffering and Struggle: Women, Men, and the Labor Movement in Minneapolis, 1915–1945* (Chapel Hill, N.C., 1991), 15.

9. Antonio Gramsci, quoted in Harvey Kaye, "Introduction," in George Rude, *The Face of the Crowd: Studies in Revolution, Ideology, and Popular Protest: Selected Essays of George Rude* (New York, 1988), 36.

10. Marcus Rediker, *Between the Devil and the Deep Blue Sea: Merchant Seamen, Pirates, and the Anglo-American Maritime World, 1700–1750* (New York, 1987). For observations on the Rediker book, I am indebted to the seminar comments of Mary Jane Aldrich-Moody. For an example of how the questions posed determine research strategy with regard to gender, see Leon Fink and Brian Greenberg,

Upheaval in the Quiet Zone: A History of Hospital Workers' Union, Local 1199 (Urbana, Ill., 1989), and Karen Brodkin Sacks, *Caring by the Hour: Women, Work, and Organizing at Duke Medical Center* (Urbana, Ill., 1988).

11. Richard Oestreicher, "Separate Tribes? Working-Class and Women's History," *Reviews in American History* 19 (1991), 228–29.

12. Palmer, 138, 140 and 87–186 *passim.*

13. Ira Katznelson, "Working-Class Formation: Constructing Cases and Comparisons," in Katznelson and Zolberg, *Working-Class Formation,* 4n.

14. Mari Jo Buhle, "Gender and Labor History," 64.

15. Gordon, quoted in Buhle, ibid.

16. Kessler-Harris, "New Agenda," 226.

17. Baron, "Gender and Labor History," 18–19.

18. Ibid., 18.

19. Ibid., 21.

20. Mary H. Blewett, "Work, Gender, and the Artisan Tradition in New England Shoemaking, 1780–1860," *Journal of Social History* (1983), 239–40. For a similar argument, see Christine Stansell, "The Origins of the Sweatshop: Women and Early Industrialization in New York City," in Michael H. Frisch and Daniel J. Walkowitz, eds., *Working-Class America* (Urbana, Ill., 1983), 78–103.

21. Thomas Dublin, "Women, Work, and Protest in the Early Lowell Mills," *Labor History* 16 (1975), 109.

22. Susan Levine, *Labor's True Woman: Carpet Weavers, Industrialization, and Labor Reform in the Gilded Age* (Philadelphia, 1984).

23. Dana Frank, "Gender, Consumer Organizing, and the Seattle Labor Movement, 1919–1929," in Baron, *Work Engendered,* 273–95.

24. See, e.g., Susan Porter Benson, *Counter Cultures: Saleswomen, Managers, and Customers in American Department Stores, 1890–1940* (Urbana, Ill., 1986); Barbara Melosh, *The Physician's Hand: Work Culture and Conflict in American Nursing* (Philadelphia, 1982); and Patricia Cooper, *Once a Cigar Maker: Men, Women, and Work Culture in American Cigar Factories, 1900–1919* (Urbana, Ill., 1987).

25. Eileen Boris, " 'A Man's Dwelling House Is His Castle': Tenement House Cigarmaking and the Judicial Imperative," in Baron, *Work Engendered,* 140.

26. David Montgomery, *The Fall of the House of Labor* (Cambridge, Mass., 1987), 139–40.

27. Alice Kessler-Harris, "Gender Ideology in Historical Reconstruction: A Case Study from the 1930s," *Gender and History* 1 (Spring 1989), 31–49, esp. 35–37; Dorothy Sue Cobble, " 'Drawing the Line': The Construction of a Gendered Work Force in the Food Service Industry," in Baron, *Work Engendered,* 216–42; Patricia Cooper, "The Faces of Gender: Sex Segregation and Work Relations at Philco, 1928–1938," in Baron, *Work Engendered,* 320–50, esp. 334–35.

28. David Montgomery, "Class, Capital, and Contentment," *Labor History* 30 (Winter 1989), 137.

29. Buhle, "Gender and Labor History," 68.

30. James R. Barrett, *Work and Community in the Jungle: Chicago's Packinghouse Workers, 1894–1922* (Urbana, Ill., 1987), 64–117, 142–47.

31. Lizabeth Cohen, *Making a New Deal: Industrial Workers in Chicago, 1919–1939* (New York, 1990).

32. Harold Benenson, "Victorian Sexual Ideology and Marx's Theory of the Working Class," *International Labor and Working-Class History* 25 (Spring 1984), 1–23.

33. Faue, *Community of Suffering,* 12.

34. E. P. Thompson, *The Making of the English Working Class* (New York, 1966), 10; Herbert Gutman, *Work, Culture, and Society in Industrializing America: Essays in American Working-Class and Social History* (New York, 1977), 3–78.

35. In this respect, I dissent from Bryan Palmer's attempt to reincorporate Thompson into his more thoroughly materialist project and from Joan Scott's self-distancing criticism in *Gender and the Politics of History* (New York, 1988), 68–90.

36. Katznelson, "Working-Class Formation," 29.

37. Amy Bridges, "Becoming American: The Working Classes in the United States before the Civil War," in Katznelson and Zolberg, *Working-Class Formation,* 157–96; and Martin Shefter, "Trade Unions and Political Machines: The Organization and Disorganization of the American Working Class in the Late Nineteenth Century," in Katznelson and Zolberg, *Working-Class Formation,* 197–278.

38. John Bodnar, "Immigration, Kinship, and the Rise of Working-Class Realism," *Journal of Social History* 14 (1980), 59.

39. Scott, *Gender and the Politics of History,* 48.

40. Mary H. Blewett, "Manhood and the Market: The Politics of Gender and Class among the Textile Workers of Fall River, Massachusetts, 1870–1880," in Baron, *Work Engendered,* 106.

41. Anna Clark, "The Rhetoric of Chartist Domesticity: Gender, Language, and Class in the 1830s and 1840s," *Journal of British Studies* 31 (January 1992), 62–88.

42. Baron, "Gender and Labor History," 38.

43. For further consideration of this theme, see James R. Barrett, "Class and Gender: The Impact of Gender Analysis on U.S. Labor History" (paper presented at the Social Science History Association annual meeting, Minneapolis, October 19, 1990).

Index

Abernathy, Ralph, 52; in Charleston hospital workers' strike, 62–66, 70, 71, 77
Abraham, A. H., 42
Adams, Henry Carter, 206, 208; academic career of, 226n17; dismissal from Cornell, 211; evangelical background of, 225n7
Adamson, Walter, 126n10
Addams, Jane, 222
Adelphon Kruptos (Knights of Labor manual), 96
AFL (American Federation of Labor): British models for, 153, 155–56; collective bargaining program of, 167n23; and court actions, 157–58; craft unionism of, 214; and demise of Knights of Labor, 109; and individual rights, 154–55; and labor republicanism, 153; relationship with intellectuals, 214; women in, 241
AFL-CIO (American Federation of Labor and Congress of Industrial Organizations): and Charleston hospital workers' strike, 63, 69; and judicial injunctions, 145, 161
Agulhon, Maurice, 180
Allgemeine Deutsche Arbeiter Verein, 181
Amalgamated Association of Iron and Steel Workers, 106
American Association of Labor Law Reform, 213
American Association of Labor Legislation, 212
American Bar Association, 144
The American Character (Gorer), 132
American Economics Association (AEA), 207, 208, 209, 226n24

American Federationist (journal), 145
American Federation of Labor. *See* AFL
American Federation of Labor and Congress of Industrial Organizations. *See* AFL-CIO
Anarchism, nineteenth-century, 181
And Keep Your Powder Dry (Mead), 132
Andrews, E. Benjamin, 228n36
Anthropology: and study of culture, 132–33, 135, 243
Anticapitalism: and the family, 140
Anti-Semitism: in American academics, 231nn69,71
Antiunionism, 52
Arbitration, 207
Artisan classes, 147, 183; British, 243; politicization of, 184; radical, 224; work ethic of, 190
Associationalism: loss of appeal of, 185
Aveling, Edward, 20
"Awakening": of labor intellectuals, 203, 210

Baker, Ella, 80
Bakhtin, Mikhail, 118, 130, 137, 141
Baron, Ava, 237–38, 245
Barry, Leonora, 107
Barry, Thomas, 25
Bellamy, Edward, 179, 204, 209; historical studies of, 222
Bemis, Edward W., 208, 212, 228n39
Benedict, Ruth, 133
Benenson, Harold, 242–43
Bennett, Isaiah, 57, 58, 61; opposition to SCLC, 63; as union advisor, 59, 60
Benson, Susan Porter, 191

Berger, Victor, 217
Berlin, Ira, 133
Berthoff, Rowland, 94
Beyond Equality (Montgomery), 222
Birnbaum, Norman, 19
Blackbourn, David, 195n2
Blair, Henry, 23
Blewett, Mary H., 191, 240–41, 242, 244–45
Bodnar, John, 189, 244
Boorstin, Daniel, 133
Boris, Eileen, 241
Boritt, S. G., 25
Boss system, urban, 103, 185
Boycotts, 95, 221; Clark's defense of, 207;
    criminalization of, 103; injunctions against,
    106, 151–52, 157
Braidwood coal miners' strike (1877), 7–9
Brandeis, Louis, 222
Breener, Robert, 10n5
Bridges, Amy, 244
Brimm, Hugh S., 75
British Amalgamated Society of Engineers
    (ASE), 148, 153, 168n26
British Trades Union Council, 153
Brody, David, 187, 236, 237
Brown, Claire G., 67, 80–81
Brown, T. H., 47
Brown v. *Board of Education* (1954), 54
Brundage, David, 25, 96
Bruner, Jerome, 137
Bryan, William Jennings, 152
Buck's Stove and Range case (1909), 158,
    167n16
Buhle, Mari Jo, 142, 239, 242
Buhle, Paul, 130, 142
Burke, Edmund, 144
Burke, Kenneth, 120

Cabaniss, Alice, 55, 65–66
Cabaniss, Joseph, 55
Calhoun, Craig, 187
Cannon, M. W., 41, 42
Capitalism: absorption of workers into, 191;
    Commons on, 4; in Gilded Age, 94, 97;
    and individualism, 122, 127, 140; Knights
    of Labor on, 90–91; and patriarchy, 239;
    welfare, 187
— industrial: hegemony of, 104; social
    implications of, 17
Carawan, Guy, 56

Carmichael, Stokely, 56
Carver, T. N., 213
Cassity, Michael J., 34
Catholic Banner (Charleston, S.C.), 74
Charleston, S.C.: black religious community
    of, 64, 71; economy of, 53; effect of hospi-
    tal workers' strike on, 64–68, 72–73, 77;
    effect of strike settlement on, 78; unioniza-
    tion in, 52–53. *See also* Hospital workers'
    strike
Charleston Council on Human Relations,
    55
Charleston Movement (civil rights), 54–55,
    64–65
Chartists, British, 98, 113n12, 177, 244–45; cri-
    tique of social problems, 180; decline of,
    185, 189
Chicago and Wilmington Coal Co., 8
The Chrysanthemum and the Sword (Benedict),
    132
Church Congress (Cleveland, 1886), 103
Citizenship schools (SCLC), 63, 83n20
Citizens party (Rutland, Vt.), 44–45, 46
Civil Rights Act (1924), 129
Civil rights movement, 118; and Charleston
    hospital workers' strike, 52–53, 55–57,
    64–65; domination by males, 130; effect of
    Charleston hospital strike on, 79–80;
    Malcolm X on, 128, 129; role of unions in,
    51; self-activity of, 142
Civil service law, 212, 213
The Civil War in France (Marx), 129
Clark, Anna, 245
Clark, John Bates, 206–7
Clark, Septima, 54, 62
Class: cultural aspects of, 131; in Gutman's
    works, 7, 9; and means of production, 238;
    role in political system, 109. *See also* Work-
    ing class
Class conflict, 29n1, 89, 221; and American
    legal system, 145; in Commons's work,
    11n5, 209, 227n29; French, 178; German,
    181; in Gilded Age, 20, 150; Knights of
    Labor on, 100, 104; language of, 121; in
    workplace, 242–43
Class consciousness, 105, 239; as basis for
    radical politics, 117; community model of,
    244; in new labor history, 132; Thompson
    on, 243; of women, 241
Class division, 185

Class formation, 131, 134, 135, 138, 238, 239, 240; and capitalist development, 237; comparative studies of, 194; gender issues in, 242; in Germany, 176

Class identity: in Germany, 182; of working class, 95–96

Class relations: and gender relations, 238, 240; in Rutland, Vt., 42–43

Clayton Act (1914), 156, 157, 167n15, 168n27, 170n37

Clement, Percival W., 47

Cleveland, Grover, 107

Cobble, Dorothy Sue, 191, 242

Cohen, Lizabeth, 242

Coles, Robert, 54

Collective action: cultural basis of, 187; residual nature of, 183

Collective bargaining: contracts governing, 158; effect of federal government on, 159–60; and industrial pluralism, 219–20

Combination Laws (Great Britain), 149

Commission on Industrial Relations (1912–15), 159, 212, 213, 218; Perlman's service to, 232n72

Committee of Concerned Clergy (Charleston, S.C.), 64, 73

Commons, Ella, 231nn69–71

Commons, Jack, 231n71

Commons, John R., 141; academic career of, 3–5, 10n5, 208–9, 212–16, 227n27, 229n46; anti-Semitism of, 217–18, 230n69; autobiography of, 215, 229n47, 231n70; contrast with Gutman, 3–4; family of, 231nn69–71; government service of, 213; and Perlman, 217–18, 231nn69–71; reputation for antagonism, 209, 227n28; on role of intellectuals in labor, 214–15, 230nn57,59

Commons, Rachel, 231n71

Commonwealth v. *Hunt* (1842), 149, 166n14

Communalism: in Gilded Age, 97

Communism, nineteenth-century, 181

Communist party, Italian, 125n10

Community: importance in labor movement, 4, 24, 122, 183–85, 187, 189, 222, 242; New England concept of, 34; role in class consciousness, 244; and worker protest, 197n20

Congress of Industrial Organizations (CIO), 17, 220, 243; effect of predecessors on, 29

Conroy, Jack, 130

Conroy, John F., 55, 71

Consciousness, 141, 146; collective, 105, 128, 190; divided, 100, 103–5, 129. *See also* Class consciousness

Consensus history, 124, 133, 194, 223

Conservatism, twentieth-century, 187

Conspiracy and Protection of Property Act (Great Britain, 1875), 155

Conspiracy cases, 151, 166nn13–14

Conspiracy doctrine, 149, 150, 170n37

Constitution, American: effect on working class, 146, 147, 152; interstate commerce clause of, 170n38; judiciary power over, 158; and labor rights, 154, 166nn13–14

Constitutionalism, eighteenth-century, 148

Consumerism: and decline of republican ideals, 187; effect on women, 192; and mass culture, 199n24

Conyers, John, 69

Cooper, Patricia A., 191, 242

Corbin, David, 189

Corbin, J. N., 101

Couvares, Francis, 192

Craft unions, 103, 110; role in working-class culture, 117, 183. *See also* Trade unions

Croghan, Reverend Leo, 74

Cultural formation, 237

Culturalism, 240, 246nn3–4; and new labor history, 236–37

Culture: anthropological studies of, 132–33, 135, 243; assimilation of, 102; counter-hegemonic, 117, 118–19; in Gutman's works, 7, 142; influence on language, 137; "movement," 112n6; relationship to power, 116, 119, 124. *See also* Working-class culture

—mass, 118–19, 120n7, 139, 188, 189; consumption by working class, 192–93; effect on working-class culture, 199n24; rise of, 190

—popular. *See* Popular culture, American

Cumbler, John, 184, 187

Darrow, Clarence, 204, 222

Davis, Leon, 51, 65, 66

Davis, Mike, 184

Dawley, Alan, 10n5, 183

Deas, Rosabelle, 68

Debs, Eugene, 183

Declaration of Independence, 145; as justification for strikes, 147; meaning to labor movement, 89–90, 120–21, 151, 153, 179, 229n52

Democratic party: in Rutland, Vt., 44–47; and working-class voters, 42

Dent, Harry, 77

Department of Health, Education, and Welfare: intervention in hospital workers' strike, 75, 76

Devine, Saint Julian, 54

Dewey, John, 222

Diggins, John Patrick, 91–92, 94, 97, 98; and concept of hegemony, 127; on cultural transformation, 136; on individualism, 140–41

Diggs, Charles, 69

The Disinherited (Conroy), 130

Doctrine of vested interests, 148

Documentary History of American Industrial Society (1910–20), 212

Dorr, Rheta Childe, 241

Doster, Lillie Mae, 58

Dred-Scott decision, 151

Dubinsky, David, 232n73

Duffy, Reverend Thomas, 74

Duplex Printing Press Co. v. *Deering* (1921), 157

Dworkin, Ronald, 146

Economists: political discrimination against, 211–12, 228n36; and study of labor, 207–9, 225n6, 227n24

Edwards, Richard, 187

Eight-hour day, 27, 106, 107, 160; campaigns of 1886, 179

Eisenhower, Dwight D., 144, 161

Eley, Geoff, 195n2

Elizabethton strike (1929), 192

Elster, Jon, 121

Ely, Richard T., 141, 204–6; evangelical background of, 225n7; radicalism of, 228n39; and railroad strikes, 212

The Emergence of a UAW Local, 1936–1939 (Friedlander), 189

Engels, Friedrich, 20–21, 141

Enright, J. T., 64

Ernst, Daniel R., 170n38, 171n44

Escape from Freedom (Fromm), 132

Ethnicity: role in political system, 109, 110, 117, 185

Evans, Sara, 129–30, 191

Exceptionalism, 176
—American, 28, 107, 147; definition of, 175

Factory system: in Gilded Age, 16

Fair Labor Standards Act (1938), 159

Family: importance to working class, 122, 123, 183, 191, 221–22, 241–42; Knights of Labor's belief in, 24, 96, 97, 98, 140

Farmer, James, 75

Farris, Carl, 63, 80

Faue, Elizabeth, 238, 243, 244

Fawcett, Henry, 210

Federation of Organized Trades and Labor Unions. *See* AFL

Ferguson, Adam, 122–23

Ferrell, Frank, 107

Fielding, Herbert U., 78

Fields, Stephen J., 93

Filippelli, Ronald L., 153, 157

Finch, Robert, 76

Flacks, Richard, 234n91

Foner, Moe, 51, 61, 69, 74, 77

Foner, Philip, 233n86

Fox-Genovese, Elizabeth, 240

Frank, Andre Gunder, 10n5

Frank, Dana, 241

Frankfurter, Felix, 168n27

Fraternalism, Anglo-American, 96

Frazier, Gloria, 70

Free speech: academic, 211–12, 228n36, 229n49

Frey, John P., 156, 214–15

Friedlander, Peter, 189

Frisch, Michael, 34

Fromm, Erich, 132

Furner, Mary, 210

Gaillard, J. Palmer, Jr., 57, 77

Gasque, Leon, 71

Geary, Dick, 181

Gender: role in labor history, 236–45. *See also* Women

Gender relations: and class relations, 238, 240

George, Henry, 4, 36, 204, 209, 215; campaigns of, 20; at Church Congress, 103; Gompers's campaign for, 151; heterodoxy of, 210; historical studies of, 222; and single tax, 22, 207–8

Germany: development of working class, 176; labor history of, 180–81

Gilbreth, F. B., Jr. ("Ashley Cooper"), 74
Gilded Age: capitalism of, 94; class conflict in, 20, 150; labor culture of, 92; labor movements during, 15–29, 109; political history of, 15; producer culture of, 100–101; social issues of, 16–18, 19
Gillespie, James, 36
Glocker, Theodore W., 165n8
Glover, Lattie Mae, 67
Godoff, Elliott, 51, 58, 74
Goldman, Emma, 229n49
Gompers, Samuel, 19, 185; on British labor, 155–56, 168n27; campaign for Henry George, 151; collaboration with industry, 156; and collective bargaining, 153–54; and Commons, 214, 230n56; correspondence of, 232n73; leadership of labor movement, 146, 154–57; and Mark Hanna, 107; stance toward injunctions, 157–58; on trade unionism, 149; voluntarism of, 157, 167n19; on workers' attitudes, 120
Gordon, David, 187
Gordon, Linda, 239–40
Gorer, Geoffrey, 132
Gould, Jay, 17, 35
Government: economic regulation by, 11n5; legitimacy of, 100; restraint of labor movements, 152; and wage-system of labor, 90, 121, 147
Graduate education: German model of, 203, 225n7
Grady, Z. L., 64
Gramsci, Antonio: concept of cultural hegemony, 91, 99–100, 123, 126–27; on "Fordism," 187; and Italian Marxists, 124; and passivity of working class, 100; prison meditations of, 123; on social formations, 92–93; terms used by, 112n9, 116, 126
Gramscianism, 116, 120
Granger, L. H., 49n12
Grant, Reverend Henry, 71–72, 78; negotiations with Medical College Hospital (Charleston, S.C.), 75
Gray, Robert, 97, 103
Great Upheaval (labor unrest), 17, 48, 203
Greeley, Horace, 215
Green, William, 157
Greenback party, 8, 20, 22
Greene, Nathan, 169n27
Guesde, Jules, 180

Gutman, Herbert G., 92, 184, 223; academic career of, 3–10; and class formation, 138; contrast with Commons, 3–4; on culture, 7, 142; death of, 131; Diggins on, 120; on individualism, 114n26; influence of, 9–10; students of, 5–6; working-class audience of, 235n92

Hadley, Arthur T., 209
Hall, Jacquelyn, 192, 193
Hall, Stuart, 127, 188
Hanagan, Daniel, 183–84
Hanagan, Michael, 178
Hanna, Mark, 93, 107
Hannon, Tom, 101
Harden, Alma, 68
Hardin, Bishop Paul, 73
Harris, Abram, 233n86
Harris, Ray, 76
Harrison, Carter, 101
Hart, George H., 154
Hartz, Louis, 93, 133, 176, 182
Haskell, Thomas L., 116, 227n24
Haymarket bombing, 106, 109; effect on labor movement, 115n33
Haynesworth, Knox, 57–58, 82n10
Haywood, "Big Bill," 185
Hegemony: instability of, 128; of middle class, 105, 123
—cultural, 91, 99–100, 102, 183; Lears on, 116, 123, 136, 139–40
Hermeneutics: and study of history, 136
Hewitt, Abram, 93
Heyward, Mrs. D. P., 67
Hill, Christopher, 6
Hinton, Richard J., 19–20
Historical blocs, 104, 116, 123, 124, 126; Diggins on, 125n9
History of Labour in the United States (Commons et al.), 212, 215, 216
Hitchman Coal Company v. *Mitchell* (1917), 157
Hobsbawm, Eric, 6, 177, 181, 190–91
Hofstadter, Richard, 133, 210, 228n36
Hogan, James F., 38
Hogg, J. S., 152
Holton, Bob, 191
Homo faber ethic, 19
Horwitz, Morton, 149
Hospital workers (Charleston, S.C.), 55–59;

benefits of strike to, 85n55; at end of strike, 79

Hospital workers' strike (Charleston, S.C., 1969), 52–53, 59–78; arrests during, 74; conclusion of, 77–78; effect on strikers, 67–68, 70; failure of, 78–80; federal intervention in, 75–77; national support for, 69–70, 77; negotiations to end, 75–77; picketing during, 60; response of black community toward, 71; support of Catholic church for, 73–74; terms of settlement, 78; violence during, 61, 65, 77

Howe, Gedney, 55, 57

Howe Scale Co., 47, 50n20

Hubalz, Reverend Leon J., 73

Huff, William, 75–76

Hume, David, 122

I Am Somebody (film), 80, 81

Immigrants: acculturation of, 186; importance of family to, 244; in Knights of Labor, 92; in labor force, 4, 16, 28, 37–38, 106

Immigration: and decline of labor movement, 111; in Gutman's works, 7, 8, 9

Immigration and Industrialization (Bodnar), 189

Individualism: of American workers, 91, 94; and capitalism, 122, 127, 140; components of, 100; cult of, 28; and decline of labor movement, 101; of French workers, 178; Knights of Labor on, 95, 98, 104, 127; and labor movement, 25–26, 110; liberal, 126–27; Lockean, 90; and republicanism, 112n10

Individual rights, 154–55, 185

Industrial pluralism, 219–20, 221

Industrial relations: Commons's study of, 4, 212; institutions of, 3; and labor legislation, 164n4; during New Deal, 159; in postwar era, 161–63; regulation of, 171n44; state intervention in, 162, 190

Industrial Relations Commission. *See* Commission on Industrial Relations

Industrial revolution: in France, 177–78; impact on New England, 33–34; impact on United States, 15–16

Industrial Workers of the World (IWW), 158, 191, 218, 232n74

Ingersoll, Robert G., 17

Injunction laws, 162, 167n15, 168n27, 221

Institute for Christian Sociology, 208

Intellectuals: activism of, 235n92; contact with workers, 210, 214–15, 222–23; and formation of historical blocs, 124; as labor historians, 131, 201–10, 234n92; in oppositional culture, 117; Progressive, 141; radical, 209, 210–11, 227n24, 228n34; religious training of, 203, 225n7; role in labor movement, 110, 203–24; workers as, 204

Interdenominational Ministerial Alliance (Charleston, S.C.), 64

International Ladies Garment Workers Union, 121

International Longshoremen Association, 76

Interstate Commerce Commission, 211

J. P. Stevens Co.: in South Carolina, 52, 77; strike against, 85n53

James, Edmund J., 208; evangelical background of, 225n7

James, John, 7–8, 9

James, William, 117

Jameson, Frederic, 118

Jarrett, John, 103

Javits, Jacob, 69

Jenkins, Esau, 54, 56, 62

Johnson, Richard, 186, 194

Johnstown County lockouts, 184

Journeymen's associations, 149, 166n13, 179; German, 182

Joyce, Patrick, 177, 190

Joyce, Reverend William, 73, 74

Judicial abstention: theory of, 155, 168n27

Judicial system, American: restraint of strikes, 150, 152, 167n15; rulings on labor movement, 154, 156–58, 211. *See also* Legal system, American; Supreme Court

Kadushin, Max, 219; and Selig Perlman, 233n78

Katznelson, Ira, 237, 239, 244

Kealey, Gregory, 95, 101

Kelley, Florence, 222

Kelloggism, 22

Kessler-Harris, Alice, 191, 237, 240, 242

Keyserling, Leon H., 160

Kimeldorf, Howard, 236, 237

King, Coretta Scott, 61, 77; in Charleston hospital workers' strike, 63, 66–67, 71
King, Edward, 24–25, 26, 204
King, Martin Luther, 62
Kirchner, William, 69
Kirkland, Lane, 161
Knies, Karl, 205
Knights of Labor, 16–18; affiliation with Greenbacks, 8; alliance with Protestantism, 103; choice of name, 26; and class conflict, 100, 104; constituency of, 17, 24, 31n16, 92–93, 123–24, 182; constitution of, 19, 20; cultural aspects of, 90–91, 102; decline of, 101–2, 104, 116, 141–42, 185, 211; diversity of, 205; and divided consciousness theory, 100; effect of Haymarket bombing on, 115n33; Engels on, 141; General Assembly of, 103, 113n15; goals of, 27, 31n21, 93, 94, 101; Great Seal of, 95, 96, 113n15; historical treatments of, 34; and individualism, 95, 98, 104, 127; moral values of, 24–26, 96, 104–5, 116; Perlman on, 216; reasons for failure of, 108–9; Richmond assembly of, 101–2; rituals of, 96, 165n11; in Rutland, Vt., 35, 36–39, 41–44, 46, 47; socialists in, 31n14; strikes by, 17, 126; and temperance movement, 24, 25, 96, 104; and value of labor, 21–22; views on capitalism, 90–91; views on marketplace, 93, 94; views on property, 93, 97–98; women in, 27, 92, 241; and women's rights, 97
Koch, Edward, 69–70
Kocka, Jurgen, 182
Korstad, Robert, 193
Kraditor, Aileen, 116, 187

Labadie, Joseph, 22, 114n26
Labor: alliance with Populists, 107; effect of American legal system on, 143n2, 163, 166n14; injunctions against, 156, 157–58; language of, 91–92, 94, 110–11, 121, 135, 142; market value of, 21–22, 28; scarcity value of, 213, 230n61; and values of the state, 147–48. *See also* Labor movement, American; Working class
Labor bureaus, 204
Labor-cost theory of value, 21
Labor culture. *See* Working-class culture
Labor force: blacks in, 84n53; heterogeneity of, 28; immigrants in, 4, 16, 28, 37–38, 106; women in, 240–42
Labor history, 120–21; and collective action, 175; European, 175–78; industrial relations model of, 220, 221; legal issues in, 146–47, 171n45; politicization of, 202; role of gender in, 236–45; twentieth-century, 108; "Wisconsin school" of, 4, 212, 215, 219, 221. *See also* New labor history
"Labor in the Land of Lincoln" (Gutman), 7
Labor legislation: and industrial relations, 164n4; twentieth-century, 156–60. *See also* Legal system, American
Labor movement: European, 176–81
—American: British models for, 153, 155–56; comparative studies of, 194; constitutional rights of, 154; cultural explanations of, 187; decline of, 27–29, 101, 106, 109–10, 211; effect of Haymarket bombing on, 115n33; failure of, 99–100, 103–4; federal protection for, 159–60; fragmentation of, 29; Francis Walker on, 209–10; during Gilded Age, 15–29, 94–95; under Gompers, 146, 154–57; ideology of, 90, 146; and individualism, 25–26, 110; leadership of, 110, 155; legitimacy of, 5; moral values of, 24–25; political parties of, 18, 36–37, 43–44, 46, 109; radicalism in, 18, 21; relation to state authority, 150–51; restraint by government, 152; rhetoric of, 91, 92, 93–94, 120; role in public life, 11n5; role of gender in, 242–43; role of intellectuals in, 110, 203–24; role of newspapers in, 26, 110; in Rutland, Vt., 36–48; stages of development, 178; universalism of, 182; women in, 25, 191–92
—British, 176; influence on American labor movement, 153, 155–56
The Labor Movement in America (Ely), 205
Labor protest: European, 181; German, 181; in Gilded Age, 109; nineteenth-century, 90, 91, 203; and political culture, 91; radical, 118, 181
Labor radicals: view of marketplace, 21–22
Labor reform: nineteenth-century, 98; political triumph of, 221
Labor relations, 219, 220. *See also* Industrial relations
Labor republicanism, 18, 90, 140, 146; and

AFL, 153; and class division, 185; demise of, 109; language of, 93–94, 111, 122; loss of appeal, 185. *See also* Republicanism
Labor system, British, 155–56
Labor theory of value, 93, 124
Labour Party (Great Britain), 177; emergence of, 190
Laissez-faire, collective, 155, 162
Land: nationalization of, 22
Landon, Albert, 38–39
Lane, Hugh, 55
Lassalle, Ferdinand, 181
Law Day (1958), 144
Lears, T. J. Jackson, 91, 102, 104–5, 137; and cultural hegemony, 136, 139–40; on Gramsci, 123, 127; and language of labor, 110; on working-class culture, 98–99
Legal system, American, 143n2, 144–47; effect on labor, 143n2, 163, 166n14; and trade unions, 145. *See also* Judicial system, American; Labor legislation; Supreme Court
Leisure, 187; effect on working class, 189–90, 192–93
Leloudis, James, 193
Lemisch, Jesse, 237
Lens, Sidney, 233n86
Levine, Susan, 90, 97
Levinsky, David, 9
Levison, Stanley, 80; in Charleston hospital workers' strike, 61–62, 83n18
Liberalism: in Gilded Age, 97; and labor movement, 19; middle-class, 92; nineteenth-century, 91, 92, 94, 181
Lichtenstein, Nelson, 161
Life, Work, and Rebellion in the Coal Fields (Corbin), 189
Lilienthal, David, 170n38
Lincoln, Abraham, 145
Lipsitz, George, 141
Lipset, Seymour Martin, 176, 182
Lloyd, Henry Demarest, 153, 204, 215; historical studies of, 222
Locke, John, 122
Locofocos, 149, 166n14
Loewe v. *Lawlor,* 167nn15,23
Low Country Newsletter (civil rights publication), 56
Lowenstein, Allard K., 69
Lum, Dyer, 154
Luther, Seth, 179

McCord, Dr. William: during Medical College strike, 59–60; modernization of Medical College Hospital, 53–54; negotiations with strikers, 75, 76, 77
Machiavelli, Niccolò, 122
McLaughlin, Anna, 49n15
McLaughlin, Daniel, 7–8
MacLeod, Daniel, 57
McNair, Governor Robert: during Medical College strike, 59, 60, 65; response to hospital strikers, 70, 75–76
McNeill, George E., 90, 121, 179, 204, 215; as Knights' executive officer, 151–52
Malcolm X, 56; on civil rights movement, 128, 129
Maloney, T. W., 44
Management: rise to power by, 27–28
Marble industry, 35, 36, 37, 41
Marginal utility theory, 206, 210–11
Marketplace, 209; effect of labor conflict on, 156; expansion of, 10n5; government regulation of, 179; views of Knights of Labor on, 93, 94, 185; and nineteenth-century labor movements, 90; views of labor radicals on, 21–22
Marshall, John, 158
Martin Luther King Labor Center, 79
Marx, Eleanor, 20
Marx, Karl, 121, 129
Marxism: British, 6; German, 148; Italian, 124
Marxism in the United States (Buhle), 130
Marxists: Neo-Smithian, 10n5
Mass media: counterhegemony in, 118
May Day, 144
Mazey, Emil, 221
Mead, Margaret, 132
Medical College Hospital (MCH; Charleston, S.C.): administration of, 57–58; effect of strike on, 70; federal audit of, 75; negotiations with strikers, 75–76, 77; segregation at, 53; and terms of strike settlement, 78; unionization of, 57–59
Memory, collective, 117, 118
Merchants: and the labor movement, 24
Metzger, Walter P., 210, 228n36
Middle class: gender ideology of, 243; hegemony of, 105, 123; individualism of, 91, 92

Middletown (Lynds), 186

Miners' National Association, 8

Minorities: in Knights of Labor, 92; unionization of, 51–52

Missouri and Texas-Pacific Railroad, 17

Mitchell, John, 157–58; and Commons, 214

Modernism: and historical development, 134

Mondale, Walter F., 69

Montgomery, David, 18, 222, 241–42; activism of, 235n92

Moore, Barrington, Jr., 98, 117

Moore, R. Laurence, 28

Morrison, John, 24

Moss, Bernard, 178, 180

Moultrie, Mary, 56, 57; contact with Local 1199, 58; and outcome of strike, 79, 80; role in hospital workers' strike, 59–60, 66, 71; as union president, 59

Moynihan, Daniel Patrick, 77

Mullen, William, 102

Mutualism, 95

National Association of Manufacturers, 107

National Civic Federation, 107

National Industrial Recovery Act, 160, 170n37

National Labor Relations Act (Wagner Act; 1935), 159–60, 161, 162, 170n38

National Labor Relations Board (NLRB), 161, 220

National Labor Relations Board v. *Jones and Laughlin Steel Corp.* (1937), 162

National War Labor Board (in WWI), 159

Nelson, Daniel, 236

New Deal, 28, 47, 146; coalitions of, 110; industrial relations during, 159; unionism of, 199n25

New England: impact of industrial revolution on, 33–34

New labor history, 131–32; and consciousness, 134–35; cultural themes of, 90–91, 131–38, 175–76, 183, 236–37, 243–45; Ira Berlin on, 133; and New Left, 221; study of tradition, 187. *See also* Labor history

New Left (1960s), 202, 223; historians of, 234n91; and new labor history, 221

Newspapers: role in labor movement, 26, 110

Newton, William Wilberforce, 103

New York City Retail Drug and Hospital Employees Union, Local 1199, 51–52; in Charleston hospital workers' strike, 69, 74; contract negotiations by, 85n55; impact of hospital workers' strike on, 78, 80–81; and unionization of Medical College Hospital, 52–53, 58–63

New York City Retail Drug and Hospital Employees Union, Local 1199B, 52, 60, 67; at end of strike, 78

Nicholas, Henry, 58, 59, 60, 79, 80; violence against, 61

Nixon administration: civil rights enforcement in, 76–77

Noble and Holy Order of the Knights of Labor. *See* Knights of Labor

Norris-LaGuardia Act (1932), 162, 170nn37–38

North American Labor History Conference (1991), 245

North Carolina: unionization in, 52

Novick, Peter, 201

Oaths, secret, 96

Objectivity, historical, 201

Oestreicher, Richard, 187, 238–39

Ohio Woman's Suffrage Association, 151

Oneita strike (Andrews, S.C.), 85n53

Operation Dixie (1946–53), 52

Oppositional movements, 117, 127, 139; culture of, 141, 187; failure of, 129; ideology of, 130; struggle for legitimation, 128

Orange, James, 63, 71; in sanitation workers' drive, 79

Organic Thinking (Kadushin), 219

Organized labor. *See* Labor; Labor movement, American

Osman, Arthur, 58

Owen, Robert Dale, 215

Palmer, Bryan D., 95, 101, 237, 238

Paris Commune, 129

Parks, Rosa, 69

Parsons, Lucy, 115n33

Parti Ouvrier (France), 180

Party politics, American, 50n27, 106; and class consciousness, 244; effect on labor movement, 15; during Gilded Age, 15–16; in Rutland, Vt., 46

Paternalism, 40; British, 177

Patten, Simon Nelson, 208, 225n7
Pearre Bill (1907), 156, 168n27
Peiss, Kathy, 192
Perkins, Frances, 220
Perlman, Eva, 231n70
Perlman, Mark, 203, 230n65, 231n69, 232n72;
   on Commons, 231n71
Perlman, Selig: biography of, 230n65; and
   Commons, 217–18, 231nn69–71; early life
   of, 216–17; family of, 231n70; government
   service of, 232n72; and Max Kadushin,
   233n78; on role of intellectuals in labor,
   216–19, 221; on socialism, 229n49; and
   trade unionists, 233n79; and Wobblies,
   232n74
Personal Politics (Evans), 129–30, 191
The Philosophy of Wealth (Clark), 207
Picketing: in Charleston hospital strike,
   60–61; judicial restraints on, 157
Pinkerton, Allan, 8
Pole, J. R., 149
Political activism: and American intellec-
   tual life, 202
Poor People's Campaign, 62, 73, 80
Popular culture, American, 108, 110, 119;
   comparative studies of, 194; Diggins on,
   91–92; effect on working class, 192–93;
   locally based, 118; twentieth-century,
   188–89. *See also* Culture
Populism, 91, 152; alliance with labor, 107;
   ambiguities within culture, 100
Populist party: defeat of, 111; fusion with
   Democratic party, 100
Postmodernism: in historical studies, 202
Poststructuralism, 135, 137, 142
Potter, David M., 133, 134
Powderly, Terence Vincent, 204; correspon-
   dence of, 17; disillusionment of, 153; on
   management, 24; Priceburg speech of,
   89–90, 92, 94, 98, 108, 109, 120, 124; and
   Richard Ely, 205–6; and Gompers, 107,
   141; on symbolism of Knights of Labor, 96;
   and value of labor, 21
Pragmatism, 232n76; of workers, 220, 221
Prendergast, Richard, 100–101, 106
Price, Richard, 177
Proctor, Emily, 49n15
Proctor, Fletcher D., 38
Proctor, Redfield, 35; and division of
   Rutland, Vt., 38–39; paternalism of, 40

Proctor, Vt., 35; government of, 39–40. *See
   also* Rutland, Vt.; West Rutland, Vt.
Producer culture, 100–101, 105
Production: artisanal values of, 178; ideol-
   ogy of, 99, 100; mass, 188; means of, 238;
   modes of, 10n5; relations of, 238, 242
Progressive party, 28
Property: as determinant of economic
   behavior, 213; views of Knights of Labor
   on, 93, 97–98
Property rights: and trade unionism, 150,
   166n14, 168n27; workers', 206
Public employee law, 58, 82n10
Public policy: workers' influence on, 4
Pullman strike (1894), 151, 211–12

Race relations: in Charleston, S.C., 54–56;
   in Gutman's works, 7, 9, 11n12
Rachleff, Peter, 98, 235n92
Radicalism, 23–24; American, 204; feminist,
   243; French, 178; monetarist, 142;
   nineteenth-century, 91; of working class,
   19–27. *See also* Labor radicals
The Radical Persuasion (Kraditor), 187
Radical Republicans, 18
Railroads: effect on New England society, 35;
   nationalization of, 160; strikes against,
   17–18
Rantoul, Robert, Jr., 166n14
Reconstruction, 47; end of, 15
Redington, W. L., 42
Reich, Michael, 187
Reid, Alastair, 177
Relationism, 224, 235n95
Relativism, 202
Religious associations: and demise of labor
   movement, 110; role of, in working-class
   culture, 117, 122
Republicanism, 124; artisanal, 147, 187; as
   civil religion, 182; classical, 94, 140; of
   French labor, 180; of Knights of Labor, 104,
   128, 151, 167n16; and labor solidarity,
   147–48; language of, 121, 122; and liberal
   individualism, 112n10; nineteenth-century,
   100; and trade unions, 149–53. *See also*
   Labor republicanism
Republican party: appeal to labor, 183; in
   Rutland, Vt., 44–46, 49n6
Restraint of trade, 146, 149, 166n13,
   170n37

Retail, Wholesale, Department Store Union, Local 15A, 57, 58
Reuther, Walter, 66, 69
Rhetoric: on Fourth of July, 140
Richberg, Donald, 170n38
Right-to-work statutes, 52
Riley, Joseph, 74
Rivers, L. Mendel, 76
Robinson, Otis, 56
Roman Catholic church: support for hospital workers' strike, 73–74
Roosevelt, Franklin D., 169n34
Rosen, Morris, 71
Rosenzweig, Roy, 193
Ross, Edward A., 228n36, 229n49
Rubin, W. B., 156, 158
Rustin, Bayard, 80
Rutland, Vt.: balance of political power in, 47; division of, 38–39; effect of industrial revolution on, 34–35; election of 1886, 36–38; election of 1896, 47; election of 1904, 46; labor movement in, 36–48; Non-Partisan caucus of, 44–45; political life of, 35–40, 43–48; wards of, 50n25. *See also* Proctor, Vt.; West Rutland, Vt.
Rutland Herald (Vt.), 38, 45
Ryan, William F., 69

Saloons: threat to labor movement, 25
Salvatore, Nick, 183
Sampson, William, 166n13
Sanderson, George, 101
Sartori, Giovanni, 48
Saunders, William: civil rights activities of, 55–57; negotiations with Medical College Hospital, 75–76; on outcome of strike, 78; and South Carolina State Law Enforcement Division, 72; as union advisor, 59, 65
Schaffer, T. A., 230n59
Schatz, Ronald, 189, 191
Schechter Poultry Corp. v. *United States,* 160
Schultz, George, 77
Scobey, David, 90, 95–96
Scott, James C., 140–41, 142
Scott, Joan W., 244, 248n35
Self-consciousness, 202; of working class, 20, 135
Self-improvement, 103; belief of Knights of Labor in, 96

Seligman, E. R. A., 207–8
Senate Committee on Labor and Capital, 23
Sewell, William, 178
Sharpe, Mack, 64
Shaw, Albert, 208
Shaw, Judge Lemuel, 166n14
Shaw, Nate, 9
Shefter, Martin, 244
Sherman Antitrust Act, 152, 156, 157, 167n15; application to trade unions, 170n37
Shlakman, Vera, 233n86
Shoe industry, 183; gender divisions within, 191, 240, 241; protests by, 147, 166n13, 182
Shopkeepers: in Knights of Labor, 26
Simons, Judge Charles E., 60–61
Singletary, Judge Clarence, 60–61, 71
Single tax, 22, 207–8
Slaughterhouse cases (1873), 93
Smalls, Vera, 67–68
Smith, Adam, 122, 123
Social formations, 92–93, 116
Socialism: Christian, 207; French, 180; German, 180–81; in Gilded Age, 97; nineteenth-century, 22, 148, 181; trade, 180
Socialist party, 28; in France, 180
Socialists: role in Knights of Labor, 31n14
Social mobility: in Gutman's works, 7
Social Question (nineteenth-century), 17, 175
Social scientists, 210, 225n6
Sombart, Werner, 176, 216
South Carolina: segregation in, 53–54; textile industry of, 77; unionization in, 52, 85n55
South Carolina State Law Enforcement Division (SLED), 71, 72
Southern Christian Leadership Conference (SCLC): and Charleston hospital workers' strike, 52–53, 62–71, 80
Southwest Strike (1886), 206
Spelling, Thomas, 156
Spellman, J. D., 44, 45
Spencer, Herbert, 227n27
Spero, Sterling, 233n86
Spheres of domination, 124, 125n9, 126
Standard of living, American, 242
Stansell, Christine, 192
Stedman Jones, Gareth, 98, 185, 187
Sternsher, Bernard, 190
Steward, Ira, 21, 204
Strasser, Adolph, 23, 214

Strikes: bans on, 52; by coal miners, 8–9, 158; effect on Knights of Labor, 109; federal sanctions for, 160; by Knights of Labor, 17, 104; railroad, 15, 16, 17–18, 211–12; restraints by judicial system, 150, 152, 167n15; southern, 85n53; by southern textile workers, 193; by steelworkers, 80; sympathy, 221. *See also* Hospital workers' strike

Strom, J. P. "Pete," 71–72, 84n40

Structuralism, 134

Strunsky, Anna, 217

Student Non-Violent Coordinating Committee (SNCC), 56

Suffrage, 146, 151

Supreme Court: actions against labor, 152, 161, 170n37; during WWII, 160. *See also* Judicial system, American; Legal system, American

Susman, Warren, 101

Sutherland Falls. *See* Proctor, Vt.

Sweezy, Paul, 10n5

Swinton, John, 17, 151, 204, 215

Sylvis, William, 179, 204

Syndicalism, British, 191

Taft, Philip, 233n84

Taft-Hartley Act, 161

Temperance movement, 15, 18; Knights of Labor on, 24, 25, 96, 104

Textile industry, southern, 77, 193

The Theology of Seder Eliahu (Kadushin), 219

A Theory of the Labor Movement (Perlman), 216

Thernstrom, Stephan, 34

Third Republic (France), 180

Tholfson, Trygve R., 19

Thompson, E. P., 138; on class, 132, 178, 223–24, 243; interpretation of culture, 133, 135; on legal system, 145–46, 163; Marxism of, 6

Thurmond, Senator Strom, 76

Tioga County lockouts, 184

Tocqueville, Alexis de, 123, 136

Toews, John E., 136, 137–38

Tomlins, Christopher, 150, 161

Town meetings, 33; demise of, 34

Trachtenberg, Alan, 100

Trade, restraint of, 146, 149, 166n13, 170n37

Trade Disputes Act (Great Britain, 1906), 155, 168n26

Trade unionism: and property rights, 150, 166n14

Trade unions, 131; and American legal system, 145; application of Sherman Act to, 170n37; balloting systems of, 165n8; British, 148, 155, 165n11, 168n26; class-based, 96; constitutionalism of, 147, 165n8; constitutions of, 147; decline of, 28–29; firing of members, 170n39; influence of voluntary societies on, 149; and Knights of Labor, 27, 109; legal rights of, 149–50; moral values of, 24–25; national, 186; in postwar era, 161–63; and republicanism, 149–53; and right of free association, 154–55, 170n40; in 1930s, 130; use of conspiracy cases against, 166n14

Traditionalism: in worker culture, 187

Tuomey, S.C.: unionization at, 85n55

Turner, Doris, 82n12

UAW–Teamsters Alliance for Labor Action (ALA), 69

Union des Chambres Syndicales Ouvrières (France), 20

Unionism: industrial, 185; of New Deal, 199n25

Unionization: in hospitals, 52, 55–59. *See also* Hospital workers, Charleston, S.C.

Unions. *See* Craft unions; Trade unions

United Labor party, 36–37; in Rutland, Vt., 43–44, 46

United Workingmen's party, 44

University enrollment: expansion of, 203, 225n6

Unterkoefler, Bishop Ernest, 73

Vermont Marble Co., 35, 40, 50n20

Violence: in Charleston hospital workers' strike, 61, 66, 77

Voluntarism, 157, 167n16

Voluntary societies, 95; influence on trade unions, 149

Voter registration drives, 56, 78

Voting Rights Act (1965), 129

Vygotsky, Lev, 137

Wages: determination of, 21–22

Wage slavery, 22

Wage-system of labor: and republican government, 90, 121, 147, 179

Wagner Act. *See* National Labor Relations Act
Walker, Francis A., 209–10
Walker, Samuel, 22
Walkowitz, Daniel, 183, 184
Wallerstein, Emmanuel, 10n5
Walling, William English, 163, 217, 232n74
Walsh, Frank, 222
Ware, Caroline, 233n86
Ware, Norman, 233n86
War Labor Board (in WWII), 159, 160; Perlman's service to, 232n72
War on Poverty, 56
Warren, Joyce W., 136
Watson, Tom, 107
Webb, Beatrice, 148, 165n11
Webb, Sidney, 148, 165n11, 168n26
Weber, Max, 123
Wechsler, James, 77
Welfare: and capitalism, 187; government sponsored, 186; reform of, 4
"We Shall Overcome" (song), 57
Wesley, Charles, 233n86
Western Federation of Miners, 152–53
West Rutland, Vt.: political life of, 40–43. *See also* Proctor, Vt.; Rutland, Vt.
Whack, Donna, 68
Whack, Virgie Lee, 68
Whigs and Hunters (Thompson), 145
White, David, 58–59; in Charleston hospital workers' strike, 63, 64
White, Naomi, 70
Wilentz, Sean, 92, 120
Williams, Hosea, 63, 77
Williams, Raymond, 6, 95
Wilson Bill (1912), 156, 168n27
Wisconsin school of labor history, 4, 212, 215, 219, 221
Wise, John E., 54
Witt, Nathan, 220
Witte, Edwin, 218
Wobblies, 158, 191, 218, 232n74
Woll, Matthew, 214
Woman suffrage, 18, 151
Women: academic degrees earned by, 225n6; class consciousness of, 241; in Gutman's works, 7; in Knights of Labor, 27, 92; in labor force, 190, 240–42; in labor movement, 25, 191–92, 230n57; working-class, 191–92. *See also* Gender

Women's rights, 97
Workers. *See* Working class
Workers, skilled, 3–4, 183; alliance with unskilled, 186; British, 148; Commons's work in, 213; decline in, 190; in Knights of Labor, 17, 26, 27, 109
Working class: and American legal system, 145–46; antagonisms among, 28; behavior of, 131; British, 103, 177, 185; and British workers, 148; collective consciousness of, 91, 128, 188, 223–24; conservatism of, 122; creativity of, 200n32; effect of constitution on, 146; European, 29, 175, 181–82; fragmentation of, 176; French, 20, 177–78, 180; German, 176, 181; ideology of, 91, 92, 93–94; institutions of, 95–96; mobilization of, 189; modern industrial, 185–86; passivity of, 100, 186, 189; political movements among, 28–29; radicalism of, 19–27; relationship with intellectuals, 214–15, 222–23; relationship with state, 144–49; self-consciousness of, 20; self-organization of, 180; social history of, 198n21
Working-class culture, 90, 131–33, 175; ambivalence to state action, 117; community in, 4, 24, 183–85, 187, 189, 222, 224; consciousness of, 189, 190; difficulties in studying, 189–90; economic basis of, 194; effect of mass culture on, 199n24; gender issues in, 242–44; Gramscian approach to, 183; in Gutman's works, 8; international, 186; Lears's work in, 98–99; traditionalism in, 187; twentieth-century, 162, 189–94, 190, 237
Working-Class Formation (Katznelson), 239
World War I: effect on industrial relations, 159
World War II: industrial relations during, 159
Wright, Carroll, 204
Wright, Frances, 215

Yellen, Samuel, 233n86
Yellow-dog contracts, 154, 157
Young, Andrew: in Charleston hospital workers' strike, 62, 63, 64, 69, 77, 83n20; negotiations with Medical College Hospital, 75; resignation from SCLC, 80

Zolberg, Aristide R., 237, 238

Leon Fink is a professor of history at the University of North Carolina, Chapel Hill. He has published numerous articles in scholarly and popular journals, including *American Historical Review, Journal of American History, Labor History, Social History, Dissent, The Nation,* and *In These Times.* He is the author of *Workingmen's Democracy: The Knights of Labor and American Politics* (1983), co-author with Brian Greenberg of *Upheaval in the Quiet Zone: A History of Hospital Workers' Union, Local 1199* (1989), and editor of *Major Problems in the Gilded Age and the Progressive Era* (1993).

Books in the Series
The Working Class in American History

Worker City, Company Town: Iron and Cotton-Worker Protest in Troy and Cohoes, New York, 1855–84
Daniel J. Walkowitz

Life, Work, and Rebellion in the Coal Fields: The Southern West Virginia Miners, 1880–1922
David Alan Corbin

Women and American Socialism, 1870–1920
Mari Jo Buhle

Lives of Their Own: Blacks, Italians, and Poles in Pittsburgh, 1900–1960
John Bodnar, Roger Simon, and Michael P. Weber

Working-Class America: Essays on Labor, Community, and American Society
Edited by Michael H. Frisch and Daniel J. Walkowitz

Eugene V. Debs: Citizen and Socialist
Nick Salvatore

American Labor and Immigration History, 1877–1920s: Recent European Research
Edited by Dirk Hoerder

Workingmen's Democracy: The Knights of Labor and American Politics
Leon Fink

The Electrical Workers: A History of Labor at General Electric and Westinghouse, 1923–60
Ronald W. Schatz

The Mechanics of Baltimore: Workers and Politics in the Age of Revolution, 1763–1812
Charles G. Steffen

The Practice of Solidarity: American Hat Finishers in the Nineteenth Century
David Bensman

The Labor History Reader
Edited by Daniel J. Leab

Solidarity and Fragmentation: Working People and Class Consciousness in Detroit, 1875–1900
Richard Oestreicher

Counter Cultures: Saleswomen, Managers, and Customers in American Department Stores, 1890–1940
Susan Porter Benson

The New England Working Class and the New Labor History
Edited by Herbert G. Gutman and Donald H. Bell

Labor Leaders in America
Edited by Melvyn Dubofsky and Warren Van Tine

Barons of Labor: The San Francisco Building Trades and Union Power
in the Progressive Era
Michael Kazin

Gender at Work: The Dynamics of Job Segregation by Sex during World War II
Ruth Milkman

Once a Cigar Maker: Men, Women, and Work Culture in American Cigar
Factories, 1900–1919
Patricia A. Cooper

A Generation of Boomers: The Pattern of Railroad Labor Conflict in
Nineteenth-Century America
Shelton Stromquist

Work and Community in the Jungle: Chicago's Packinghouse Workers,
1894–1922
James R. Barrett

Workers, Managers, and Welfare Capitalism: The Shoeworkers and Tanners of
Endicott Johnson, 1890–1950
Gerald Zahavi

Men, Women, and Work: Class, Gender, and Protest in the New England Shoe
Industry, 1780–1910
Mary Blewett

Workers on the Waterfront: Seamen, Longshoremen, and Unionism
in the 1930s
Bruce Nelson

German Workers in Chicago: A Documentary History of Working-Class Culture
from 1850 to World War I
Edited by Hartmut Keil and John B. Jentz

On the Line: Essays in the History of Auto Work
Edited by Nelson Lichtenstein and Stephen Meyer III

Upheaval in the Quiet Zone: A History of Hospital Workers' Union, Local 1199
Leon Fink and Brian Greenberg

Labor's Flaming Youth: Telephone Operators and Worker Militancy, 1878–1923
Stephen H. Norwood

Another Civil War: Labor, Capital, and the State in the Anthracite Regions of
Pennsylvania, 1840–68
Grace Palladino

Coal, Class, and Color: Blacks in Southern West Virginia, 1915–32
Joe William Trotter, Jr.

For Democracy, Workers, and God: Labor Song-Poems and Labor Protest,
1865–95
Clark D. Halker

Dishing It Out: Waitresses and Their Unions in the Twentieth Century
Dorothy Sue Cobble

The Spirit of 1848: German Immigrants, Labor Conflict, and the Coming
of the Civil War
Bruce Levine

Working Women of Collar City: Gender, Class, and Community in Troy,
New York, 1864–86
Carole Turbin

Southern Labor and Black Civil Rights: Organizing Memphis Workers
Michael K. Honey

Radicals of the Worst Sort: Laboring Women in Lawrence, Massachusetts,
1860–1912
Ardis Cameron

Producers, Proletarians, and Politicians: Workers and Party Politics in Evansville
and New Albany, Indiana, 1850–87
Lawrence M. Lipin

The New Left and Labor in the 1960s
Peter B. Levy

The Making of Western Labor Radicalism: Denver's Organized Workers,
1878–1905
David Brundage

In Search of the Working Class: Essays in American Labor History and
Political Culture
Leon Fink

<u>overall</u>

excellent writer (but tight / full of detail ?/s
excellent citational wk –
        learn great deal w/ footnts (some updat
intellectual w/ broad range of interests BA-B
w/i LH field spanning knowledge of (. hist
British (comparative) by labor law hist (
to depth on K of L & early life – als
& 1960s * → today ± depth labr/politic
asks thoughtful ?s (eg. life w/ wages but ?
& weans shows evidence on both sides/deba
    + making gd use of his knowledge
    of K of L & politics & 1199's 60s story
                                        (themes?)

<u>relevance to current debates</u>   peculiarité
1b. w/ thew labor law   – 6   (LF: of the amei
2b. race/gender & class   – 4/9   (LF: contexts fo p
2a. amer. class conflict – 2 & 3   (LF: contexts fo
1a. pessimism of US labor – 5   power)
        wi scholarly rejoinders   (LF: peculiarit
                                                of the amei
3. LH craft – 1/5/7/8/9   (LF: strategie
   in 80s/90s   reinventio
   (2nd generation of New LH)   of the amei
   aimed to ...   wk)

   about Commons & Gutman & gender analysis

   (chpt #1 tribute)

_____

Some chpts mostly accessible only to other LH * & certainly a G
not for students other than PhD candidates
exceptions = chpt. 6? & most of 8 or for undergrads as hist
    of LH field in 1880's-20s + role of intell (2.4) in labo
most useful to LH not Wk Ed / ? but a tough read
    (exceptions 4 & 8)   + chpts 4 accessible to most as
                                        LH stores